A Conversation at the home of Jean Prouvé

Stefan Devoldere, Iwan Strauven
In preparation for this book on Robbrecht en Daem architecten, we invited Paul Robbrecht to talk to us in a building he considers a major point of reference for their work. The one he chose was the home of Jean Prouvé, which this architect built with his own hands on a hill in Nancy in 1954. Prouvé lived there until 1984. It was a suitable setting for a conversation about the motifs and motivations in the work of Robbrecht en Daem. And what does their oeuvre have in common with that of Jean Prouvé?

Hilde and myself are not really adepts of Jean Prouvé, but what I find interesting about him is that he was a real 'constructor'. His family had a large steel construction company here in Nancy. I like to see a meaningful approach to construction and that can be seen here in a variety of forms. It is a sort of low-tech architecture that starts from the construction, and that is precisely where it derives some of its eloquence. This house is dominated by a sloping ceiling that envelops and defines the space, with a large beam as its clearly marked backbone. Prouvé liked to make the interplay of forces visible, and that actually resulted in a typical Prouvé form. I am also fascinated by the scale he used for this project. It is very tangible on the hill side – you can touch the ceiling with your outstretched arm – and on the other side it opens onto the landscape. All with the very moderate use of scale. That is also a characteristic of architecture in general. There is always something comprehensible about the construction of houses and buildings. Architecture makes use of a knowledge that is shared by many and which everyone knows something about.

If the essence of architecture has something to do with this comprehensibility, do you think this also implies the modernist notion of 'honesty'?
That's a very ambiguous matter. I also love the Baroque and that involves a lot of trickery with all sorts of things. And not only technically speaking; baroque architecture also plays around with the perceptions. Our work includes both aspects. But of course I tend to like everything I see. There are nevertheless limits to the honesty and dishonesty of architecture. Using things to distort or make things disappear in architecture must always be done in the right way.

In which way is this house a point of reference for the work of Robbrecht en Daem?
We have a tremendous penchant for the shed, shack, cabin and suchlike. The first time I heard about

Laugier's hut... that's the way the architectural world is made. We took up that theme again in the design for the Woodland cabin, the idea that everything should be a sort of hut. Even the Concertgebouw. In the shape of the roof. In the beginning of the design process we ourselves talked about the pastoral aspect of the building. Bruges is one of the few Flemish towns with a real landscape around it. And the idea was that the building is slid into the town from that encircling landscape, thereby introducing a pastoral quality into the city. It goes back to Laugier, the start of tectonic thought, and also a basic instinct, an intuitive way of experiencing and creating architecture.

Are there any parallels with the design for your own home, which you are currently building?
I have always liked ceilings, because they are the architect's exclusive domain. The ceiling is the place where the architect shows himself completely. The rest of the building, the floor and the walls, are taken up by life itself. This can also be seen in the design for my own home, where the ceiling consists of an impressive structure of beams in plywood. There's no point in my dreaming of building my own house like Prouvé, but I am fascinated by DIY. You can see this in my fondness for plywood, the perfect DIY material. Plywood also makes marvellous use of wood. Every part of the tree is used. Adolf Loos once wrote that cutting through stone exposed the soul of the material. I feel the same about plywood, though of course it's a poorer version. I can look at it with a certain pleasure. DIY, cabins, lean-to roofs and suchlike. This house is actually just a lean-to roof. It has so little pretension in the way it looks.

And what about the location of your offices in combination with your own home? Here too there are tall blocks of flats in the background, just like the place you found in Ghent in the shadow of some large blocks.
Yes, perhaps you're right. When we were looking for a place for our offices – and so also for my own home – these blocks of flats were not an objection at all, on the contrary. I don't know exactly why it attracts me. I don't live in them of course, but they are nevertheless beautiful to look at. Their appearance is also constantly changing. In the winter they give off a warm glow. They are something like warm urban radiators. As oversized partitions they offer some kind of shelter. And there I sit, down below, in my own hut. It reminds me of pictures of metropolises in India and South America, where the original building in the foreground has a tense relationship with the metropolitan upheaval in the background. I have a very good feeling about such major differences in scale; they give the place a charge. It makes a place stronger. I once developed an idea for the City of Art. It was like an arena oriented towards the sea and at its heart was the National Museum of Art. In order to be allowed into the city as an inhabitant, you had to steal a masterpiece in your own country and hand it over to the museum. This proves your loyalty to the city. The artists live adjacent to the flanks of the arena, on its outermost edge, each in a sort of nest that looks out over the city. This house of Prouvé's has also established itself against the slope. With a view of Nancy, a city with a pronounced urban planning structure, a true Enlightenment city. This City of Art is a fantasy I occasionally talk to artists about. A city with ramparts around it. At the gate you have to show the work of art you have stolen in order to be allowed in. This art serves as a sort of shield. They can't bombard it because the world's heritage is housed there. (*Laughs*).

To what extent does art act as a shield in your projects? As a sort of passport, booty hidden under your coat?
Not as a shield for myself, perhaps more as an alibi. But not too explicit. The presence of art in our architecture really grows out of necessity. Art comes up for discussion very early on in a project as a

sort of critical presence. Its role therefore is that of executioner, 'the other' with regard to the architectural space. This space may be charged with all sorts of preoccupations – our architecture also involves stories – but essentially it displays architecture and nothing else. While a work of art actually displays an image rather than a work of art. There is an interesting tension between this rigidity in the architecture and the critical presence of the work of art.

For Hilde and me, being an architect is a fantastic alibi for penetrating deeply into various cultural fields. The fact that we have had relationships with various artists has marked our lives considerably. They were fabulous encounters. The range of environments you come into contact with as an architect is huge. It is this that makes our profession so fantastic. I really wanted to become an artist, but then I did not take account of my father, who steered me towards architecture. In the fifties the economic situation finally began to improve and he felt that I should first concentrate on being able to earn my living. And you could earn your living as an architect.

And now art plays a critical role in your architecture?
Well, we have always aimed for a certain elegant cohabitation. This critical tension is necessary, but at the same time you have to guarantee a certain accessibility for the users. We always try to display a certain flexibility in this dialogue so that people don't get a slap in the face. A good point of reference here is Mozart. His music is pleasant to listen to and everyone loves it, but it also has a sharp undertone. He presented his music in theatres where people mainly came for entertainment. Similarly, we recognise few critical possibilities in architecture because we believe that architecture should give people a sort of satisfaction.

Do you mean the usefulness of architecture?
No, more the satisfaction, comfort in the broadest sense of the word. Even the barracks in Auschwitz offered people shelter. These were not the instruments used to torture people. Architecture is never aimed at causing people discomfort, while art has the right to be very, very black.

Is this provision of shelter then the essence of architecture?
In this sense the architectural models made by the artist Thomas Schütte in the early 80s had a profound influence on us. In his '*bunker für kunstler*' I was very much aware of our need to create architecture. It is essential that a house offers protection, but on the other hand the house is a vehicle for understanding the world. There is the world and here I am protected. The house as an observatory, an instrument you create all around you to observe the greater reality and to learn to understand. In our earlier work this is very evident in the roof flat we did for the Meert Rihoux gallery in Brussels. It is a sort of observation post from which you can look at the city.

Another important influence comes from painting. Architecture irrefutably has three dimensions but I find the idea that architecture should be sculptural to be a sickness. And in the case of spectacular architecture, whose most extreme exponents at the moment are Zaha Hadid and Frank Gehry, I even consider it truly a mistake. As if the purpose of architecture was to display an enormous plasticity. I do not deny architecture's three dimensionality but I feel more kinship with the masterpieces of the Flemish Primitives such as Van Eyck, with their foregrounds and backgrounds, their depths and views. There is something very direct about sculpture. There is a sort of energy that is condensed into a sculptural work. In architecture this energy is inverted. Architecture opens something up, it is divergent rather than convergent. Painting is also very illusory. Something is suggested by using colour on a flat surface. You can't stick your hand into it, but still. This is also the case in abstract painting; the paintings by Mark

Rothko radiate towards the spectator. I find colour very stimulating.

How do you introduce colour into your architecture?
Colour is sprinkled into it, like a myriad. This is definitely true of the colour accents in the Concertgebouw. Colour is strange. Of course it is paint, but in great painting – think of the pointillist Seurat for example – colour becomes something else: not a material but a sensuality that immediately overwhelms you. On the one hand the colour accents create a heightened awareness of the materiality and solidity of the building and on the other they provide a flowing ephemeral presence like a sort of wind blowing through the space.

Is it all about contrast?
We love material. Our buildings must be sturdy because we believe that this makes people happy. You can touch it, use it, stamp on it, rub it. It is something you can hold on to. Colour strengthens this. It stimulates you. And by juxtaposing a series of colours you intensify this stimulus. You also see this in Seurat's work, where the dots of colour together form a single impression in which there is a literal scintillation. I have at certain times been very much involved in this. And then I discovered *une polychromie architecturale*, which is the title of a book on Le Corbusier's use of colour. This word led me to the *Farbenklavier* or Colour Piano, and I immediately saw it start to flow. Colour used with the tingling directness of music. You could almost describe it as chords.

Do you use the same range of colours in different projects?
No, in principle it is always different. We try to find a criterion for the choice of colours that can be made objective. In the case of the Concertgebouw it was the complementary colour to the terra cotta, a sort of blue-green, from which we singled out several colours.

For the High Views the range of colours is based on the local birds. We wanted the High Views to have the effect of a multicoloured bird you suddenly come across in the landscape. Like a strange being, sparkling colours in that green landscape. The observation towers are static constructions, but they are also machines you can ascend. There is also trickery that makes climbing them more dynamic: the steps are not all the same. The first steps are initially very wide but gradually become narrower. In this way you experience a sort of glissando. A changing rhythm as you mount the stairs.

Measurement is very important in your architecture. You have even developed your own series of numbers which the firm uses a measurement system. Did you apply this system right from the start?
No, it only developed later. But now the system, known as Loue, is applied very rigorously. We used it throughout the design of the Concertgebouw.

Does it guarantee the consistency or coherence of the building?
For us it is a way of making design decisions very quickly. It is a very useful instrument. You have to start somewhere when making choices regarding depth and then height. Above all, it guarantees a sort of ease. Things fit into one another, they are easily arranged. But it undoubtedly also has to do with my superstitions. For example in the swimming pool I only go in changing cubicles that have a number in the Loue series, just like the number of seconds I use to heat up something in the microwave. However, apart from this superstition I have always loved geometry. The Loue is ultimately a geometric game: the series of numbers increasing exponentially creates a natural geometry. In my view the Loue also refers to archetypes. The first three numbers are so archetypal; 3, 5 and 7, they are real characters. I

also love the number 105. This is a base number because 3 x 5 x 7 is the multiplication of the first three numbers. This number is also our silent opposition to the metre, which was forced on us during the Enlightenment and has become a very authoritarian measurement. 105 centimetres is therefore our version of the metre, a faulty metre.

Can you explain exactly how the series works?
The 'Loue' series of numbers begins with the numbers 3, 5 and 7 and continues with every possible form of multiplication of these numbers – and the successive numbers in the series. Which means there is not a single even number in it. Because 5 is one of the numbers in the series, there is a decimal element which allows us to work with standard building materials. So it has not made us completely unworldly. Proportion is essential and that has to stay the same.

Does this remove the reservations about sometimes oversizing certain elements, because of the Loue number, and giving them a sturdiness they possibly don't need?
Yes, we certainly do not try to constantly make things as fine as possible. For example, the windows in my house are heavier than they need to be because they comply with the Loue proportions. But I also like the grain patterns you see in wood and they only become visible when you make your window frames wide enough.

This unusual system of measurement may not make the firm unworldly, but it does make for a context of its own that is coherent in itself. Does the application of this series of numbers also respond to the expansion of the firm, so that as a design tool it holds the various designs together?
Maybe. We joke with job applicants telling them that if they wish to work here they have to calculate fifty new Loue numbers. We are now in the thousands and it is no simple matter not to miss a few. But the Loue is a very easy instrument to use. In principle I also like the Fibonacci series, but it ascends too rapidly. The Golden Section is also very good but is extremely difficult to apply. I use it when I can: the floor plan of my own house follows the Golden Section, but using Loue measurements.

This fascination with measure and rhythm is also found in other arts that have inspired you.
Yes, Béla Bartók for example, who composed music based on the Golden Section. Anne Teresa de Keersmaeker uses it a lot in her dance performances. In fact, she finds our Loue distasteful. As far as she is concerned only the Golden Section and Fibonacci will do.

In his music Bartók also imposes classical measurement on folk themes and melodies. Is your aim to achieve something similar in your architecture?
Bartók is my favourite 20th-century composer. I really love his combination of classical and folk. We also see this in the work of the painter Seurat: he uses a highly scientific colour system and the compositions he creates refer to very classical poses. At the same time, and this makes it very interesting, the work has a very contemporary social content. You often see factory chimneys in the background. It is this strange connection of different layers of meaning that interests me. I refer here to Seurat, but you also see this stratification in others. Mondrian's Boogie Woogie paintings are the same. They are abstract and mathematical, but are painted very physically, with adhesive tape that has been pulled off.

What about stratification in your work?
In our work there are many ideas and references that have little meaning for many people. When we were designing the High Views for example, I was fascinated by people who live in trees. Very old trees ultimately become quite hollow inside. This idea of a trunk into which you can crawl has therefore found

its way into this design. Stories like this charge up the design process but they are in fact not important to the final result; nobody needs to know these things.

So you like to confront a geometric, scientific character with all sorts of personal references and inspirations, sometimes hidden?
But it is a scientific character that is not too difficult, more like 'science for dummies'. When I was a student I read a work by Lionello Puppi, which really affected me, about Palladio's sources of inspiration. Puppi states that Palladio's ideas are based on three main principles. First there is Plato, the pursuit of the prototype, the ideal form. Secondly there is Aristotle, who represents science. Among other things Palladio carried out archaeological studies, but he also worked out his own numerical system. He used three measurements in a room, adopted two of these measurements for the next room and so on. A third principle is called elastic humanism: 'Architecture must be practical, easy to use.' In Villa Emo, for example, there is an imposing sloping surface that leads to the central building, but this surface is also a threshing floor on which the husks roll smoothly to the bottom. Architecture must fit like a glove. This scientific character is important, but to be honest, isn't architecture a fairly simple science? Lucid, comprehensible, in the here and now. Even the theory of the strength of materials is something I can deal with. But when we are dealing with a really difficult science I get lost very quickly. I decided to stick to architecture.

Robbrecht en Daem
Pacing through Architecture

Maarten Delbeke
Stefan Devoldere
Iwan Strauven

Kristien Daem, *photography*

Bozar Books
Verlag der Buchhandlung Walther König

3   A Conversation at the home of Jean Prouvé
    Stefan Devoldere, Iwan Strauven

        I   Rubensplein
        II   Concertgebouw Brugge
        III   Gaasbeek
        IIII   Colombier
        IIIII   Robbrecht en Daem Offices
        IIIIII High Views Lincolnshire
        IIIIIII Woodland Cabin

181 Ephemeral Principles
    Maarten Delbeke

195 Projects

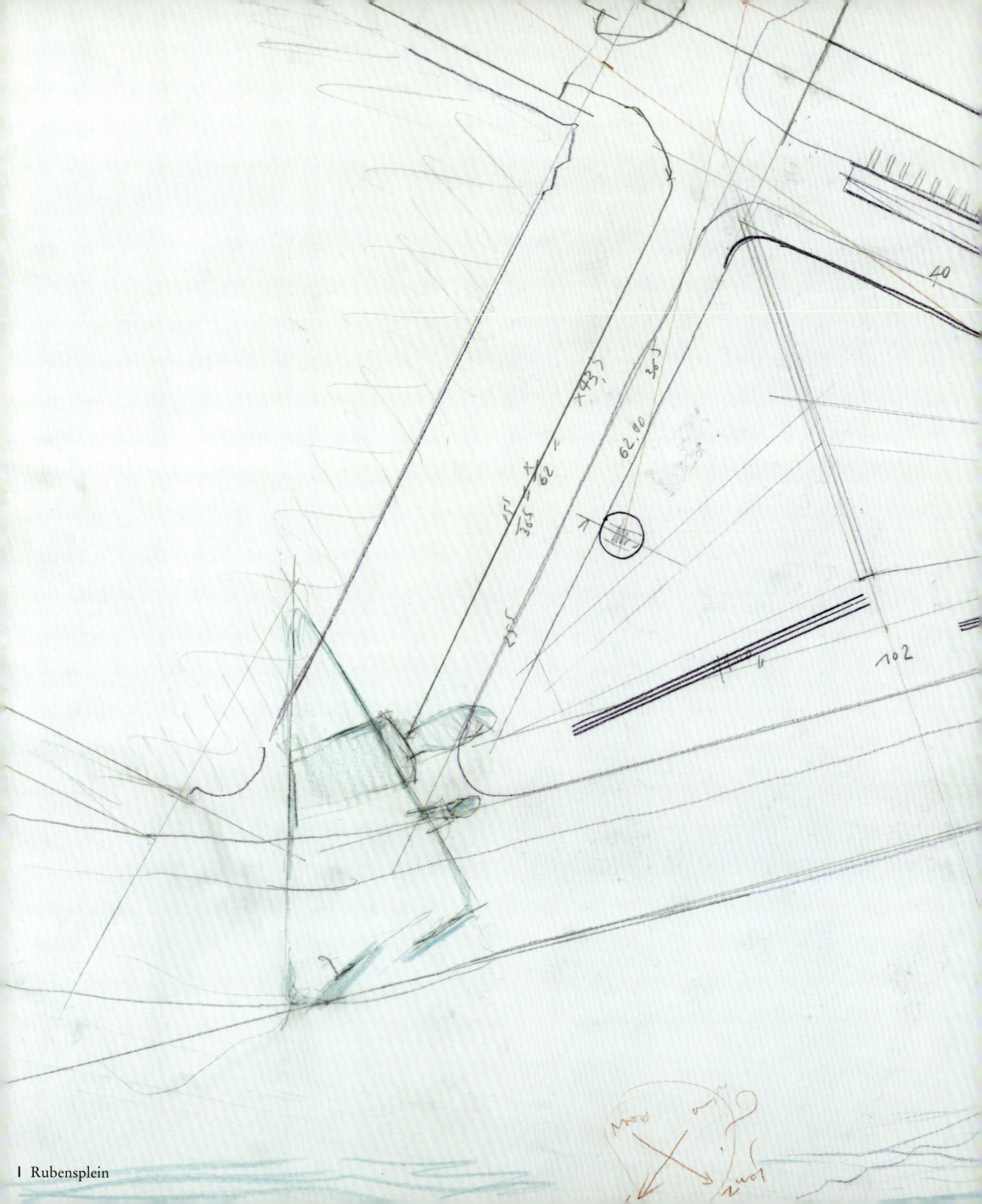
1 Rubensplein

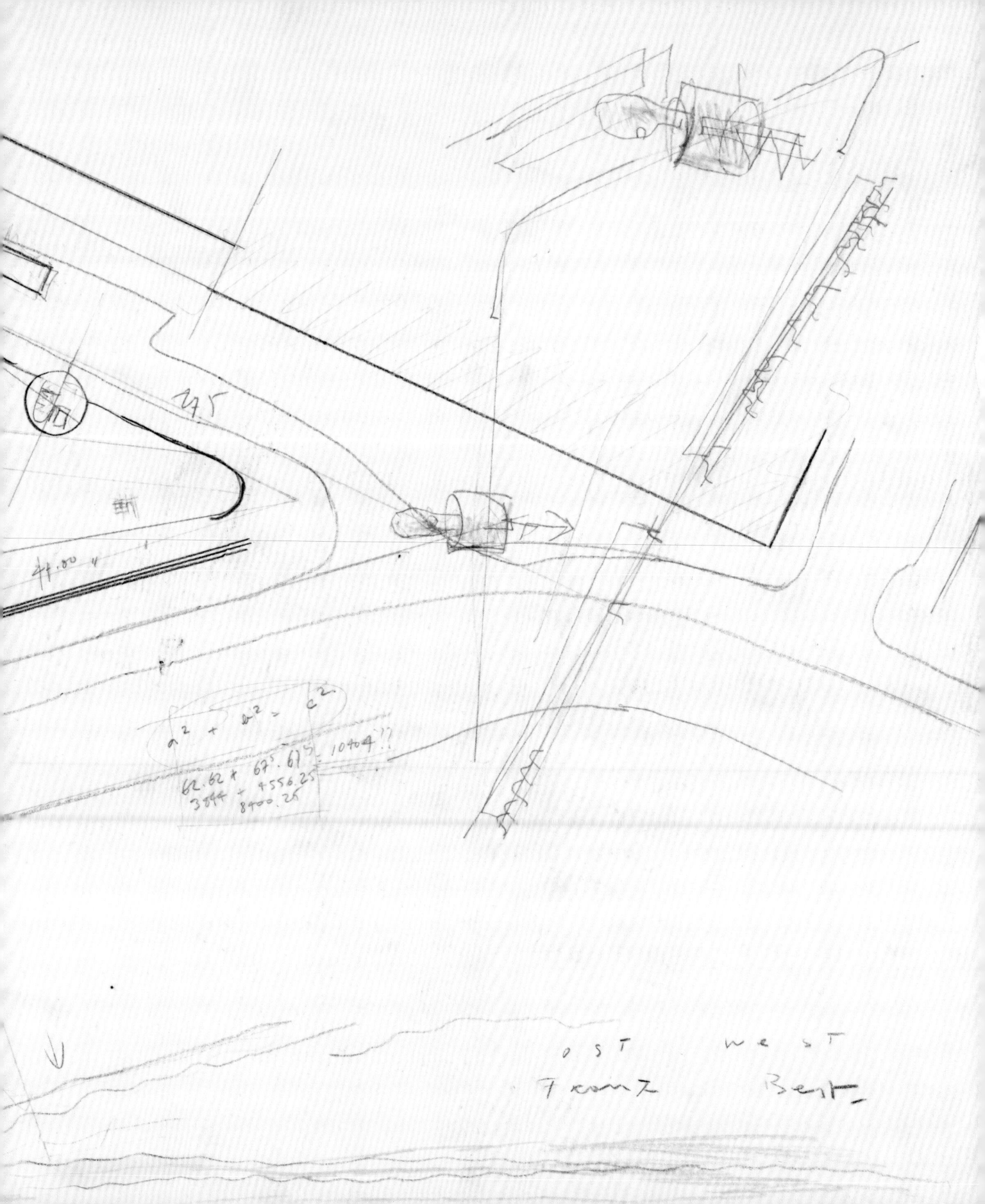

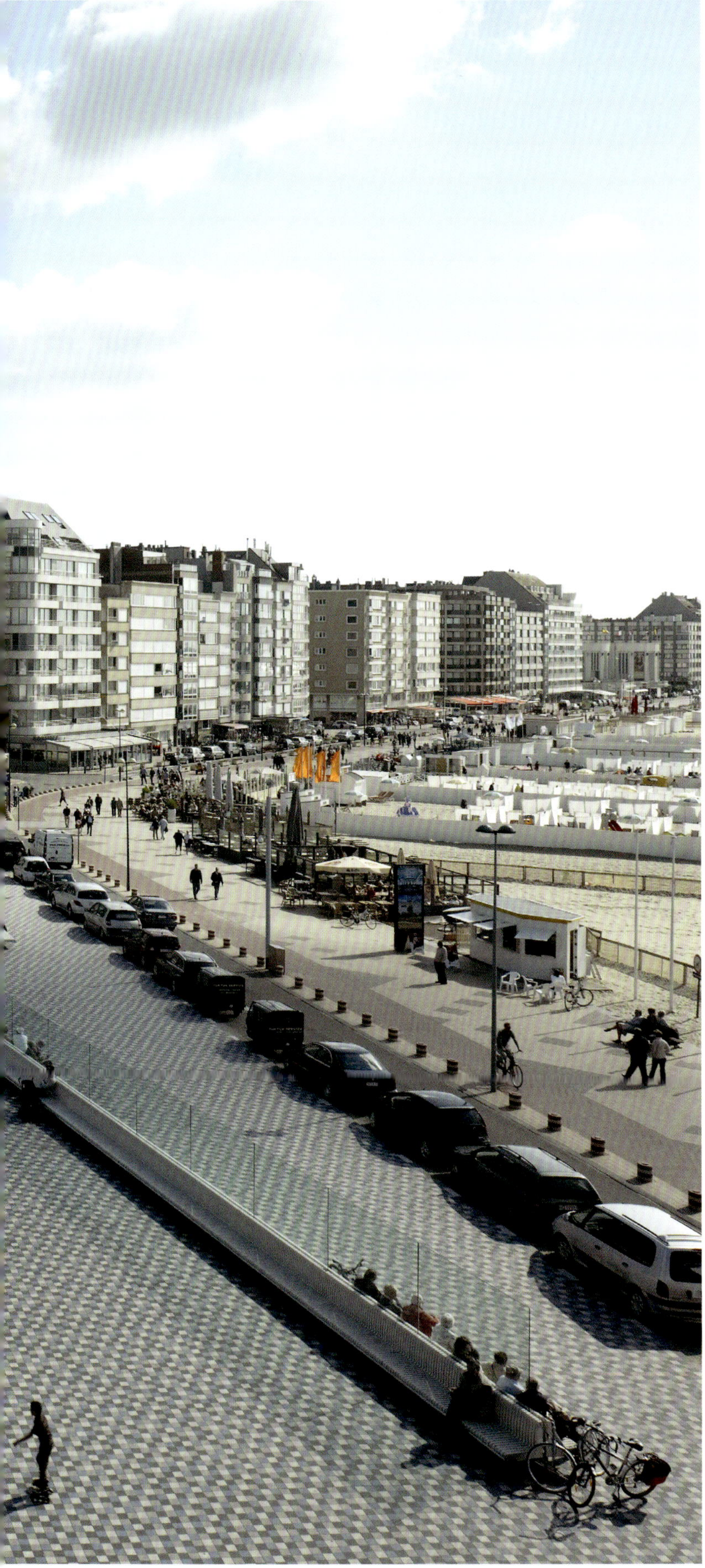
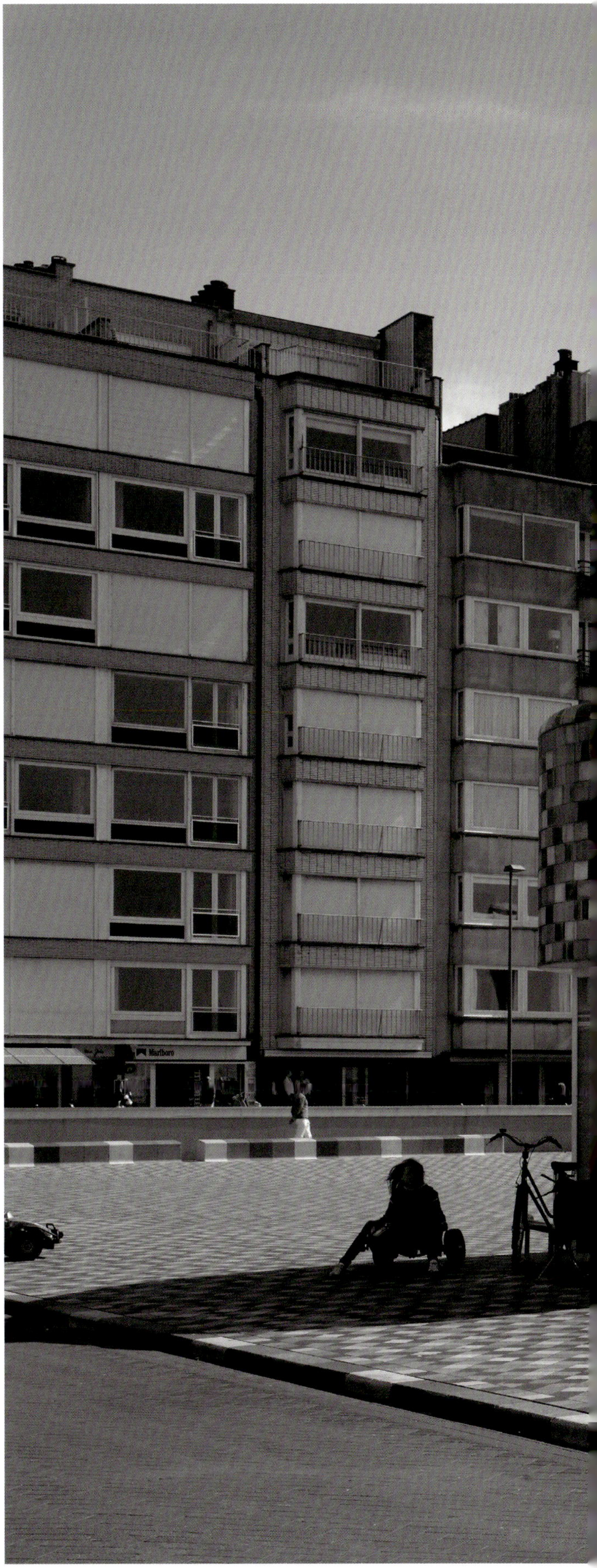

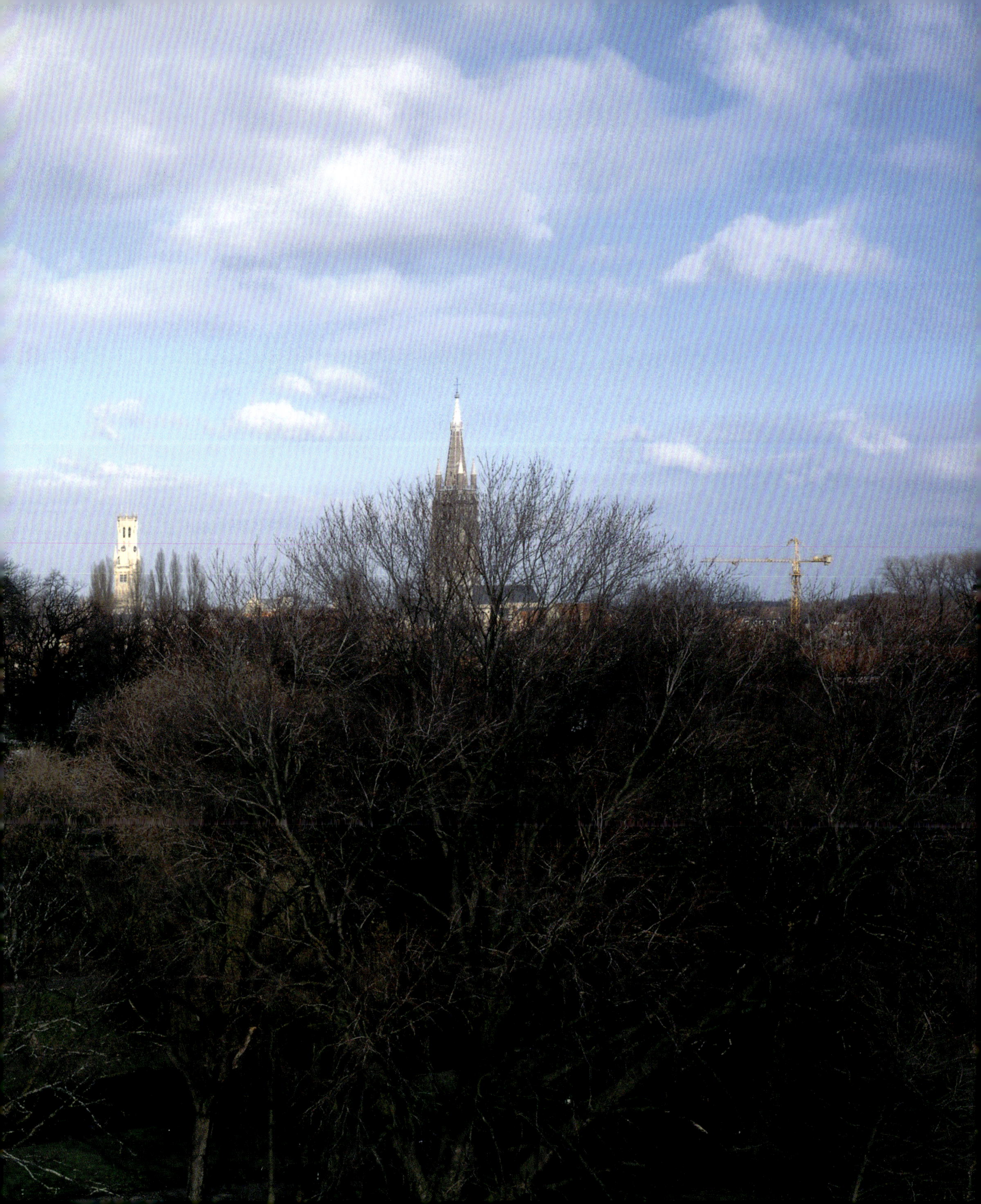

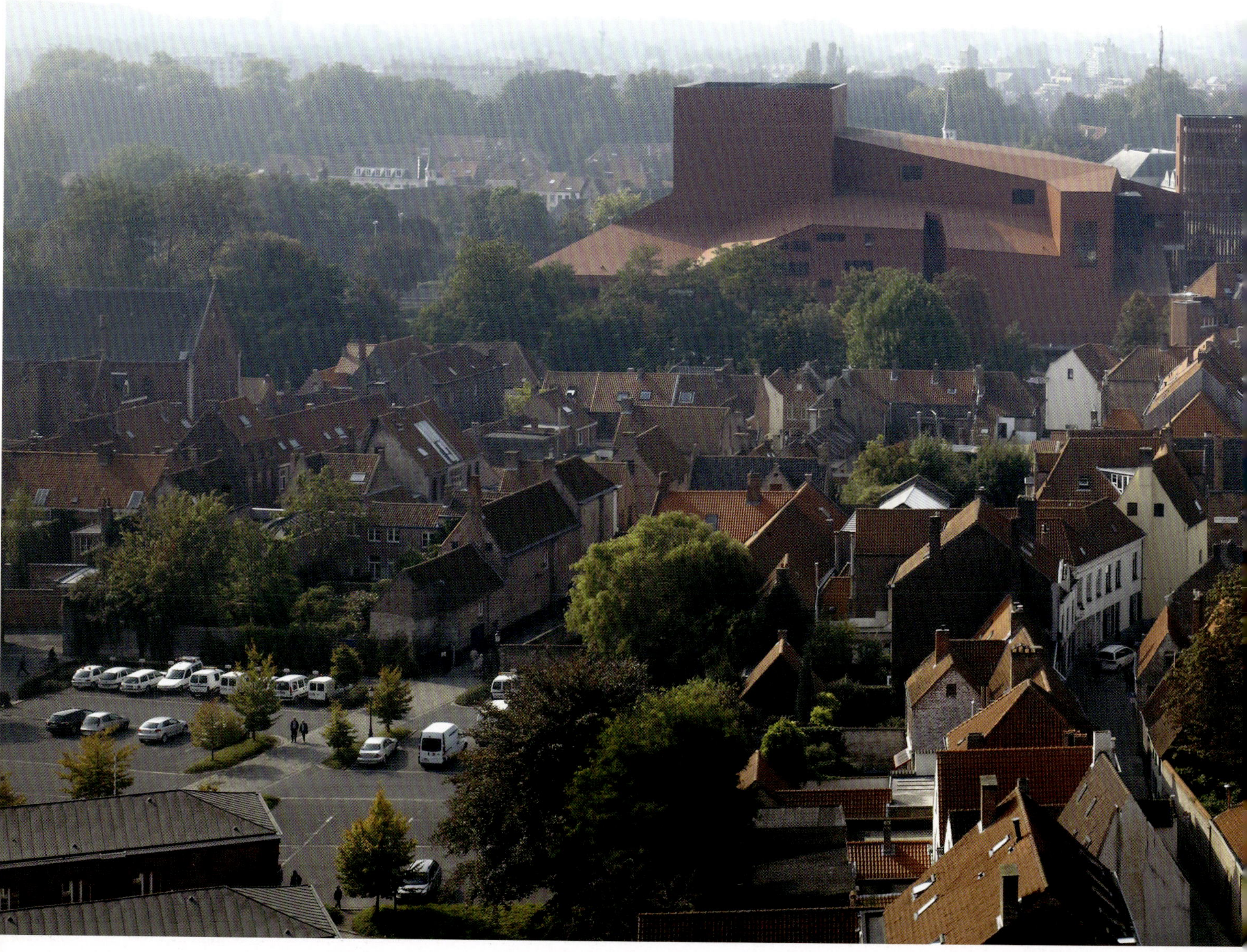

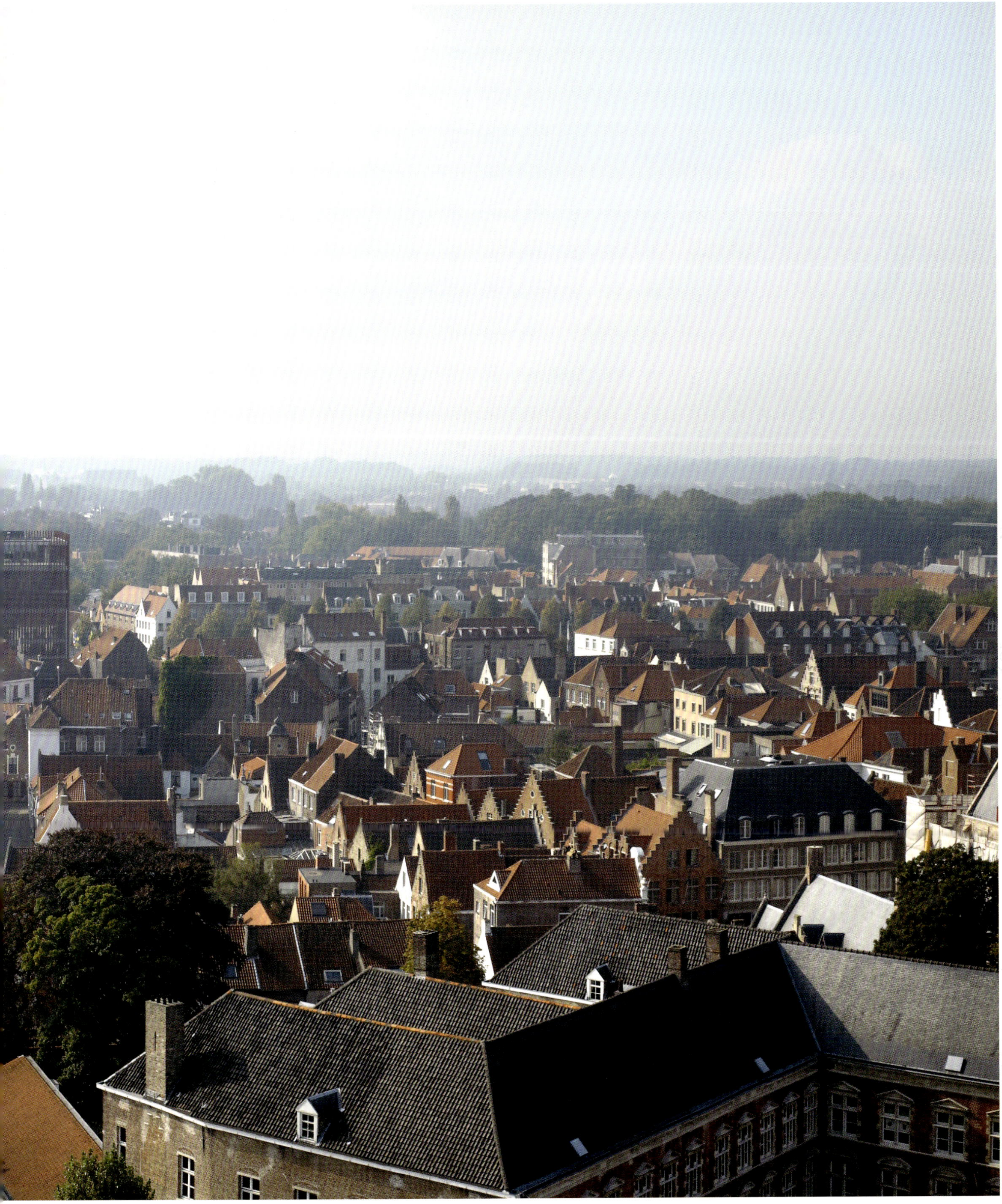

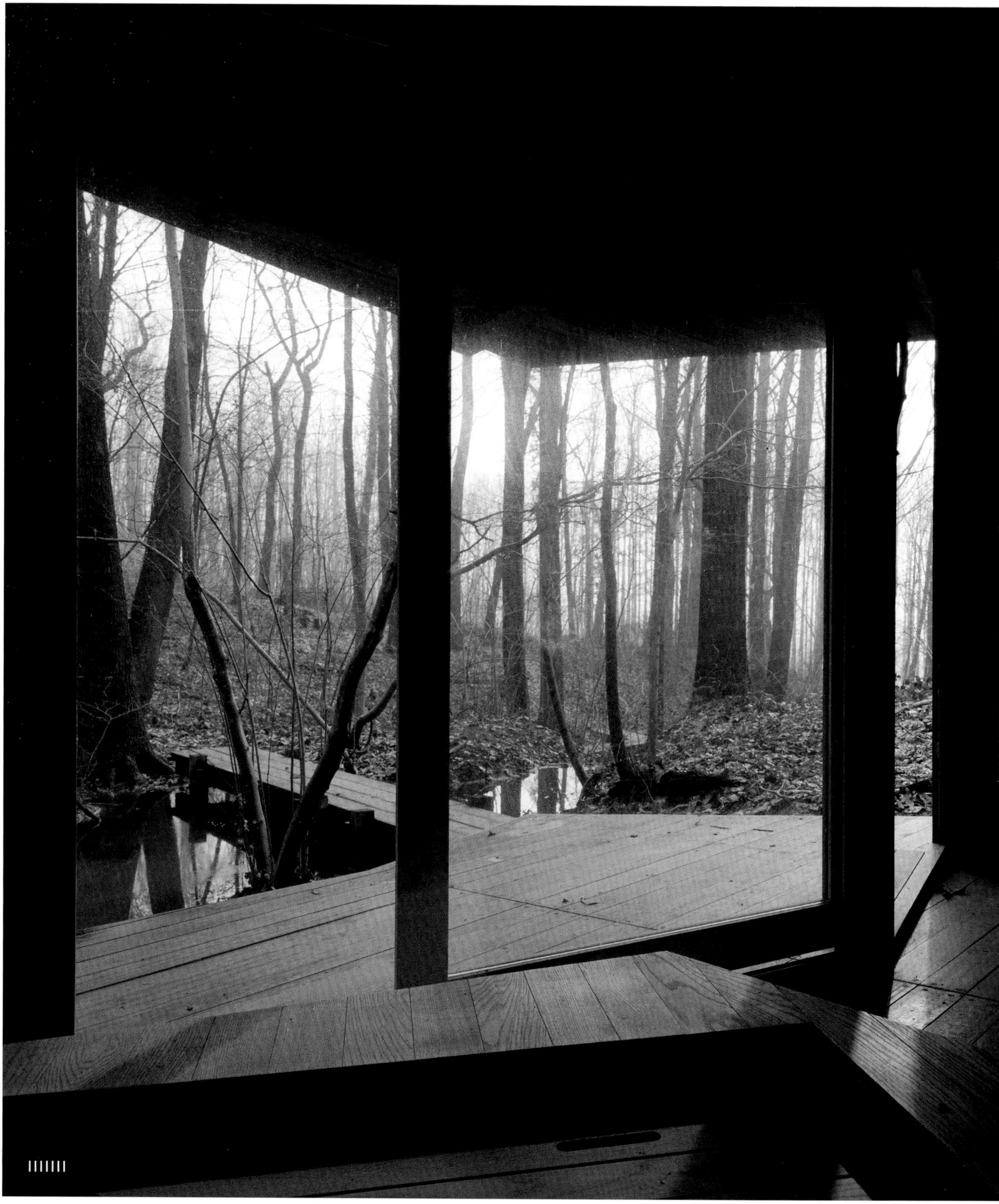

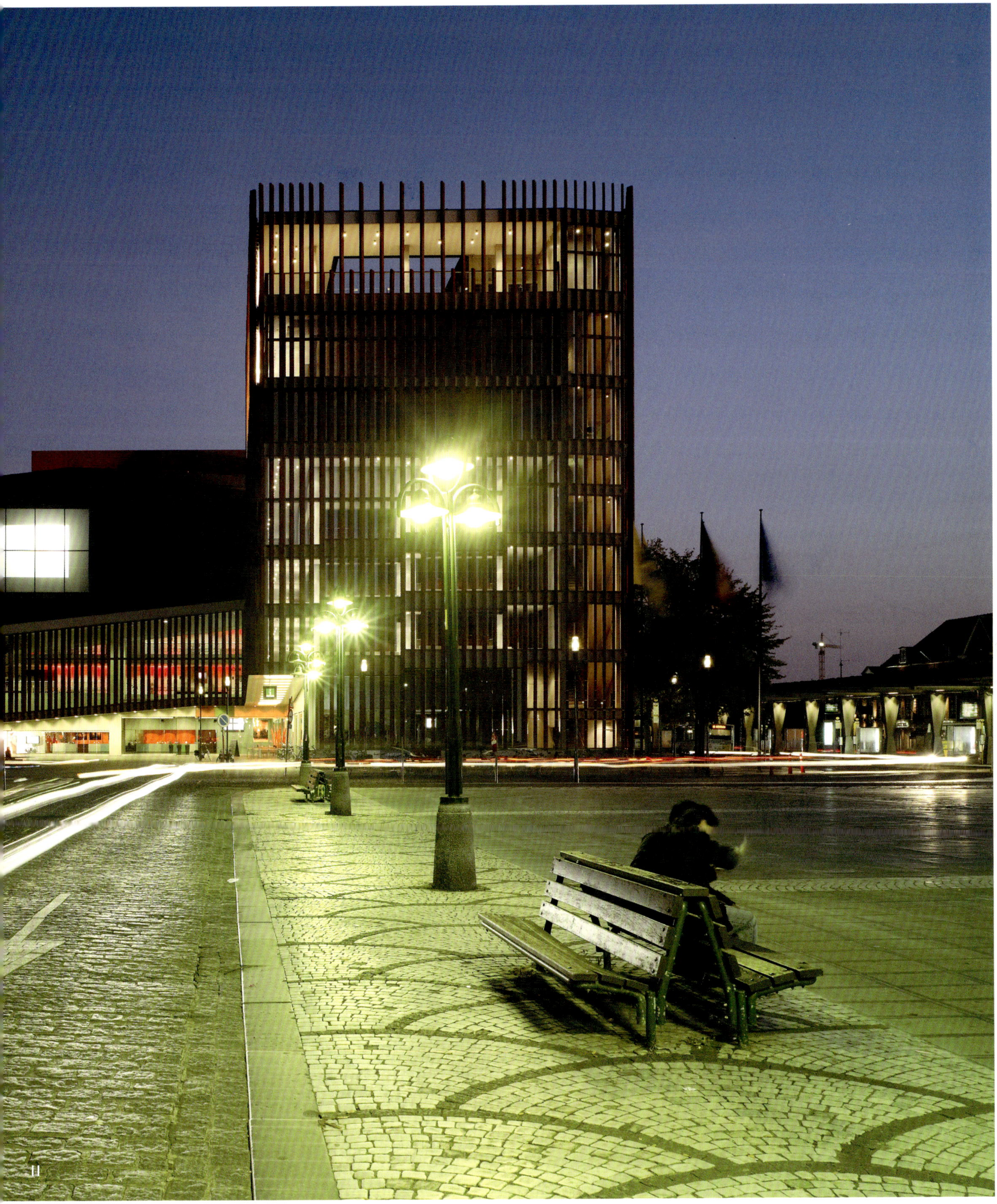

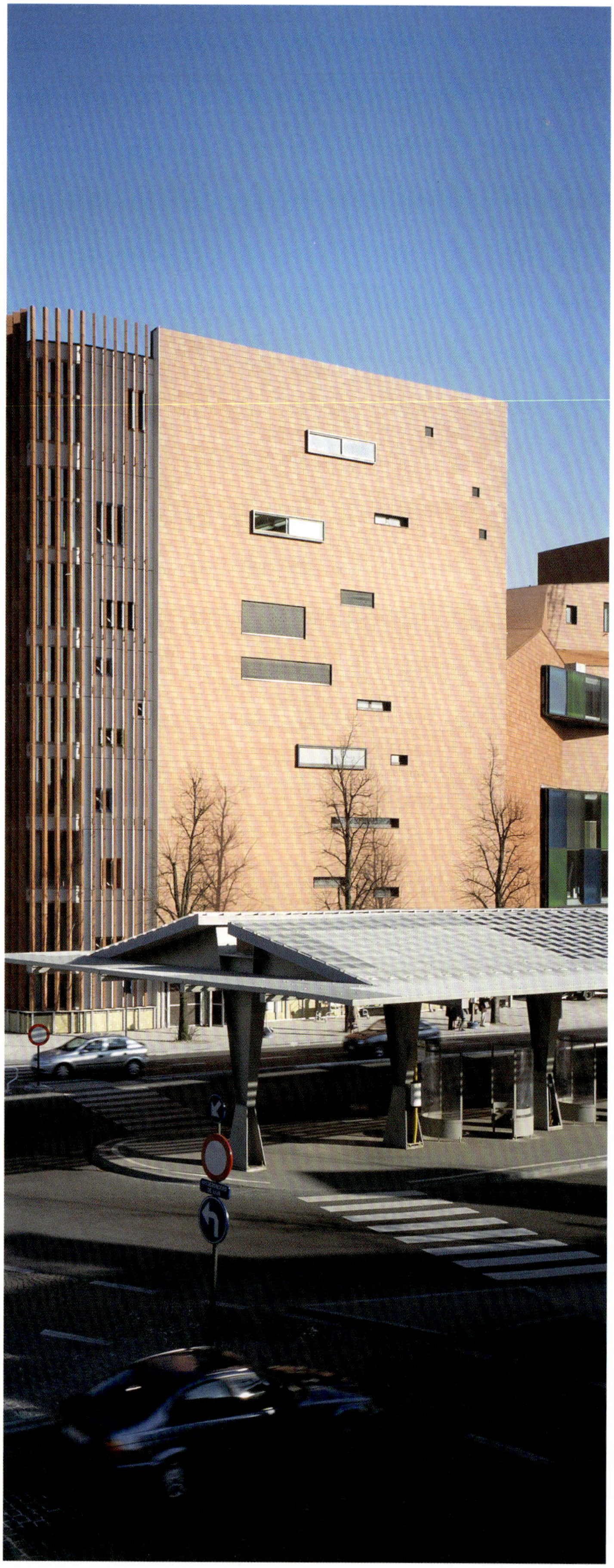

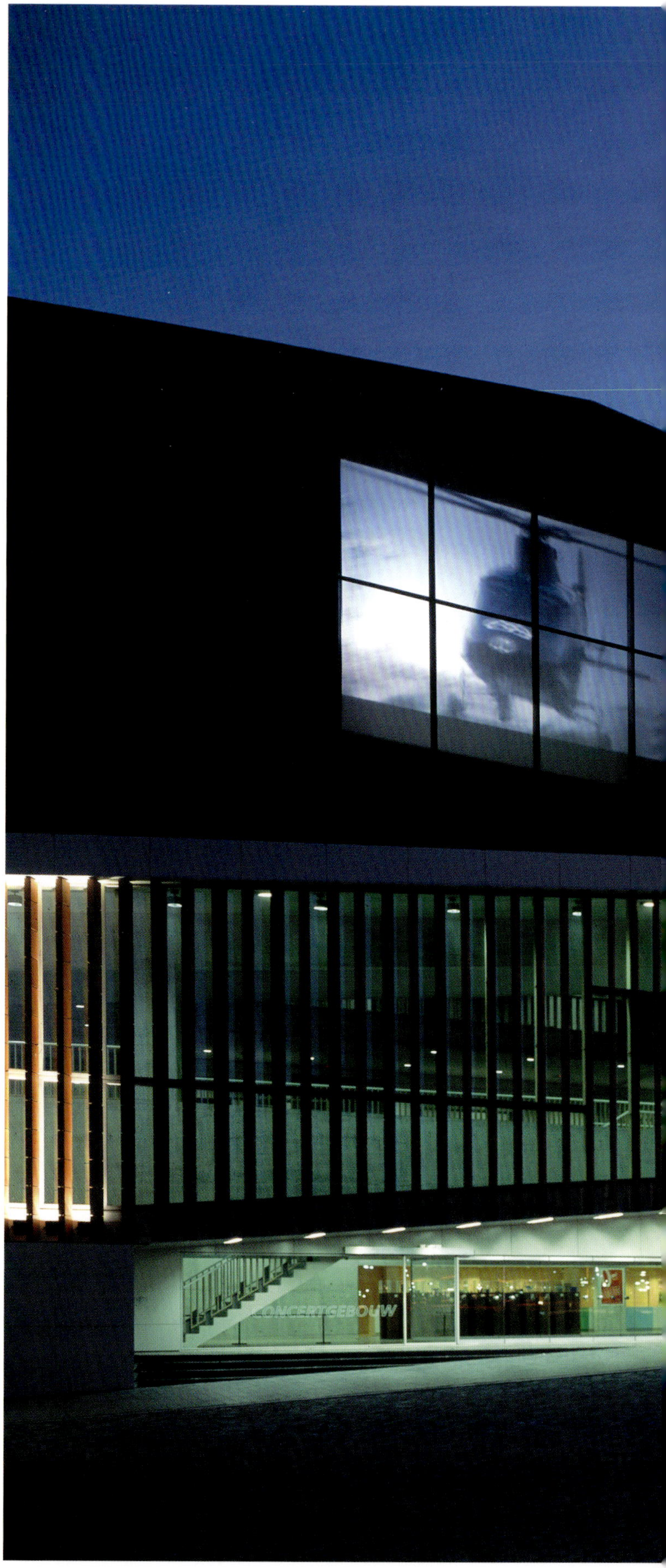
CONCERTGEBOUW

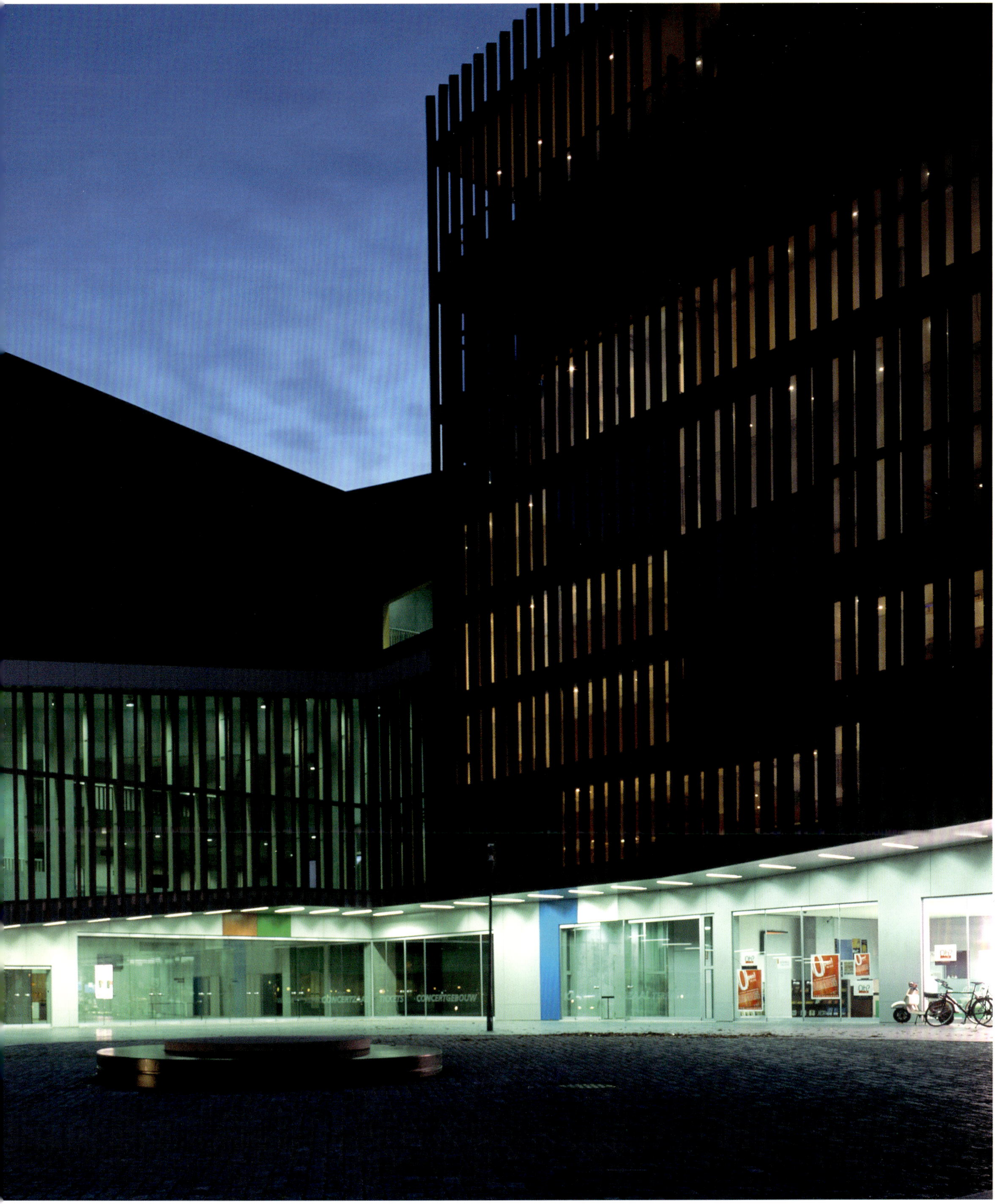
CONCERTGEBOUW

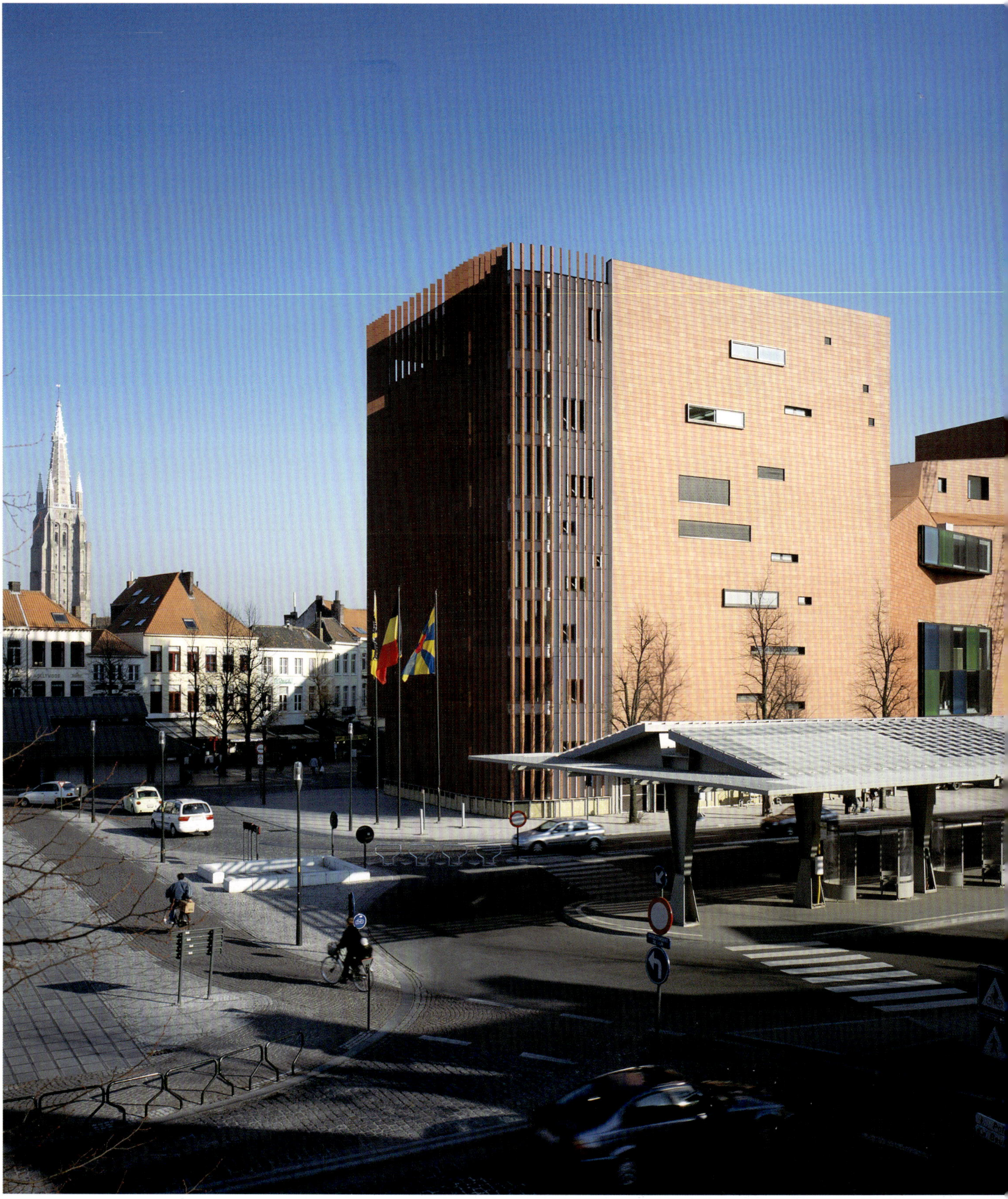

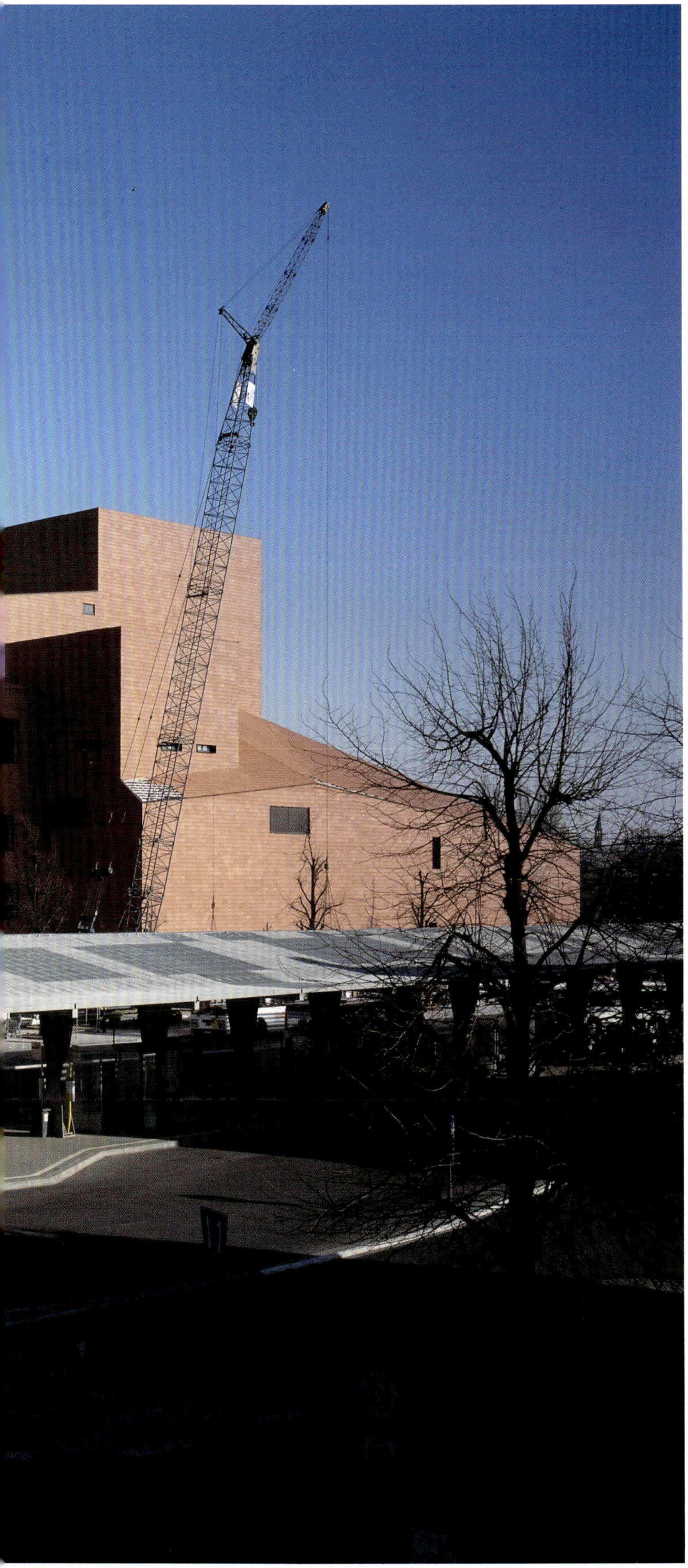

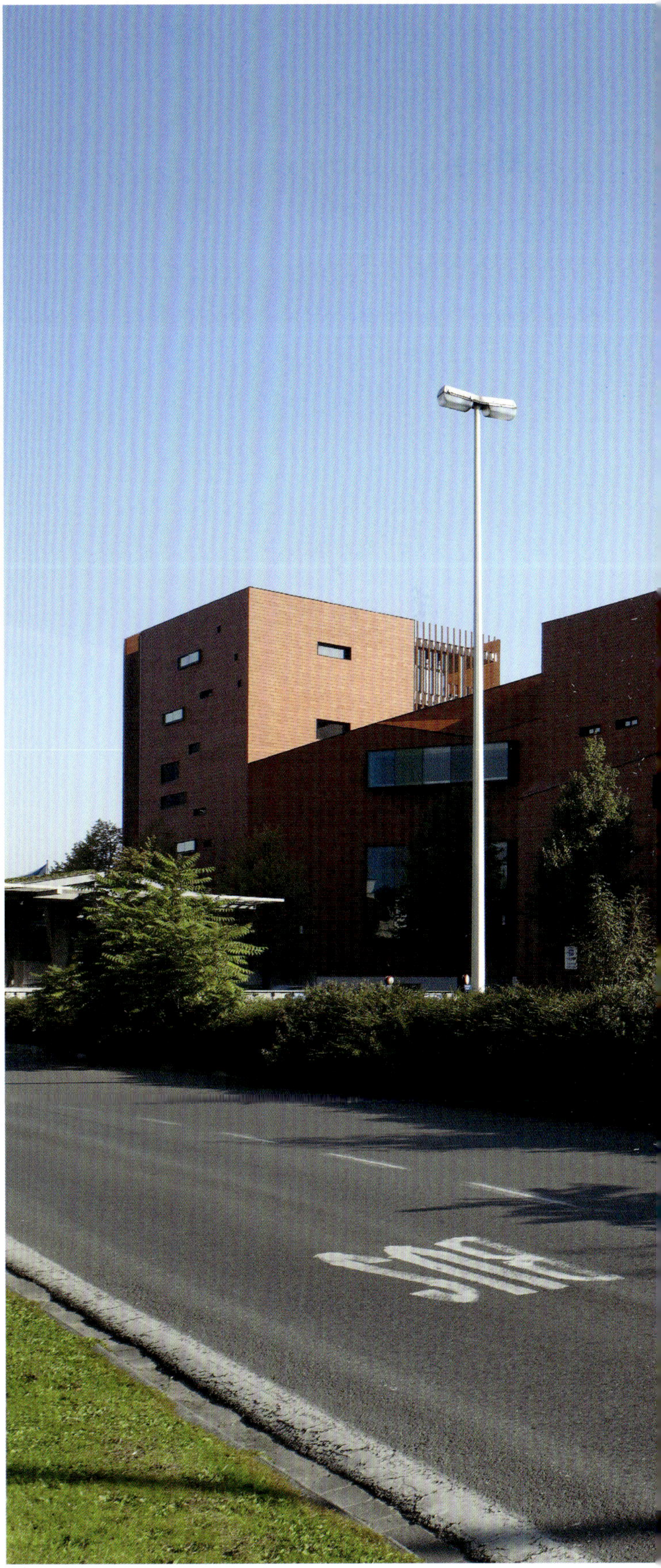

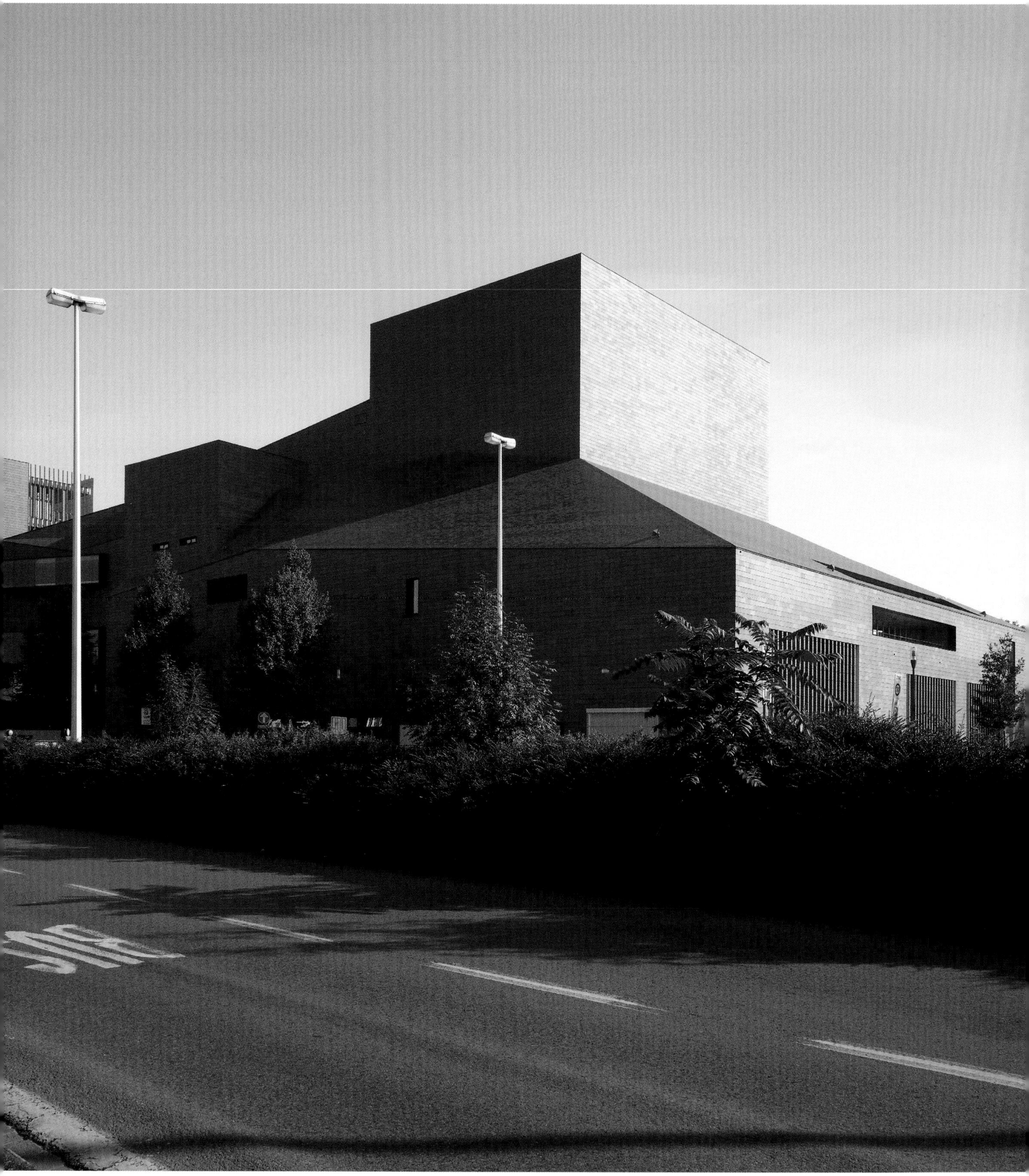

47

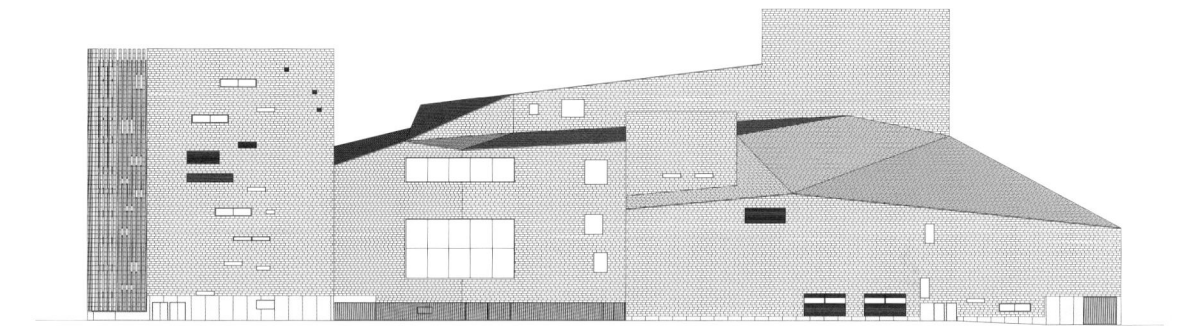

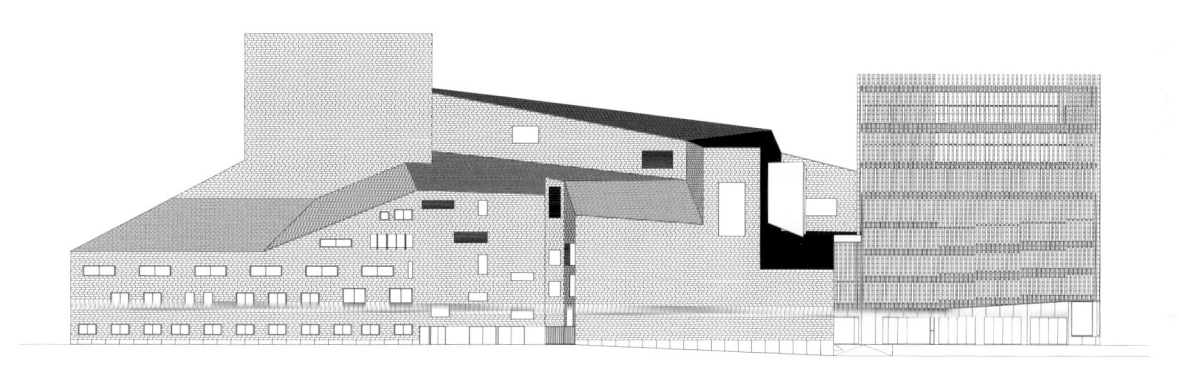

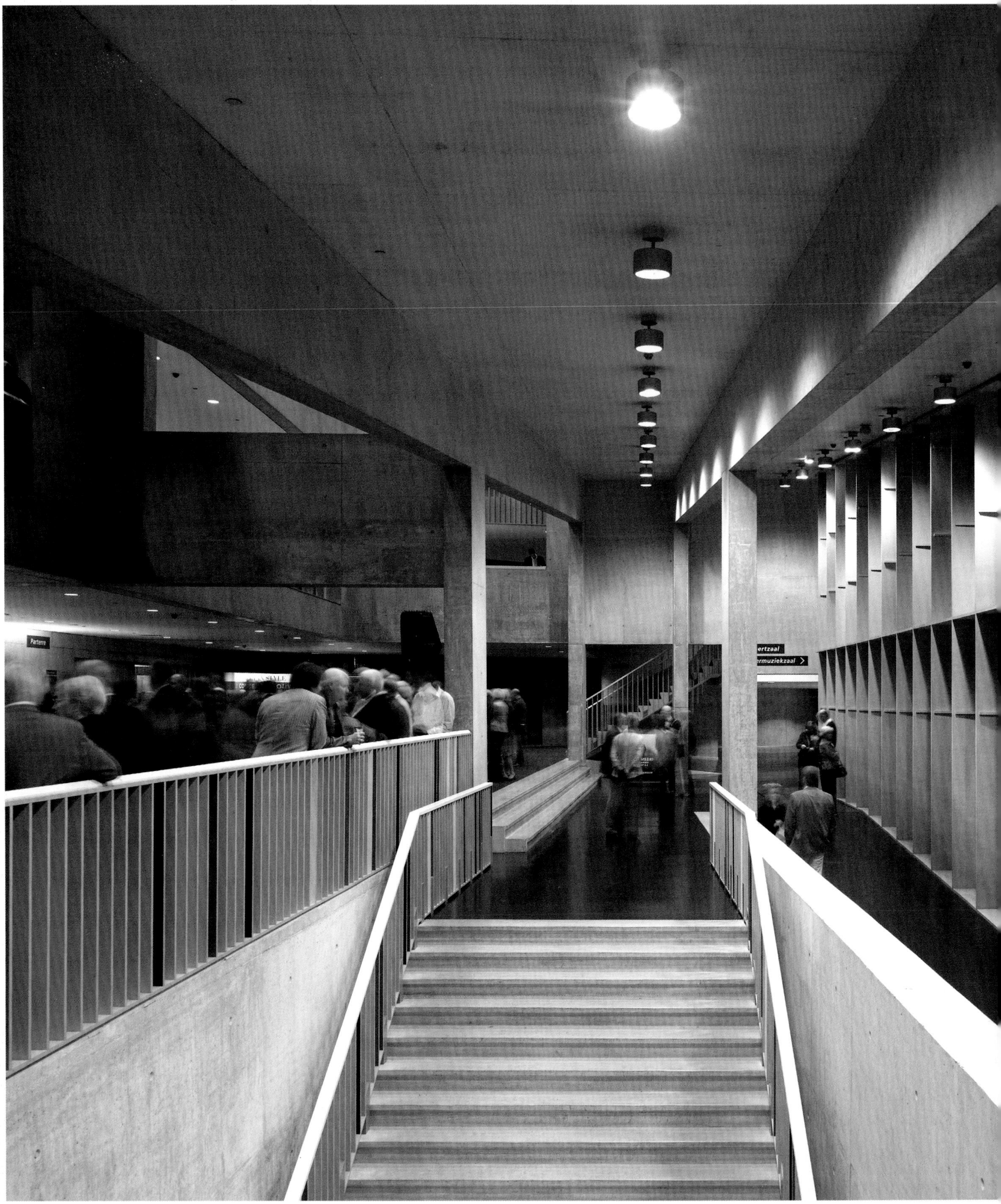

Parterre
ertzaal
ermuziekzaal

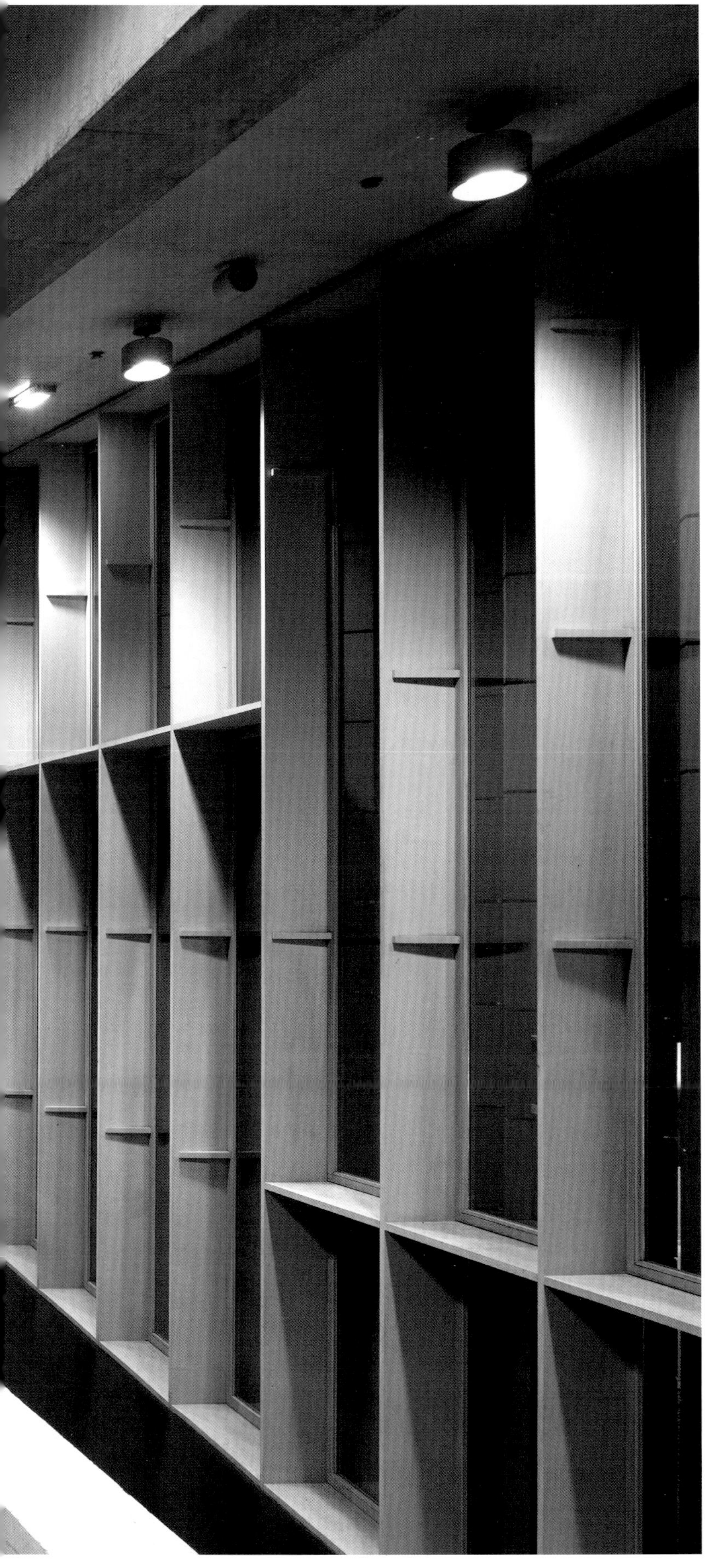

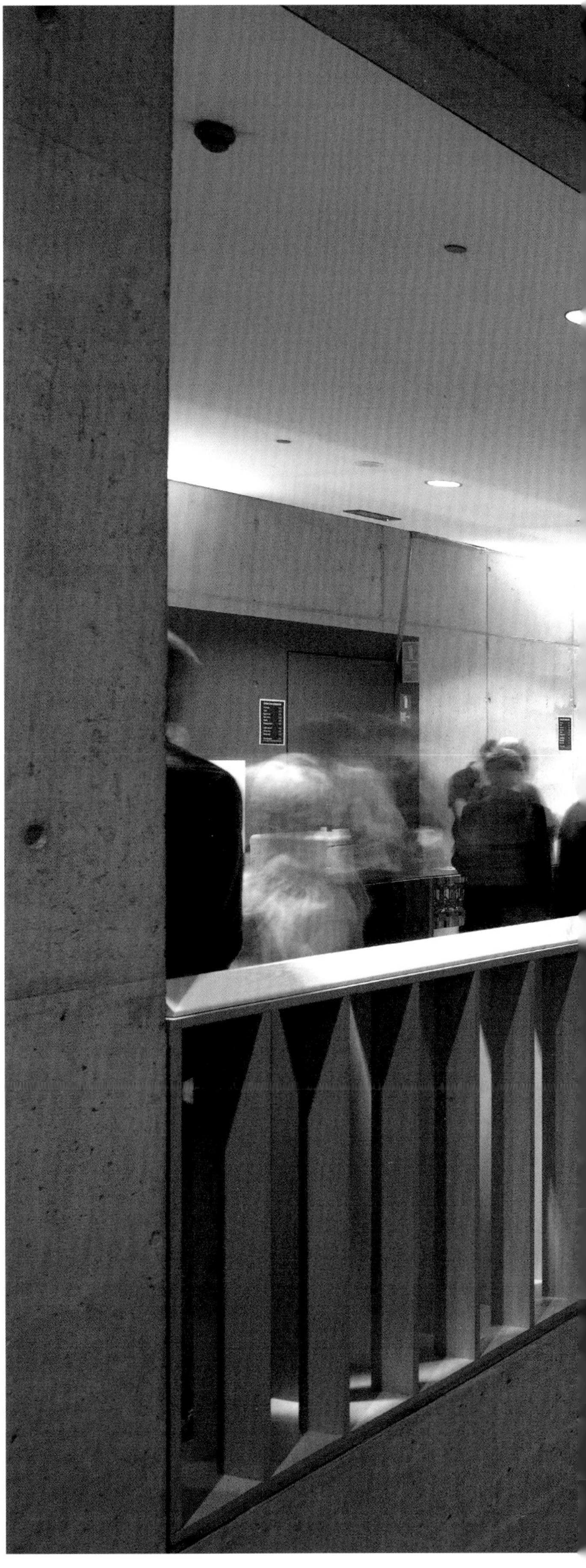

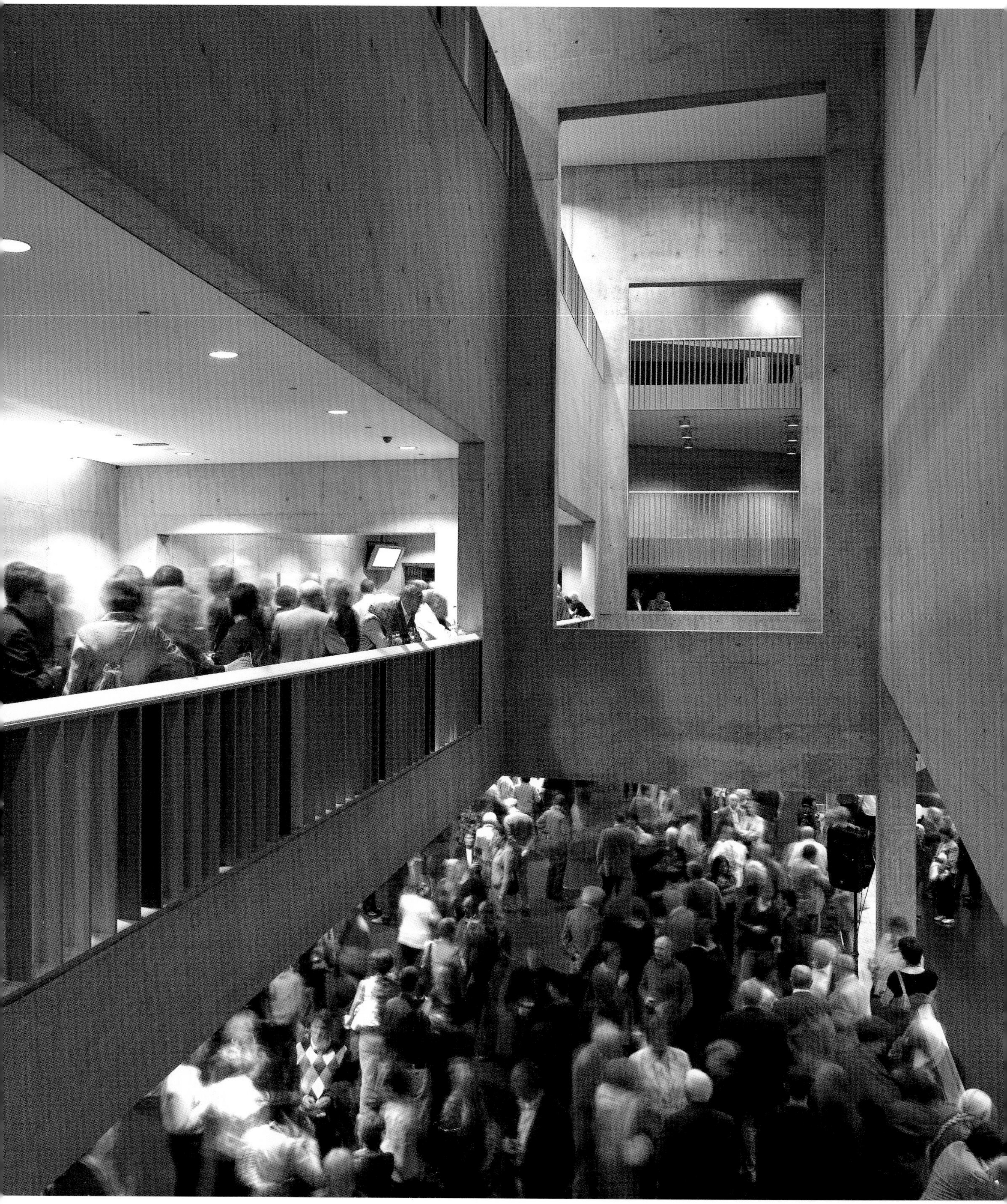

artiesten foyer | repetitiezaal

scene
orkestschelp

vista dwarsheen foyer

blik oost
stad Brugge

Lantaarntoren

blik noordzee

Het P lein

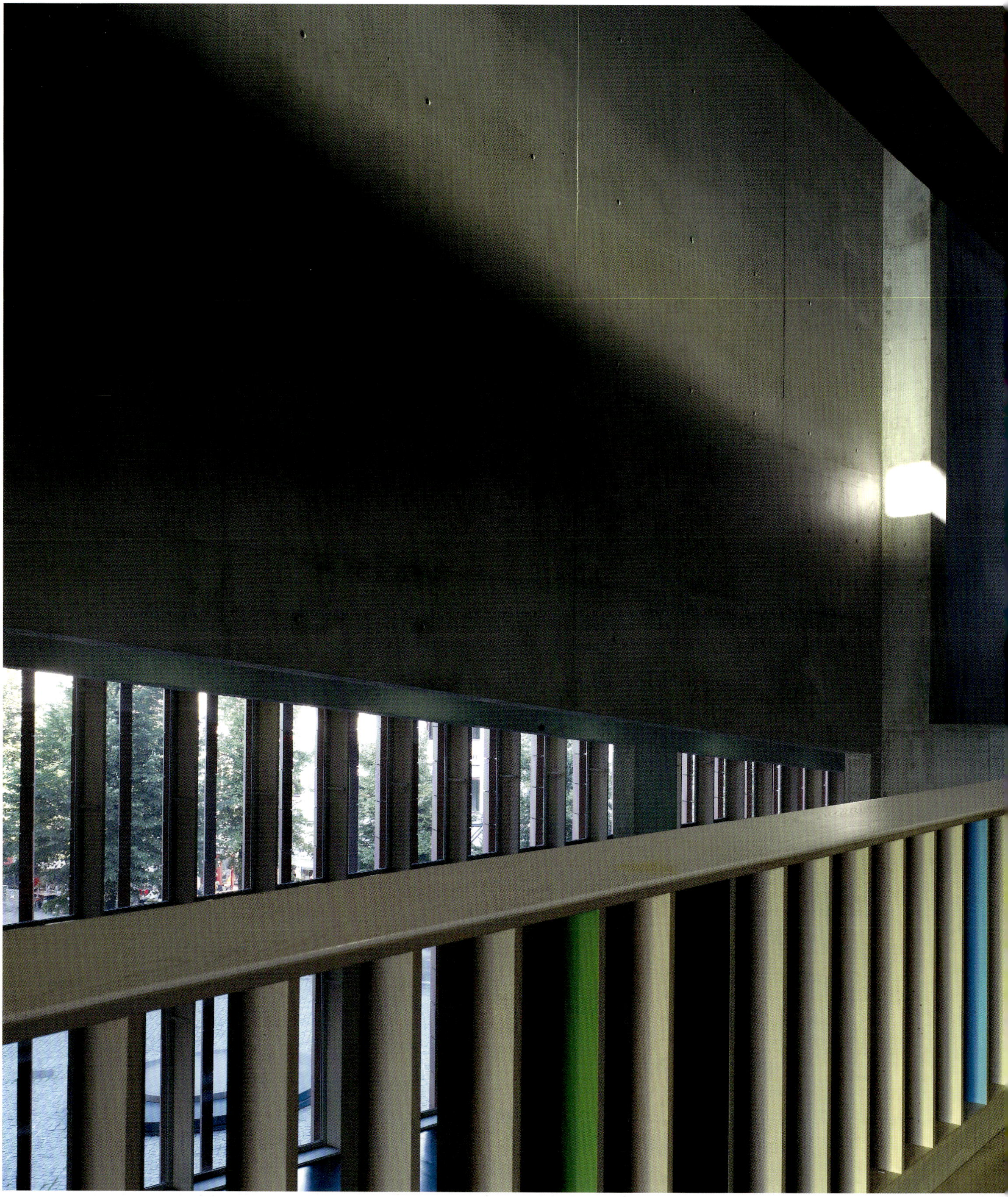

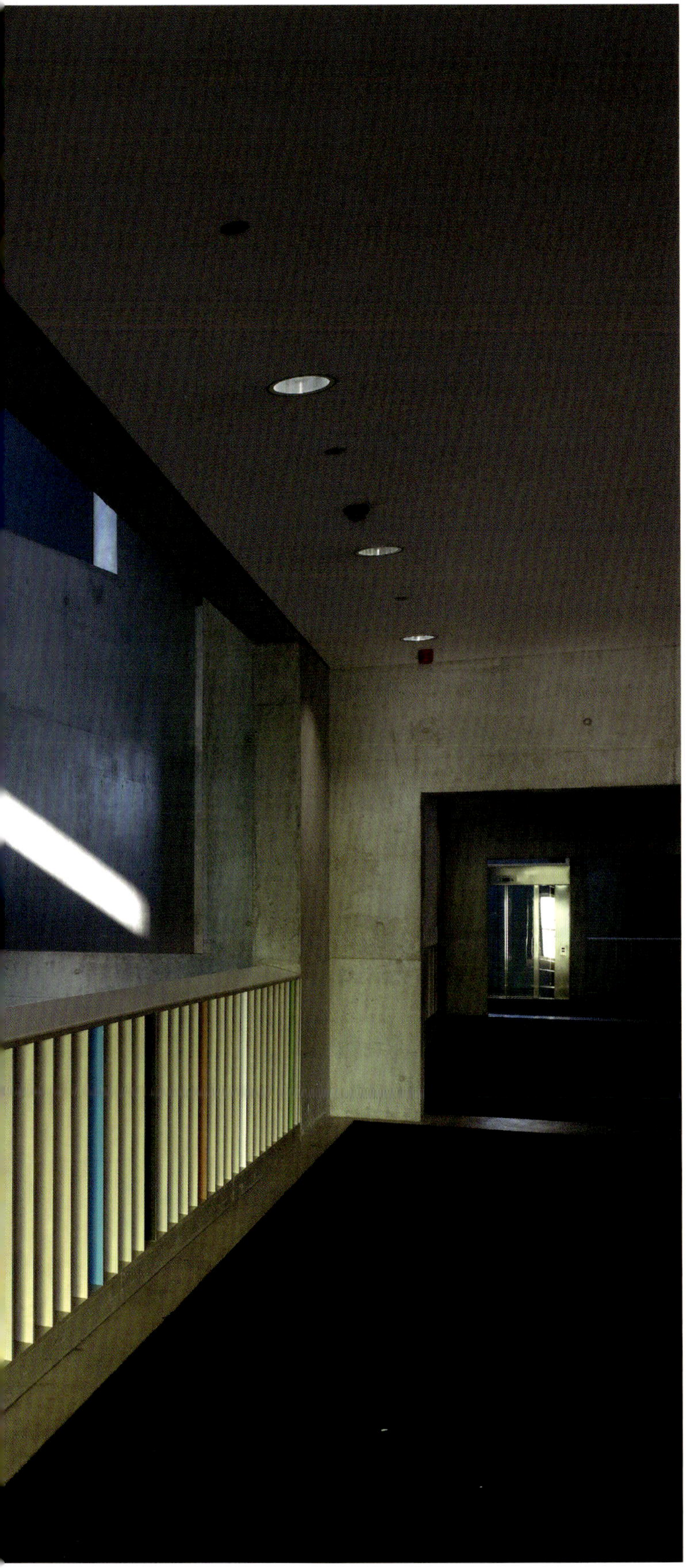

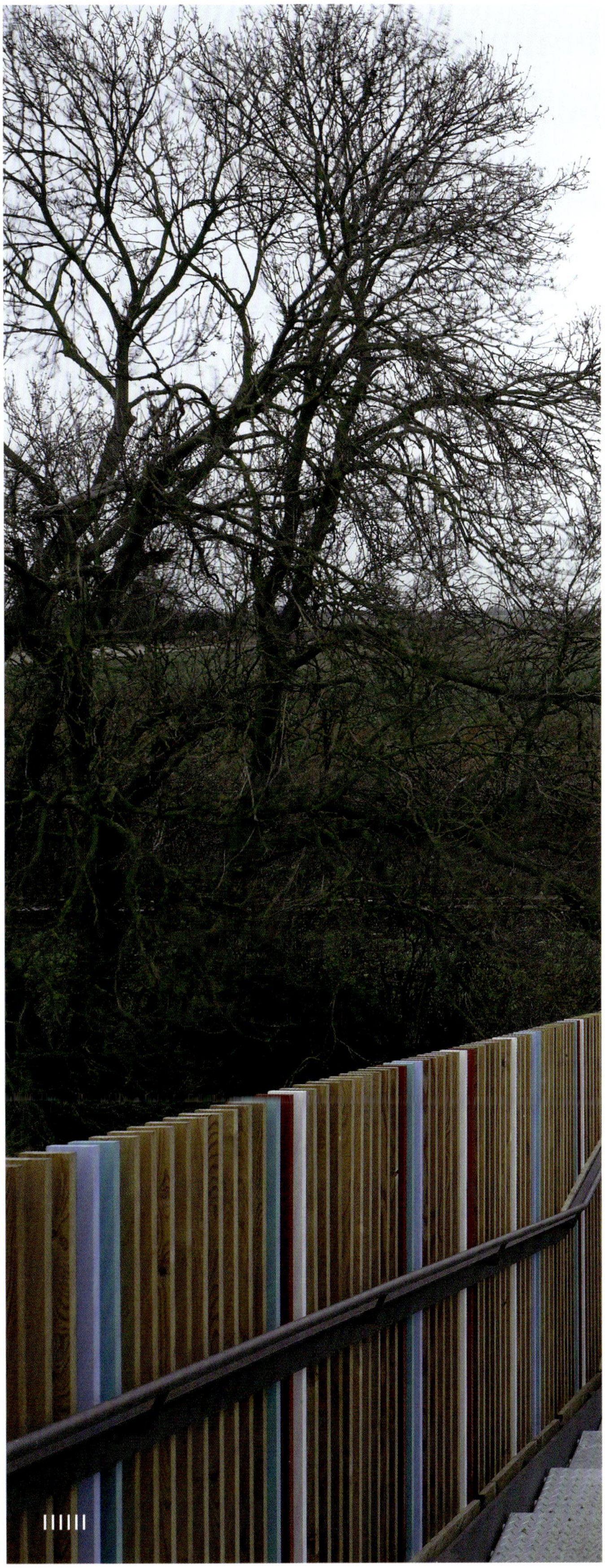

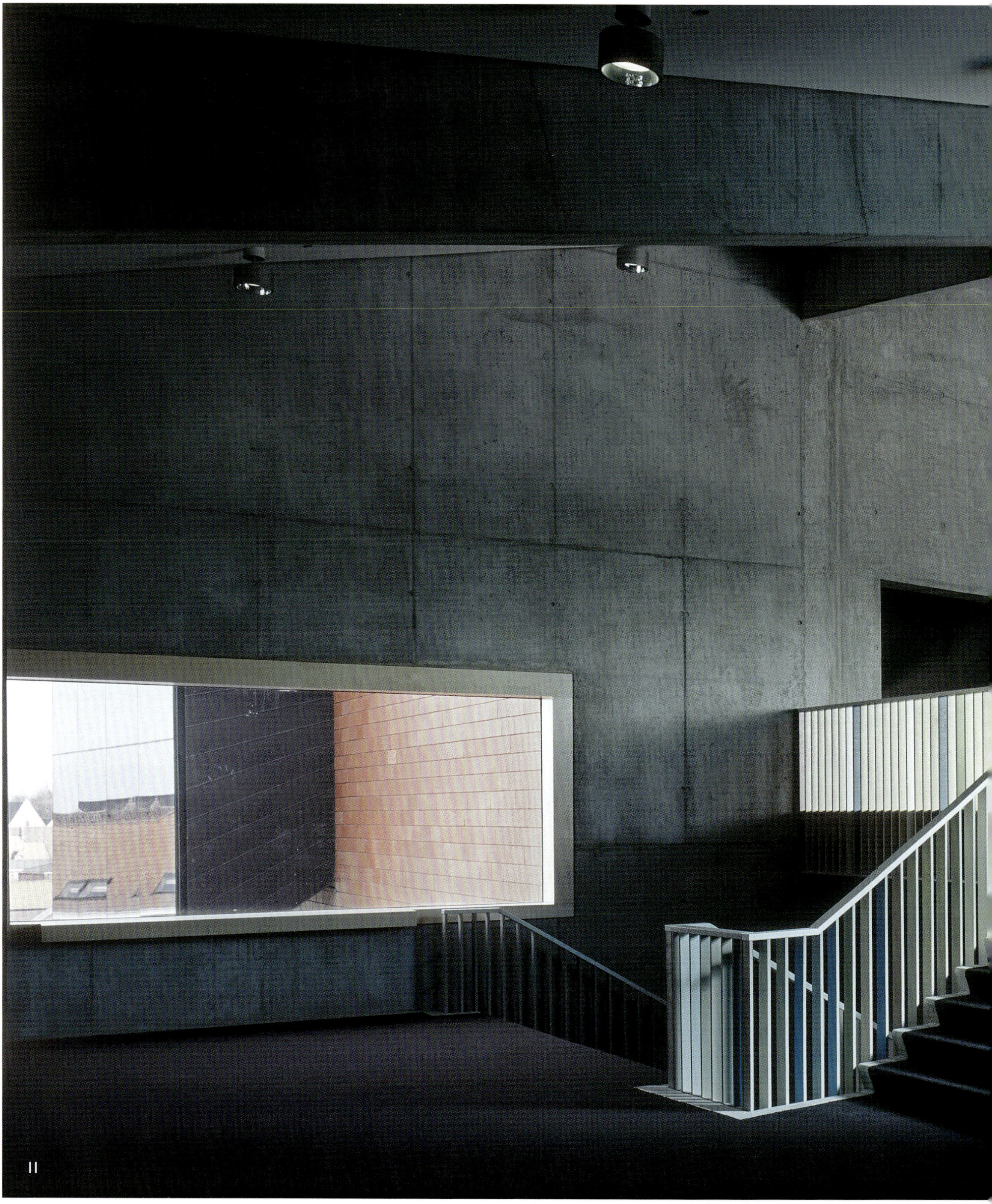

2 de Balkon

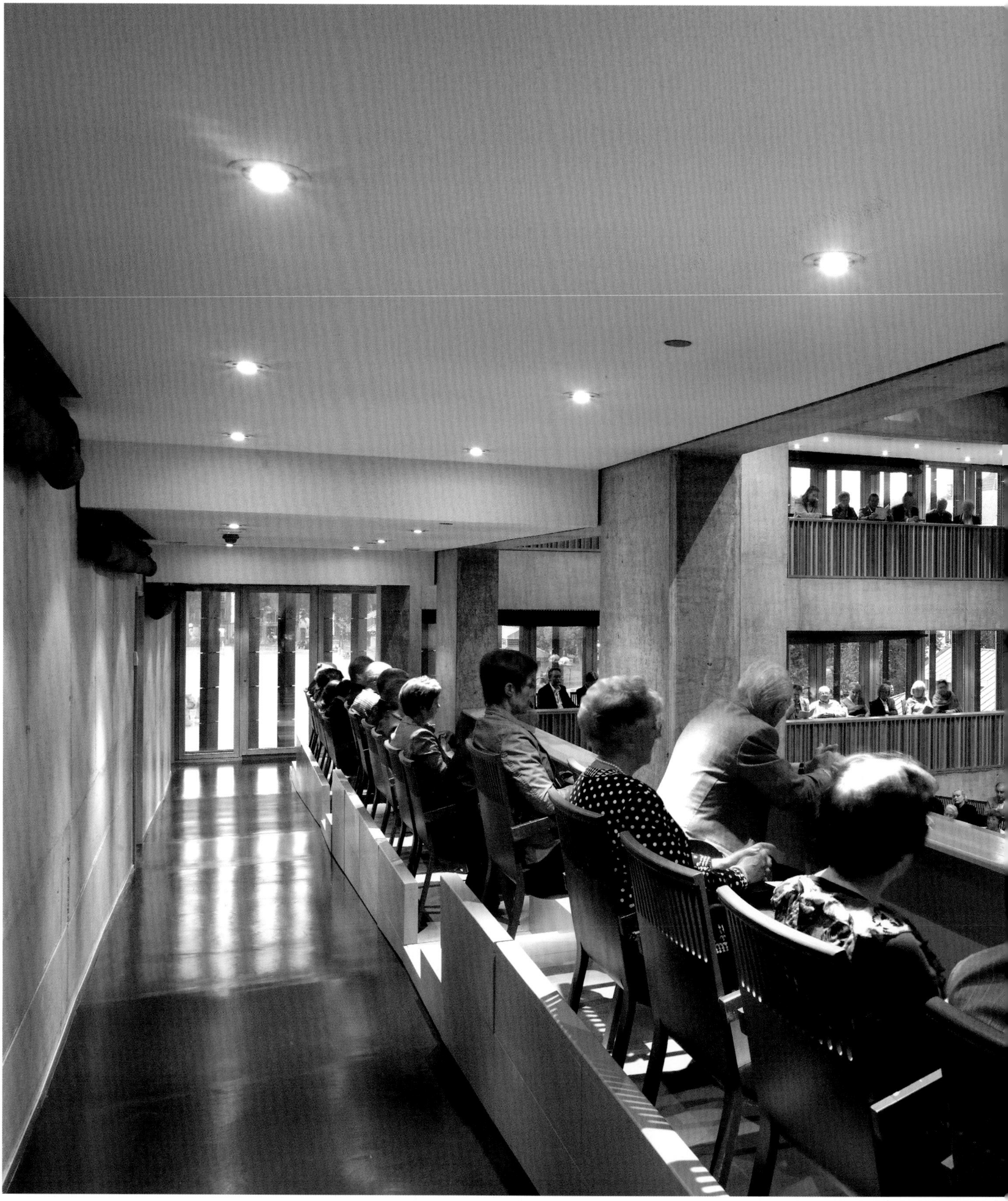

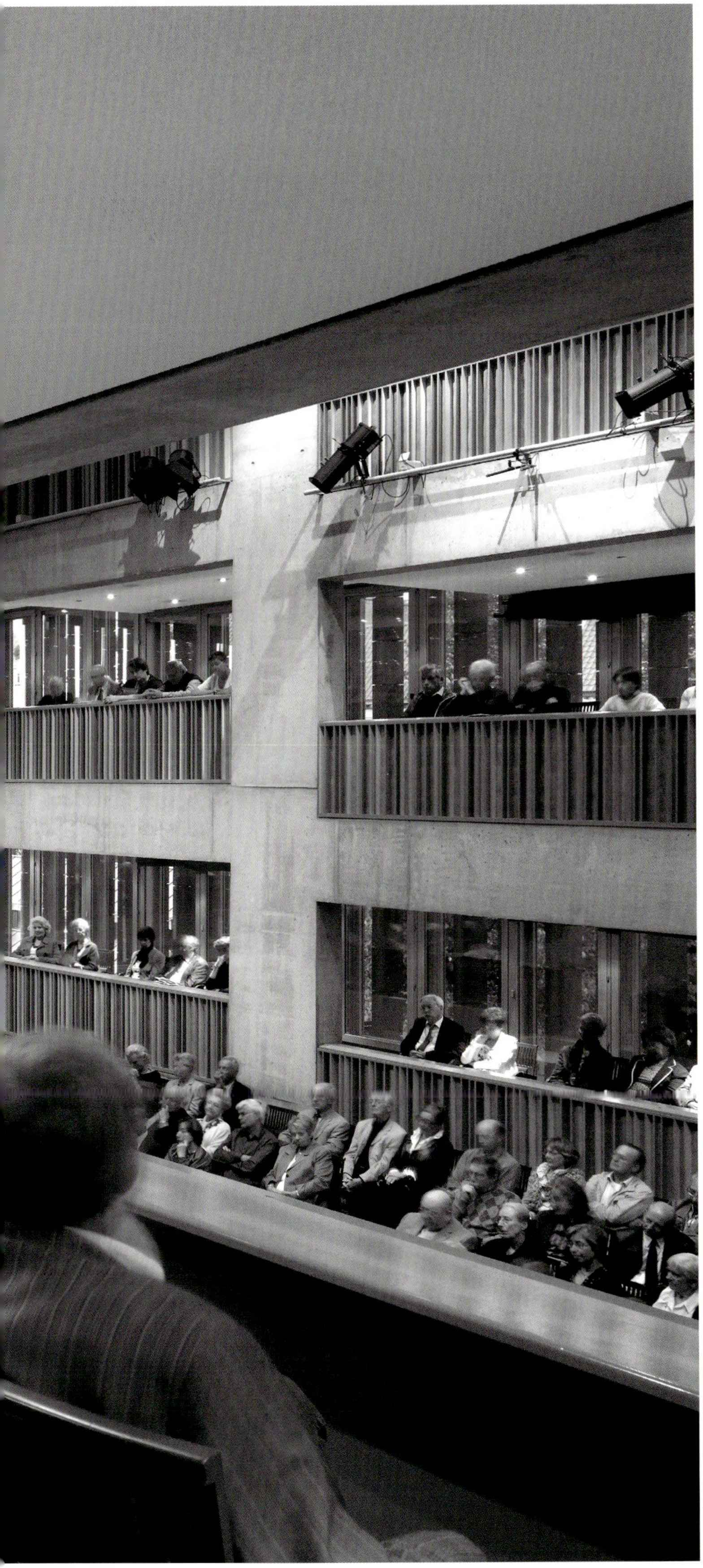
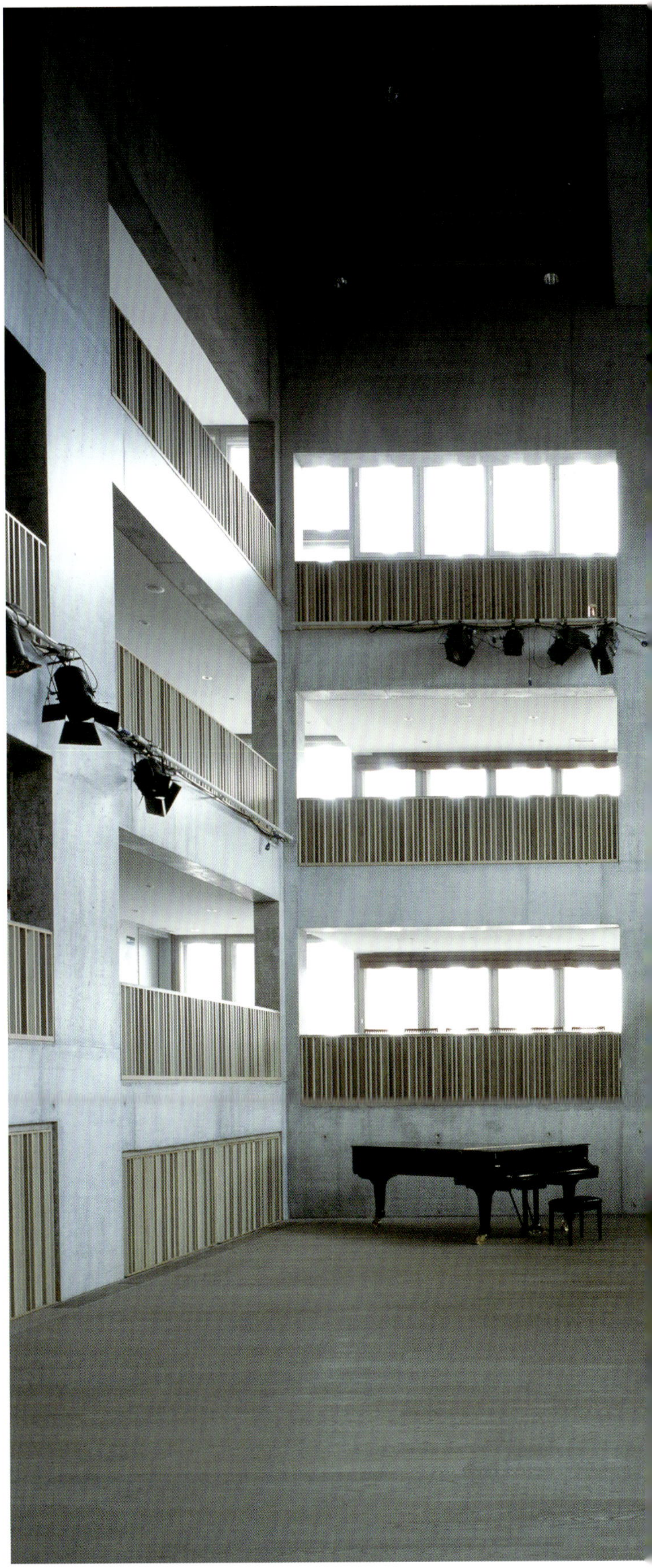

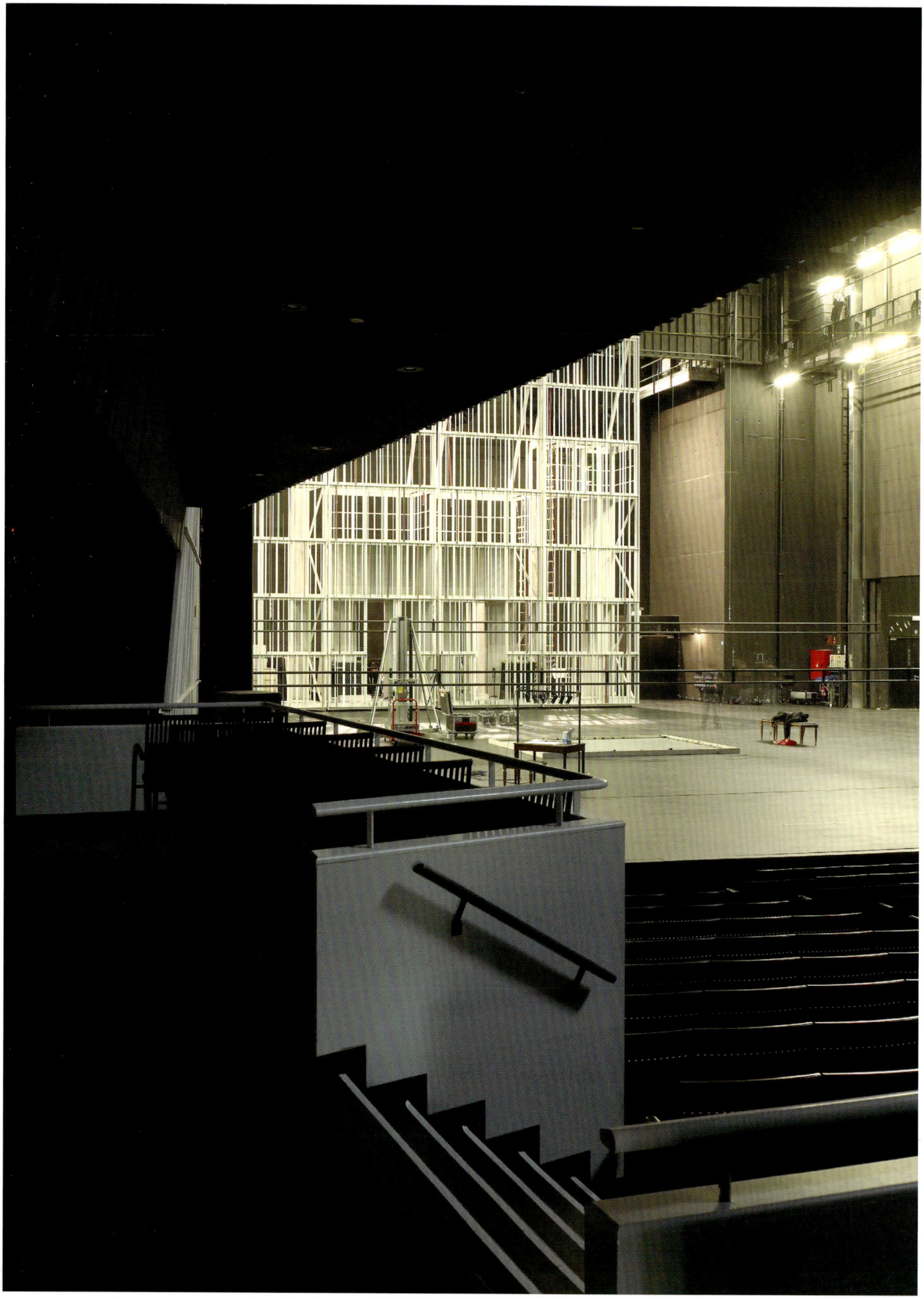
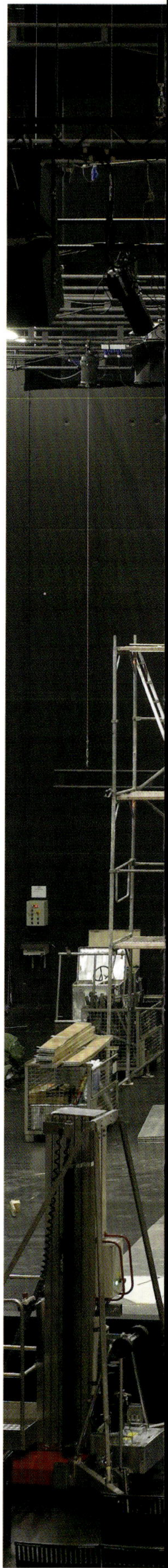

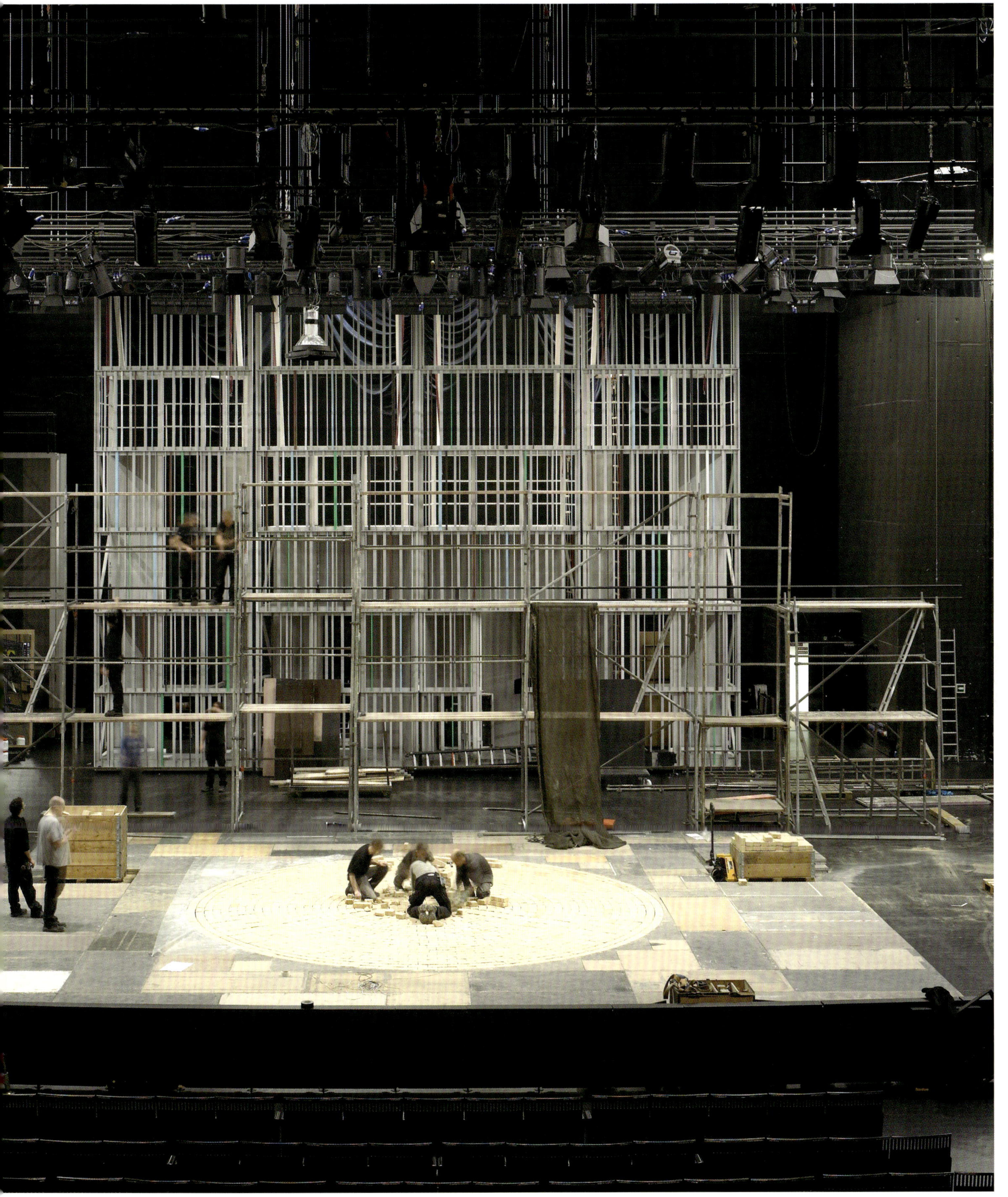

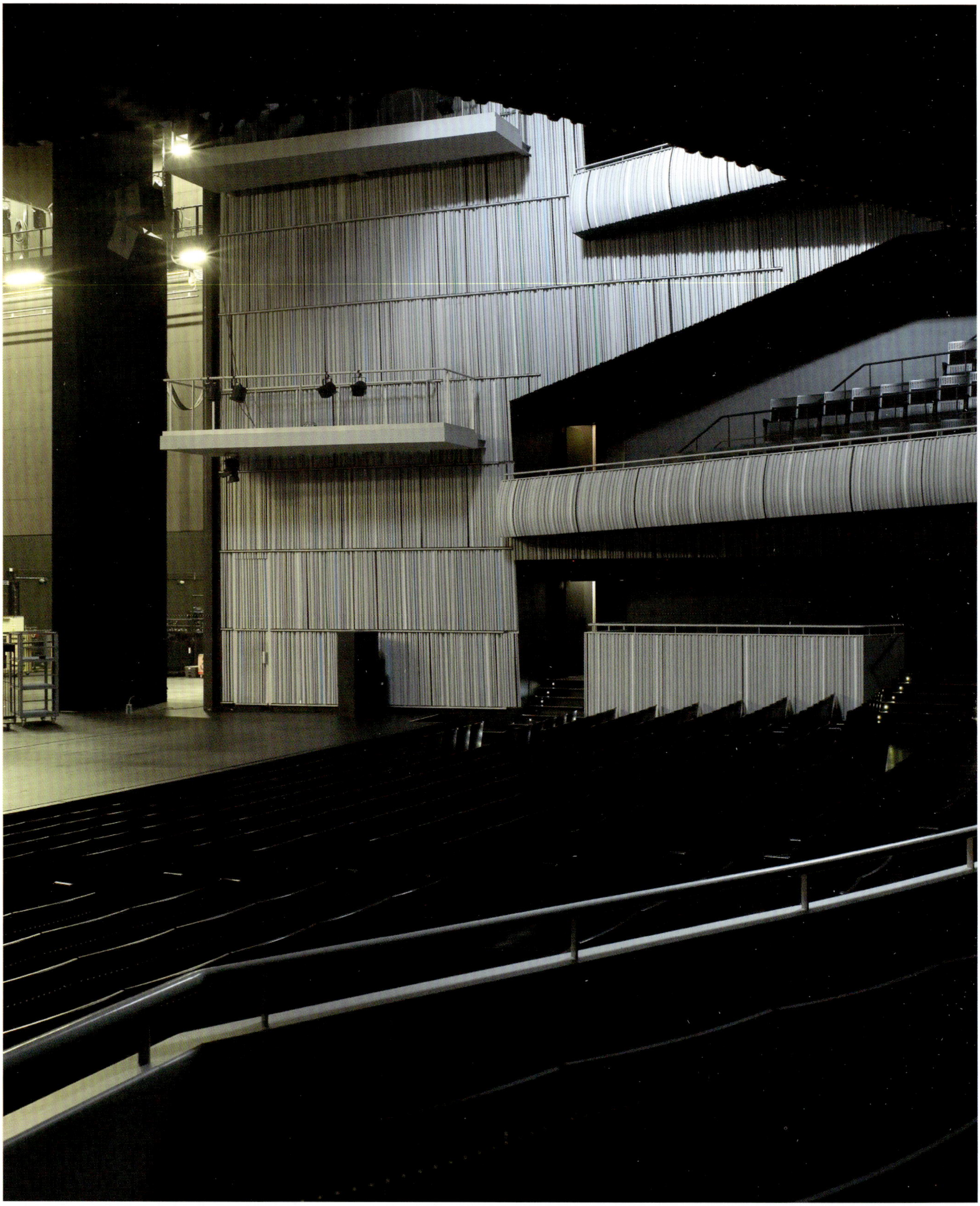

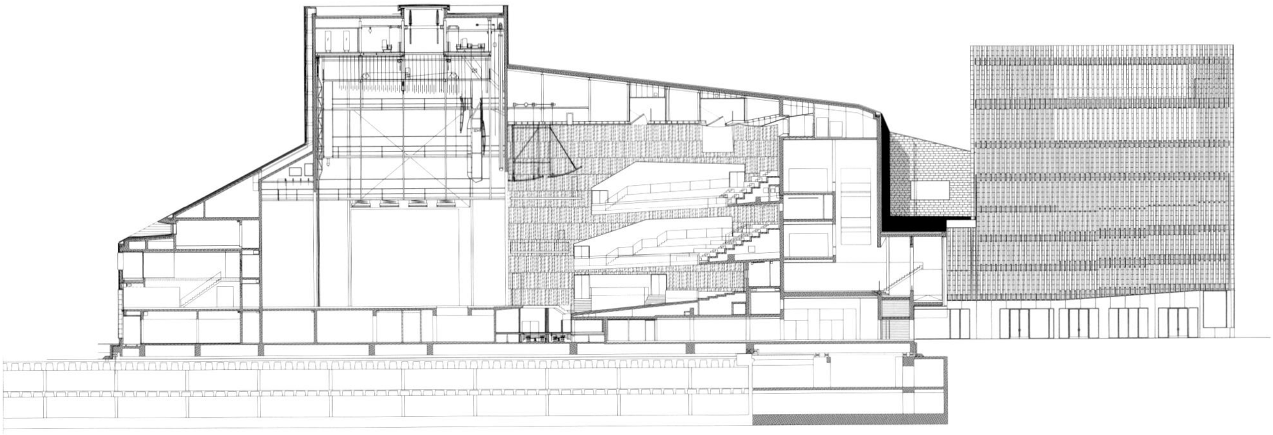

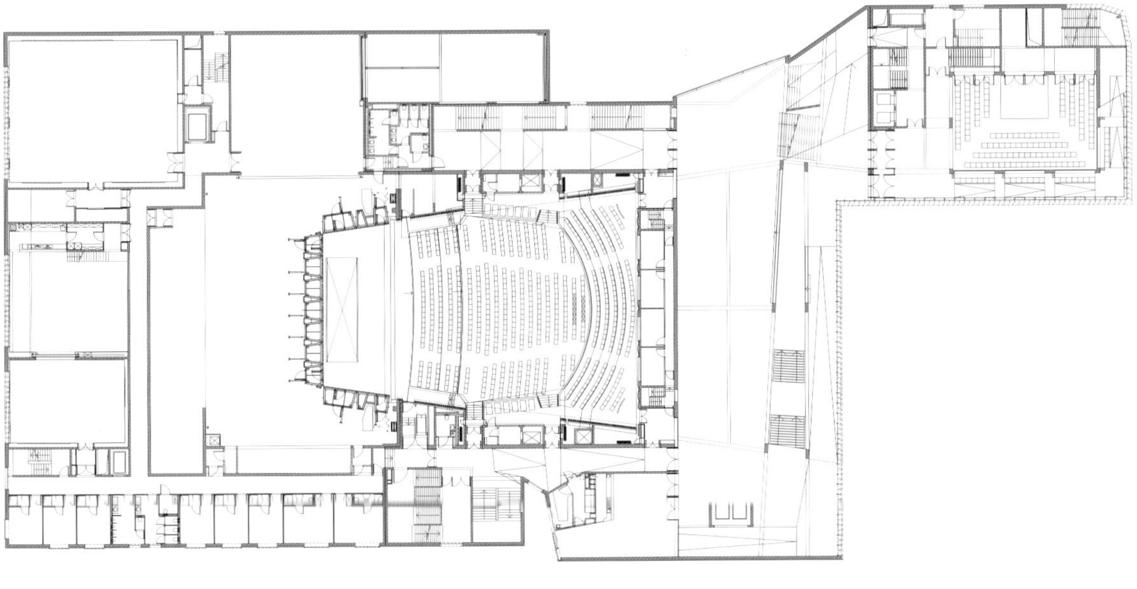

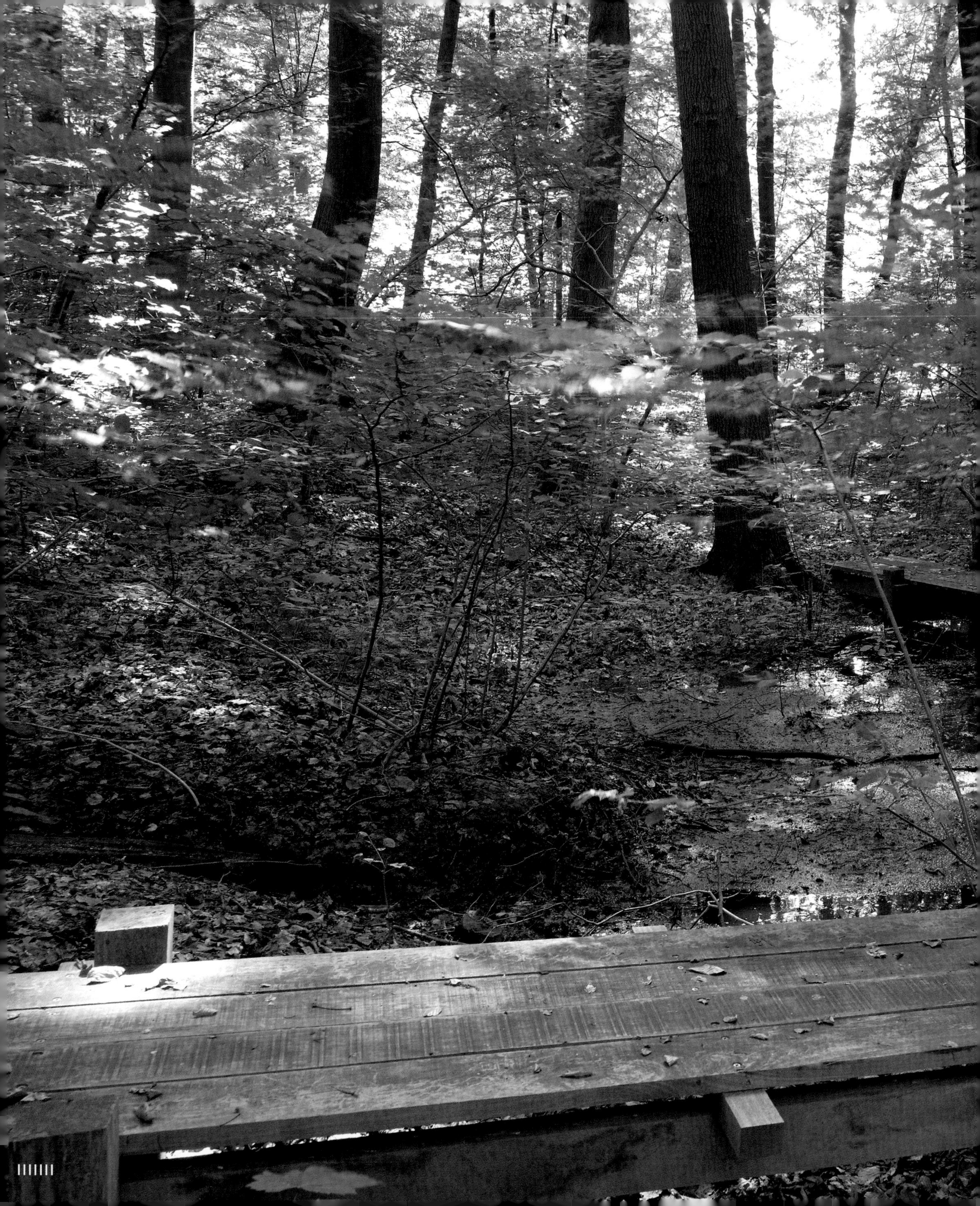

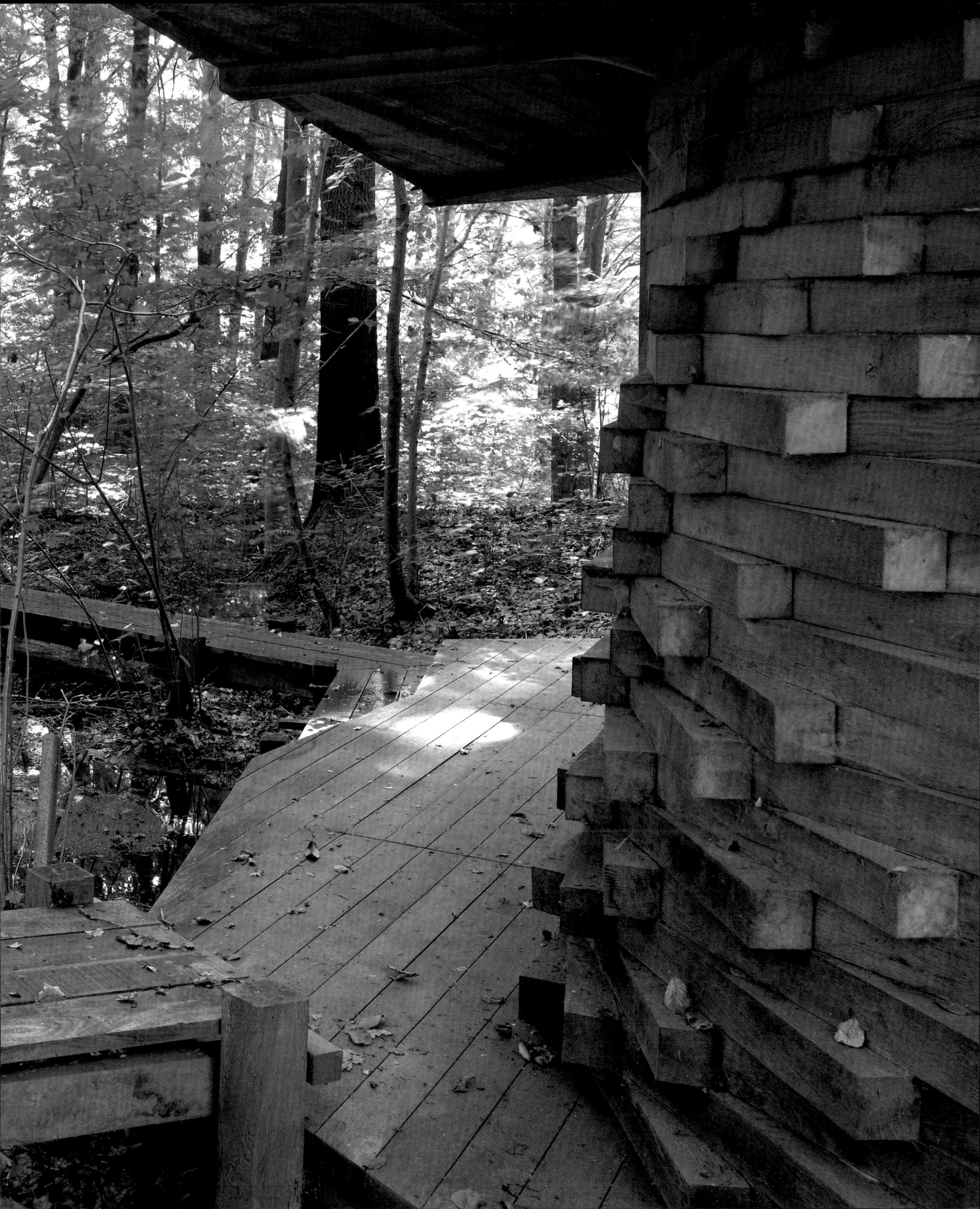

kamermuziekzaal

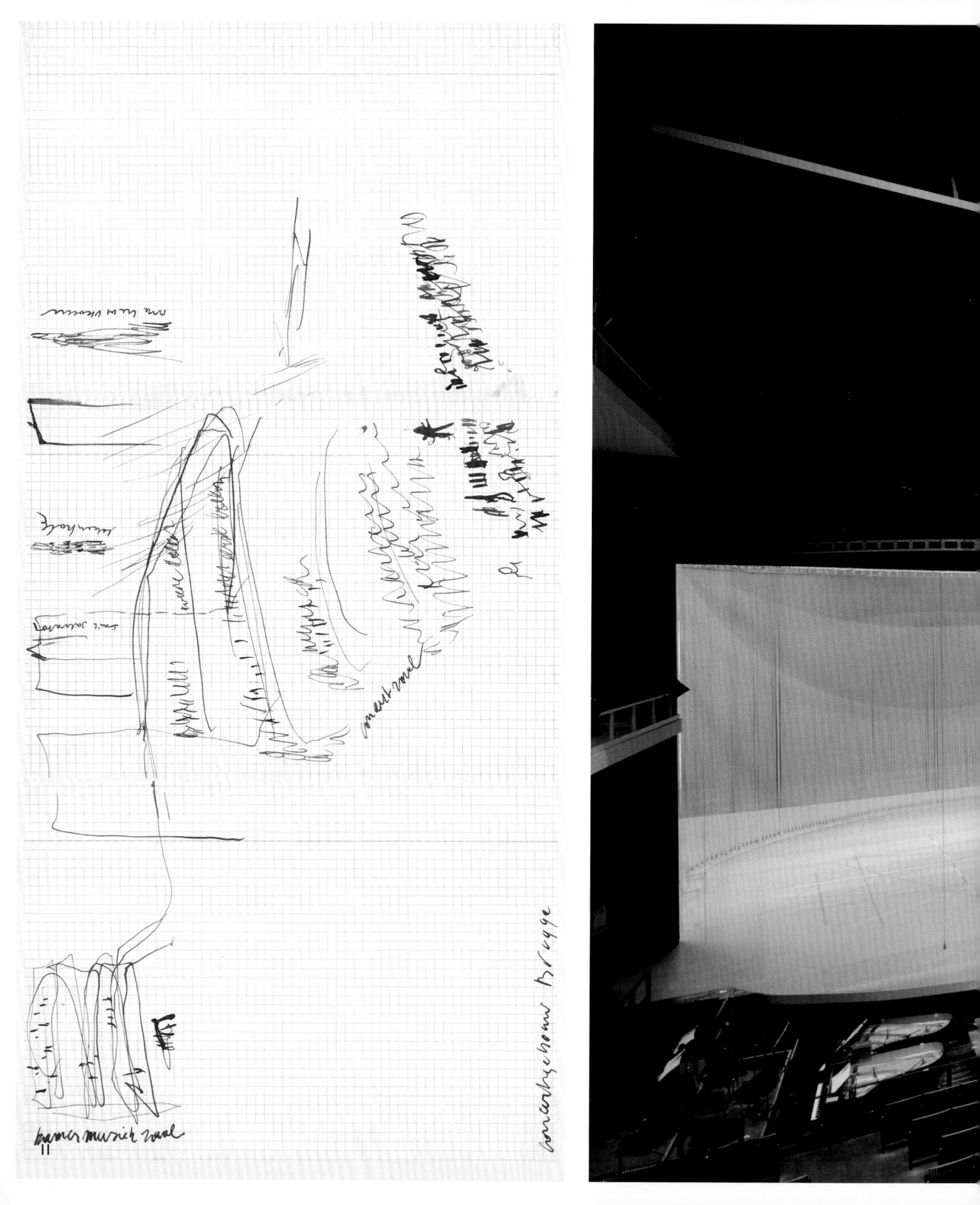

concertgebouw brugge

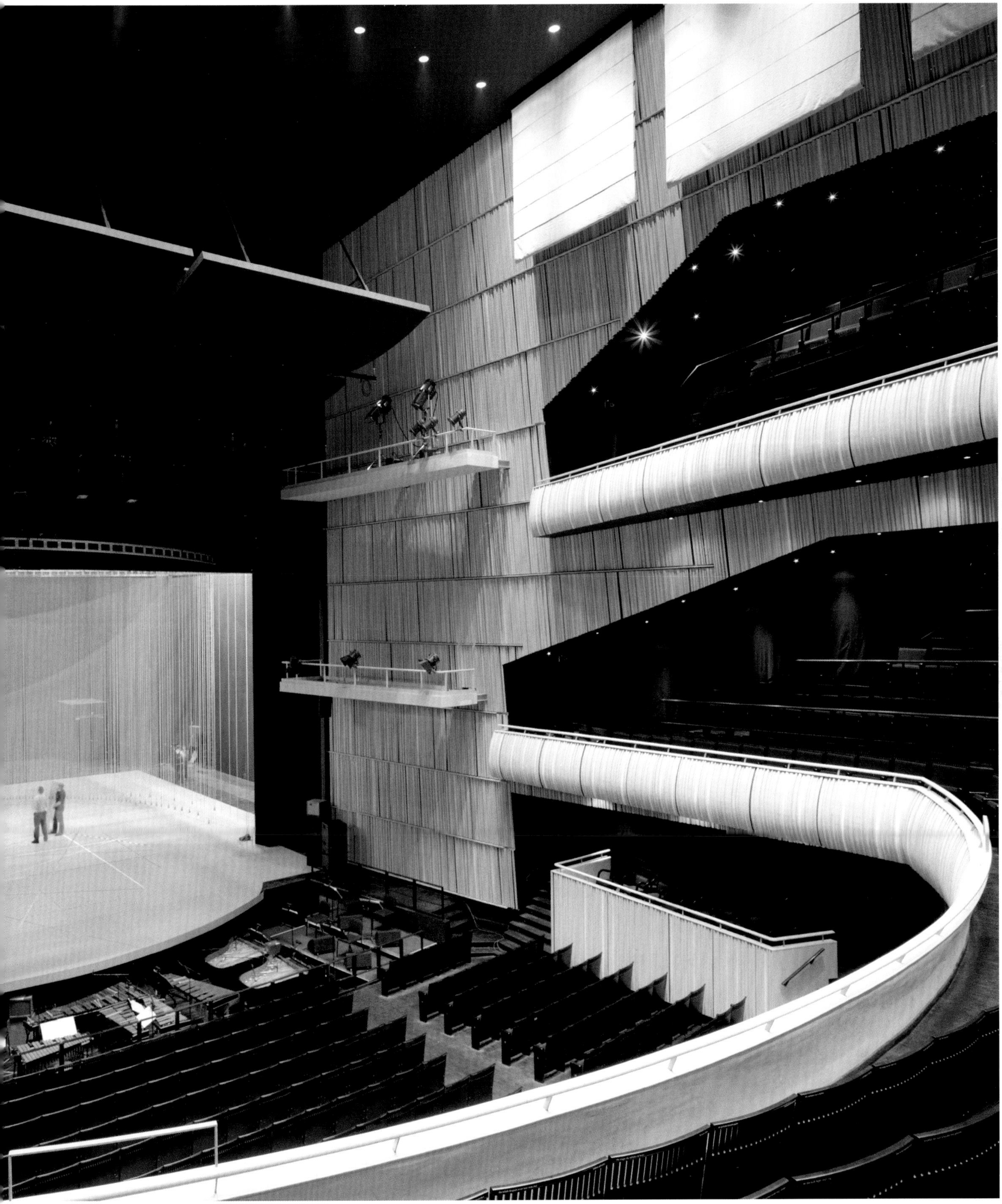

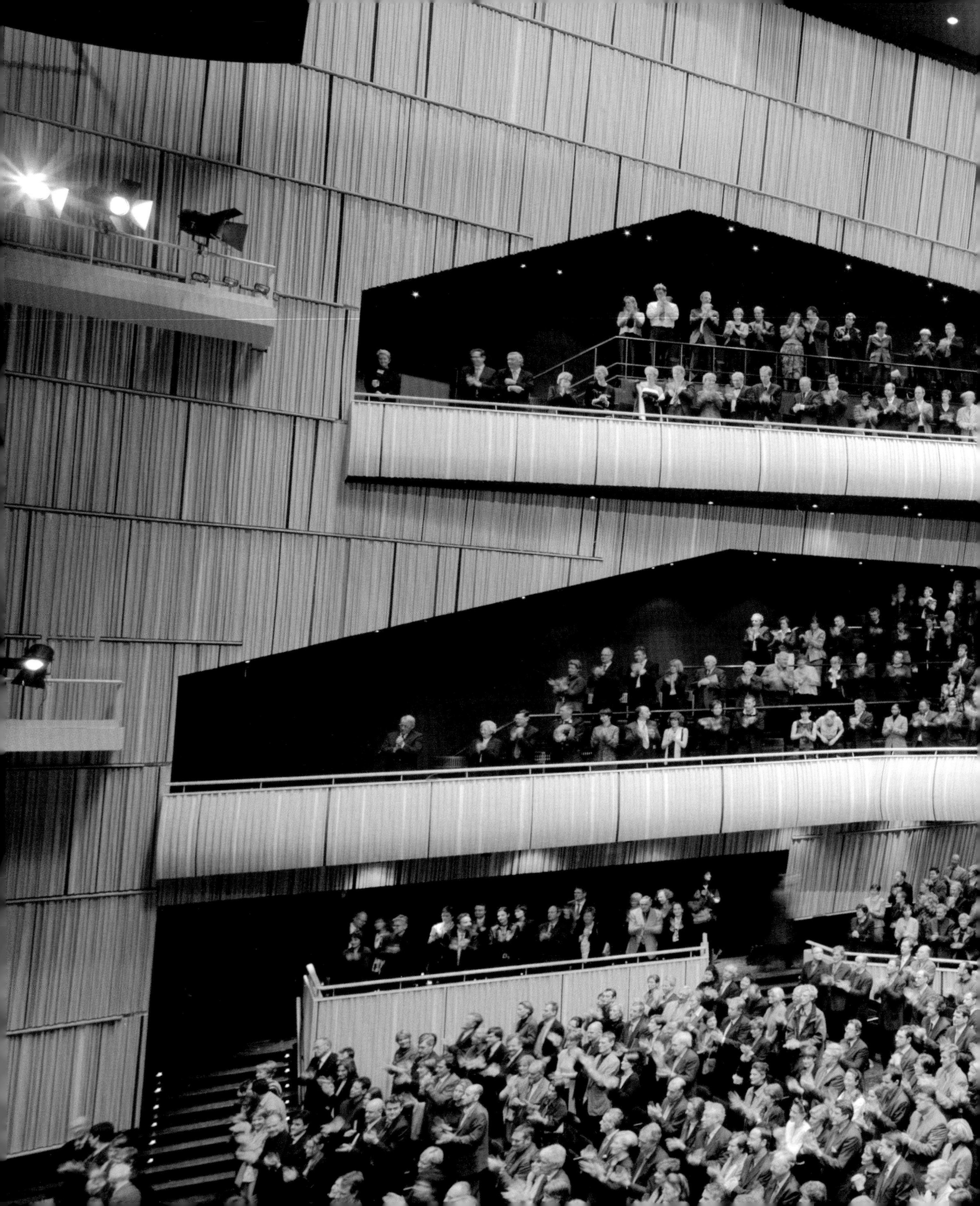

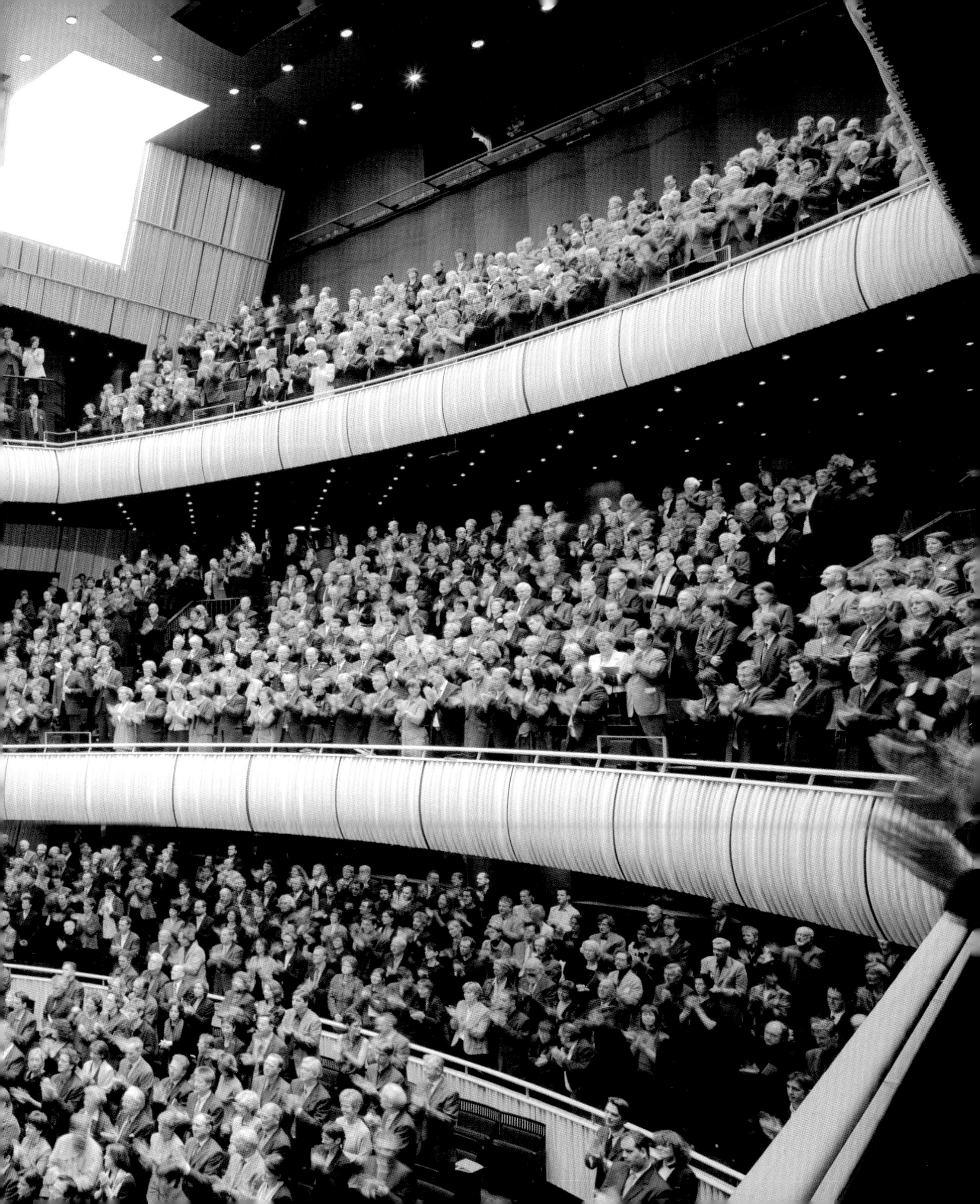

111　Gaasbeek

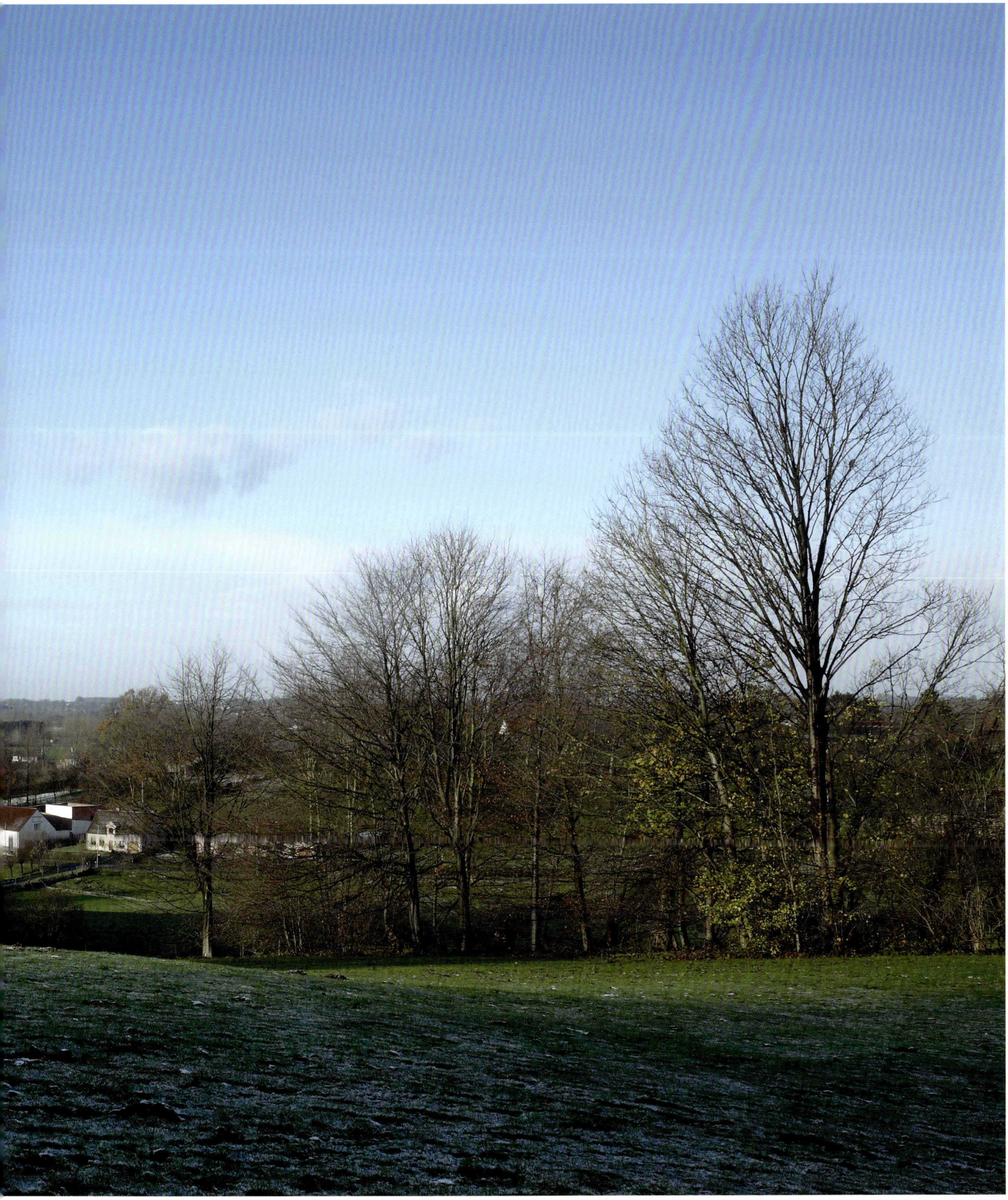

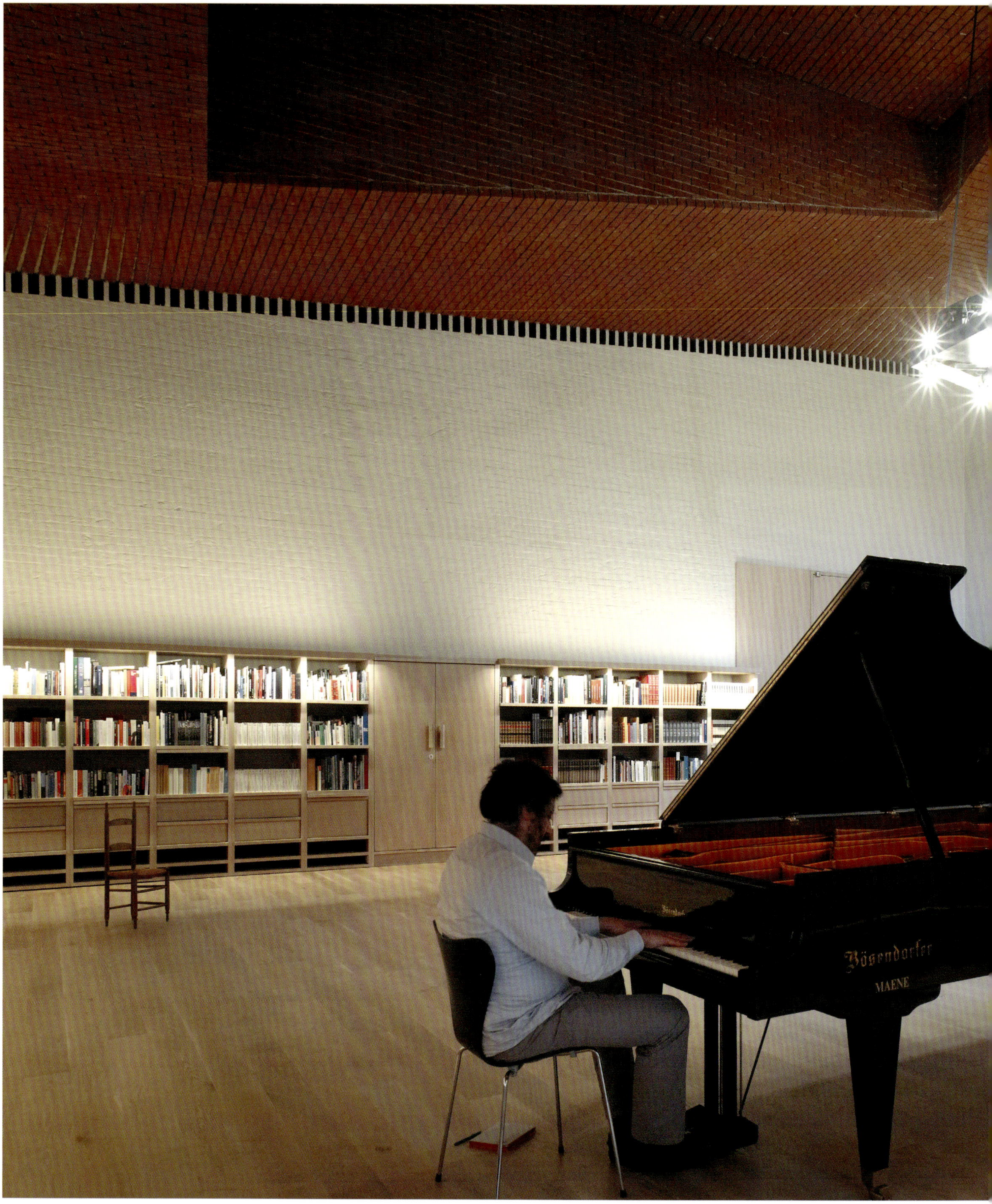
Bösendorfer
MAENE

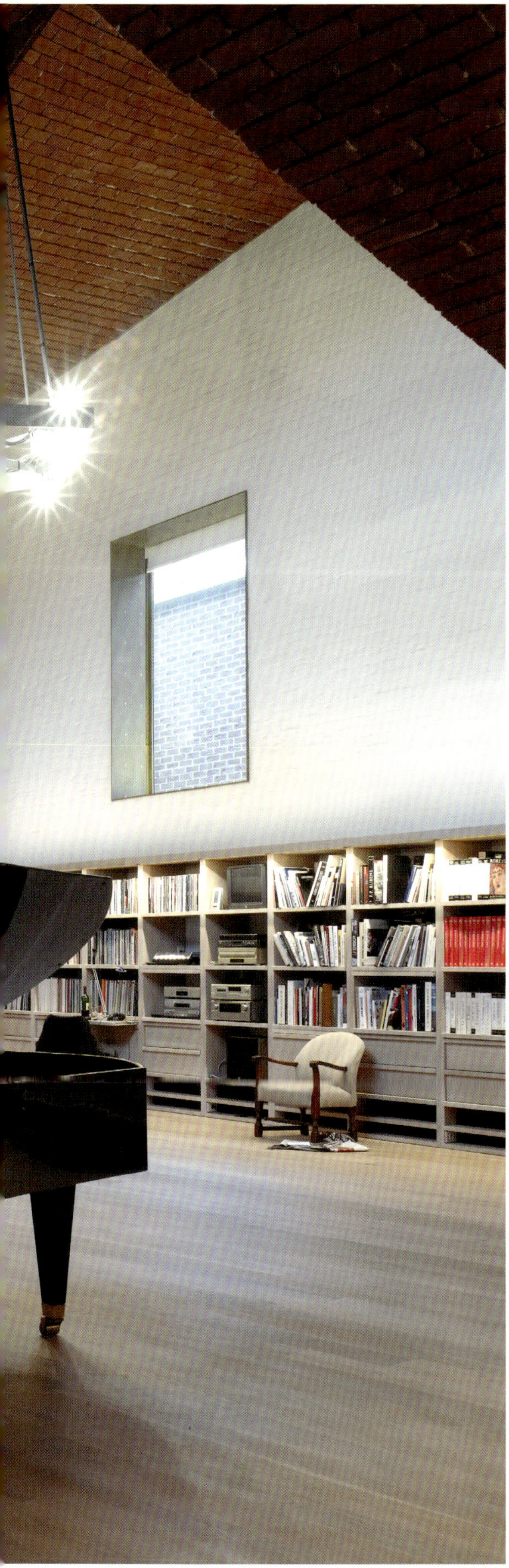

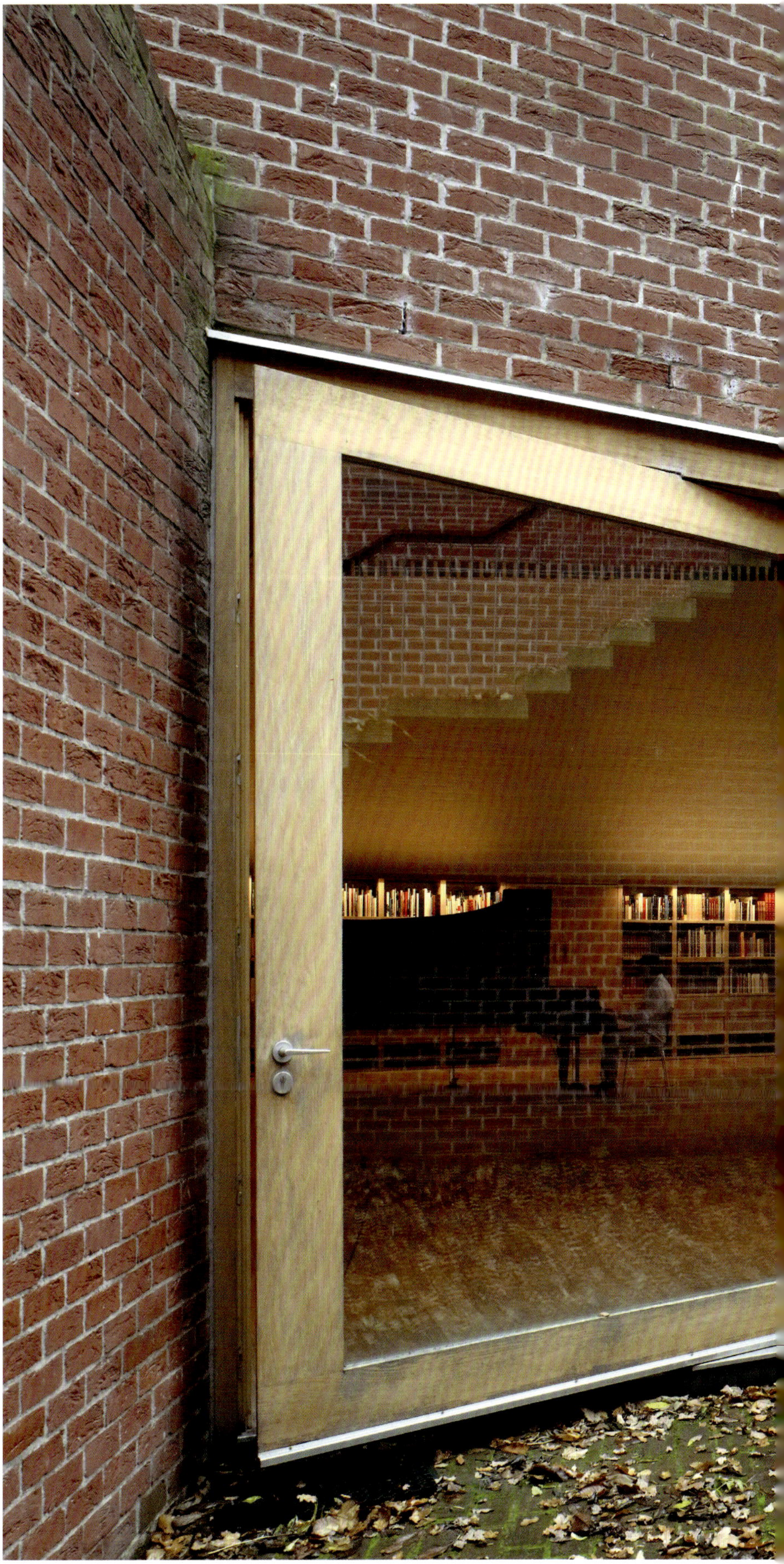

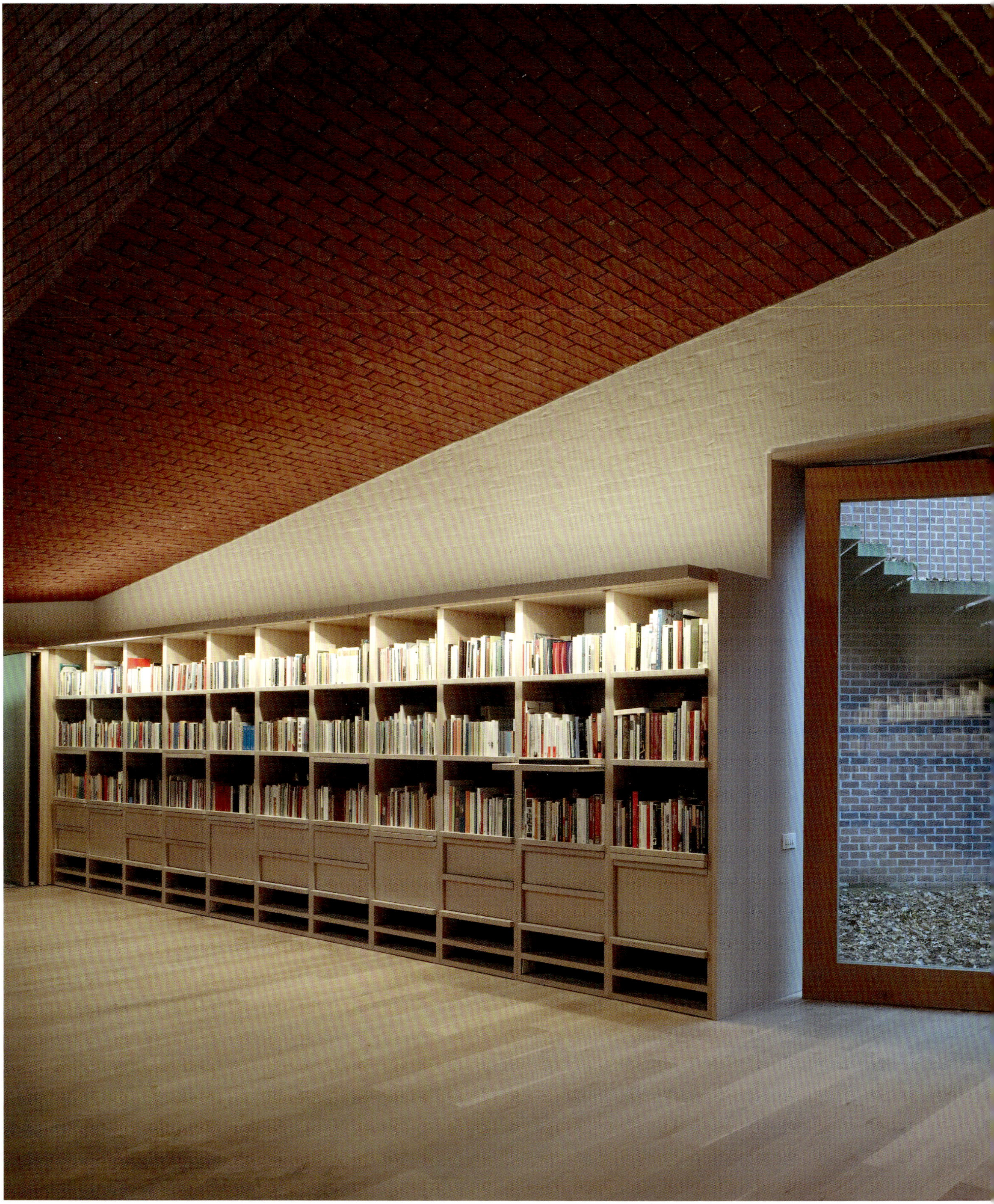

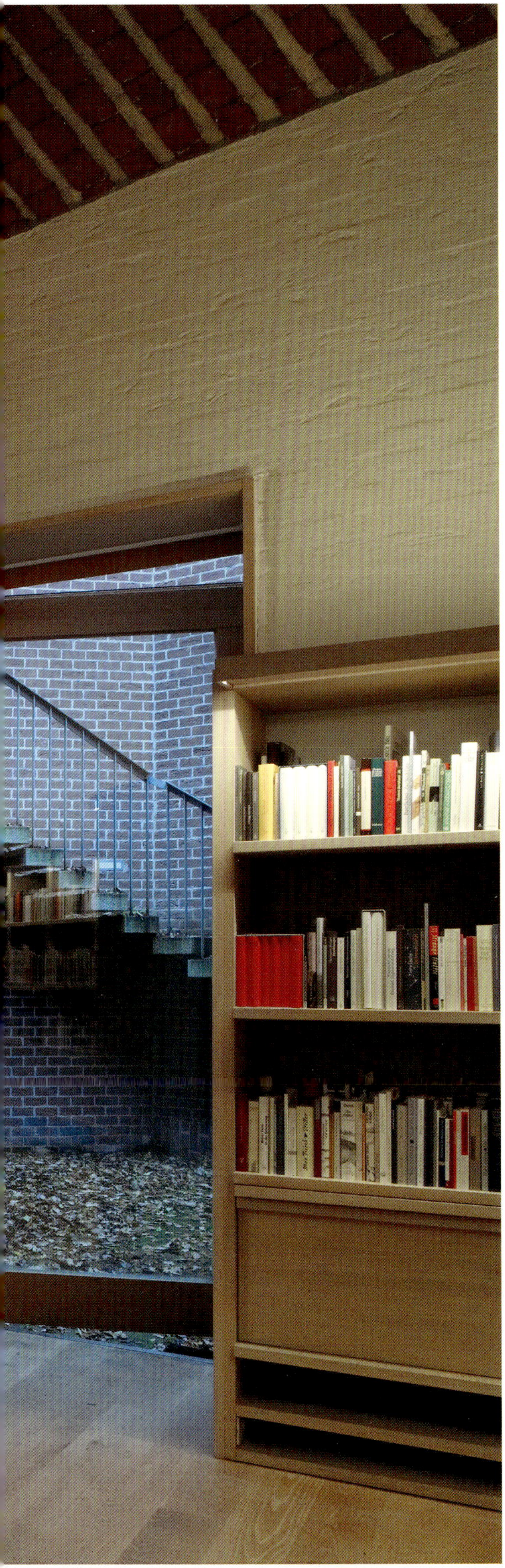

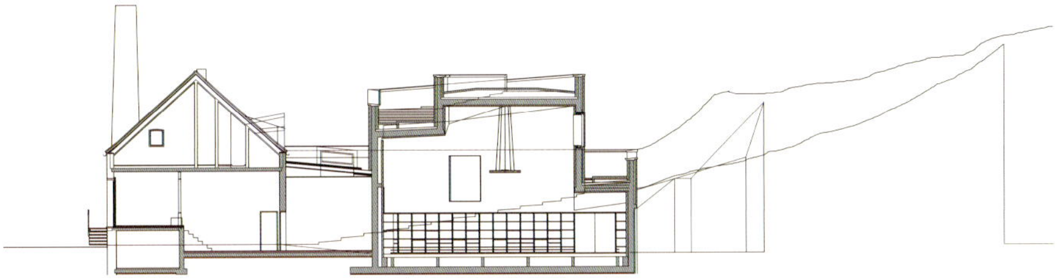

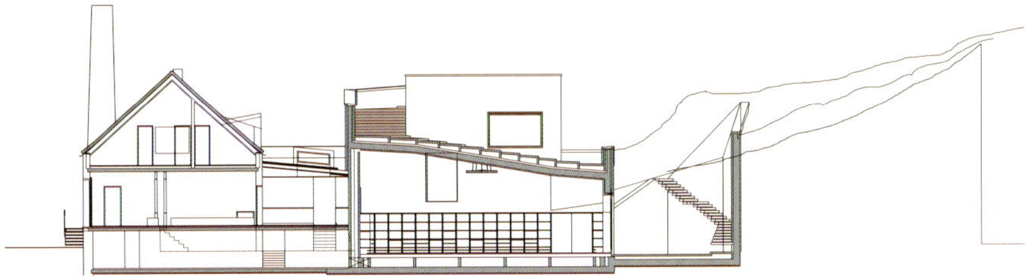

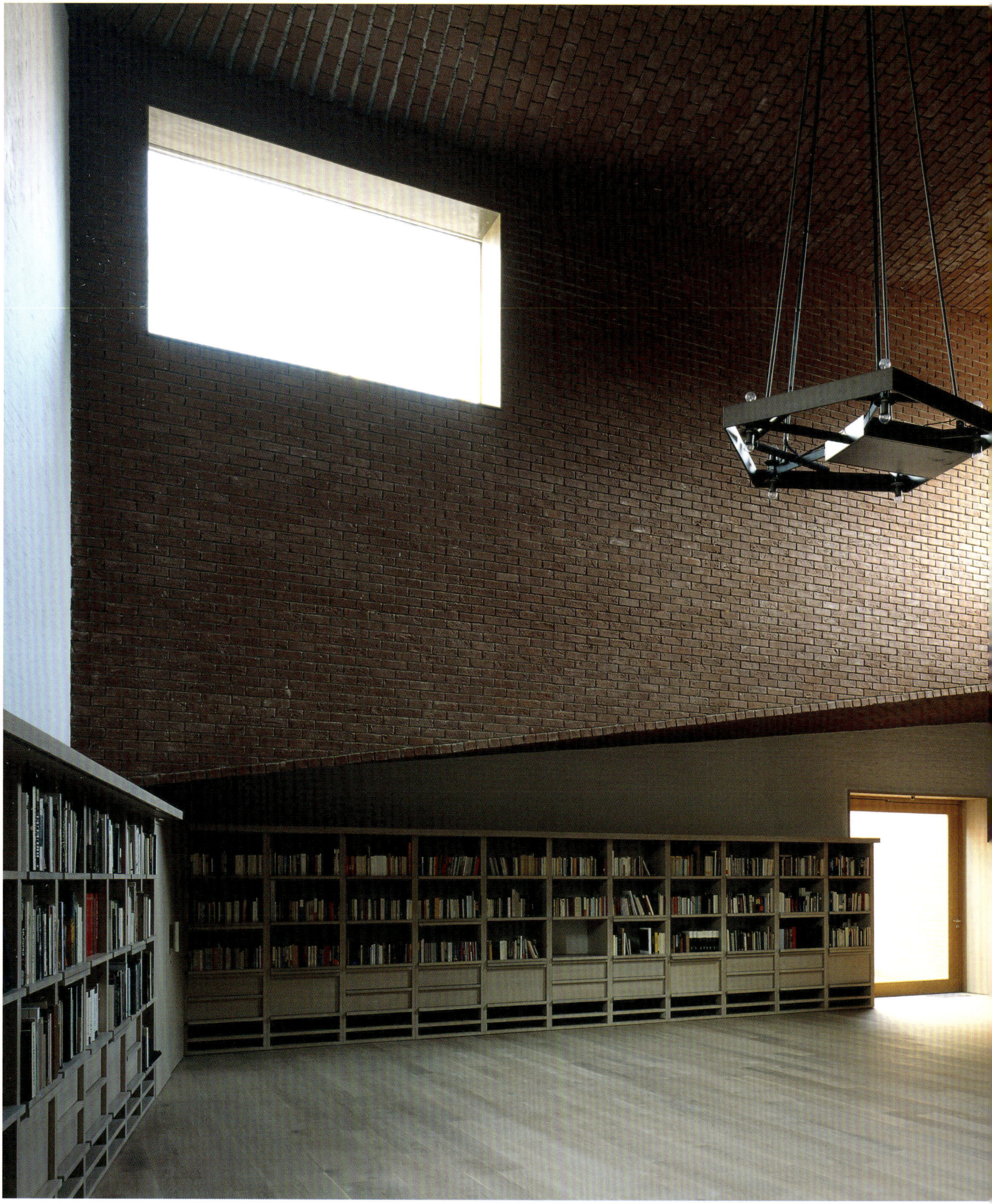

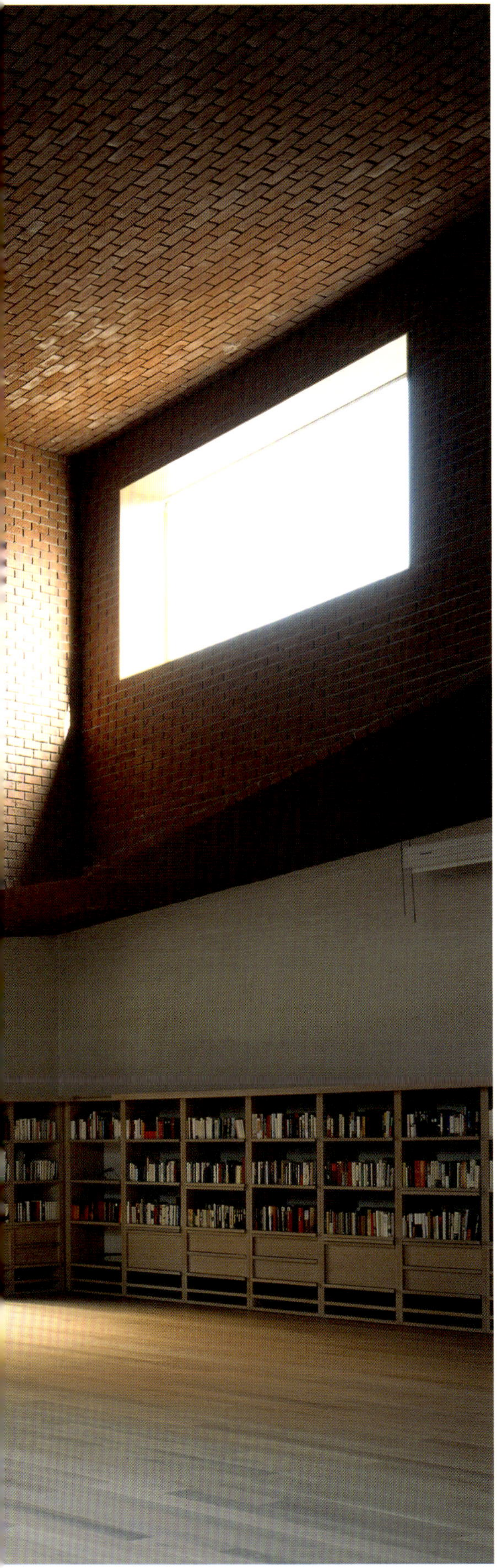

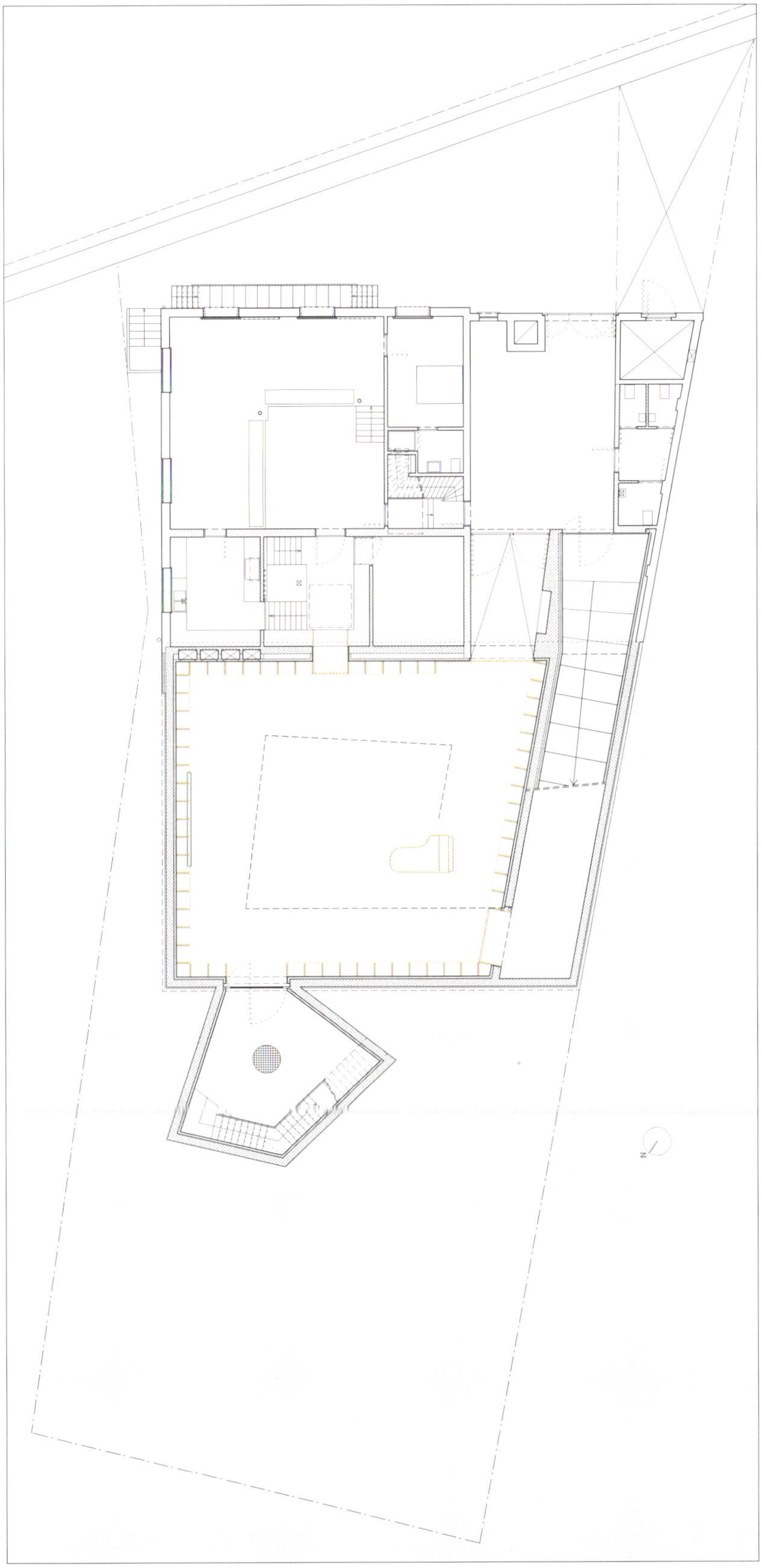

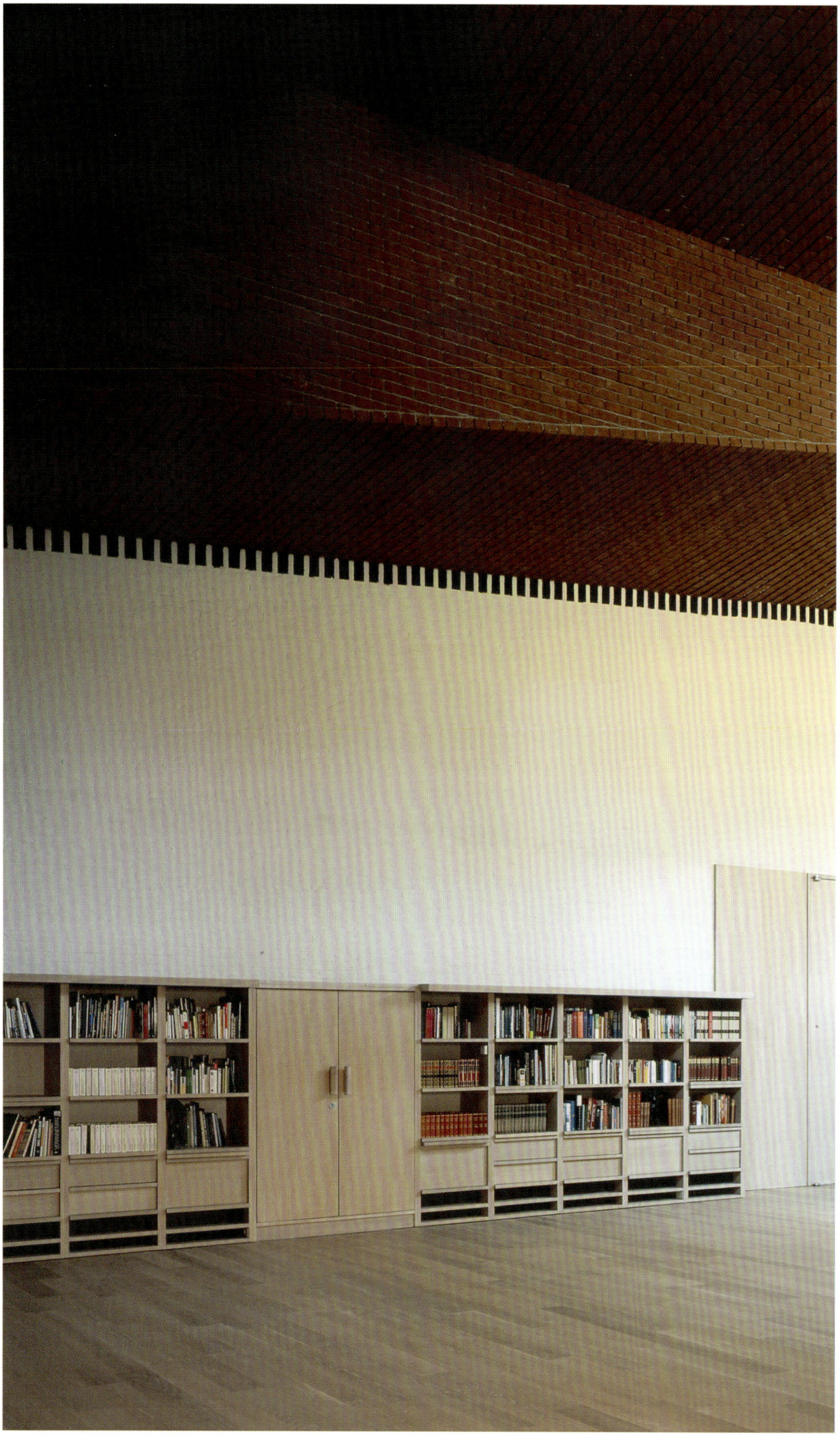

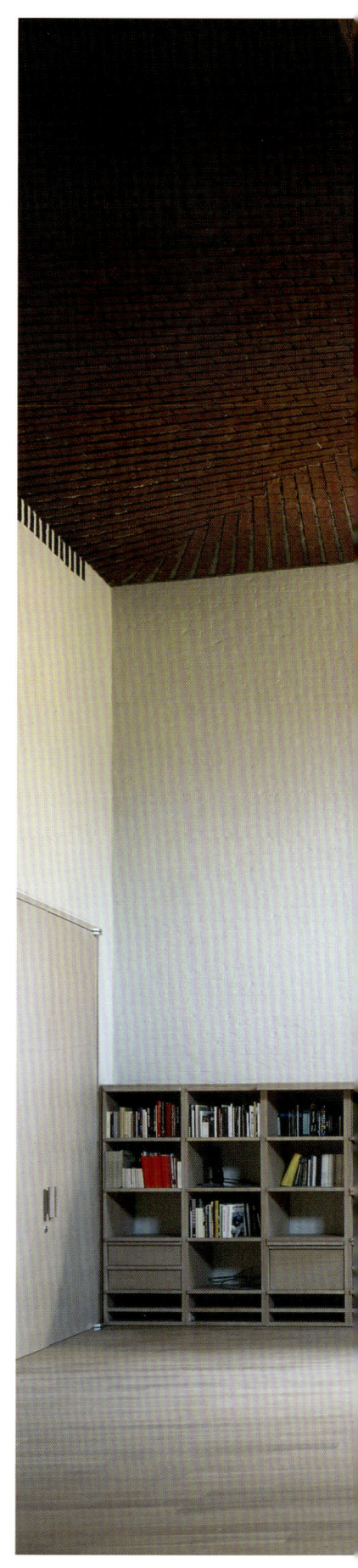

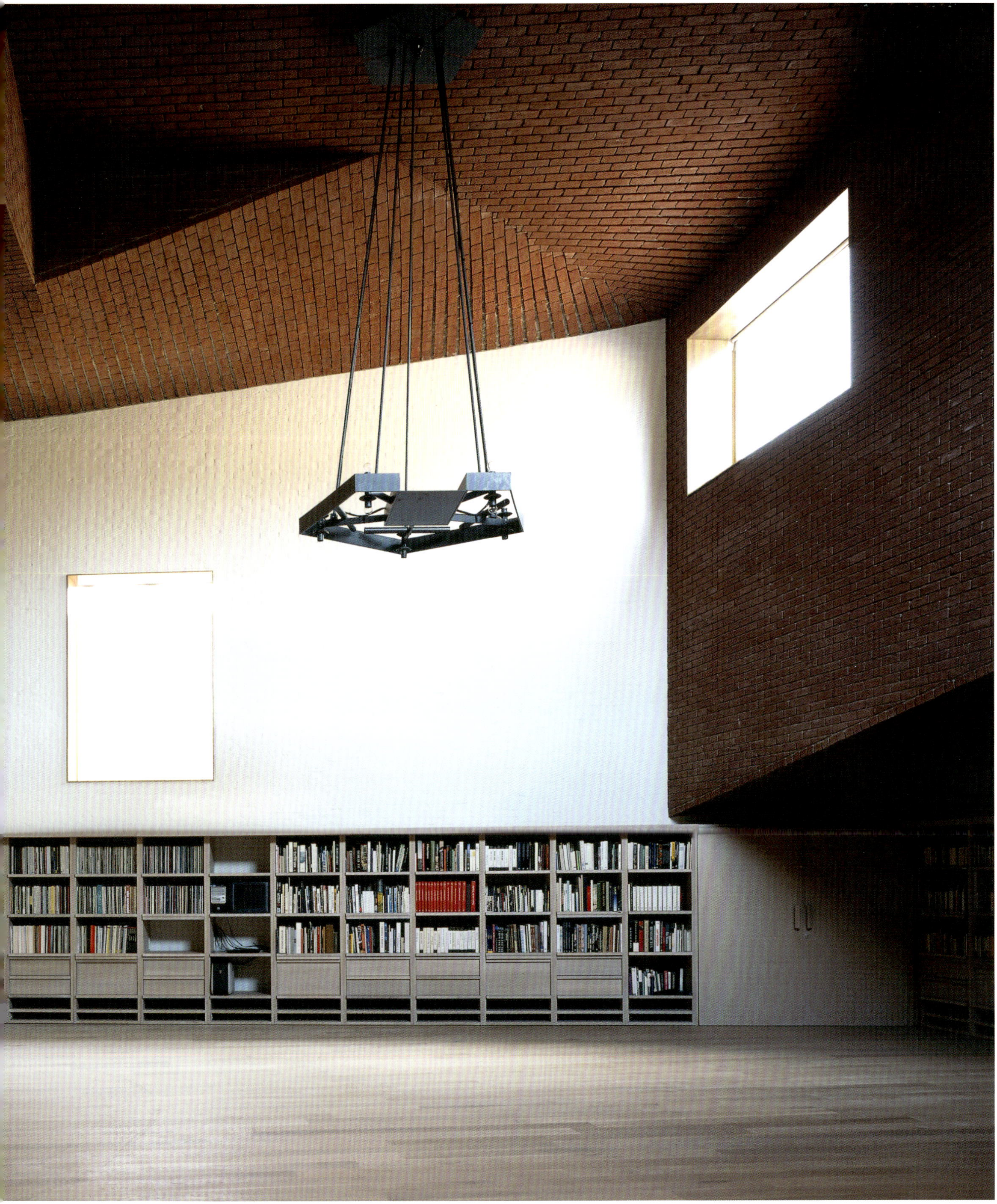

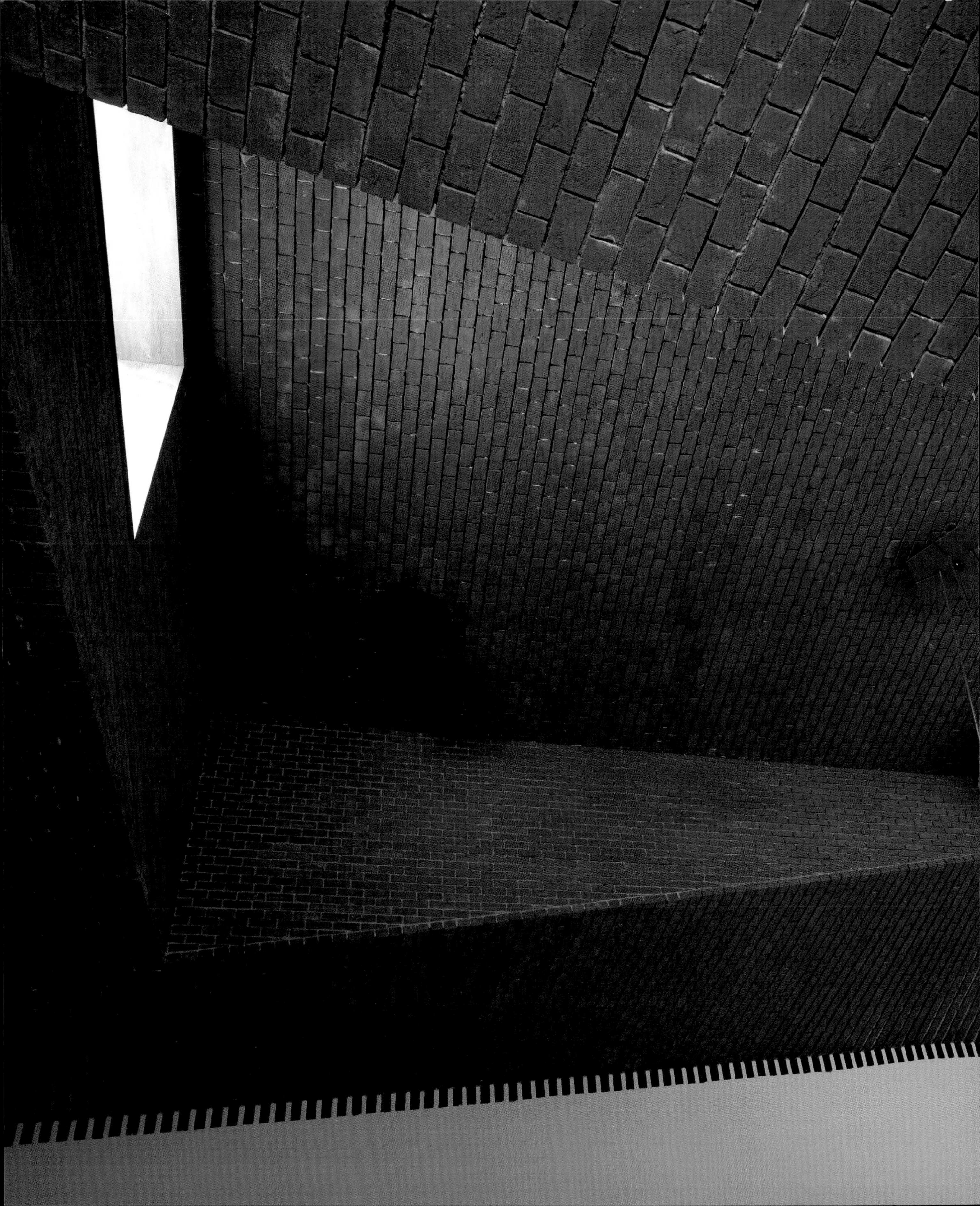

79

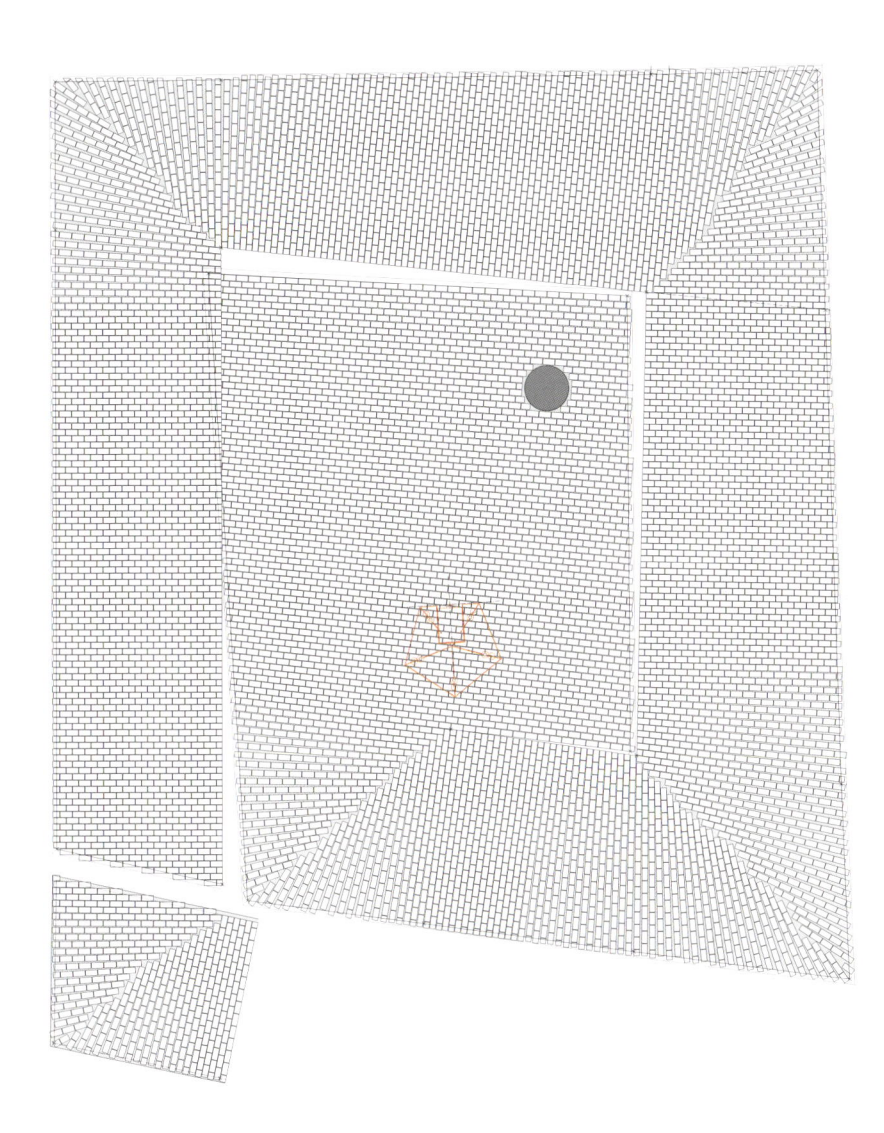

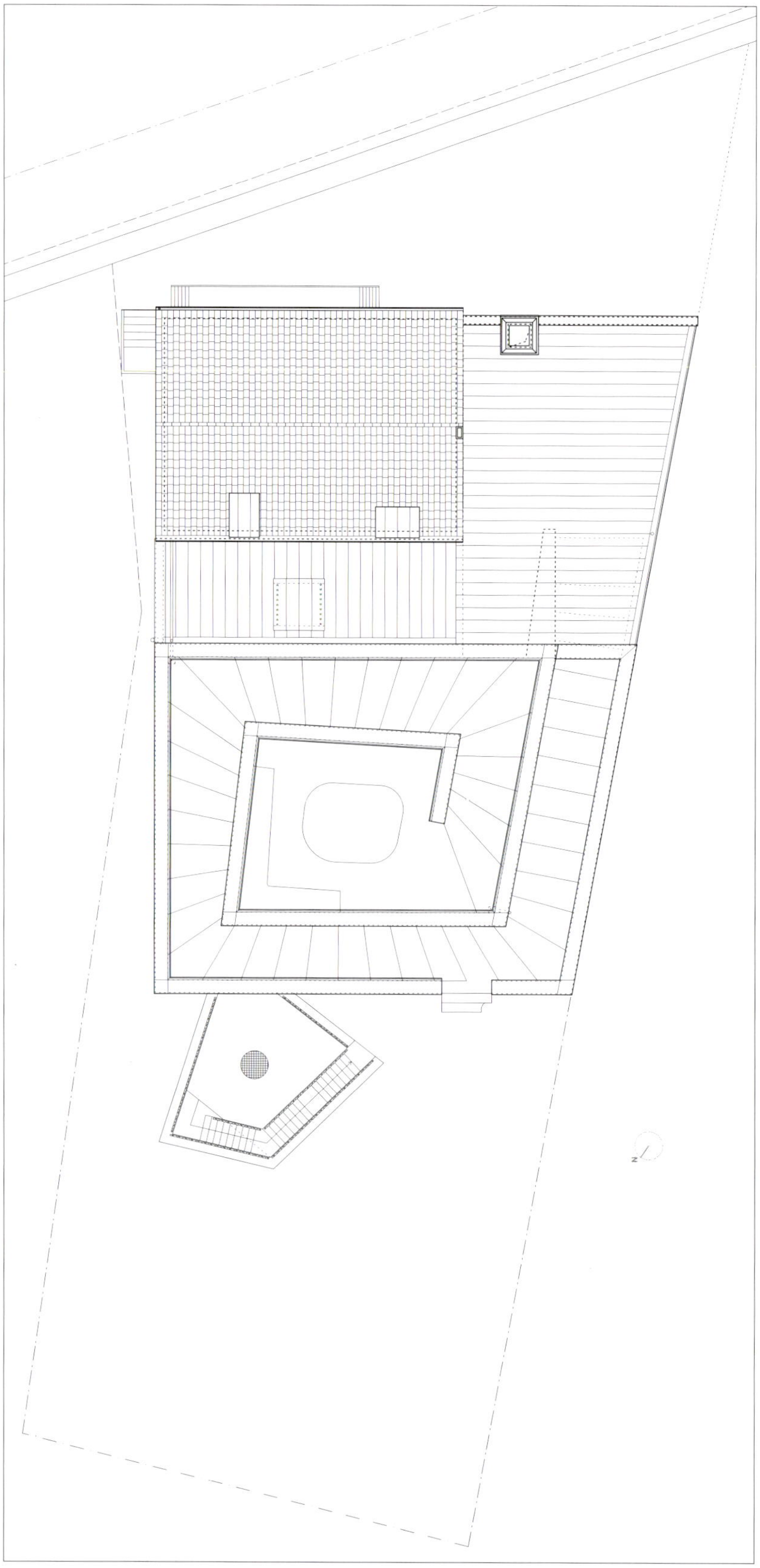

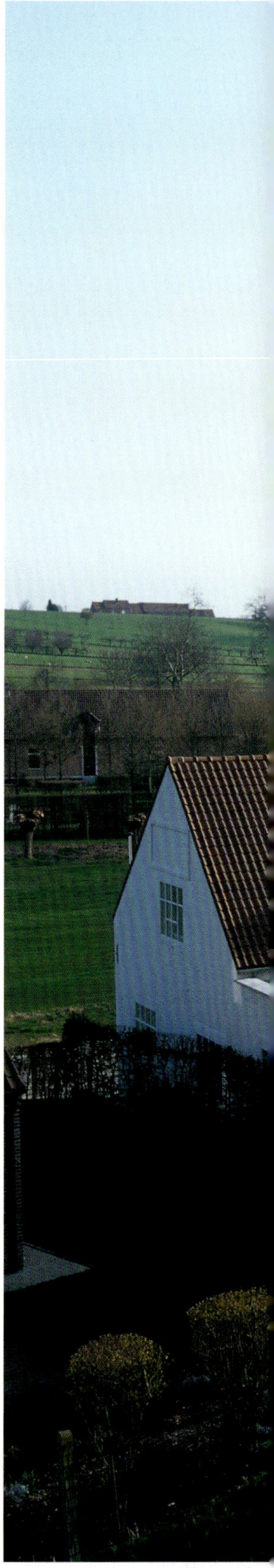

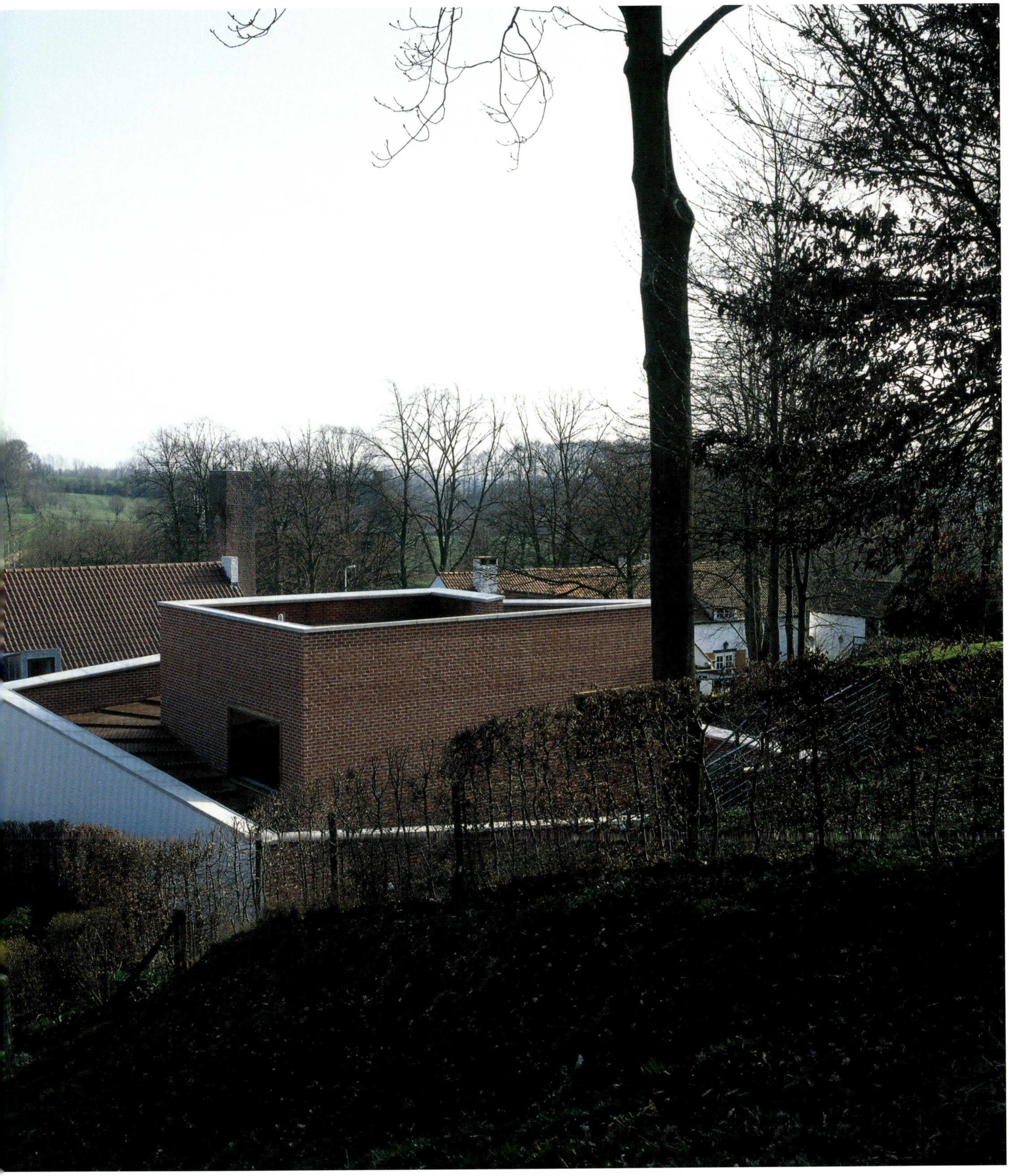

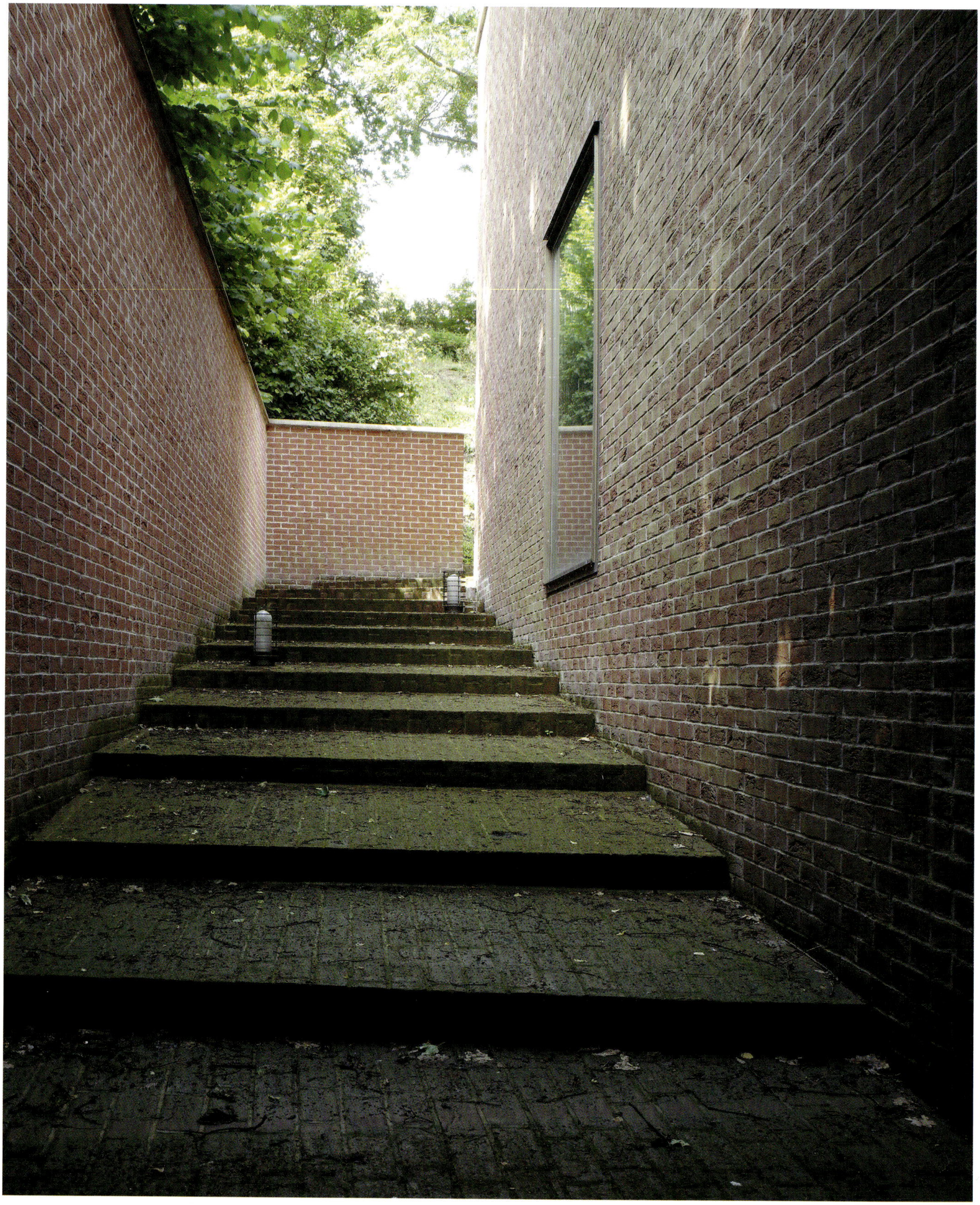

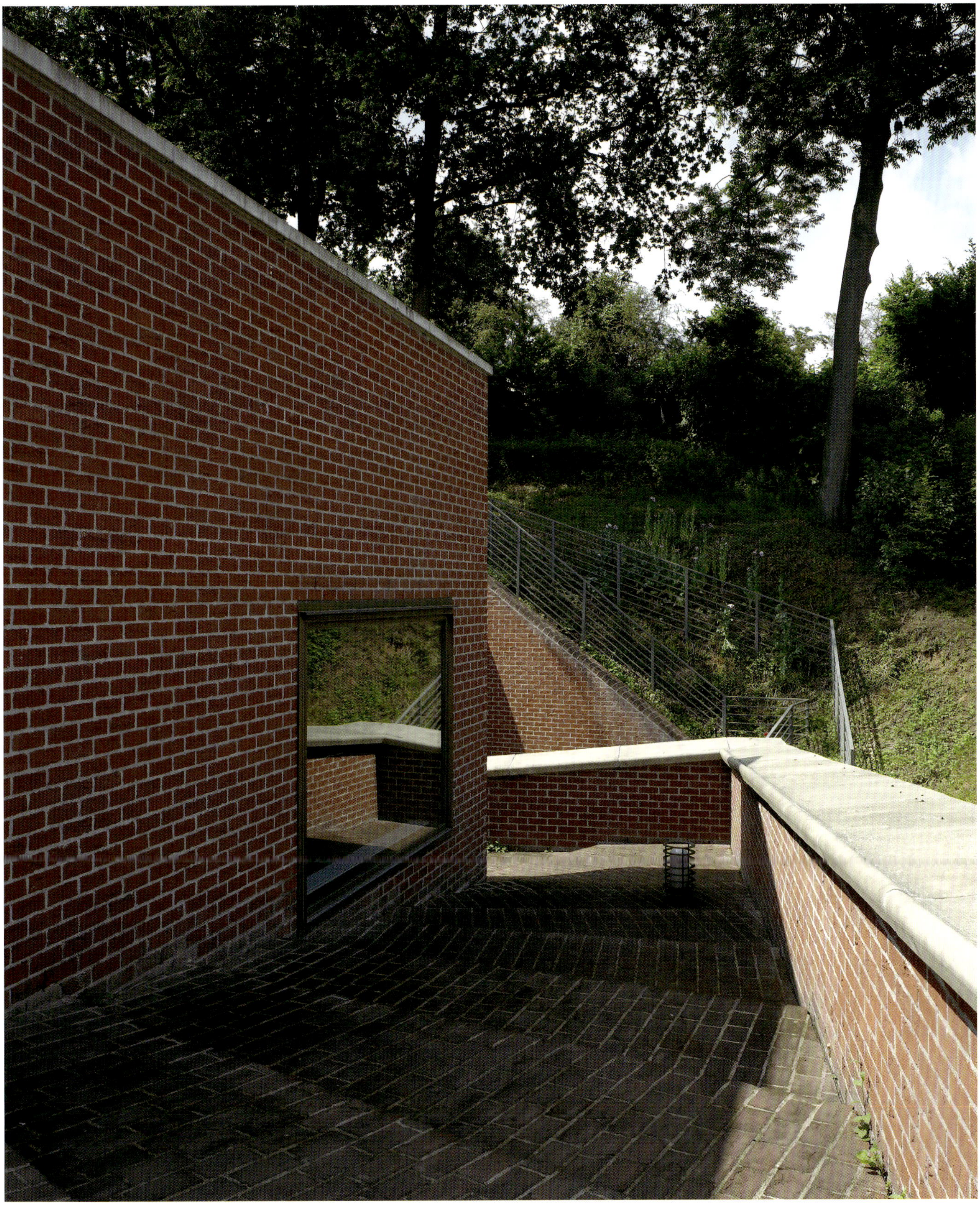

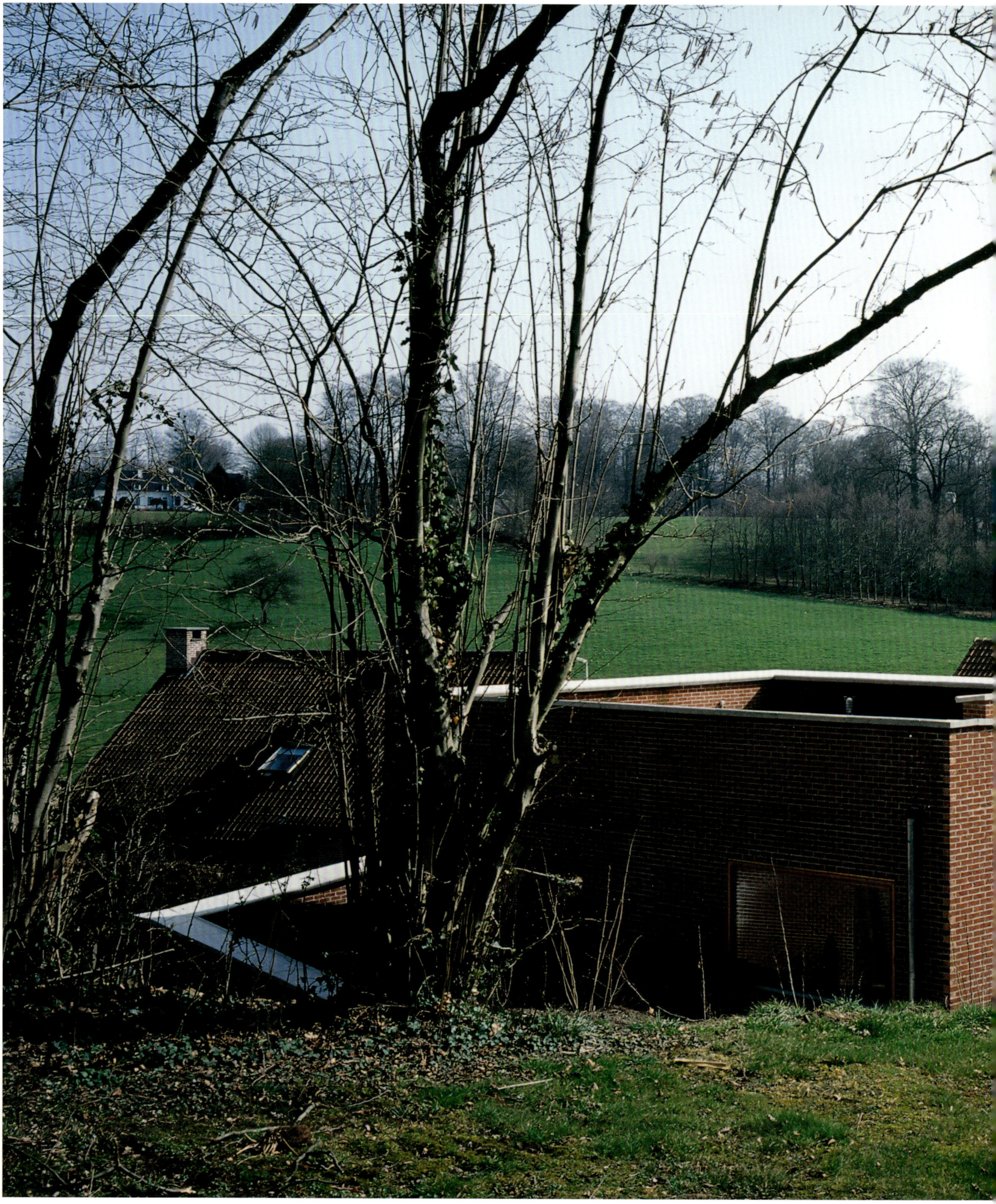

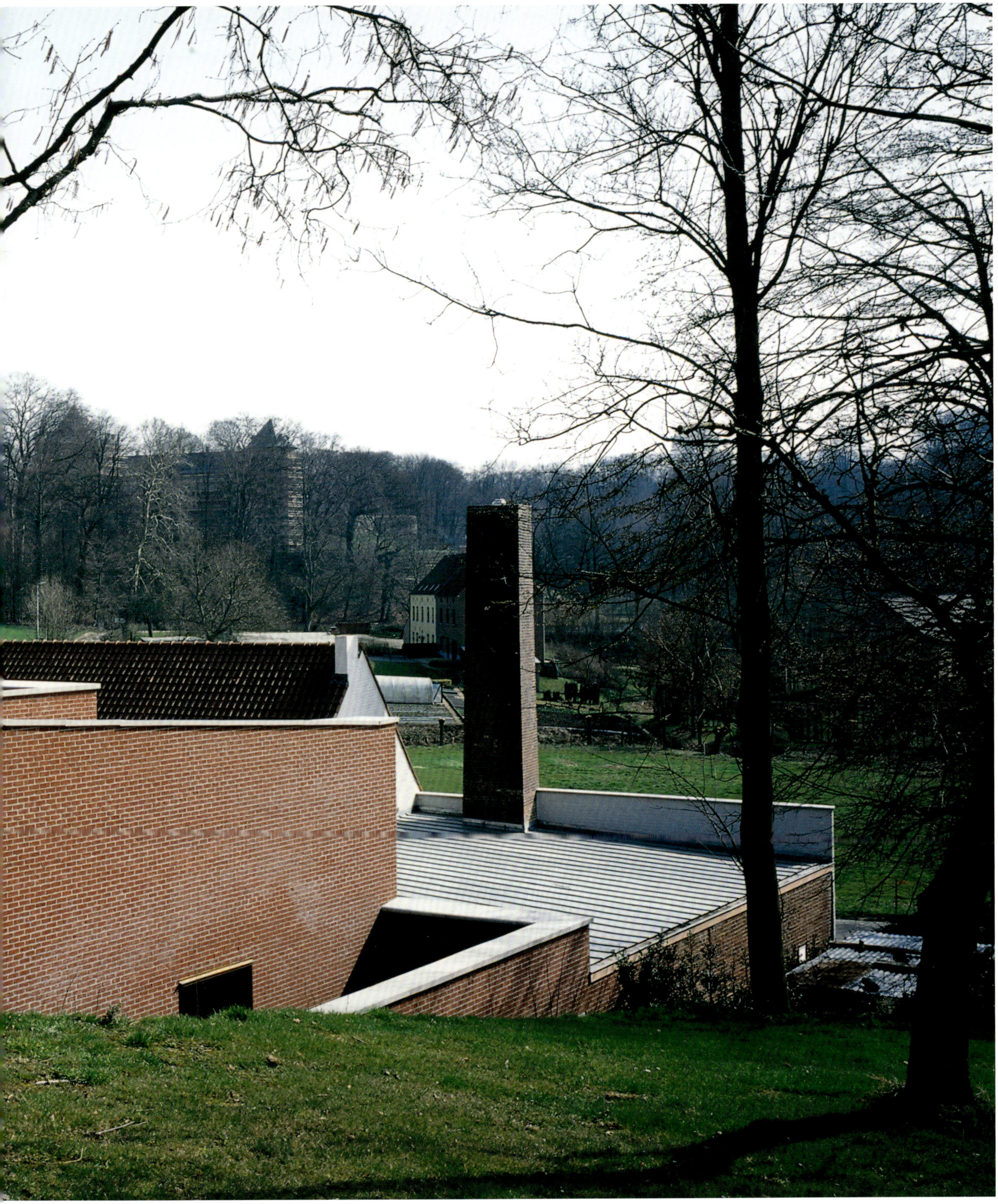

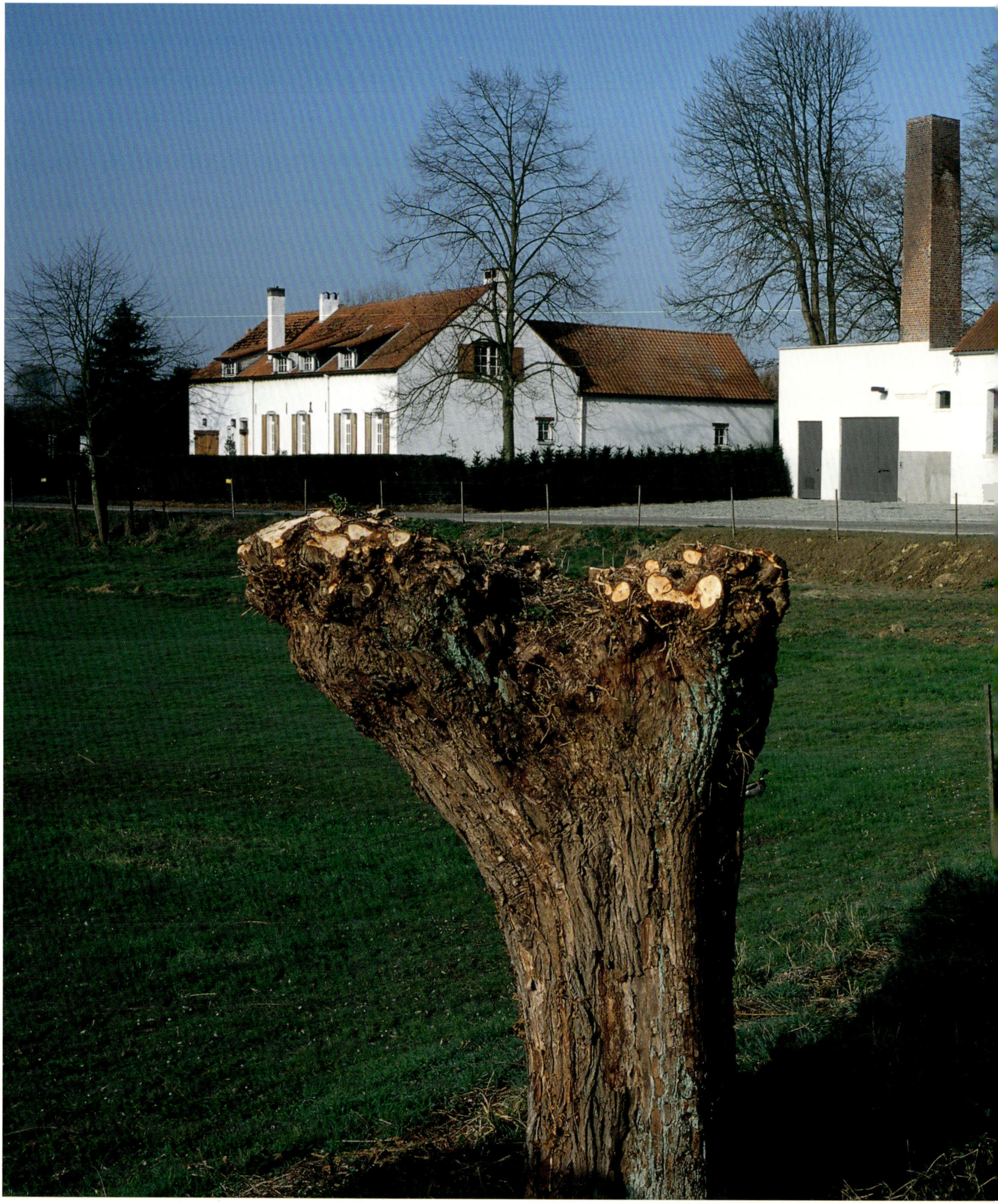

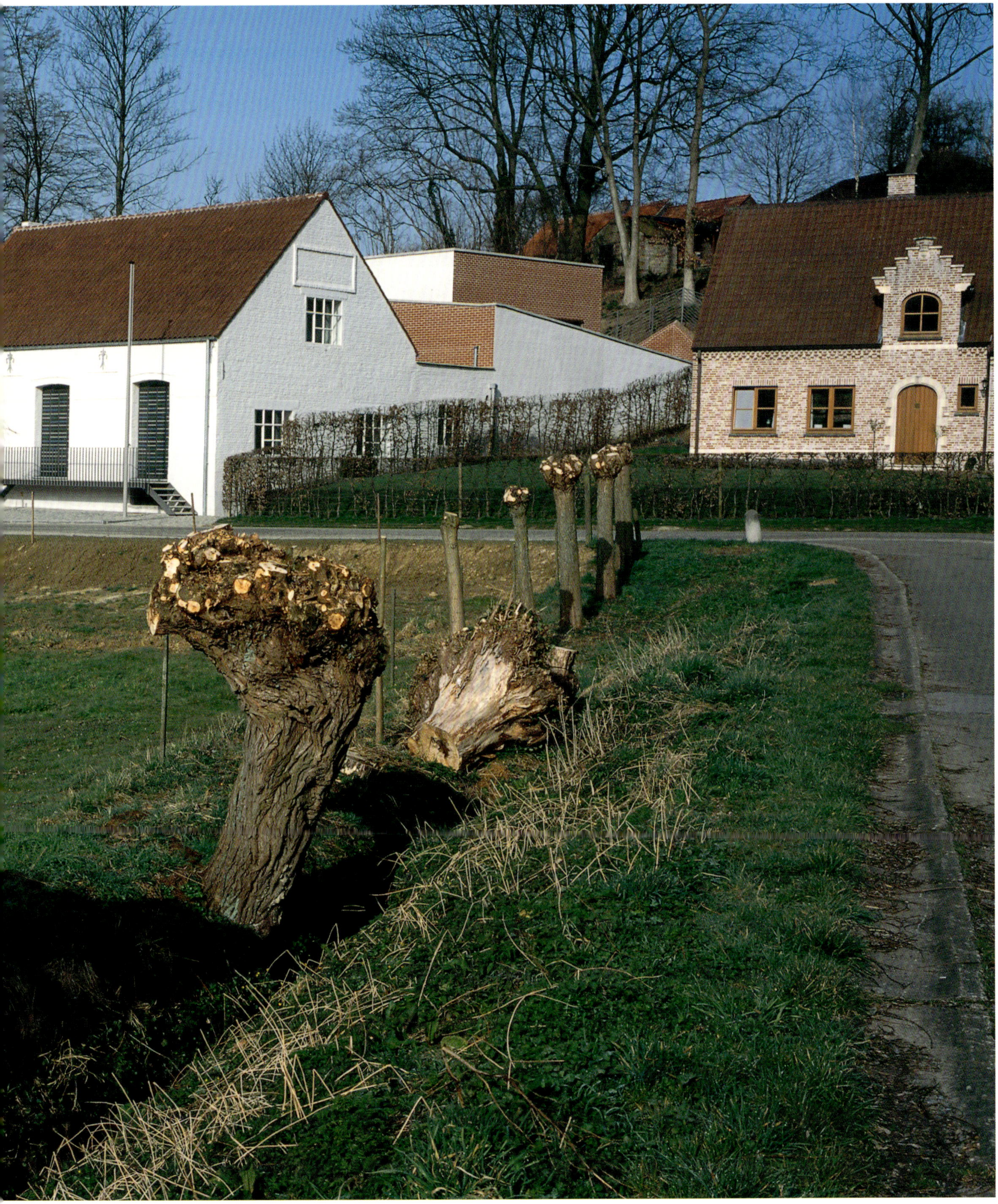

IIII Colombier

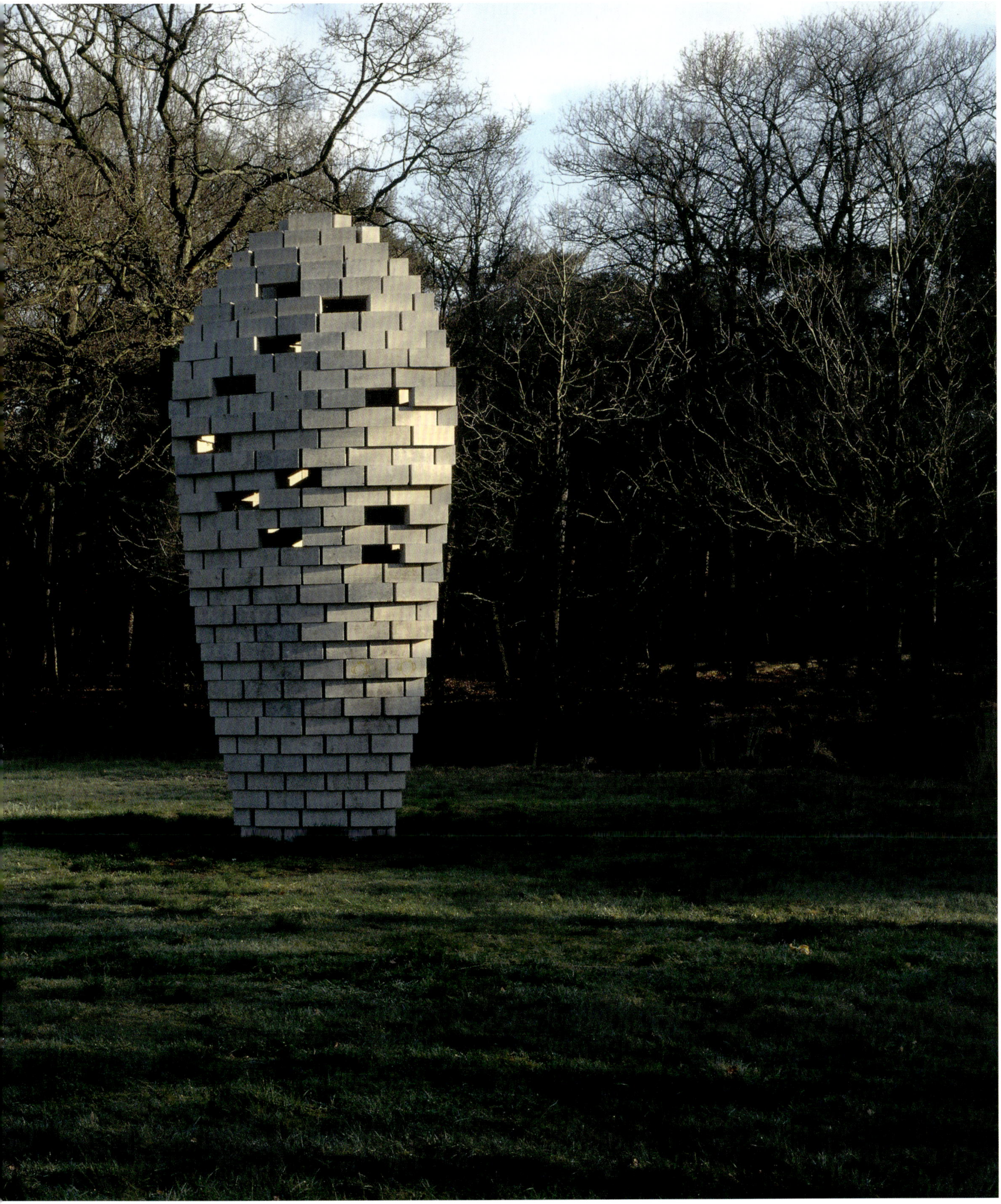

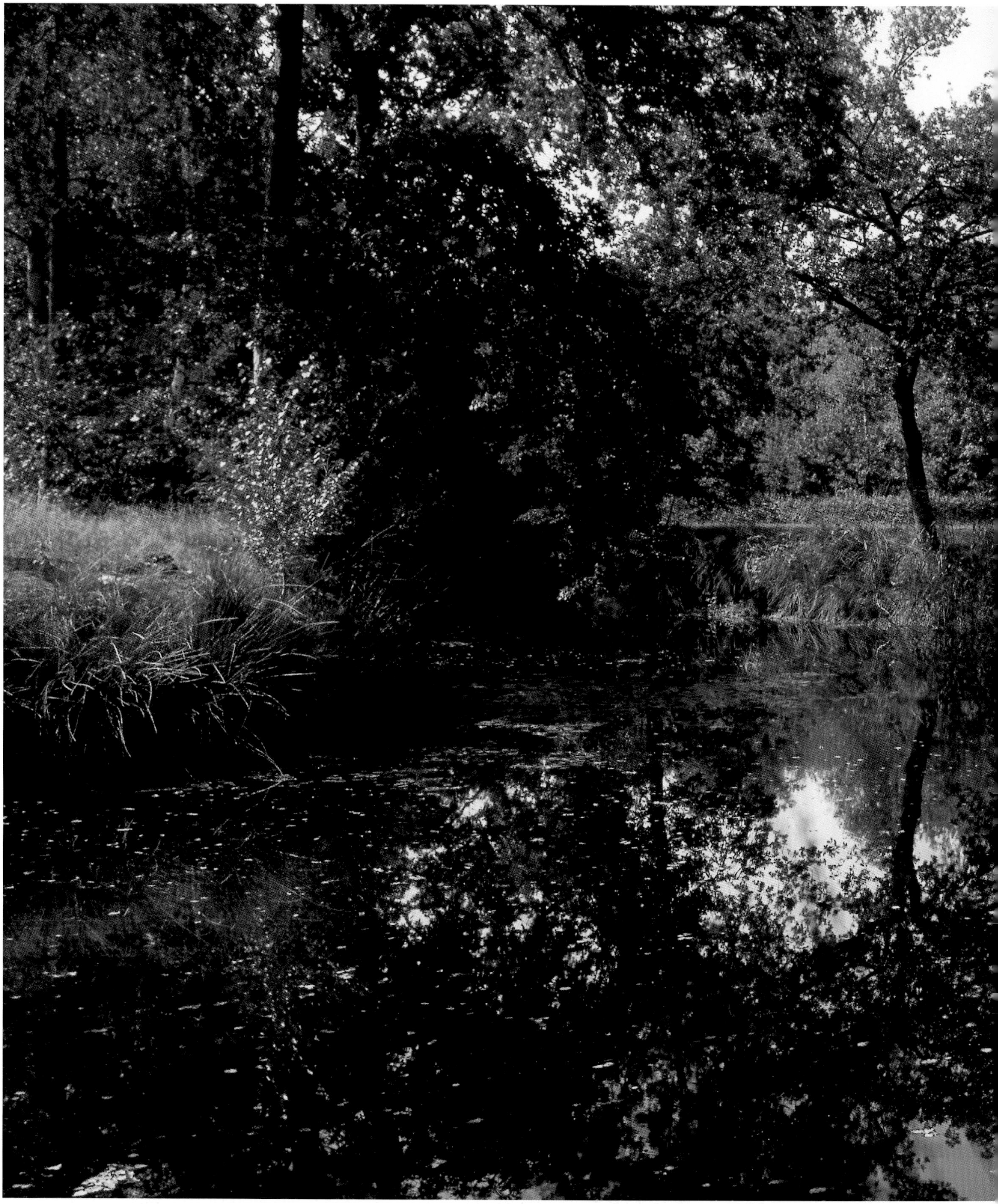

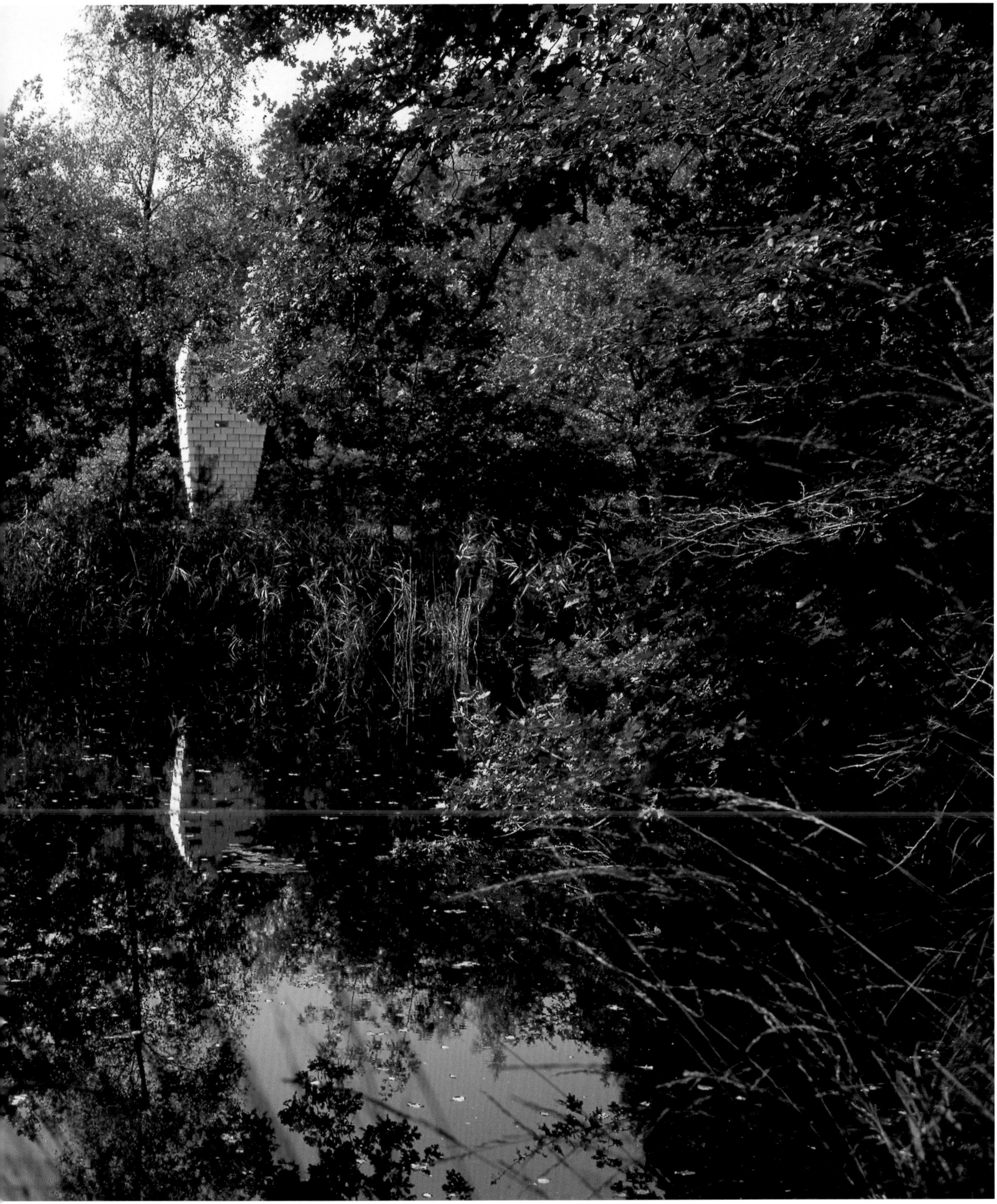

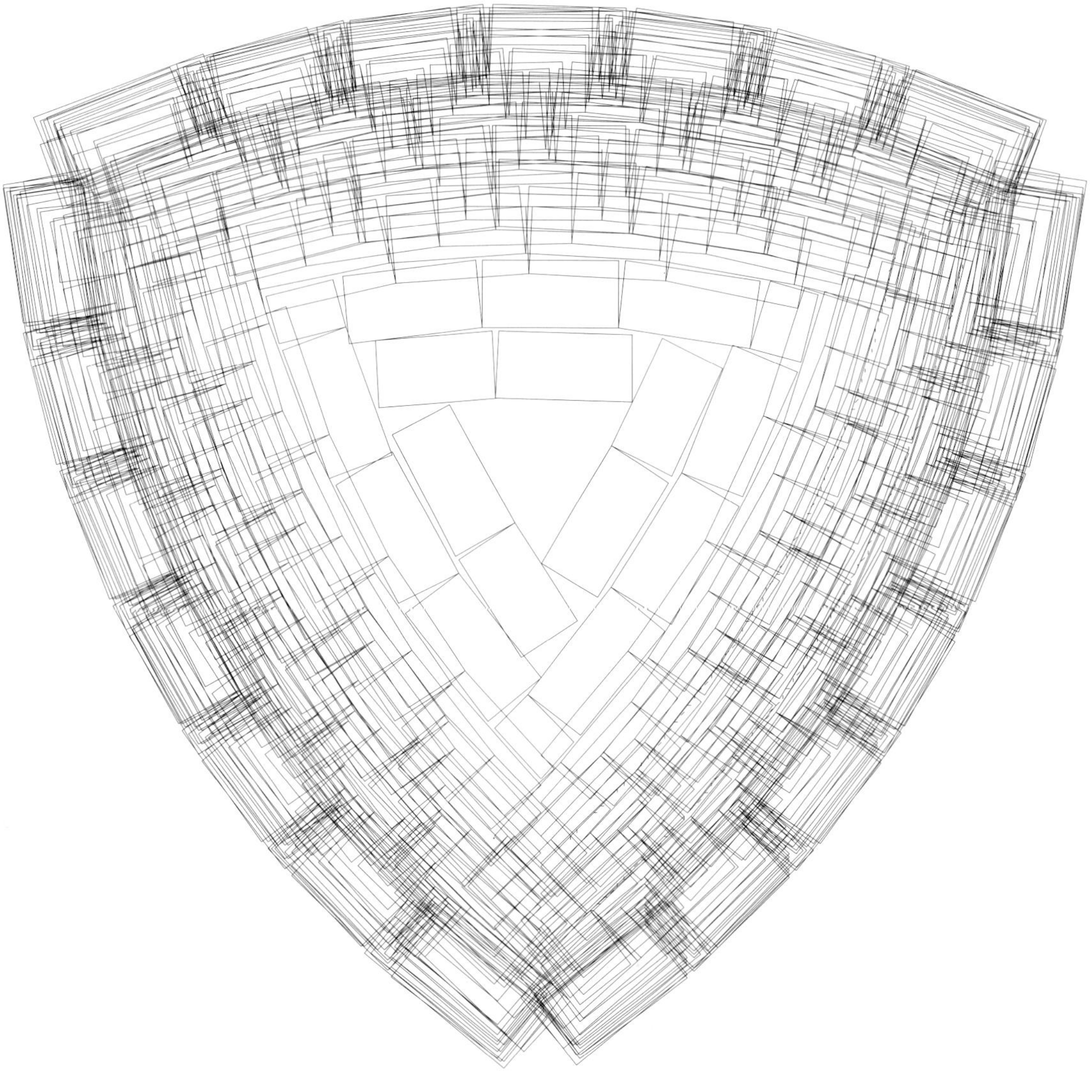

Robbrecht en Daem Offices

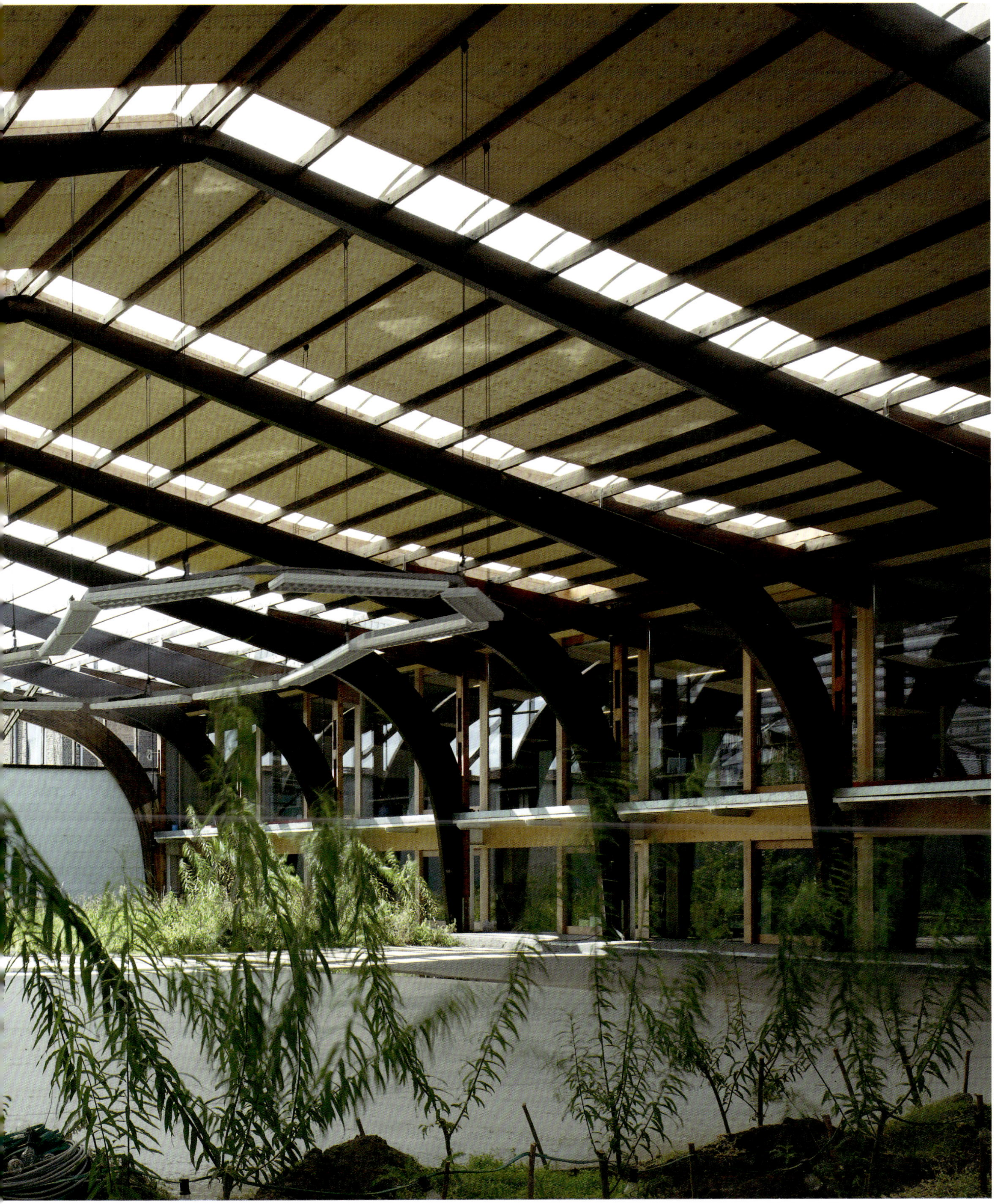

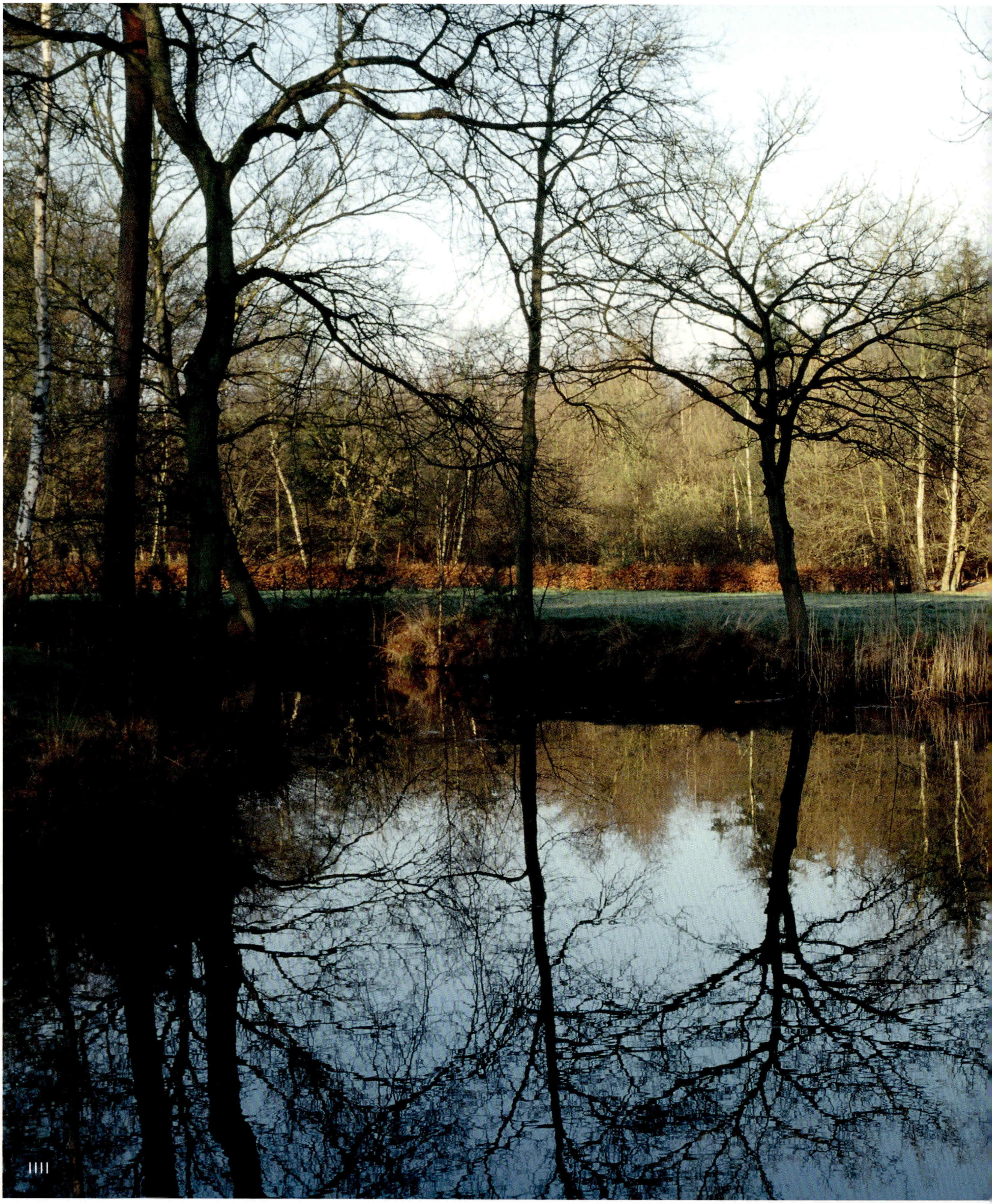

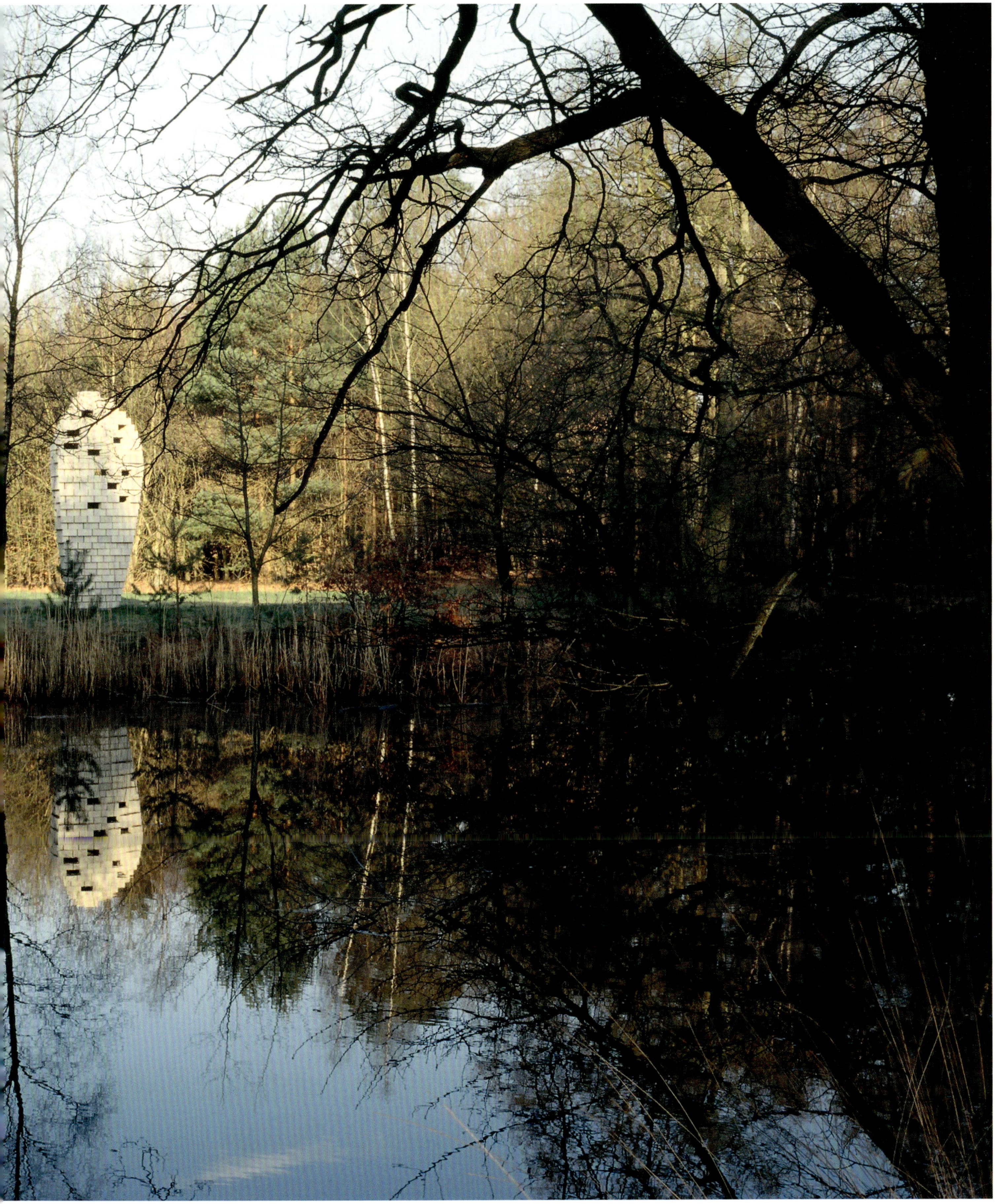

overwacht

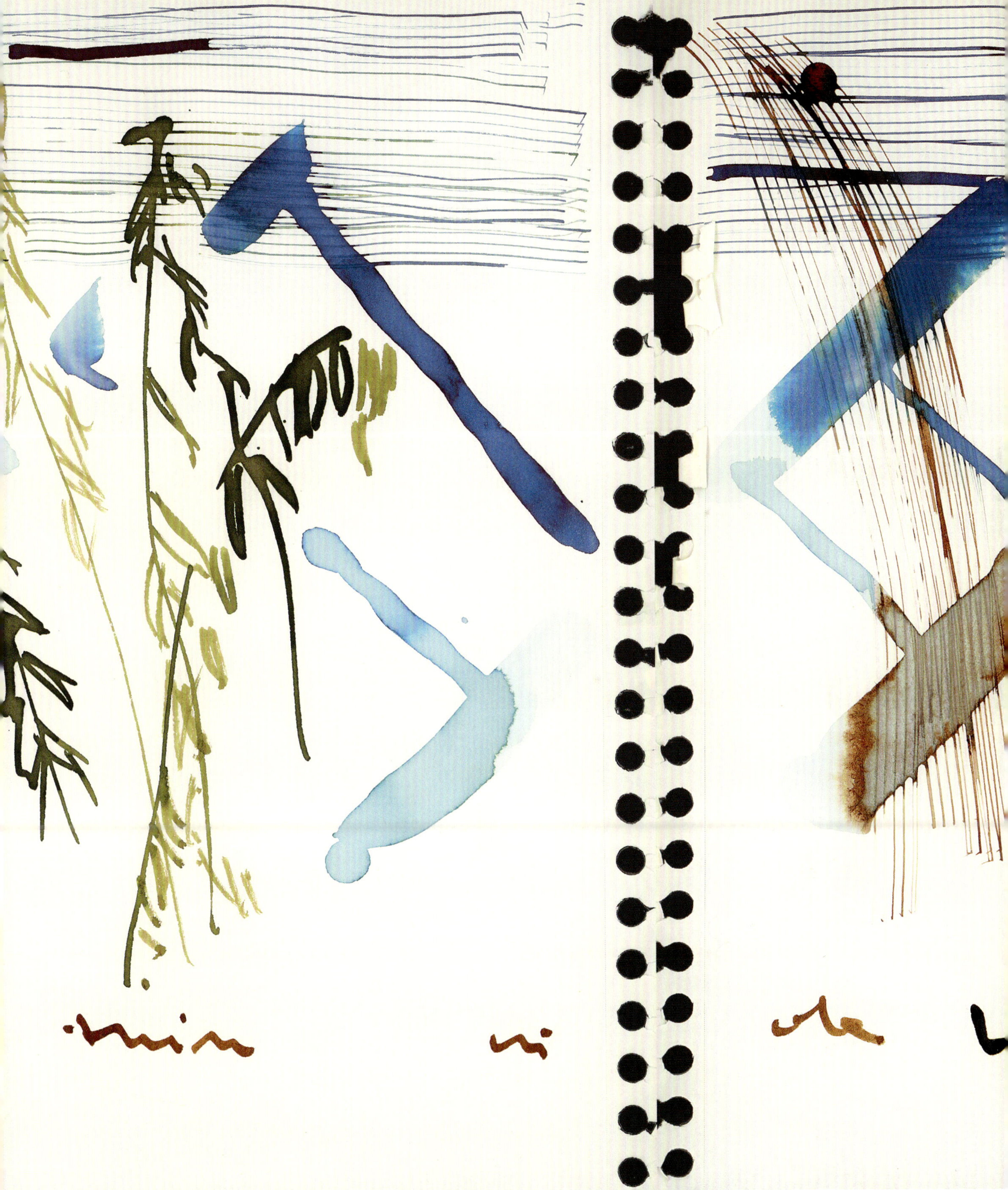

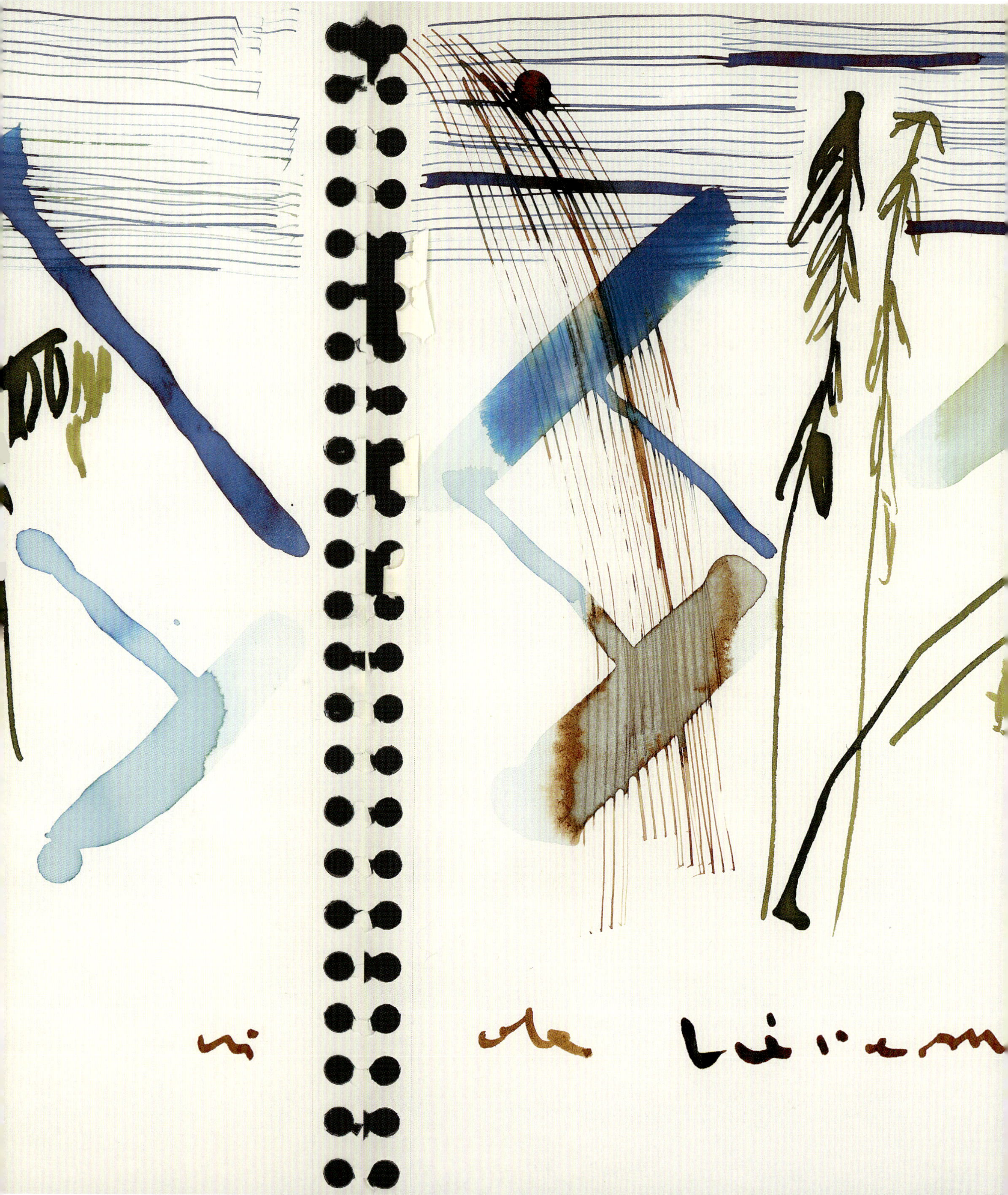

abstract   Sept. 2008

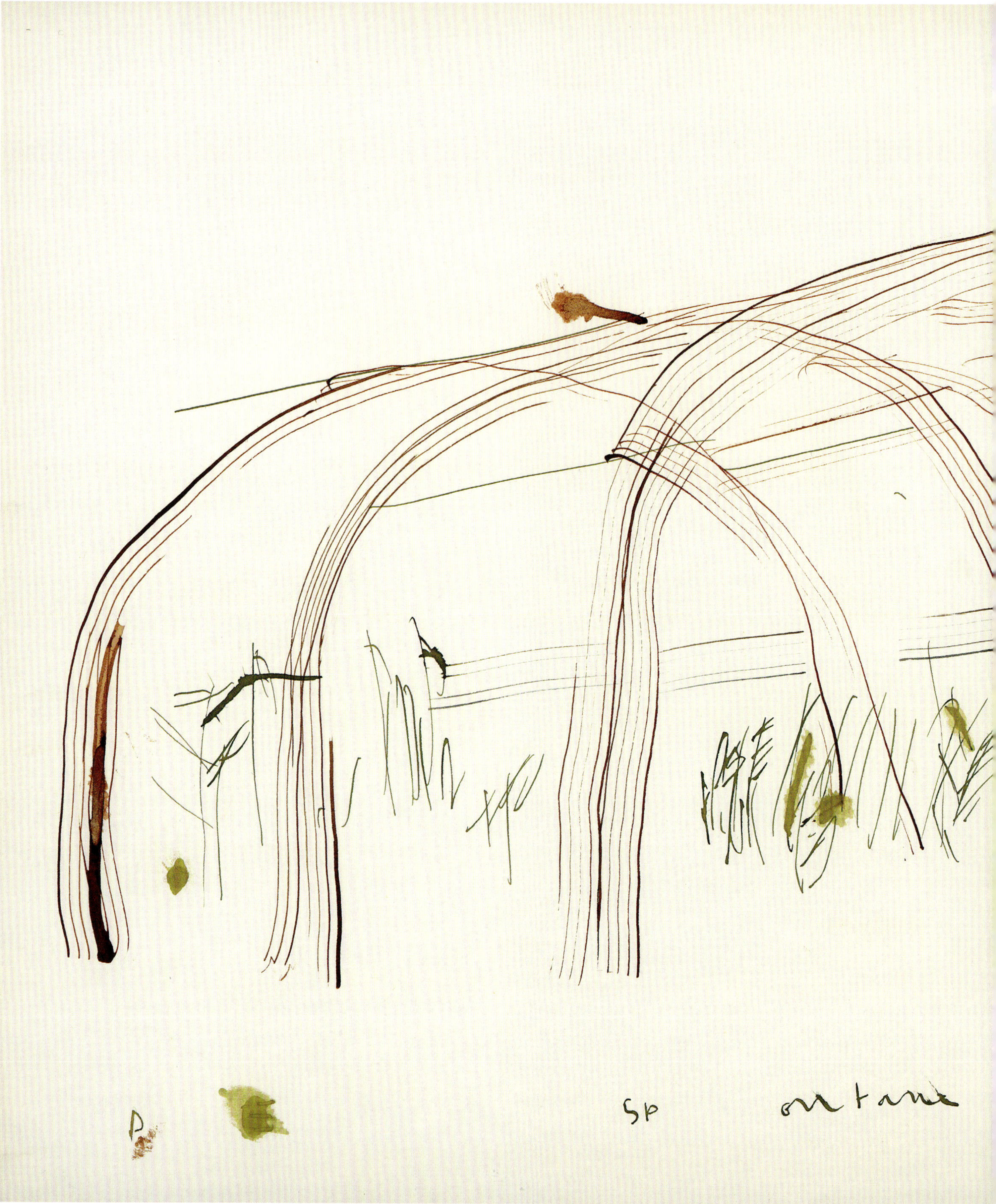

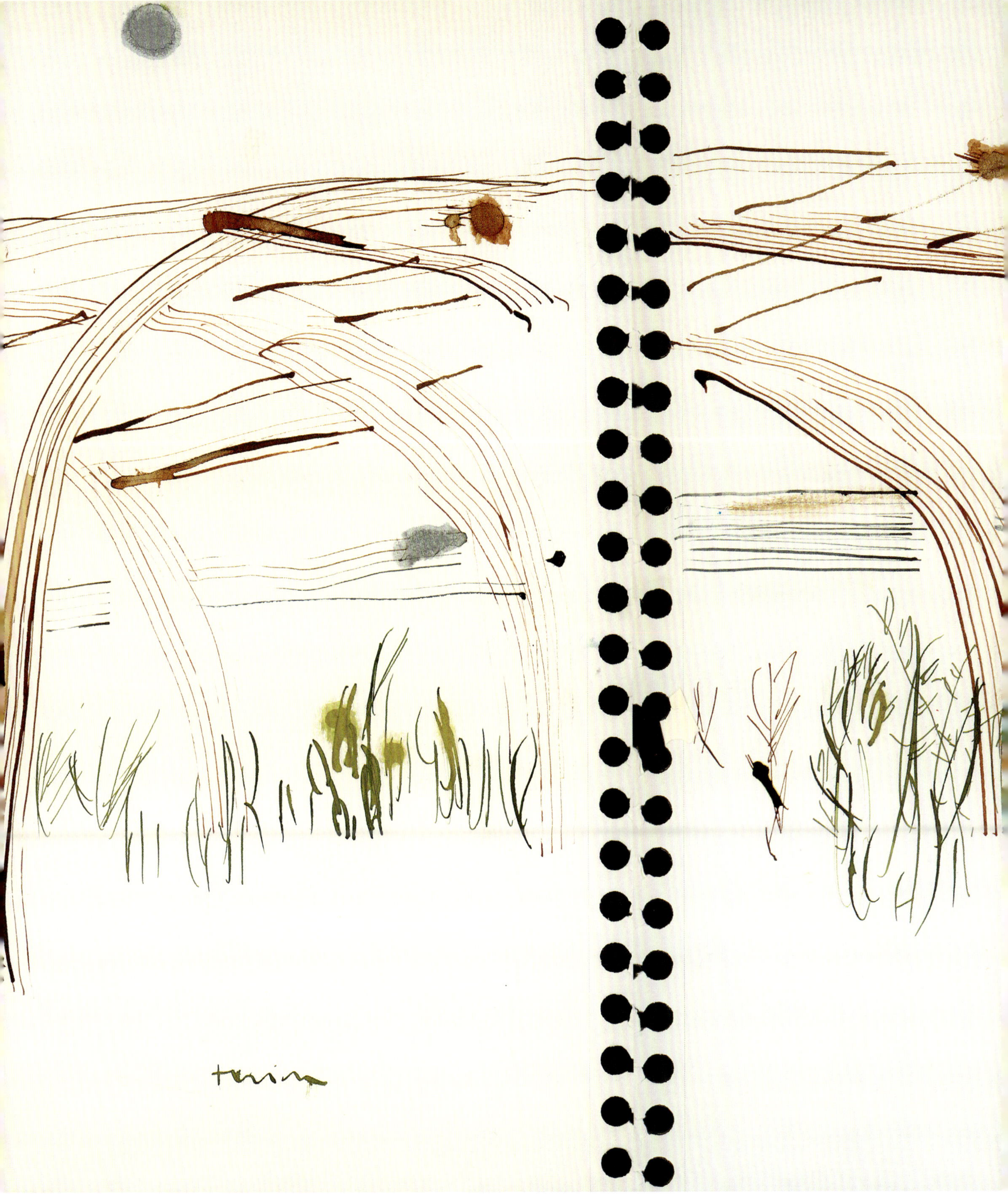

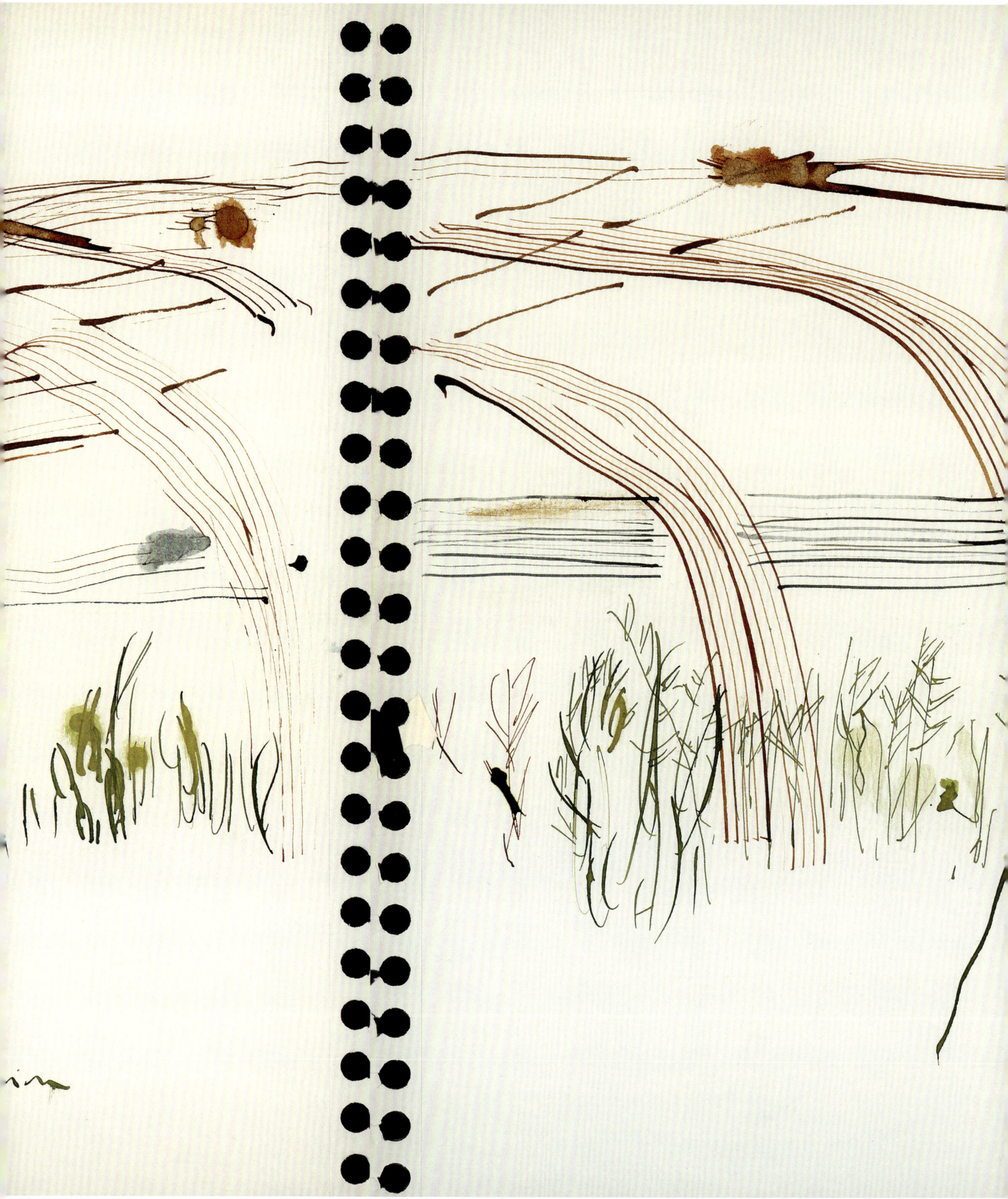

10.9.08

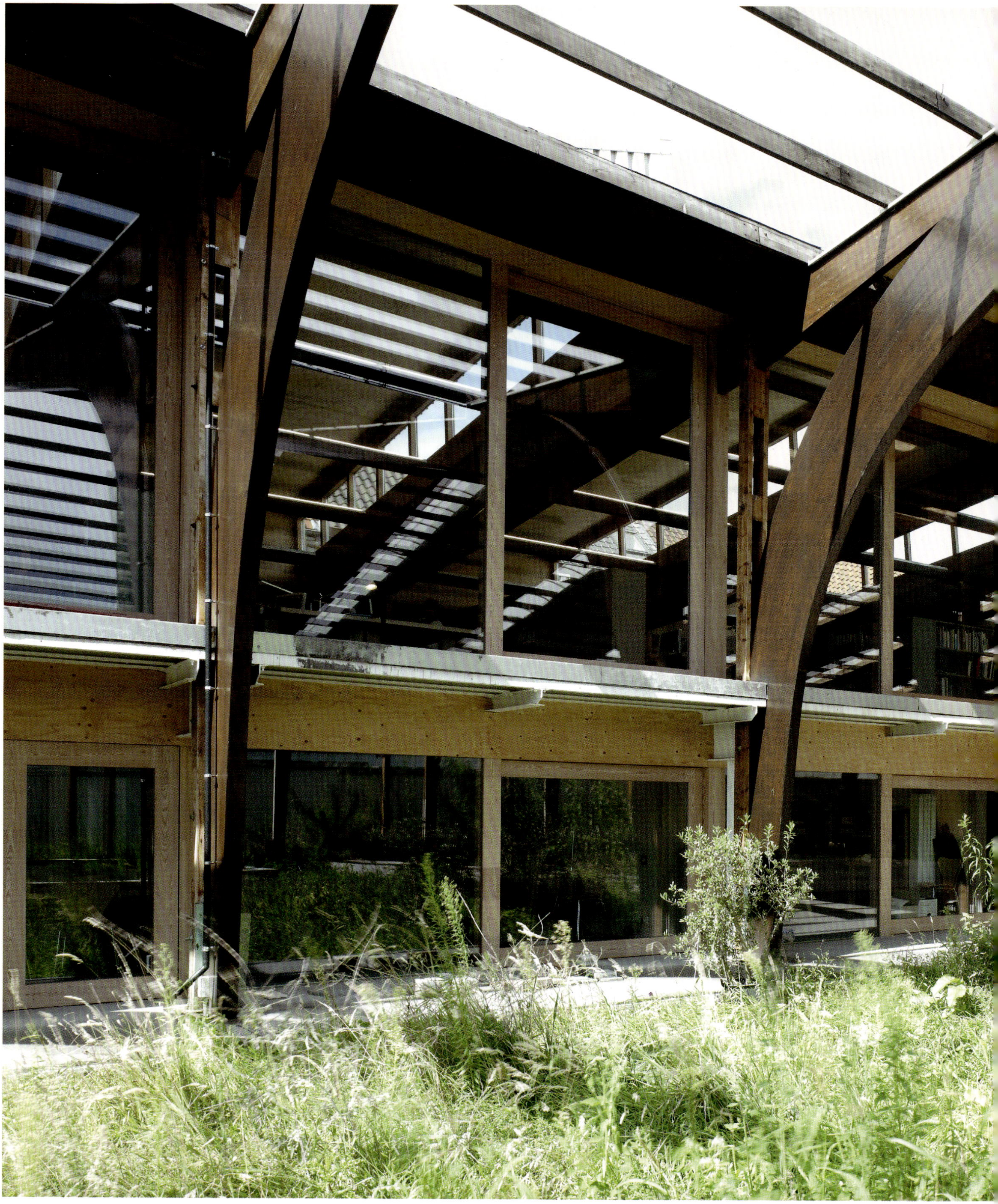

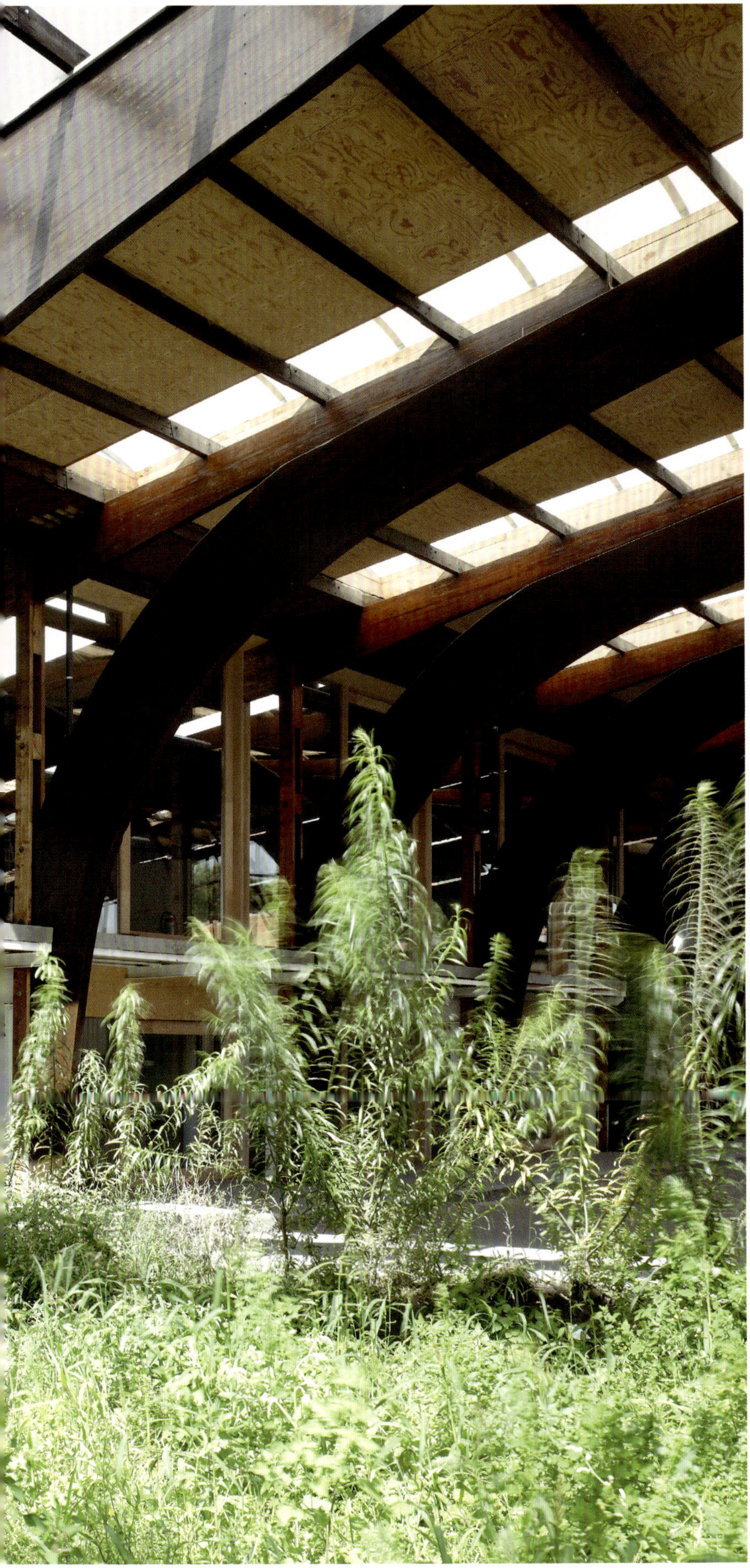
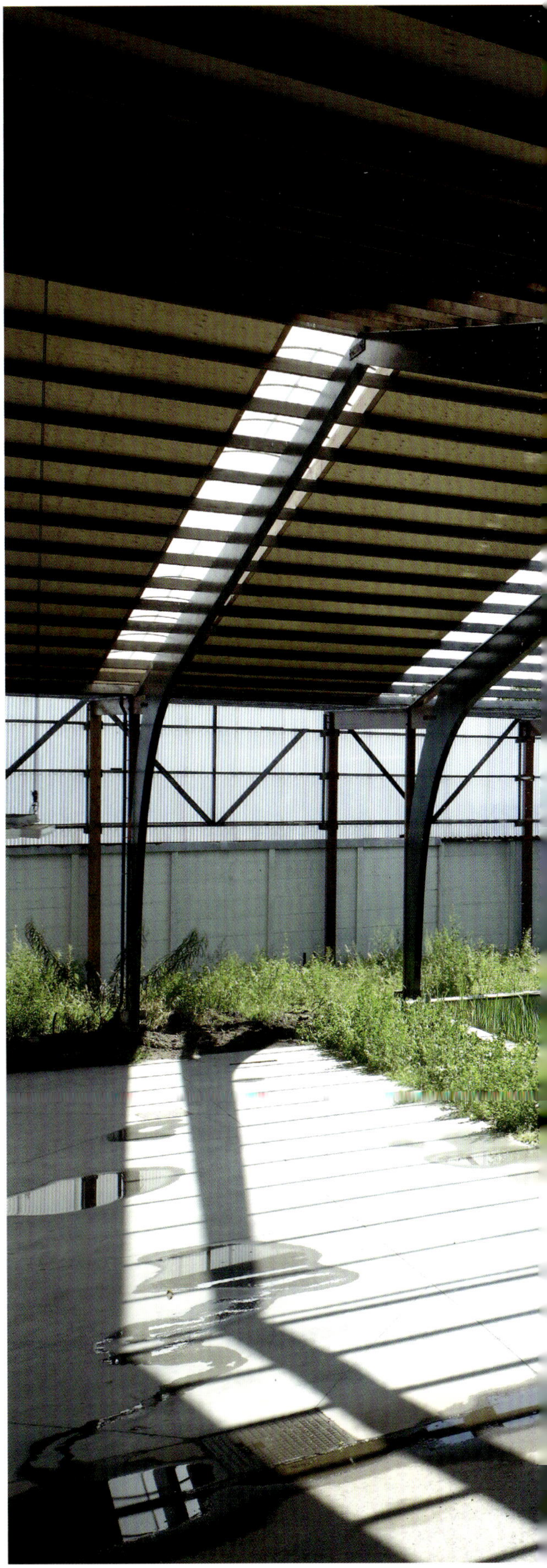

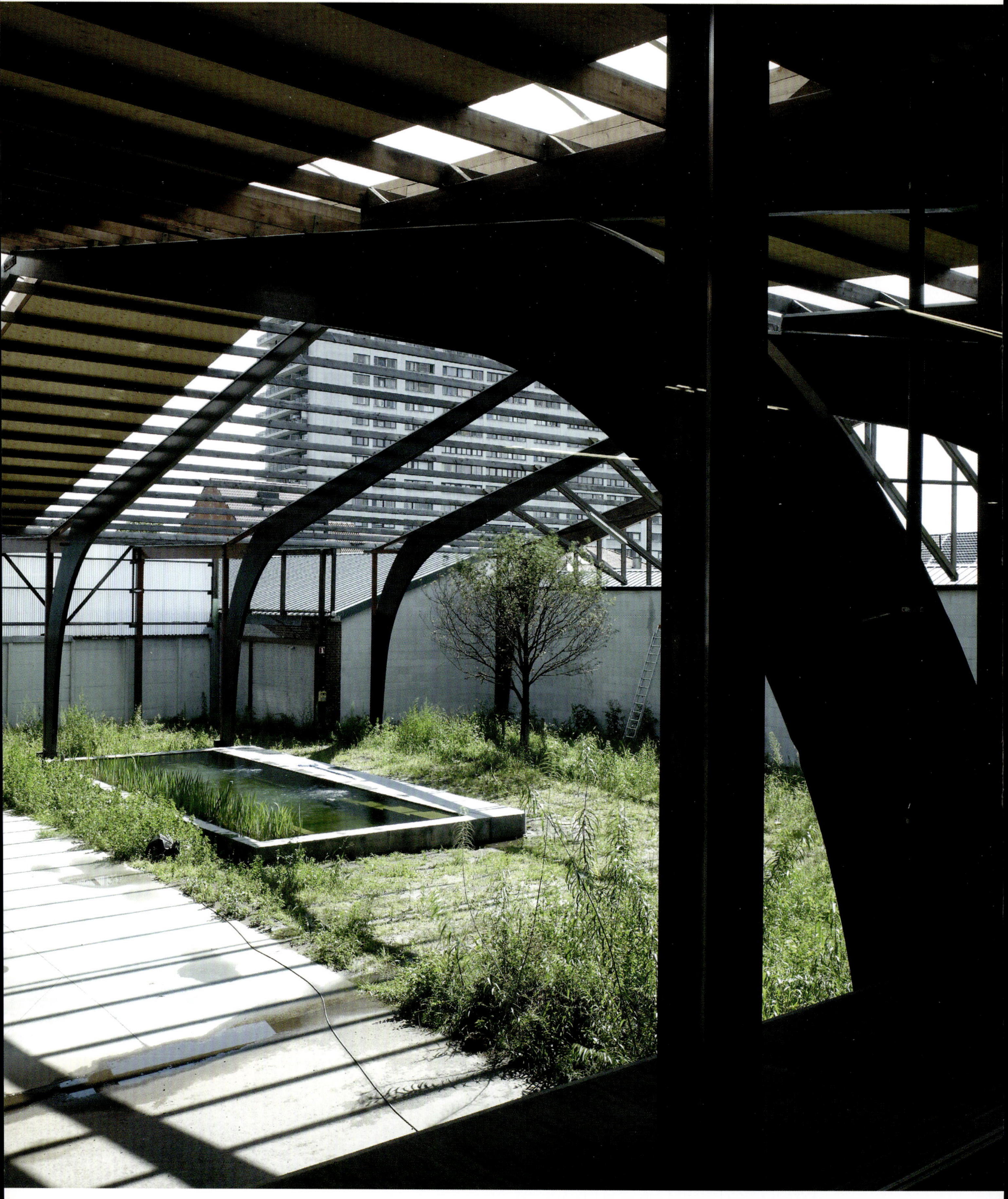

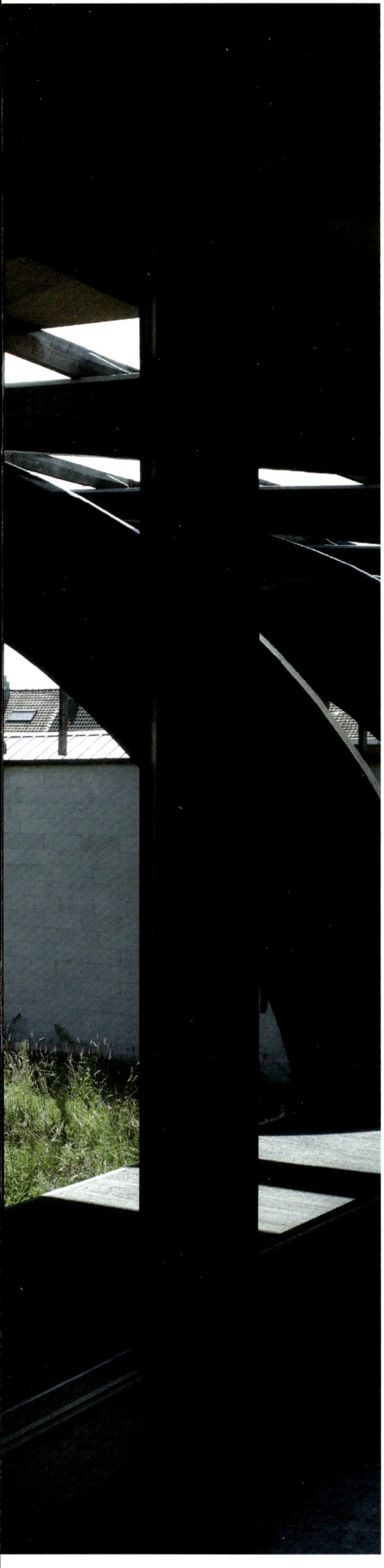
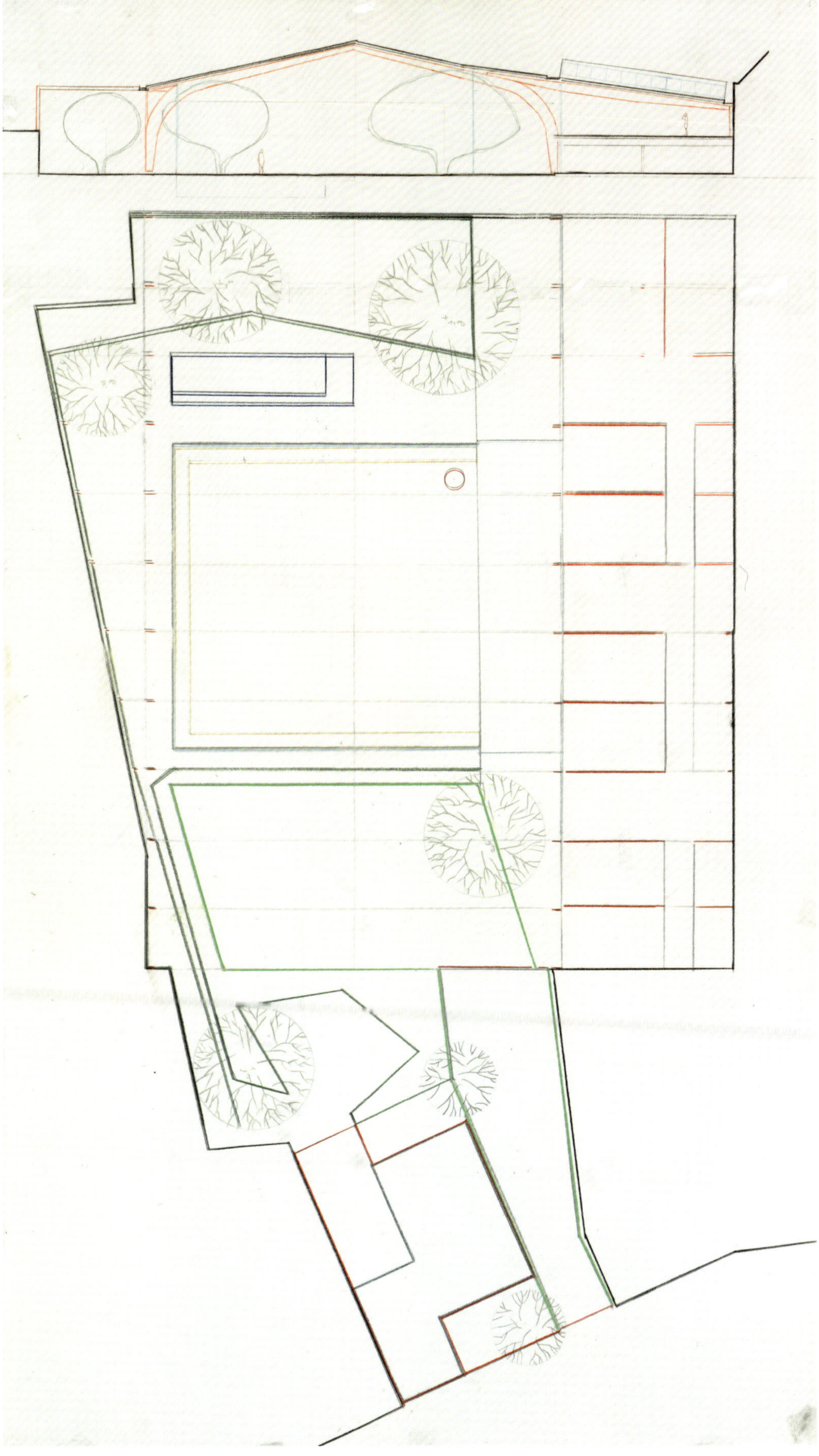

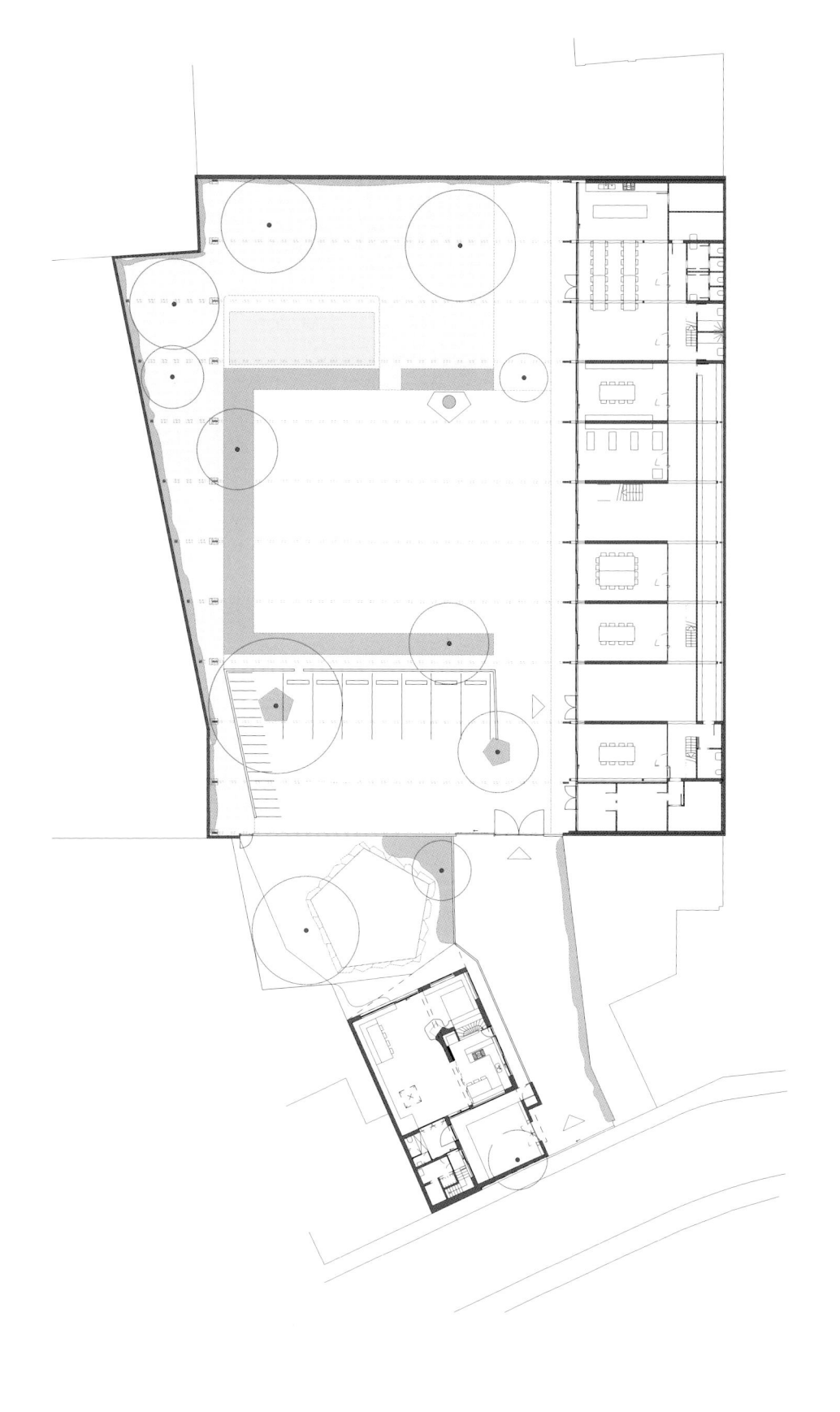

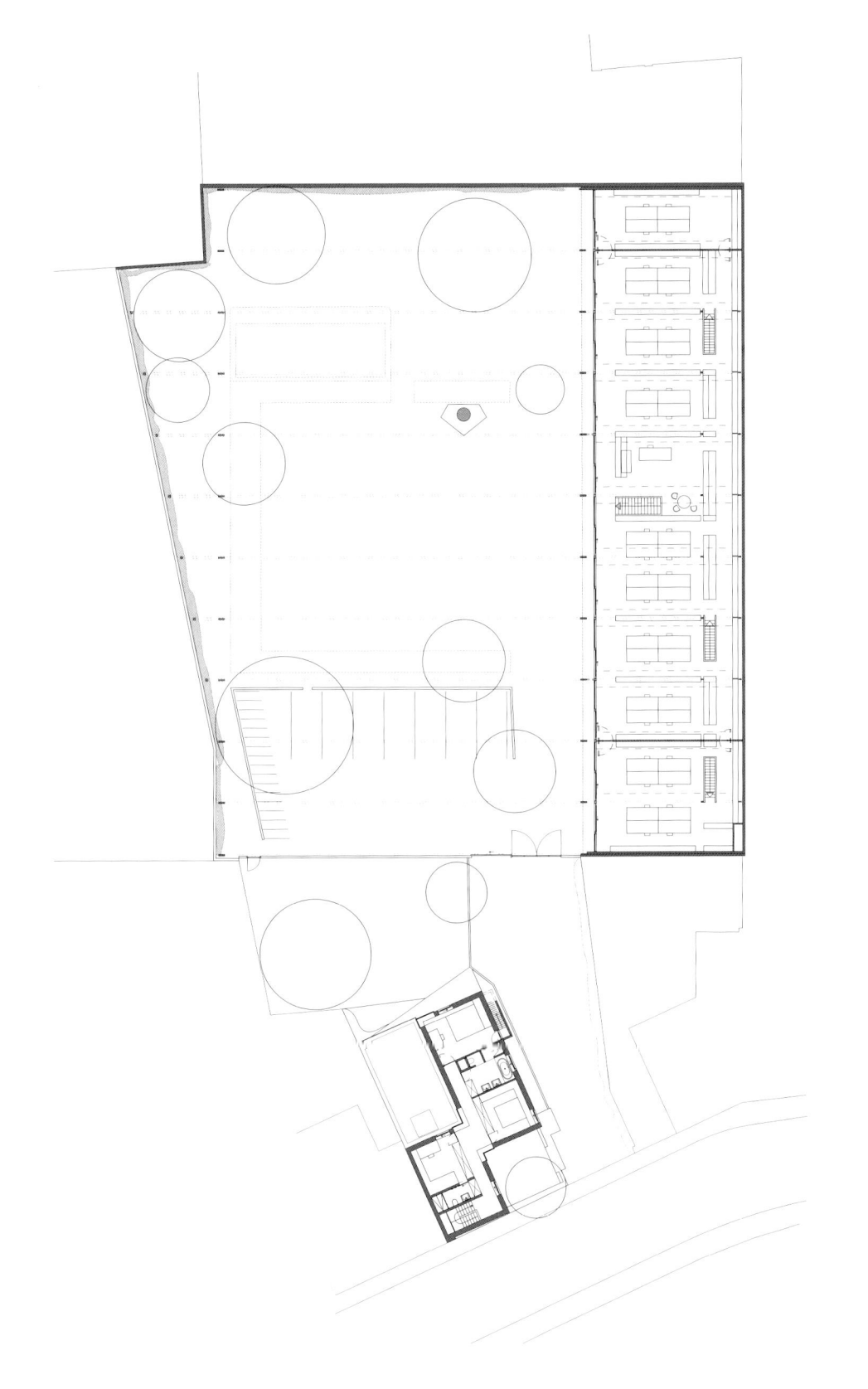

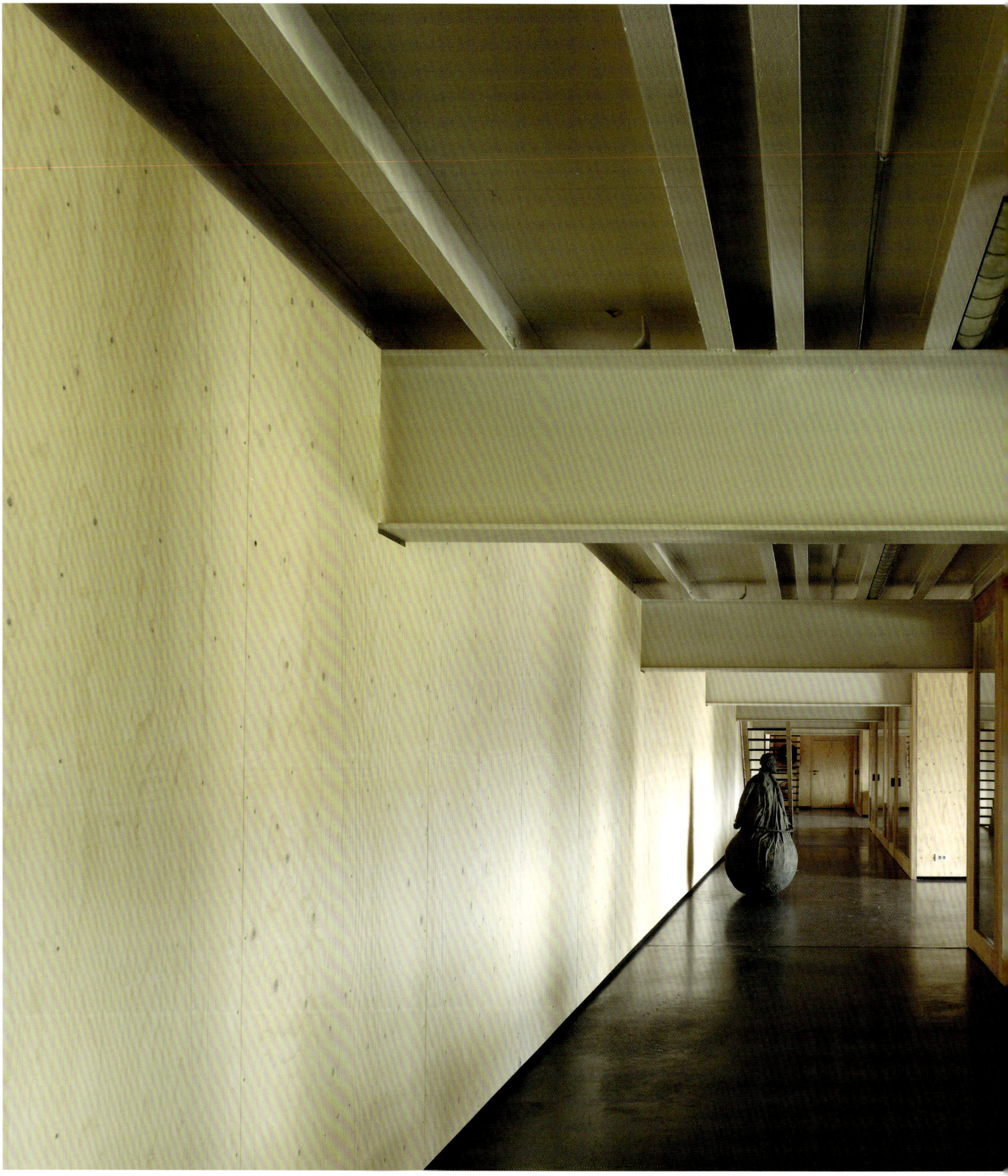

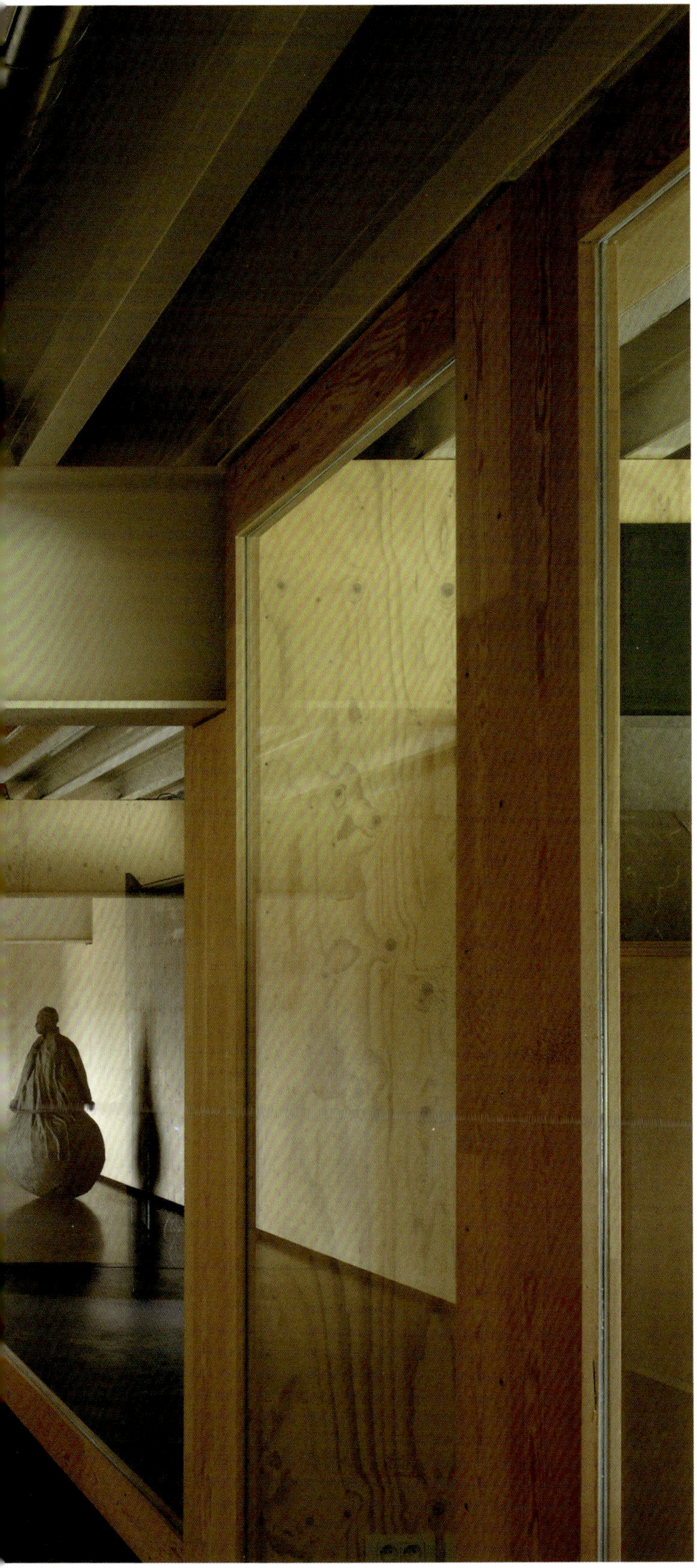
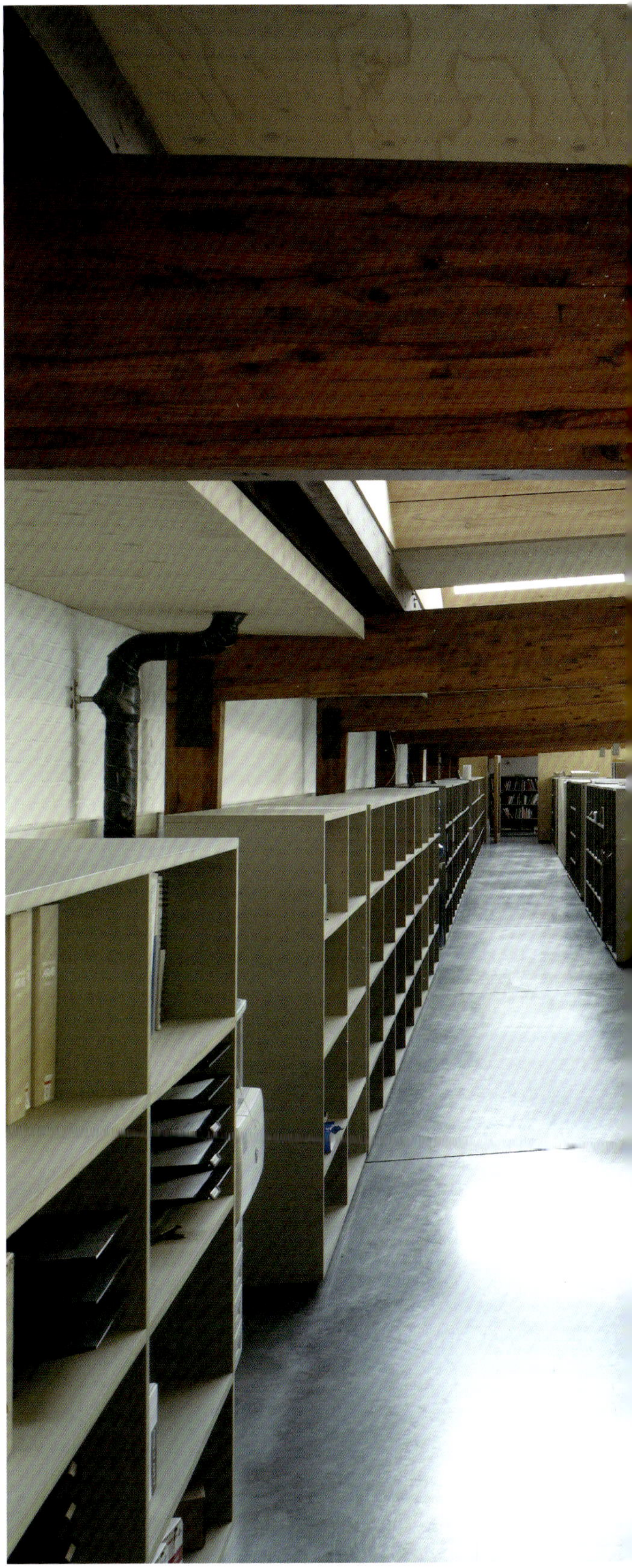

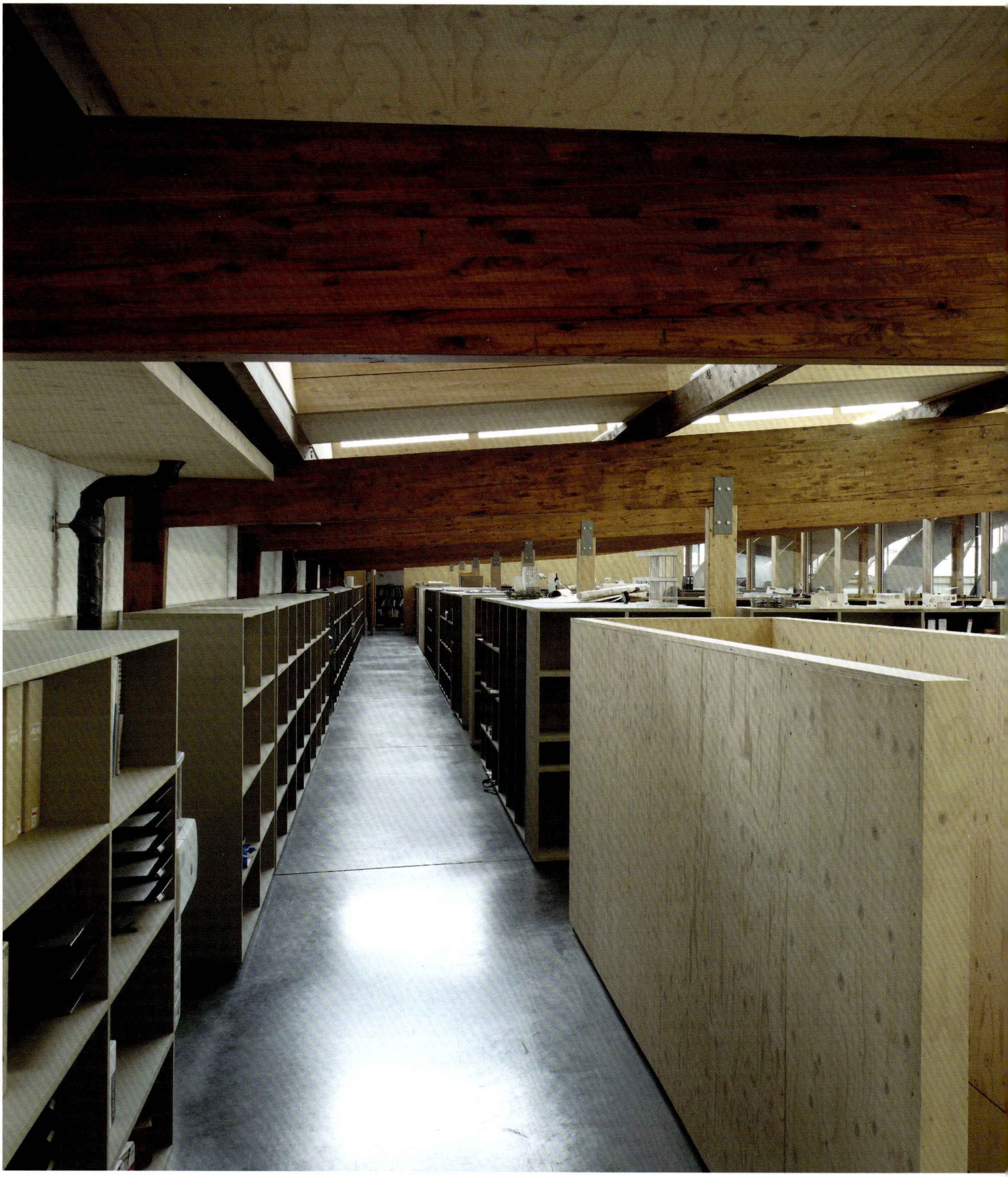

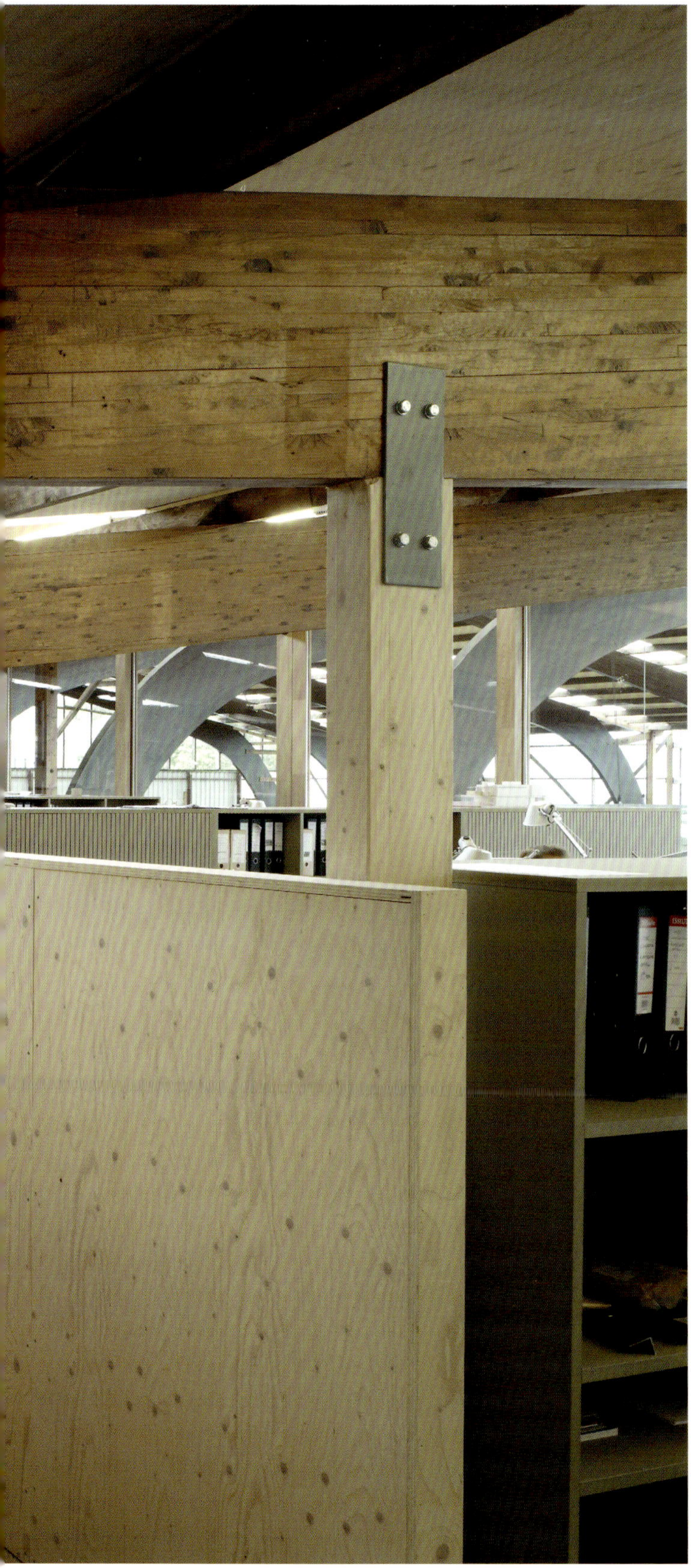

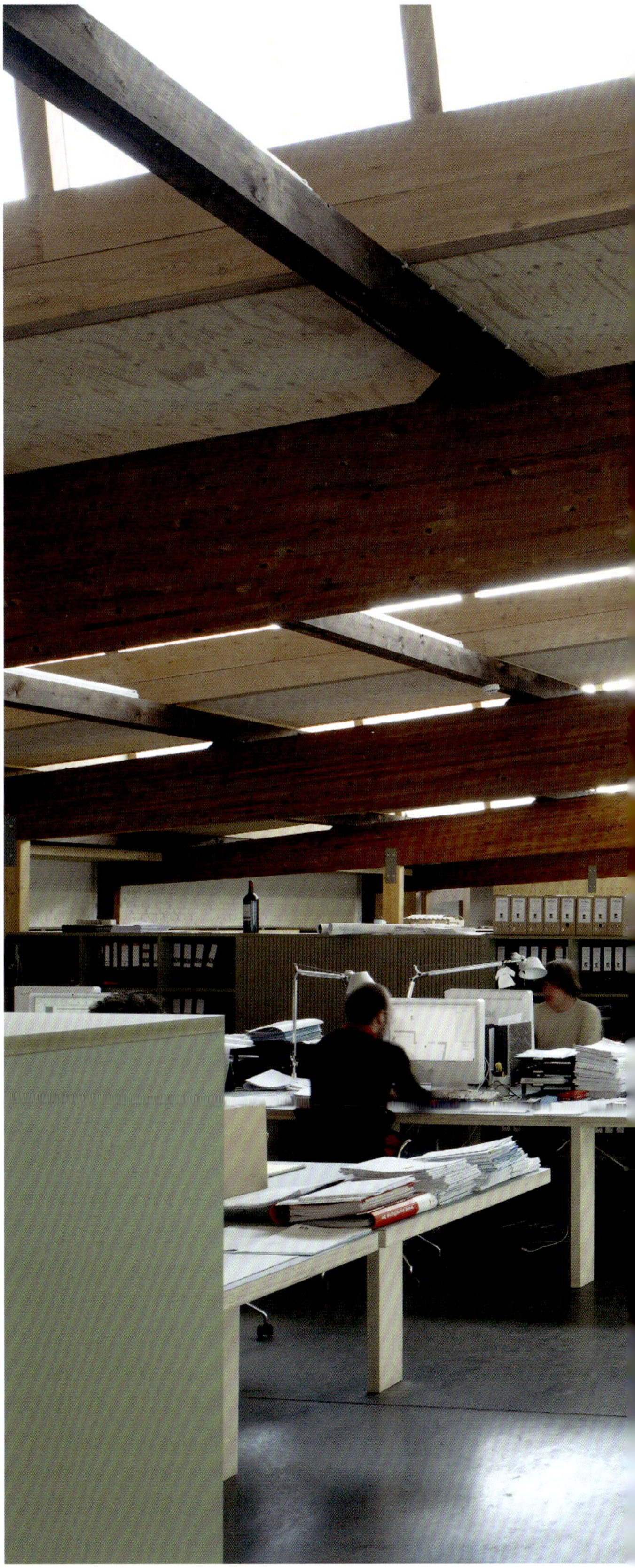

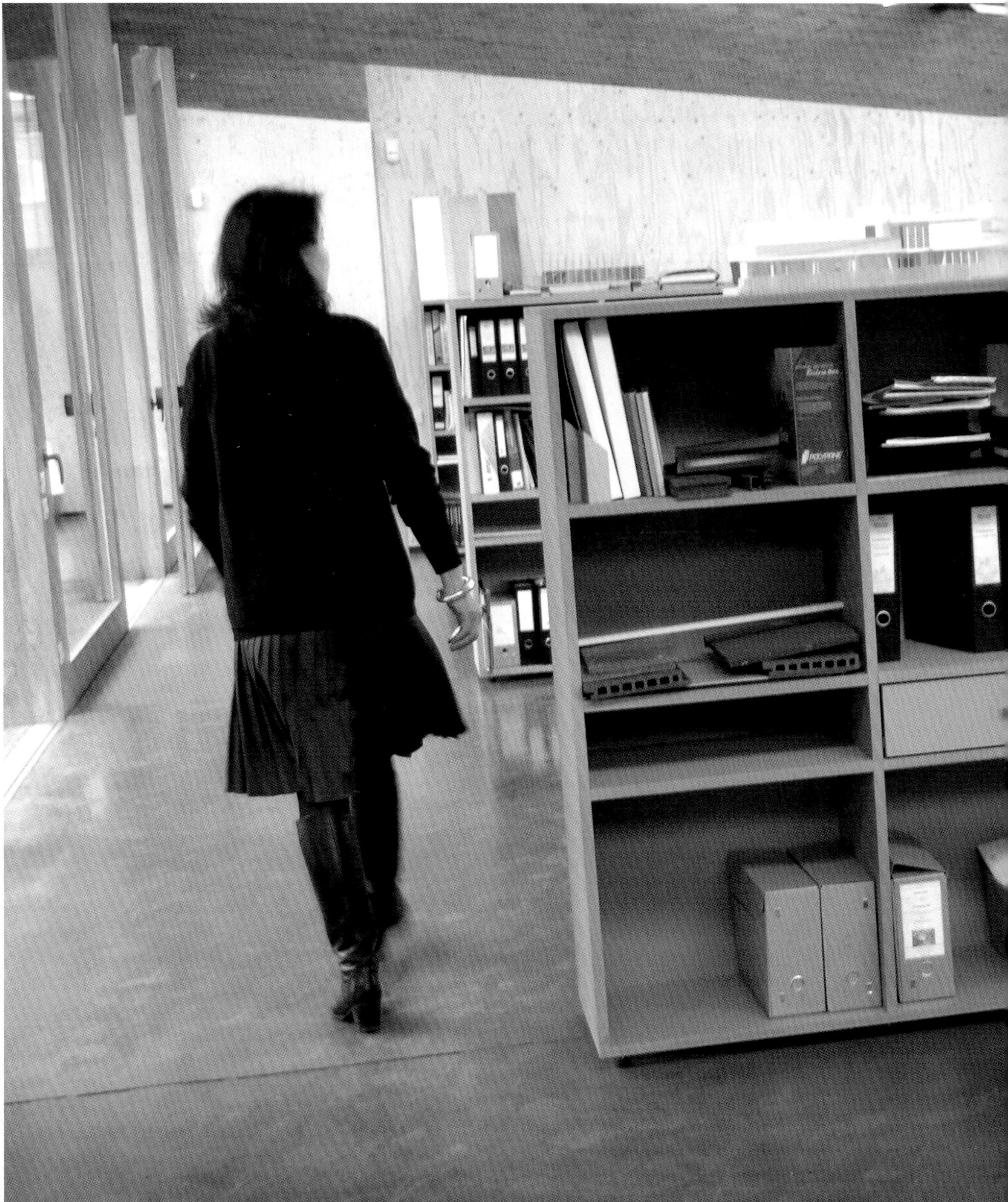

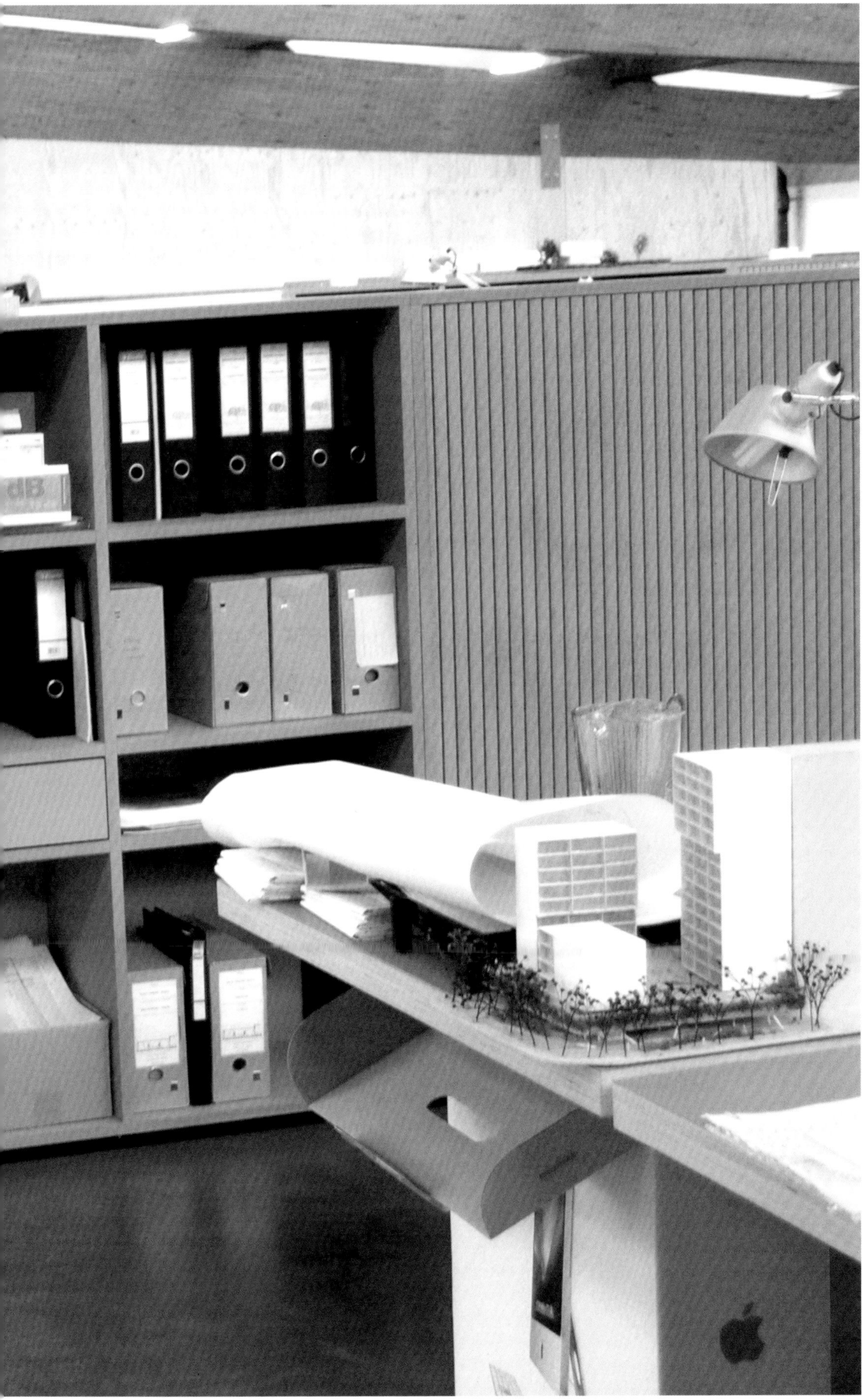

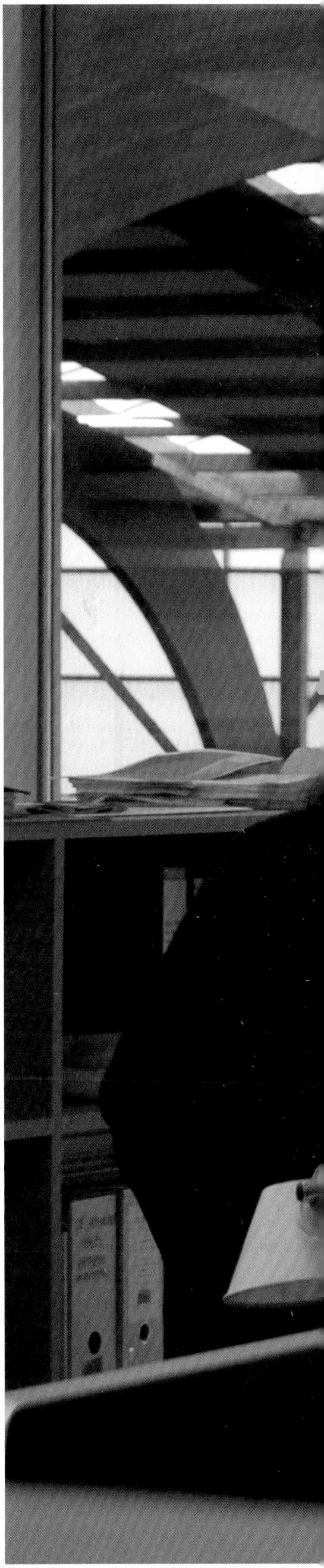

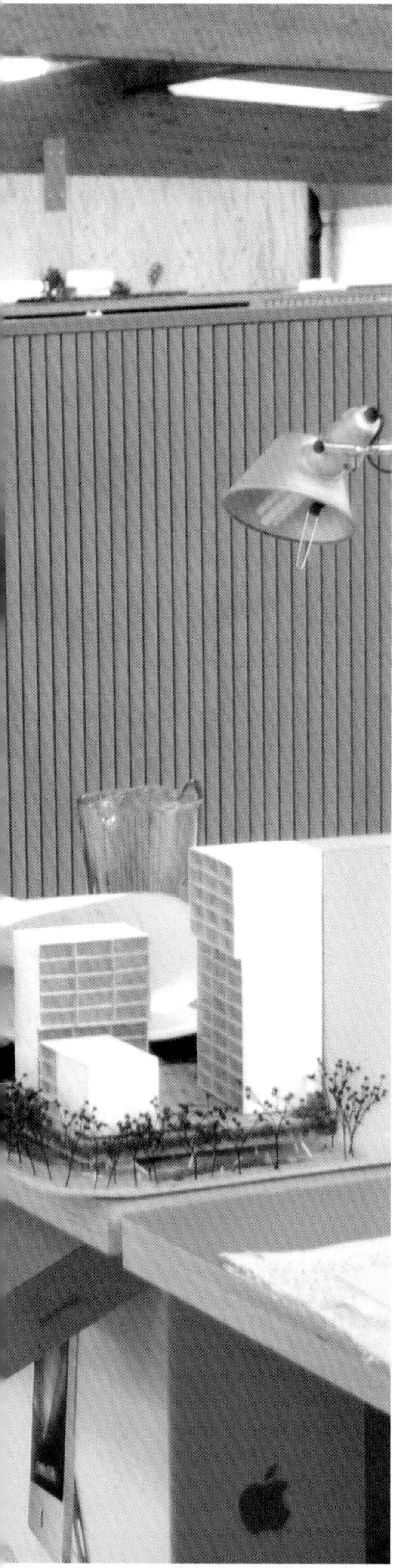
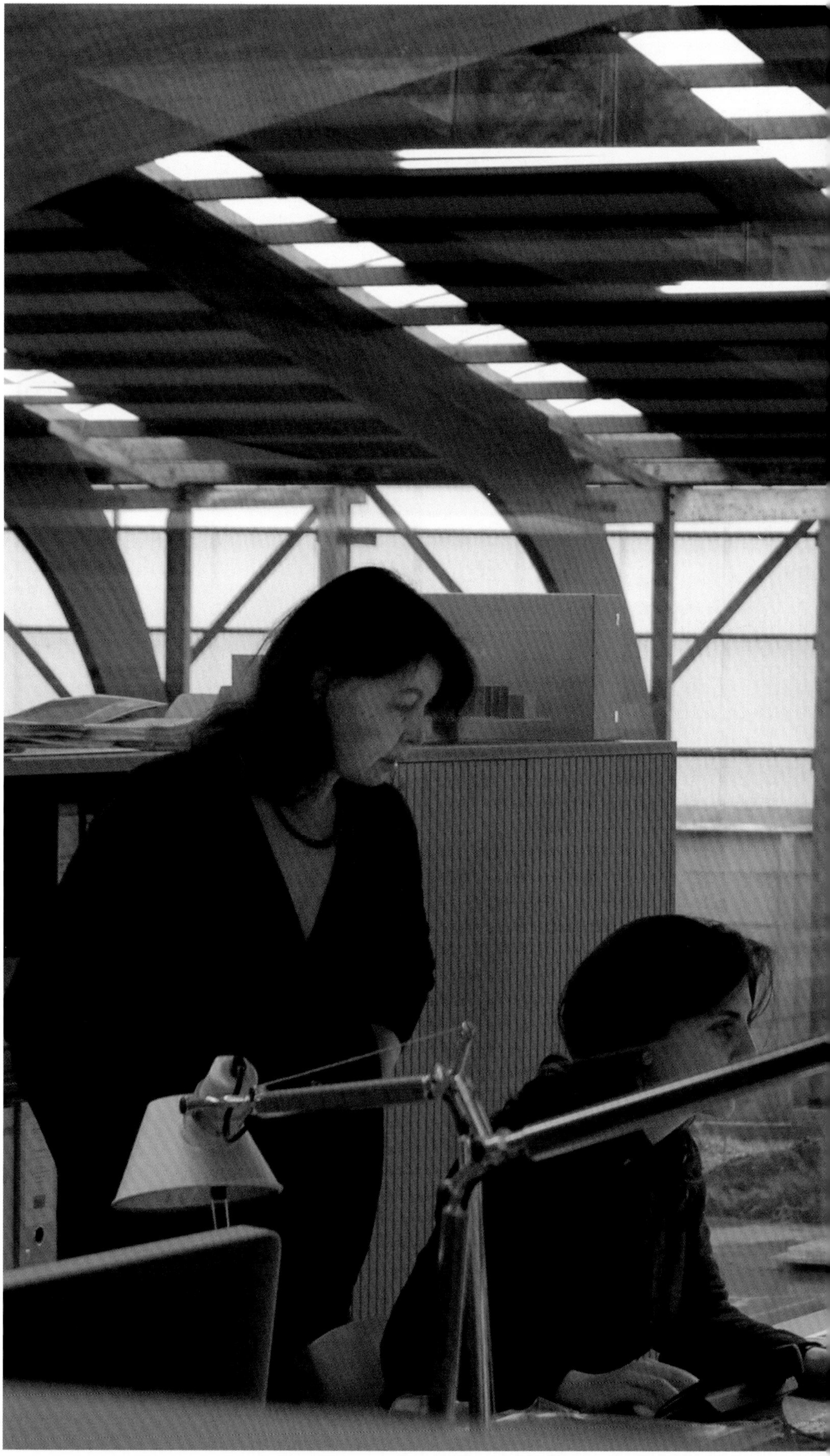

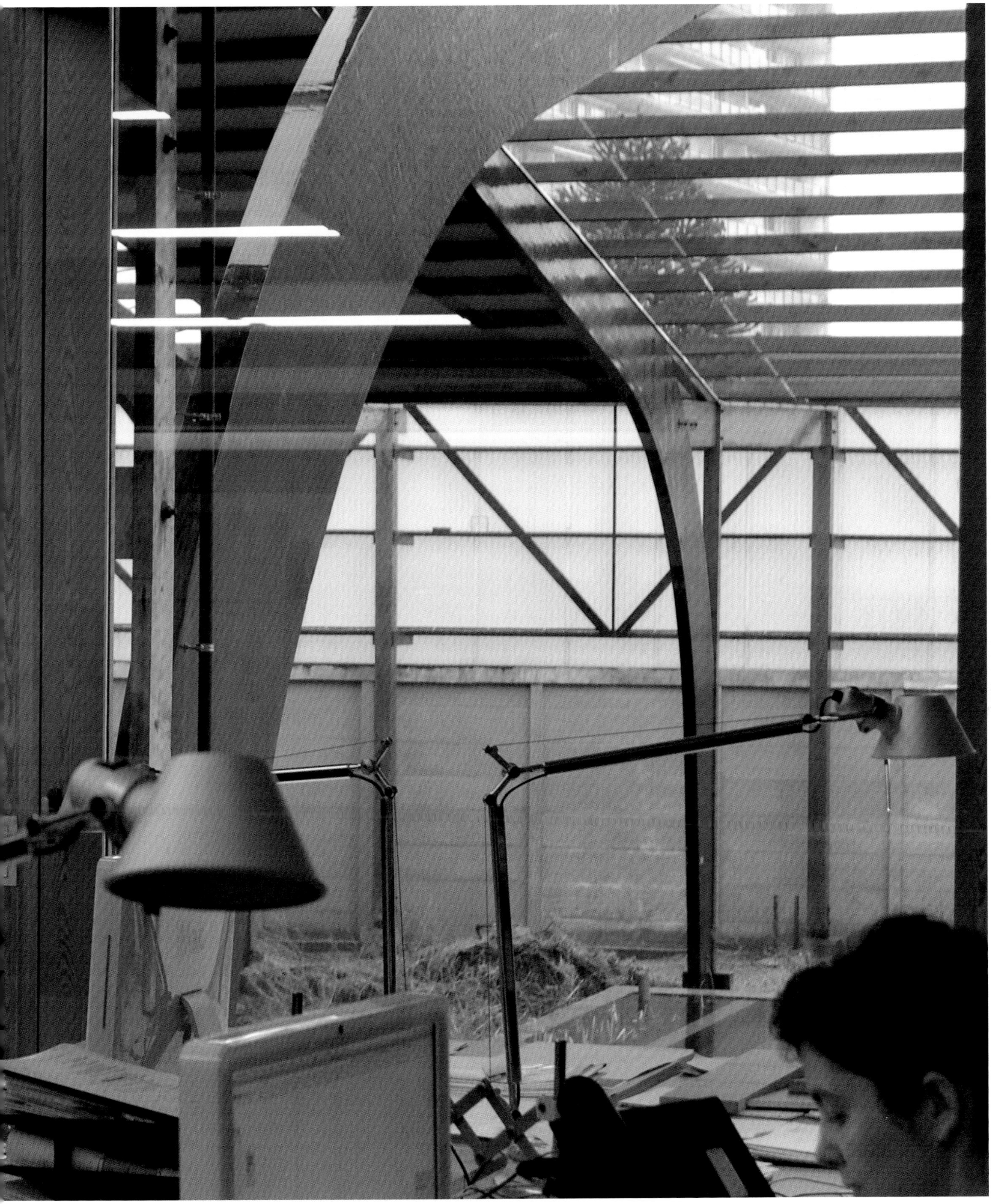

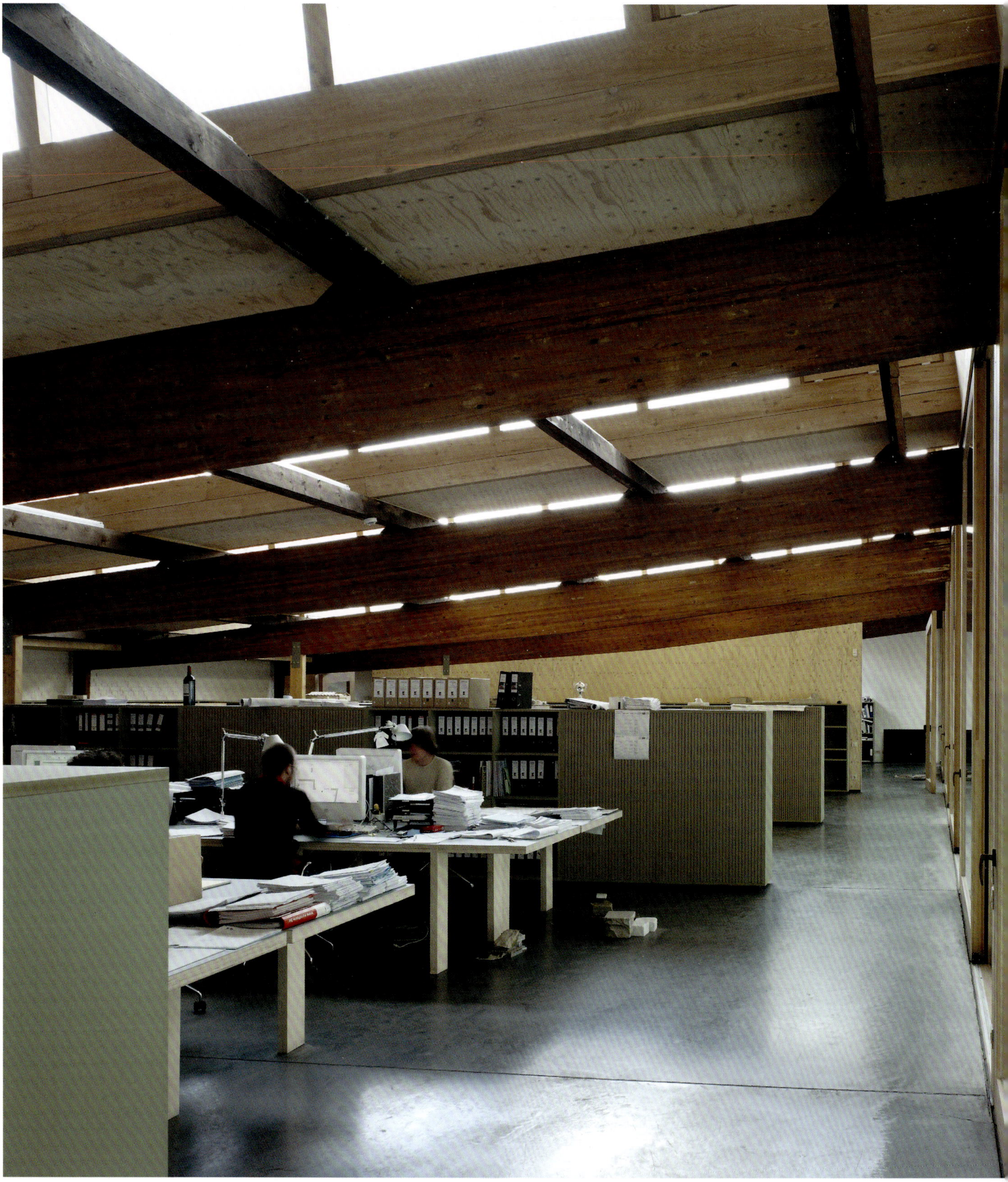

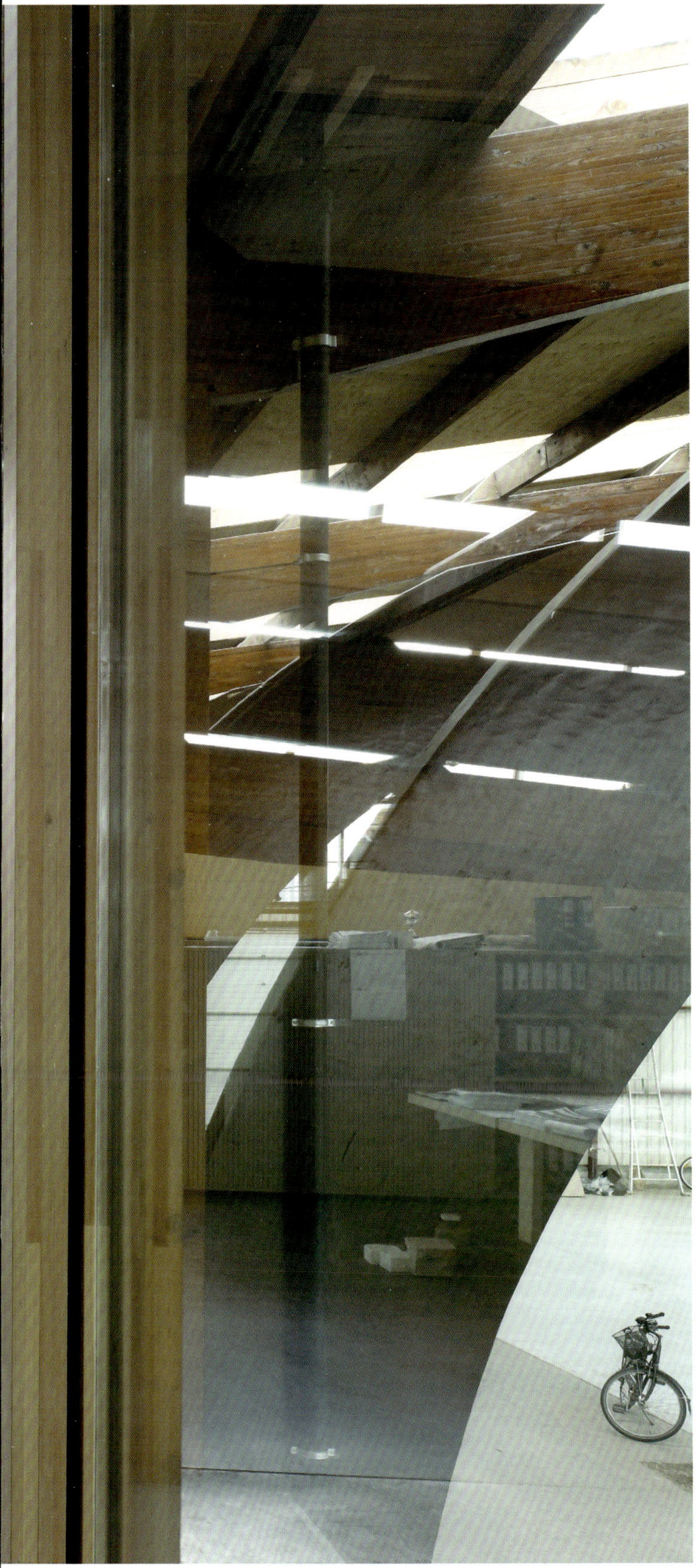

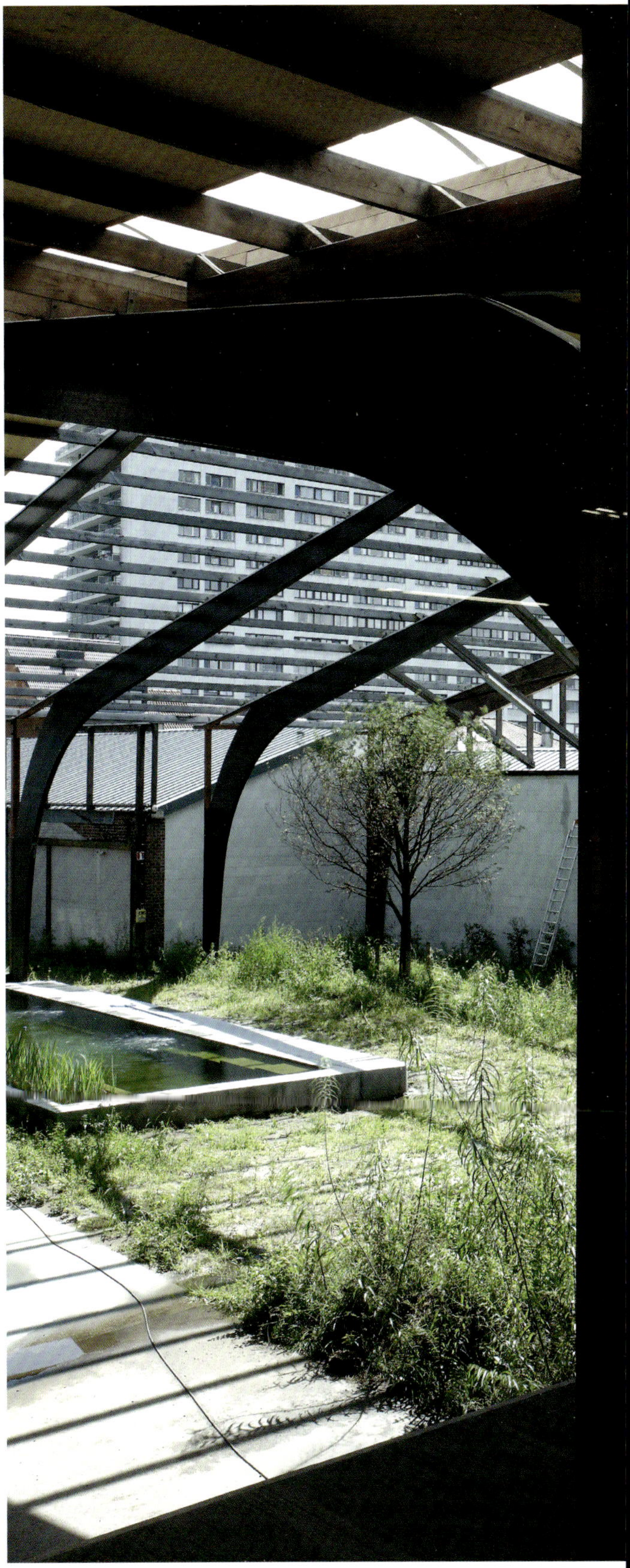

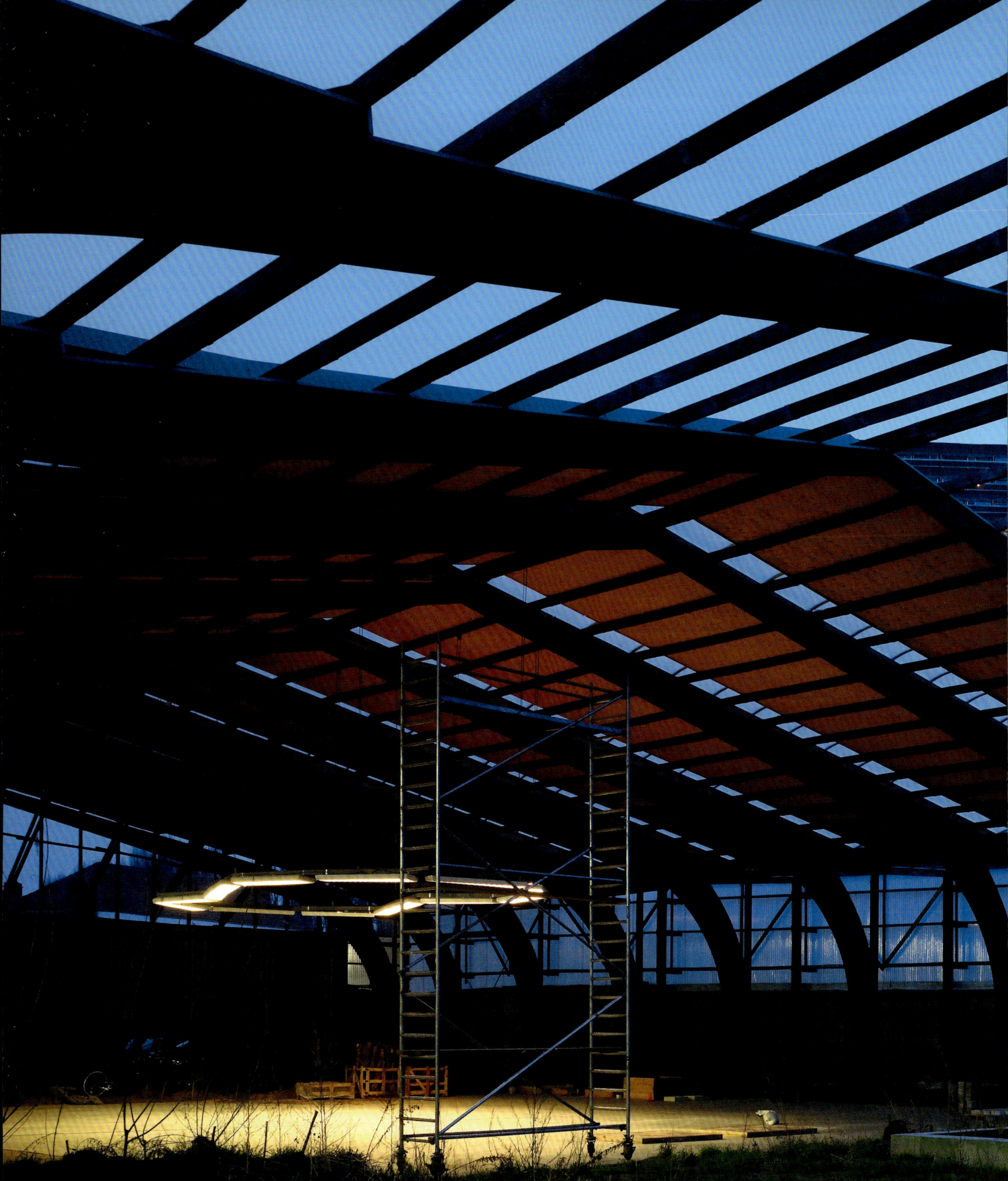

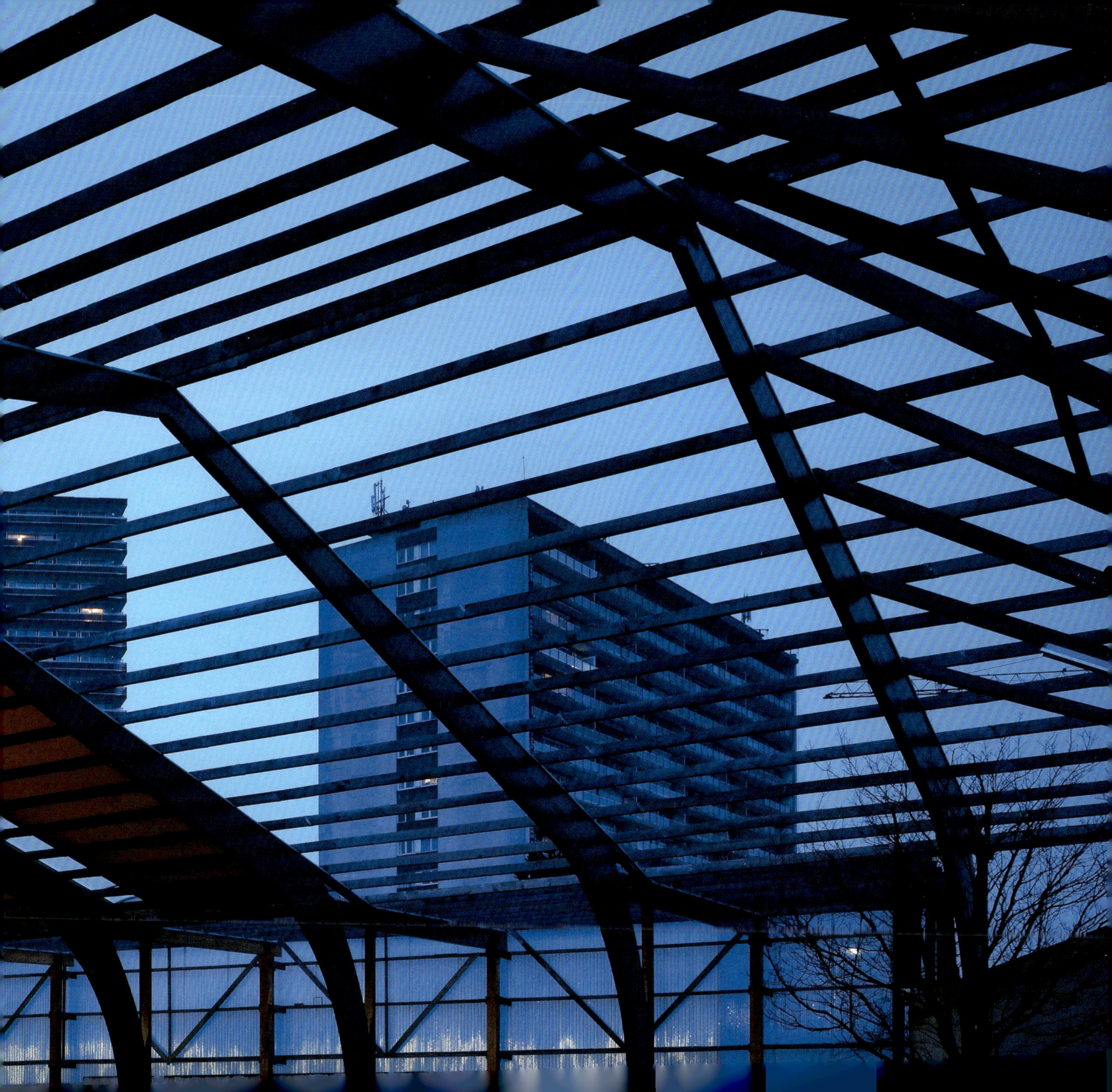

IIIIII High Views Lincolnshire

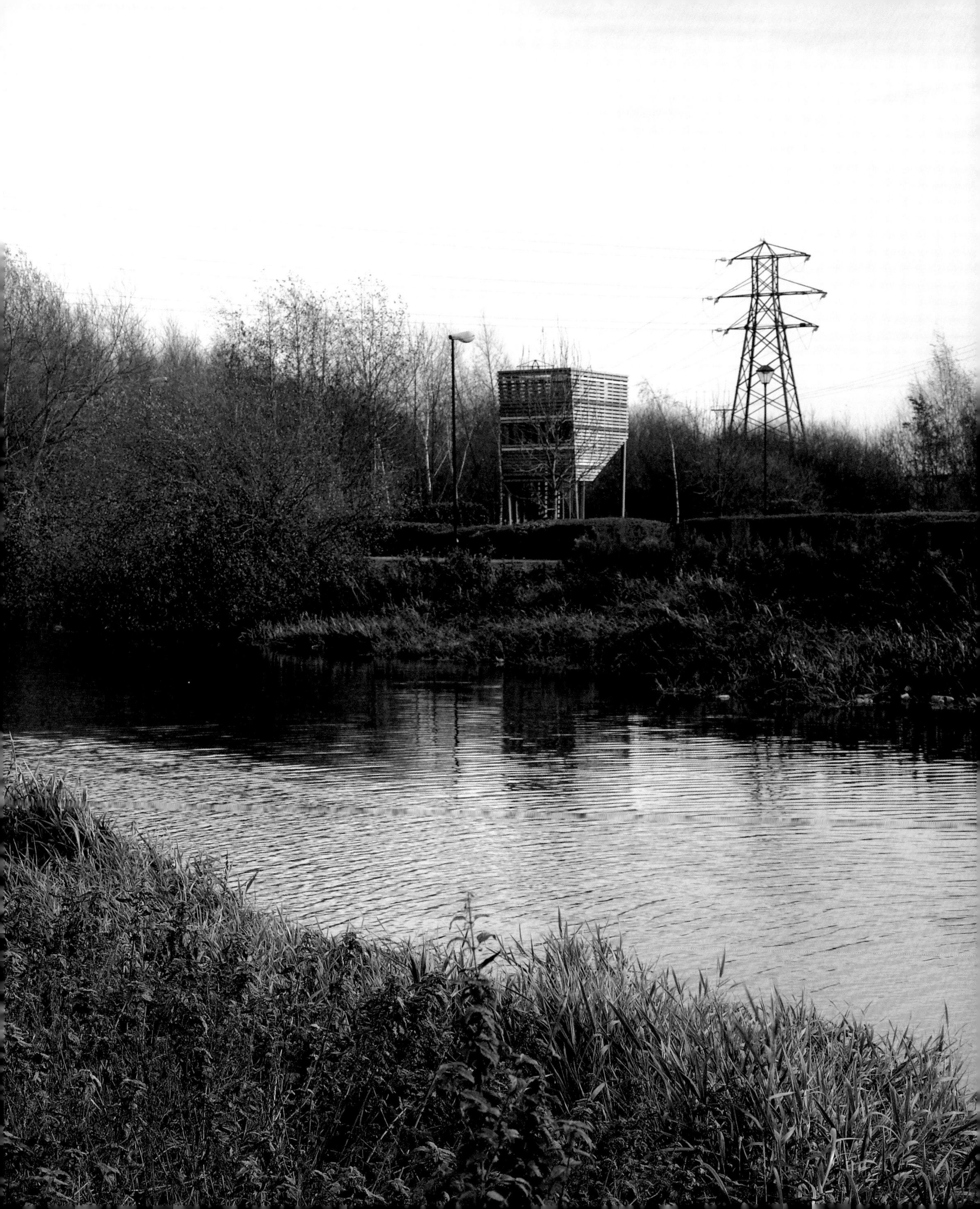

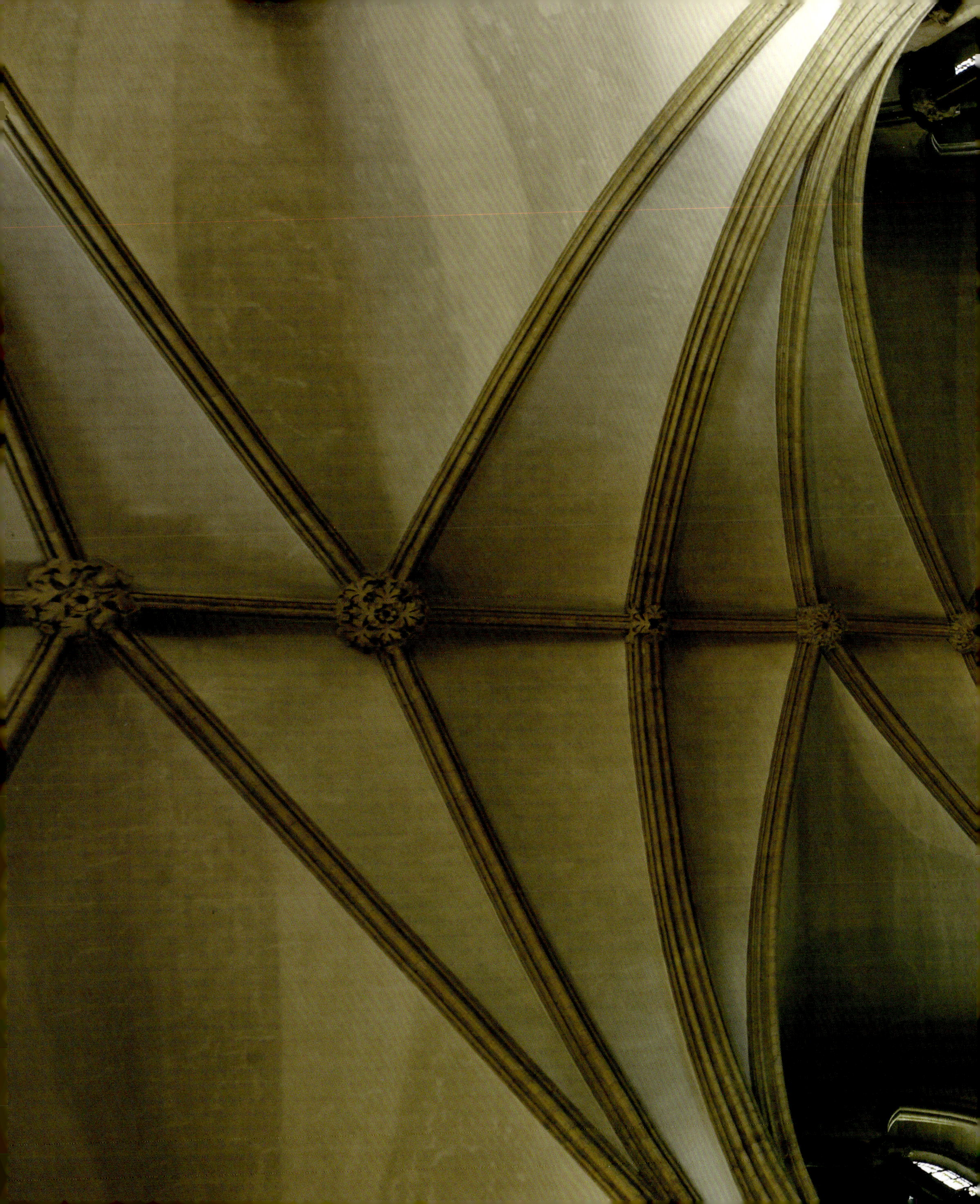

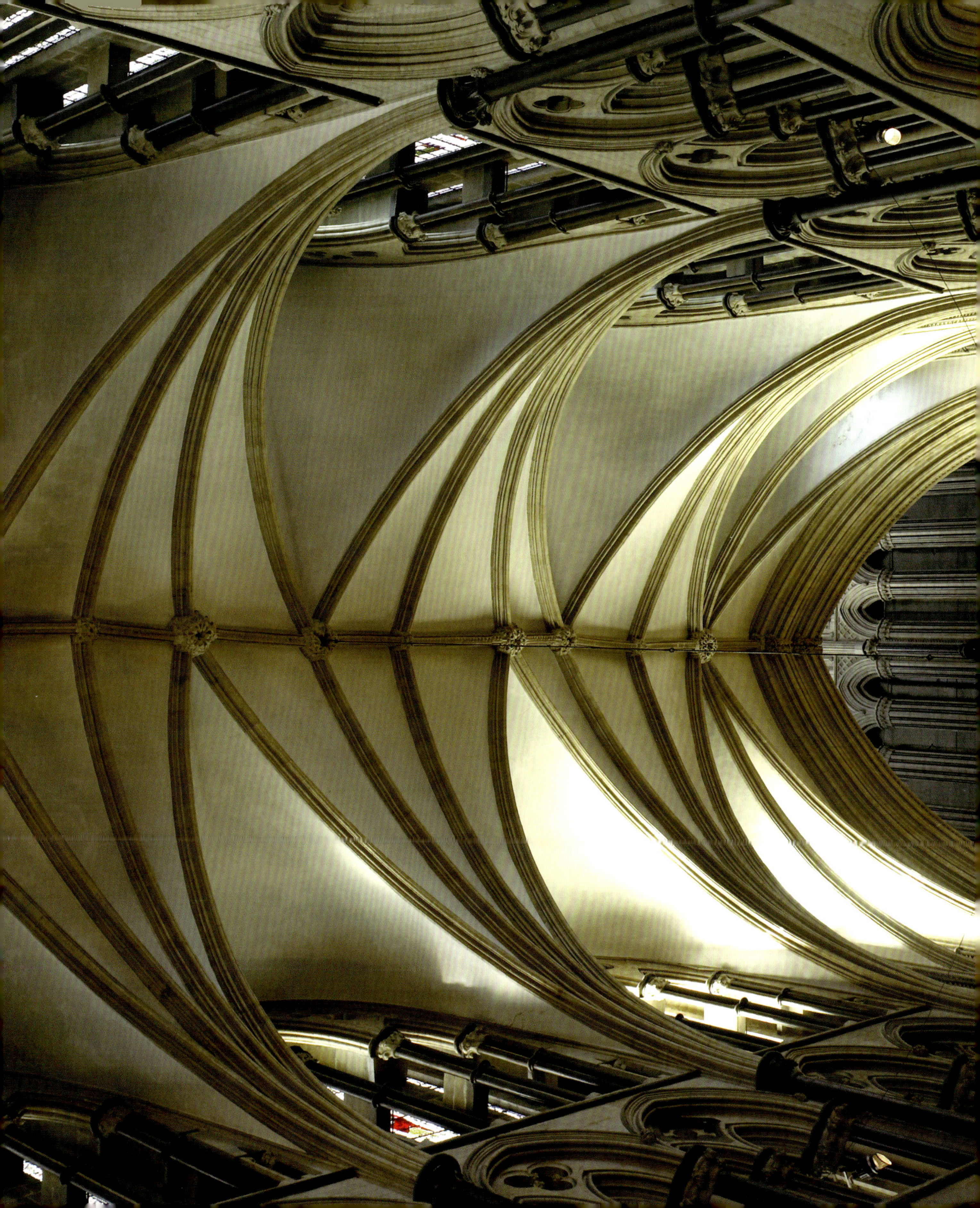

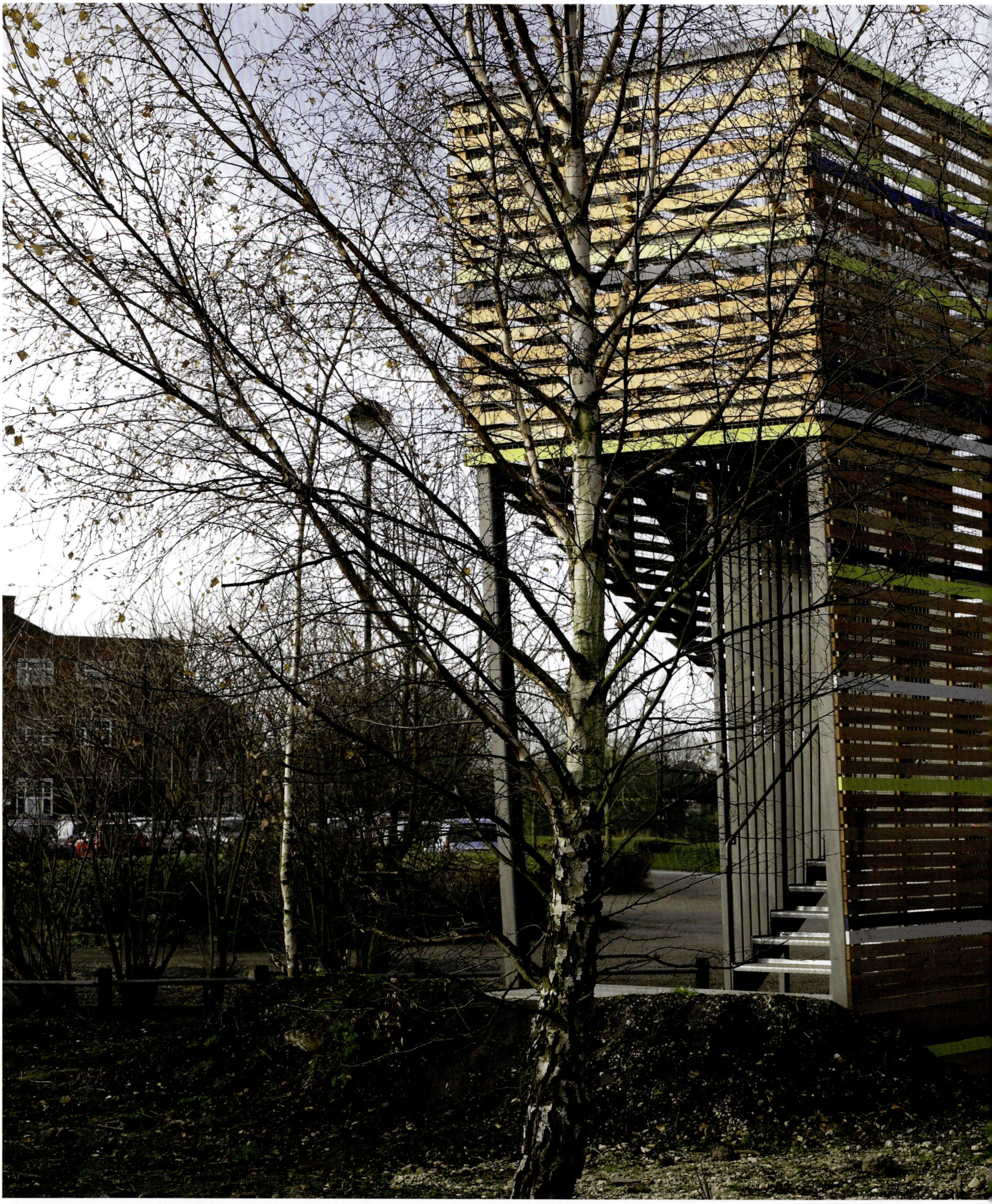

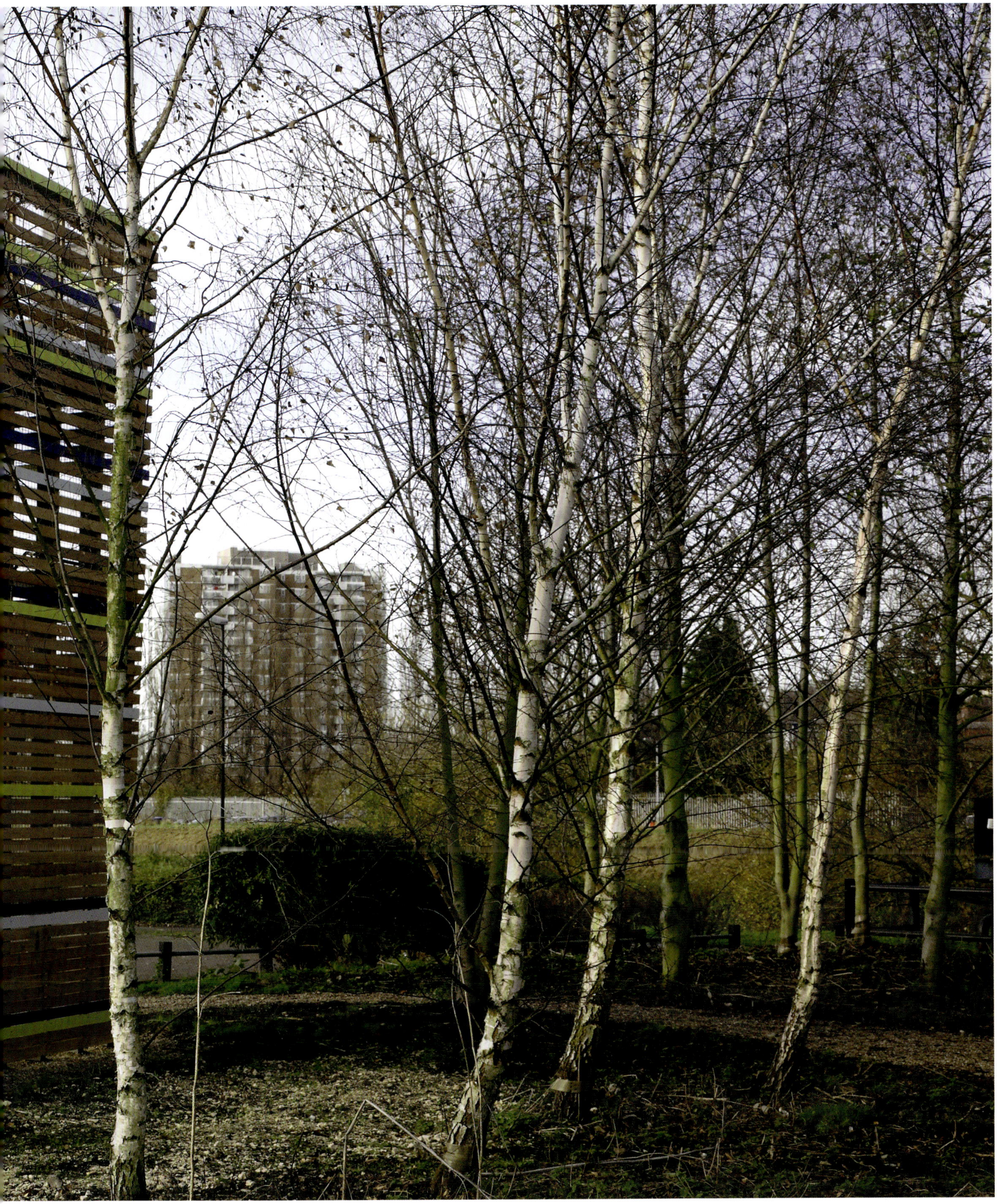

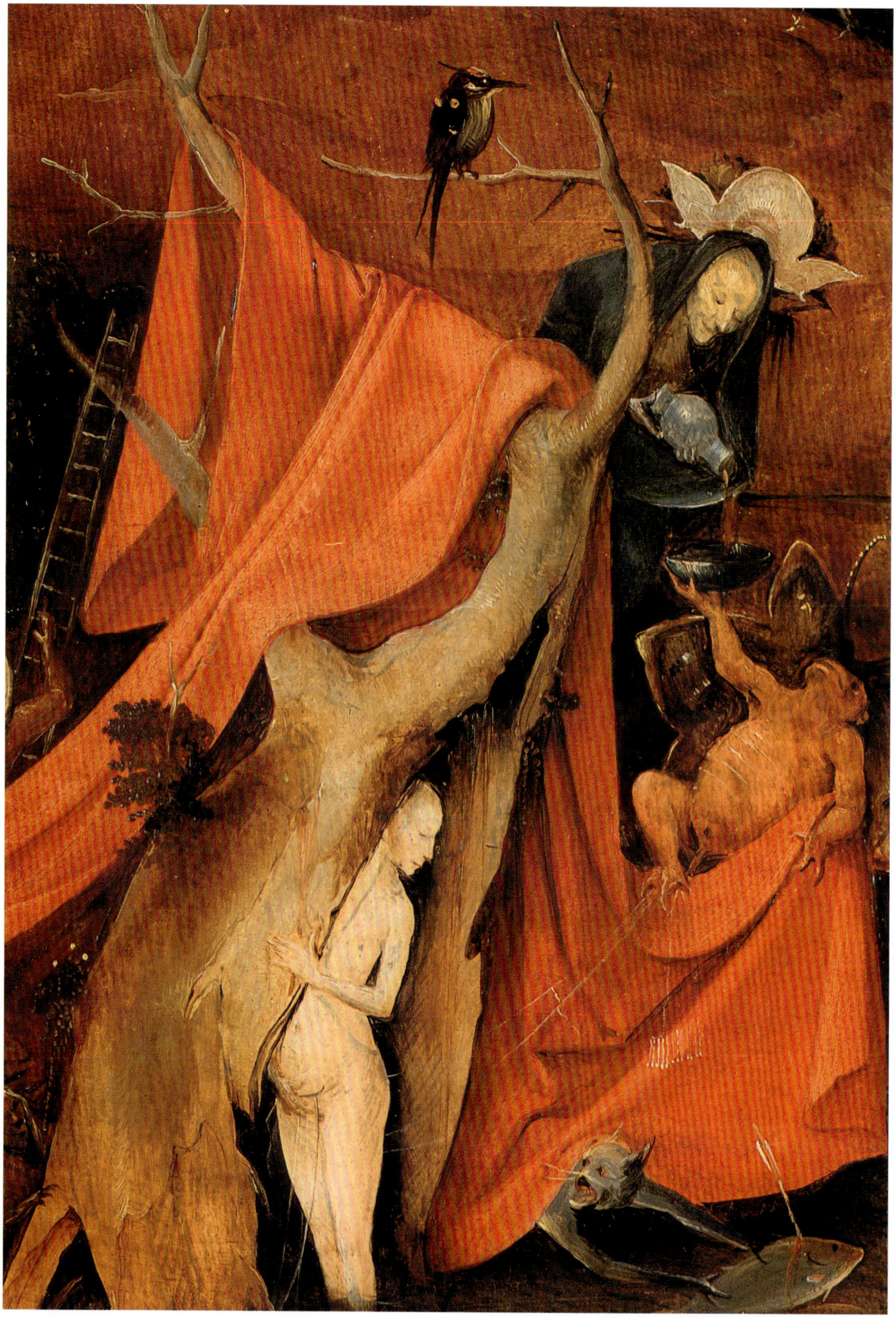

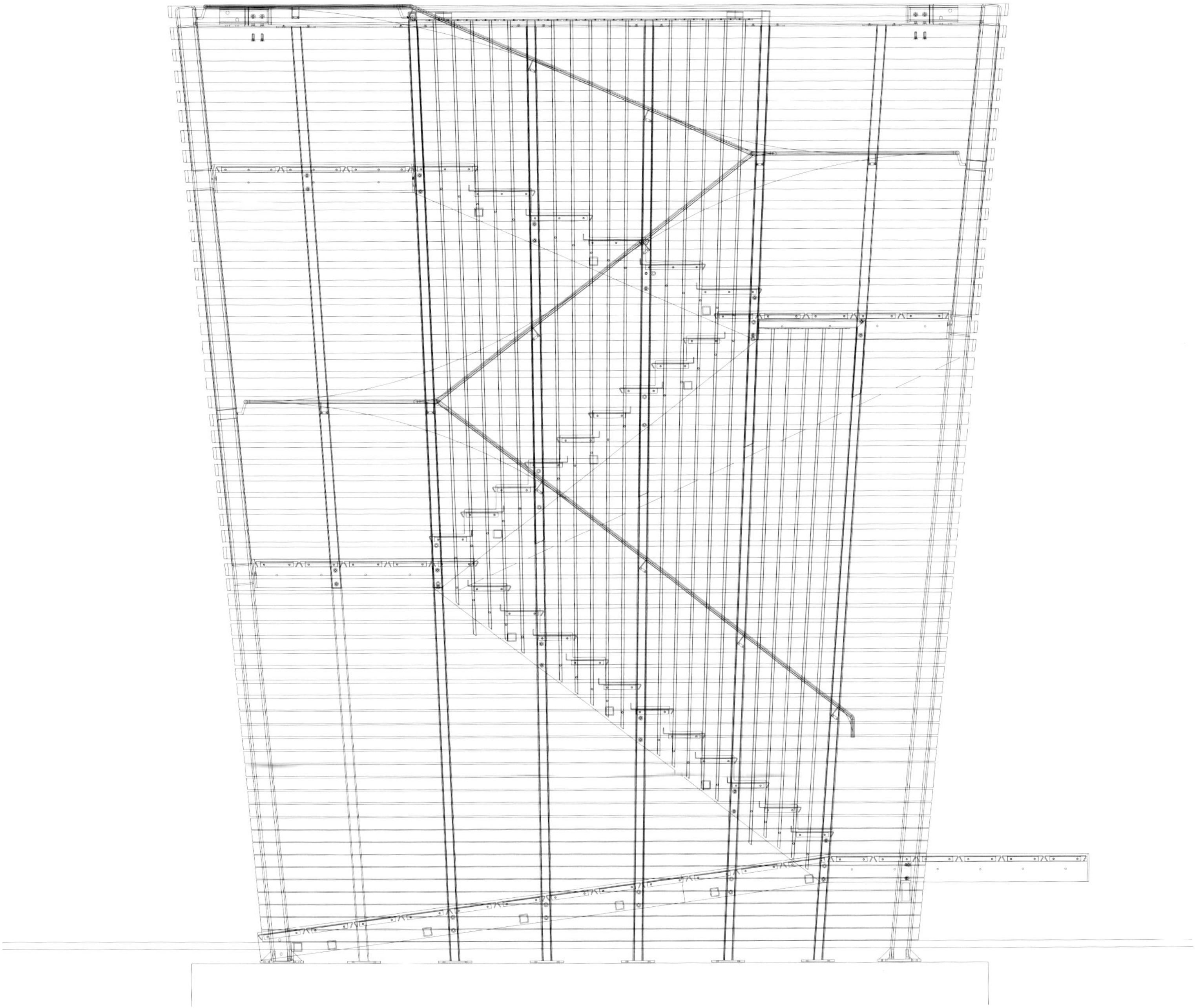

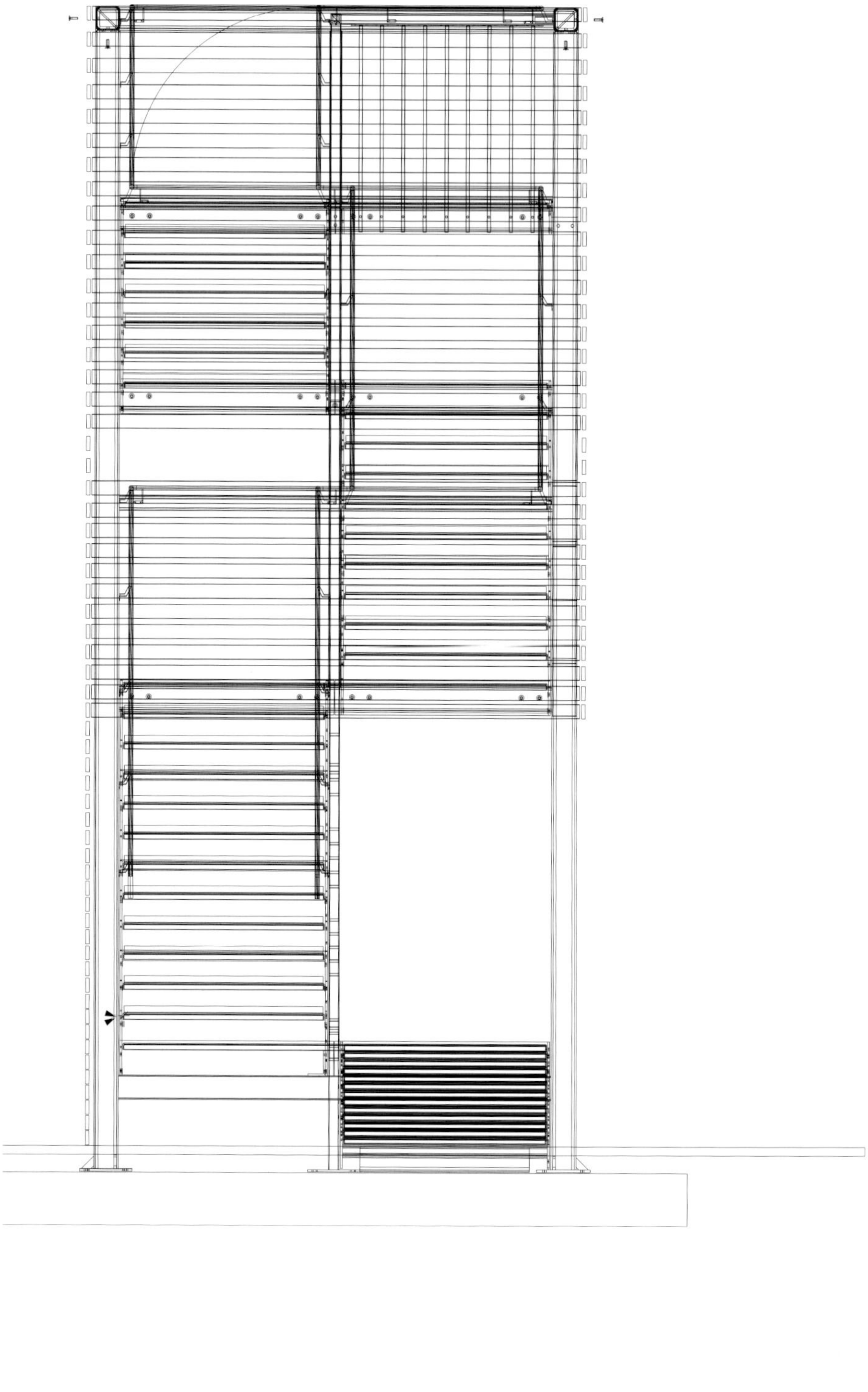

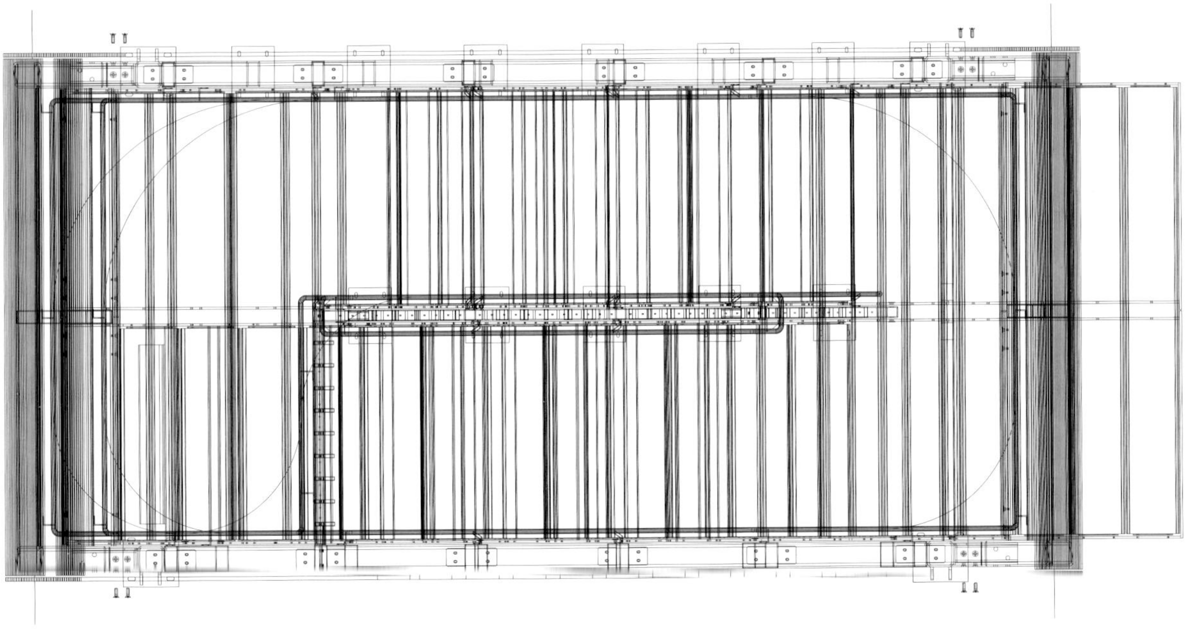

bishops eye

Lincoln Seligman

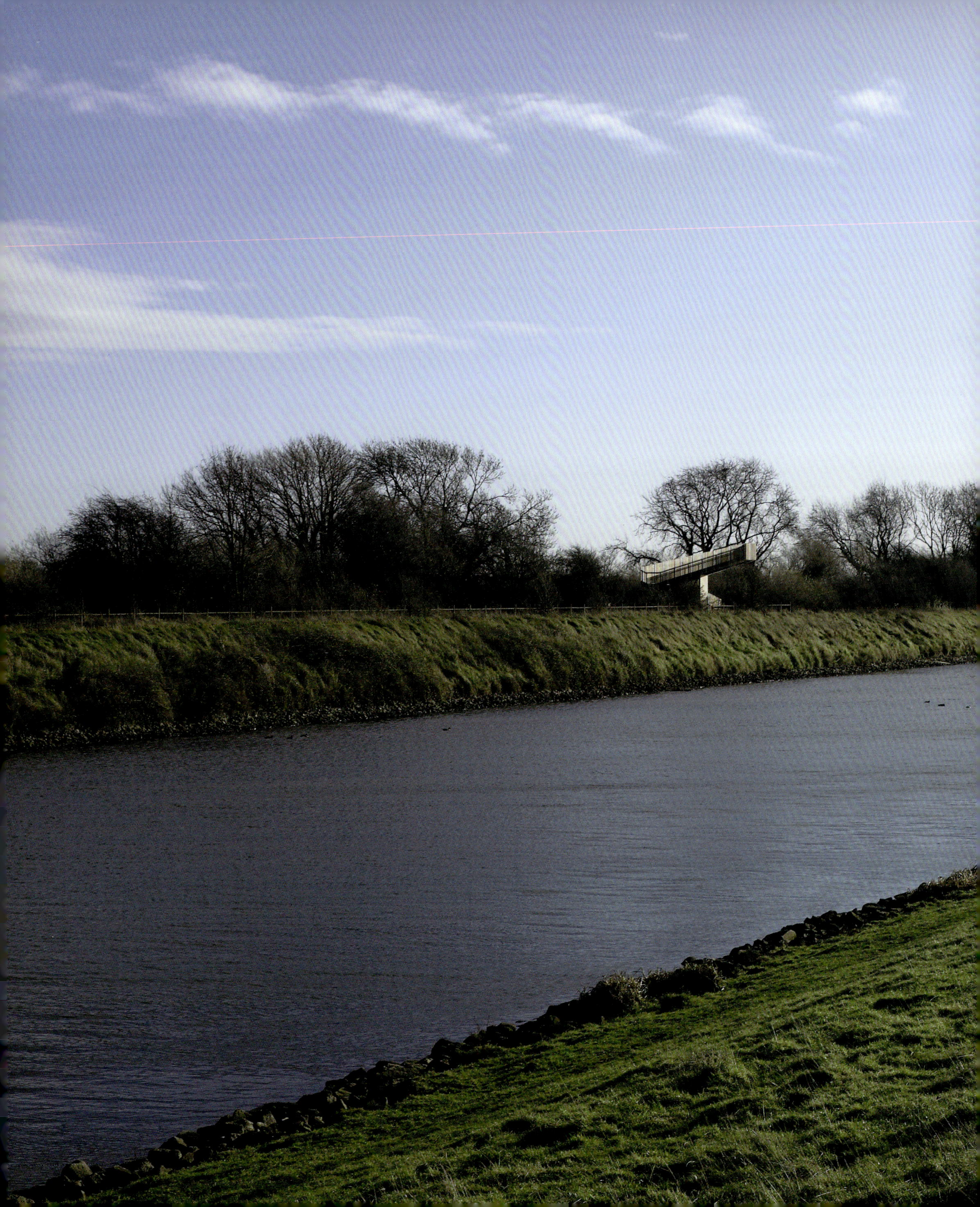

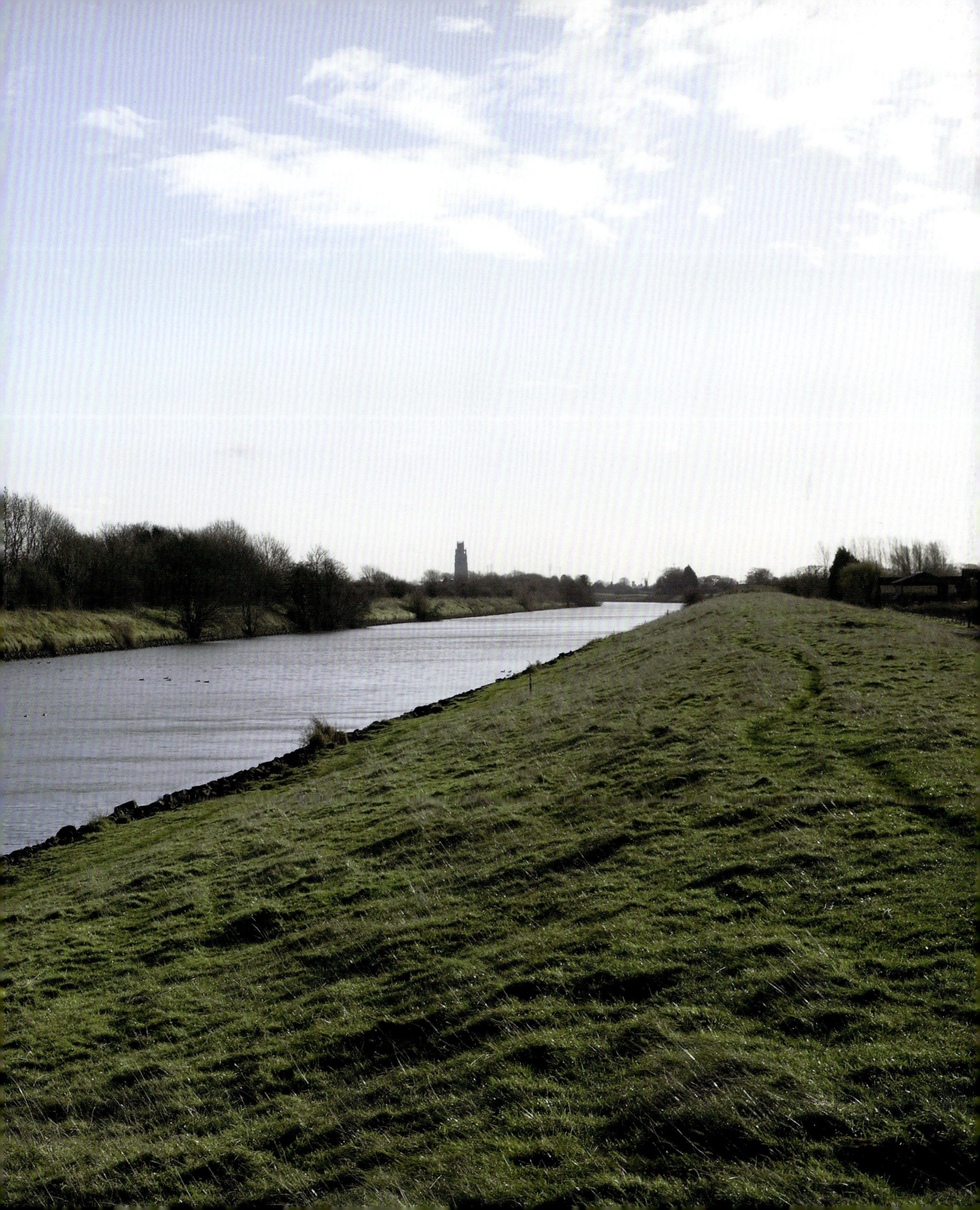

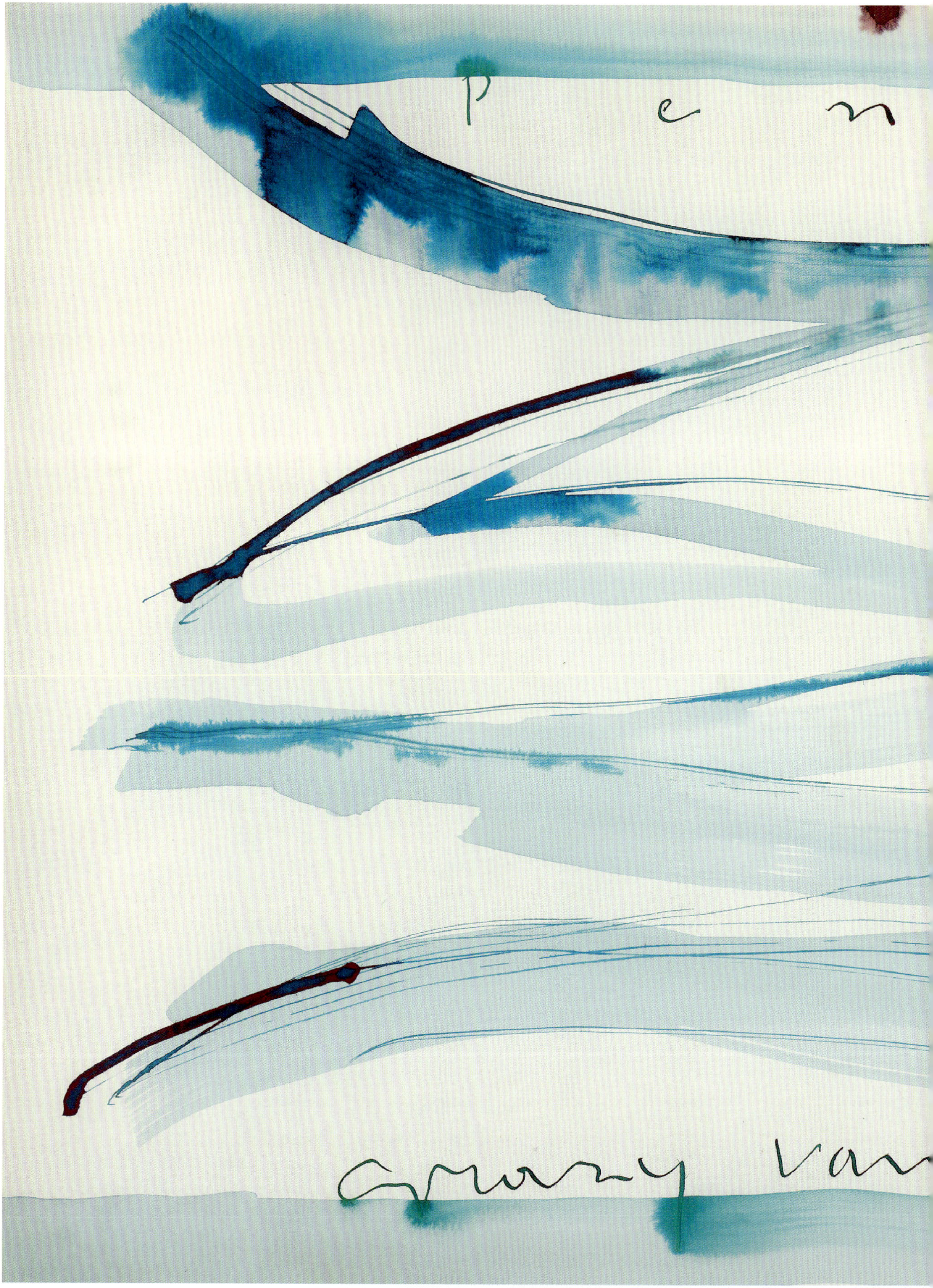
p e n

oculum

lrg

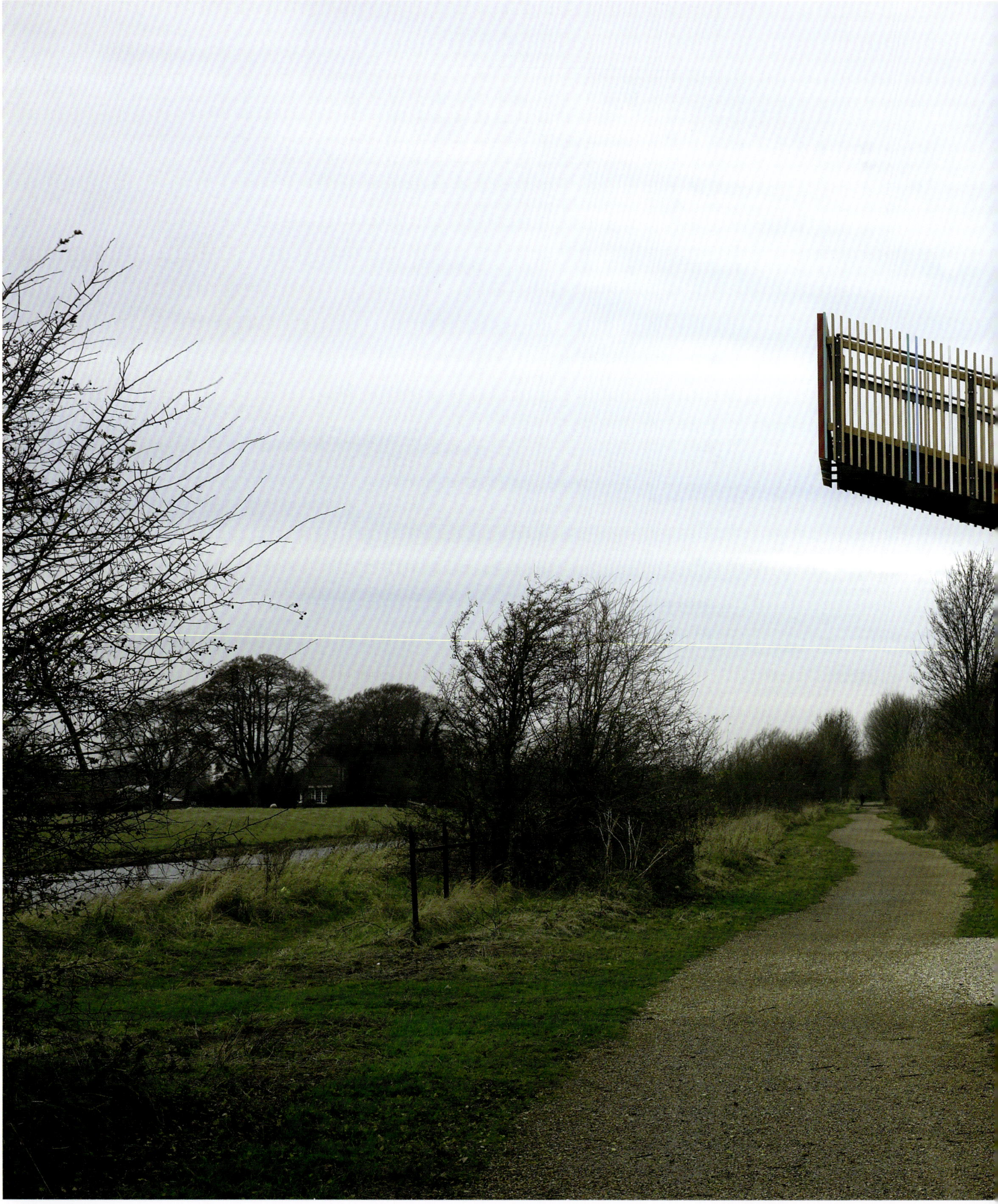

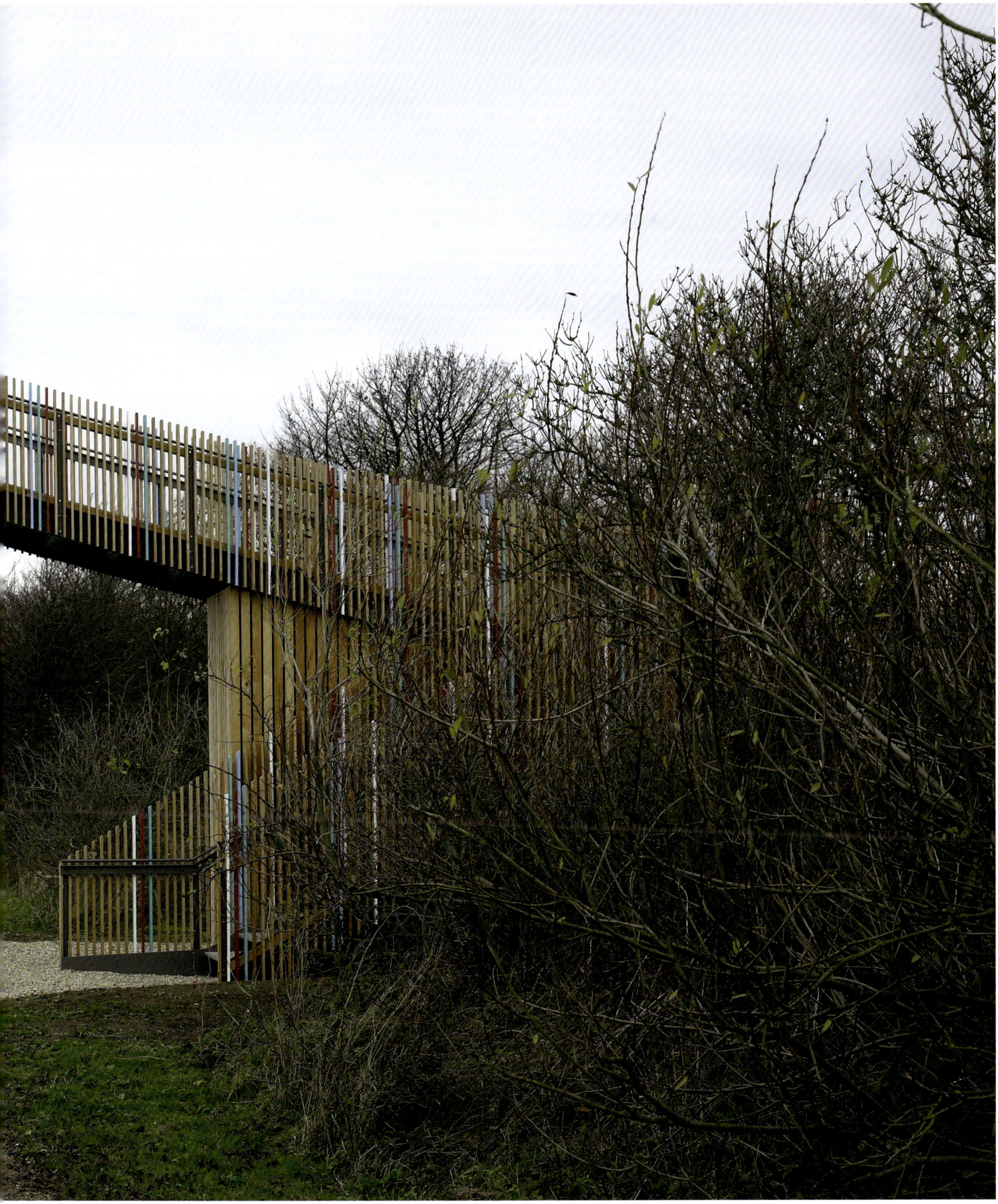

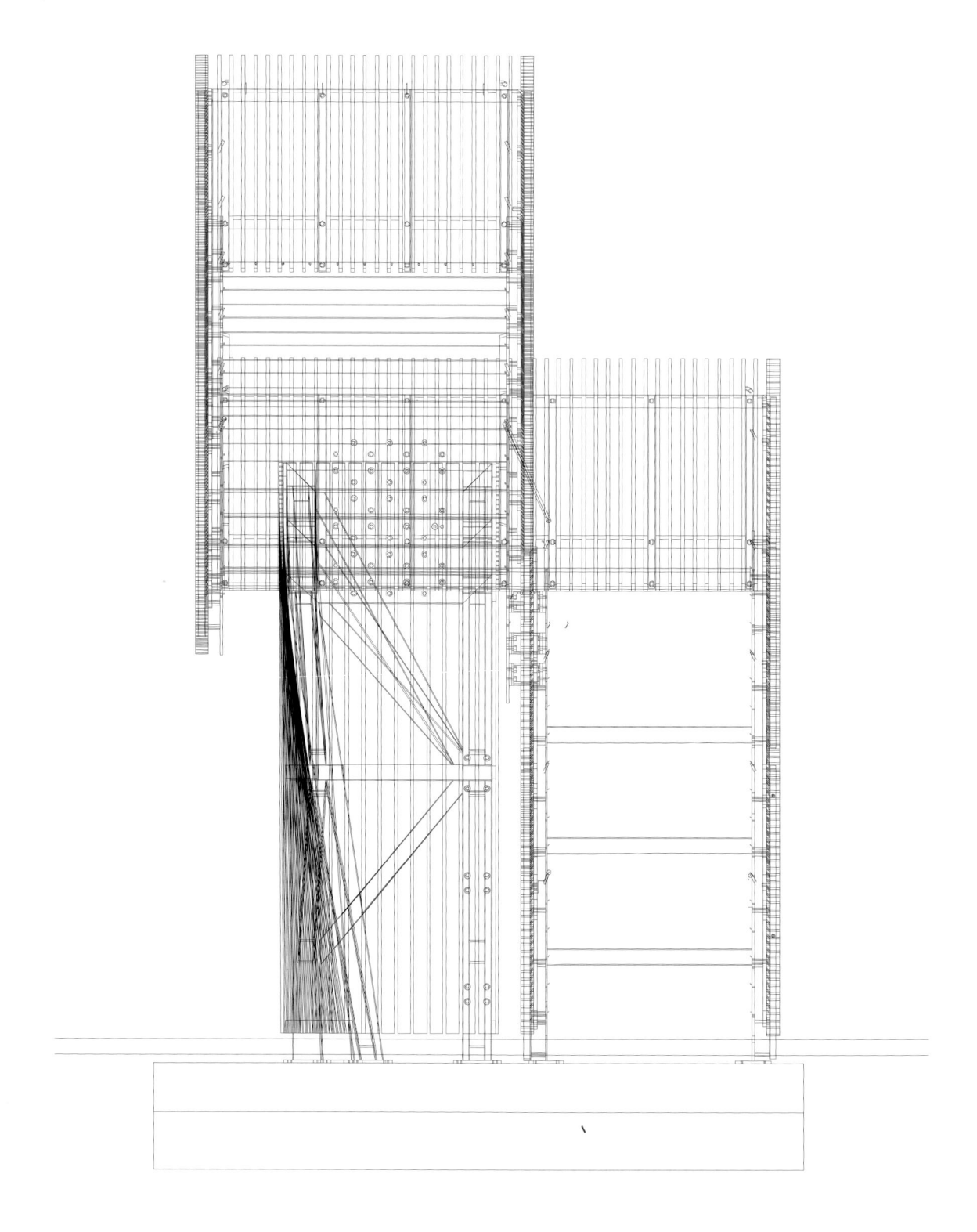

143

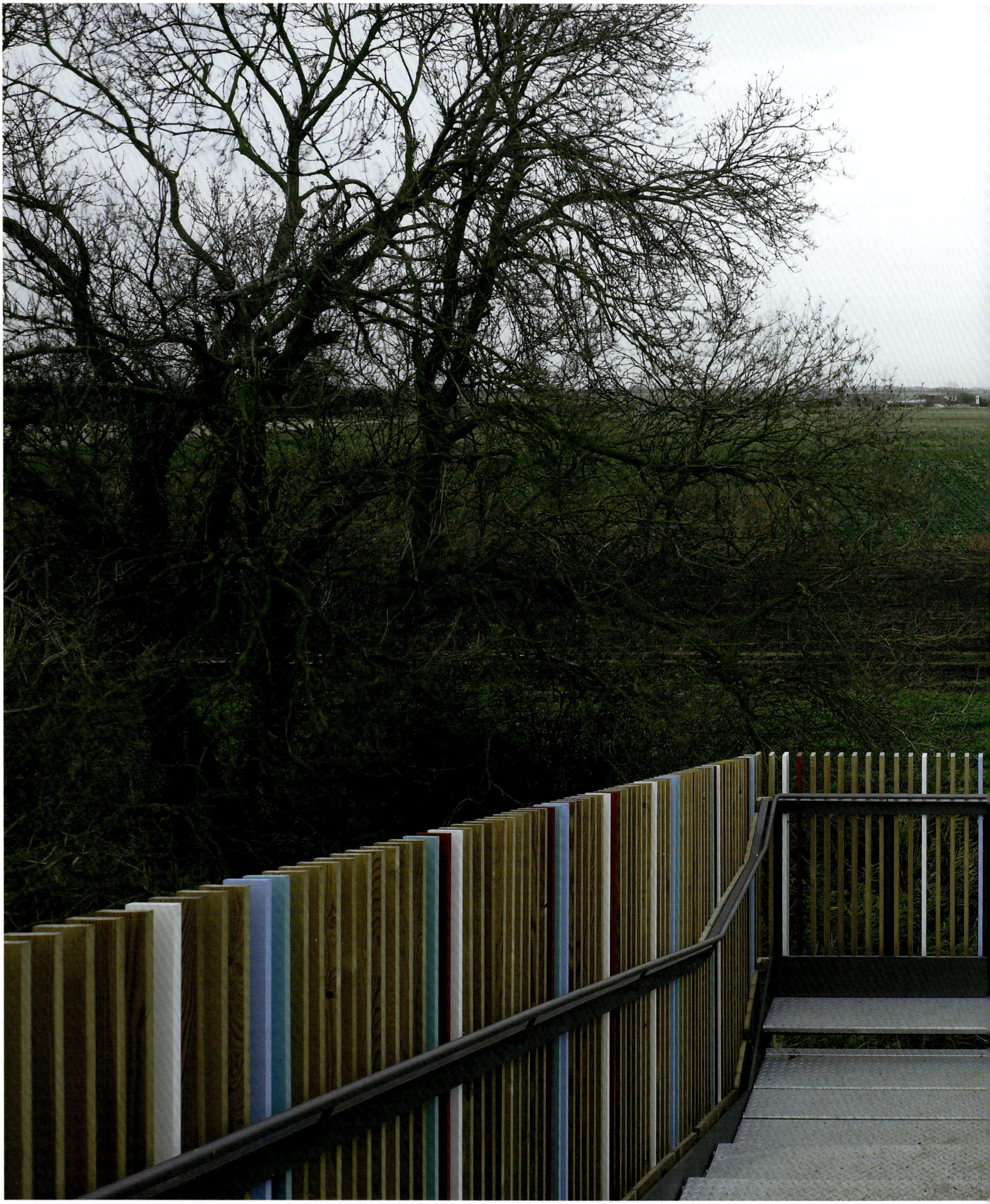

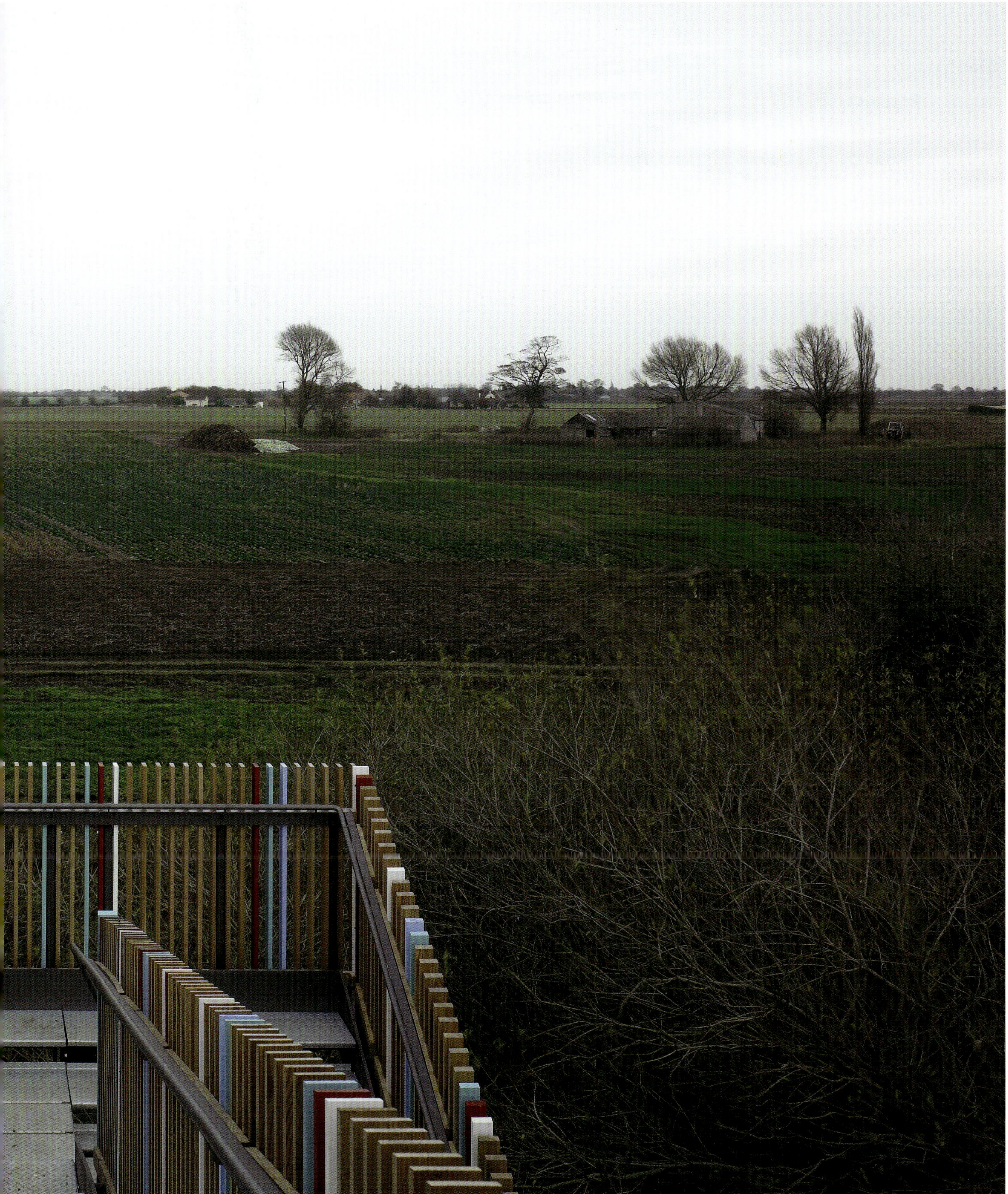

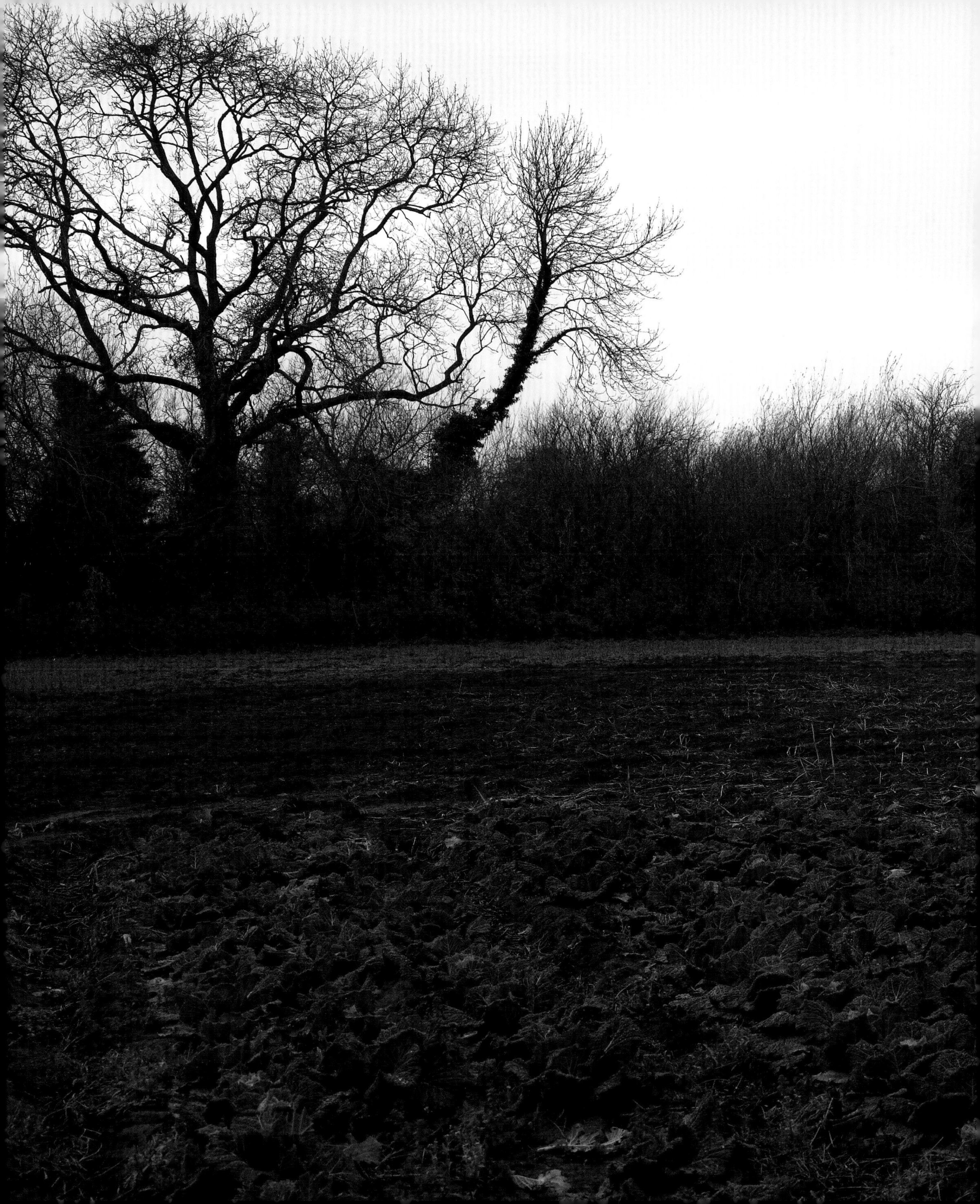

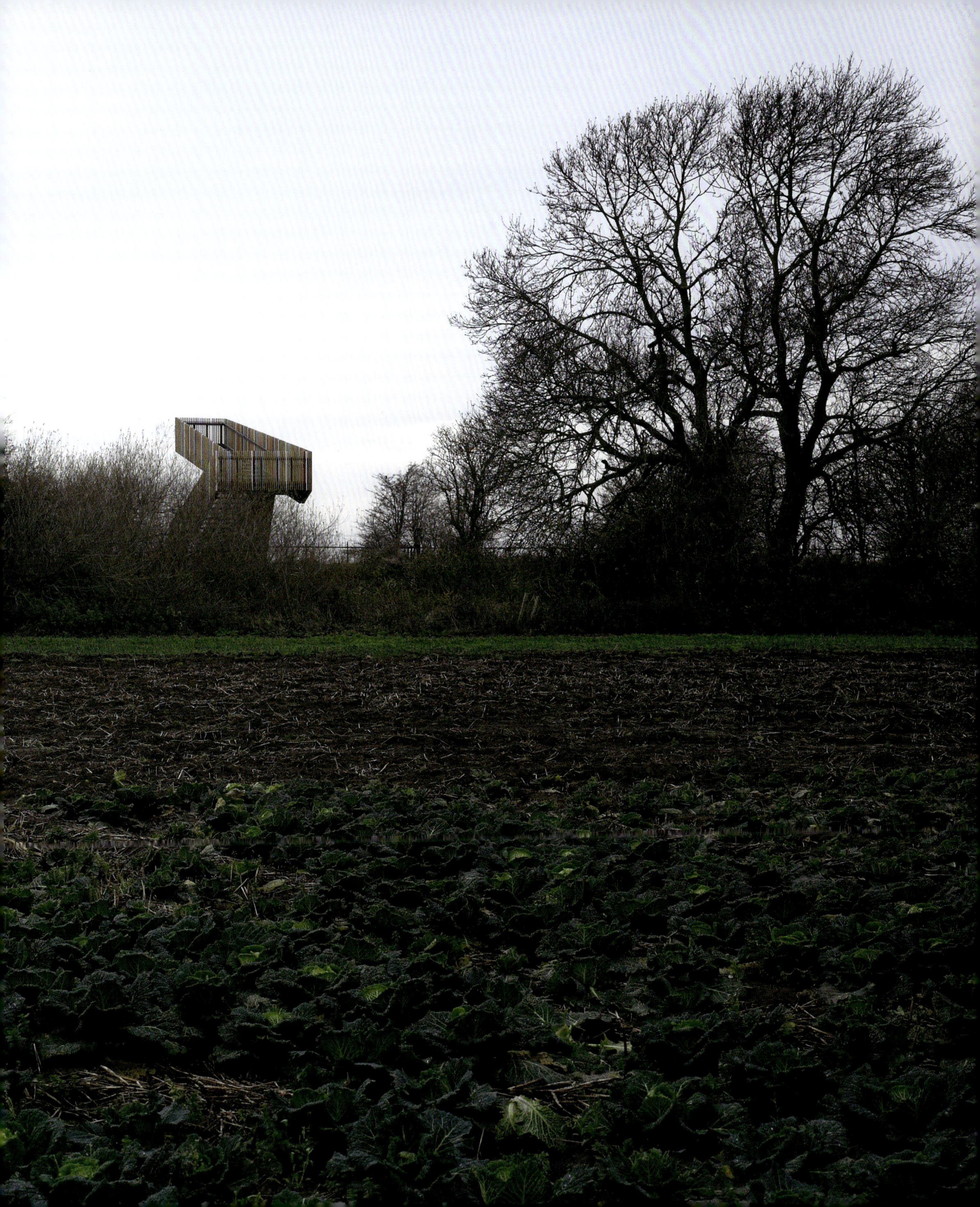

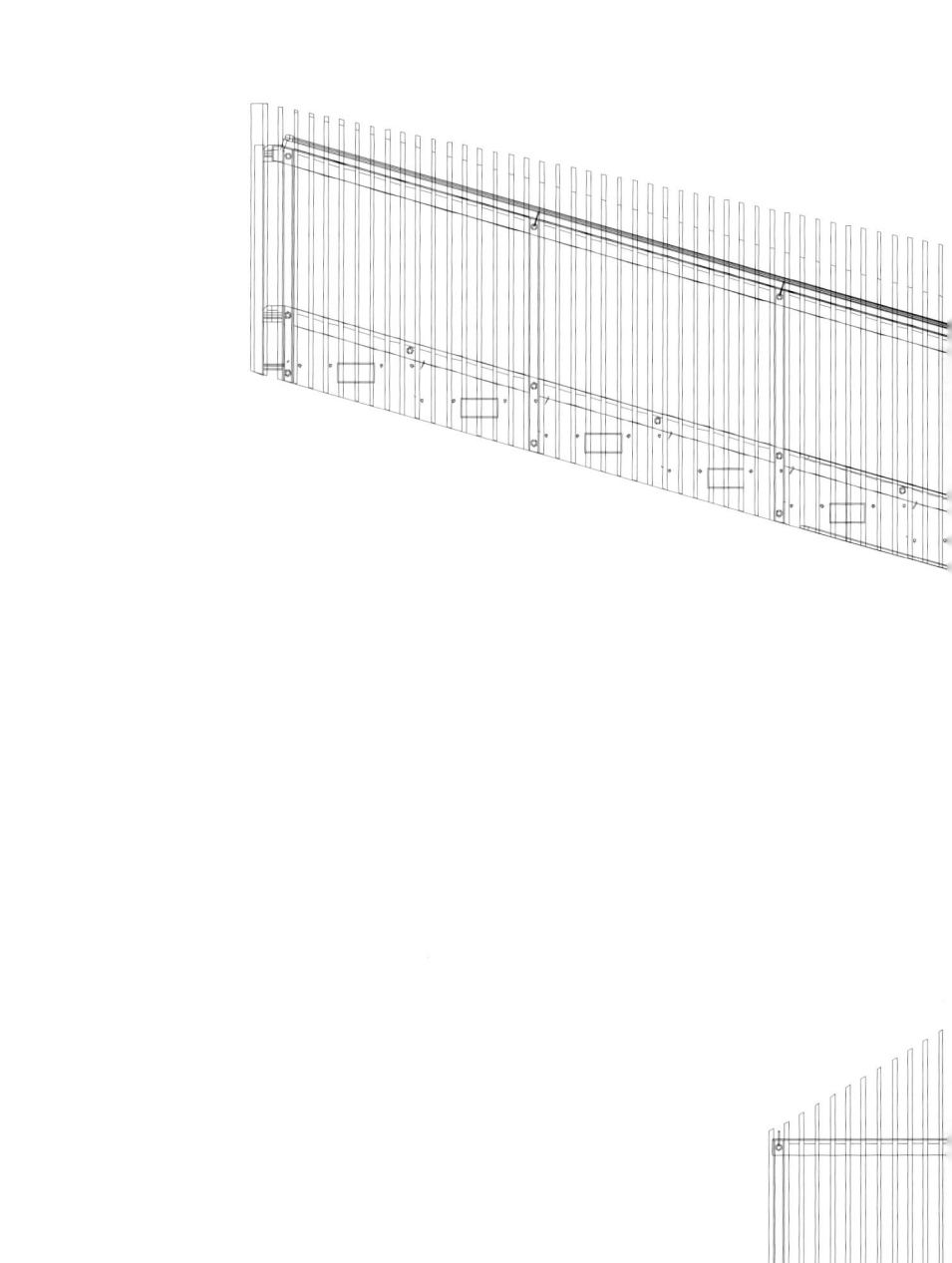

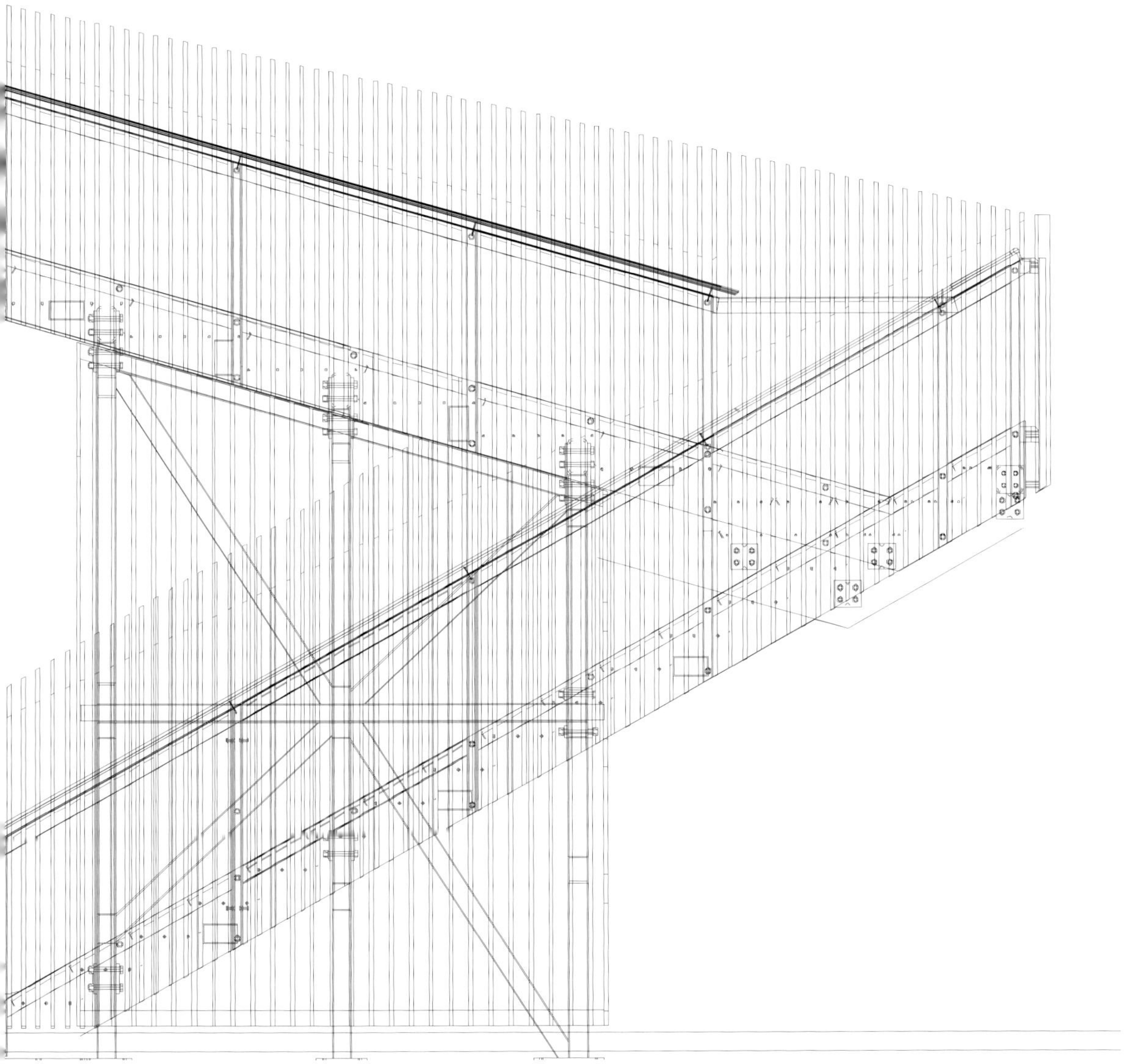

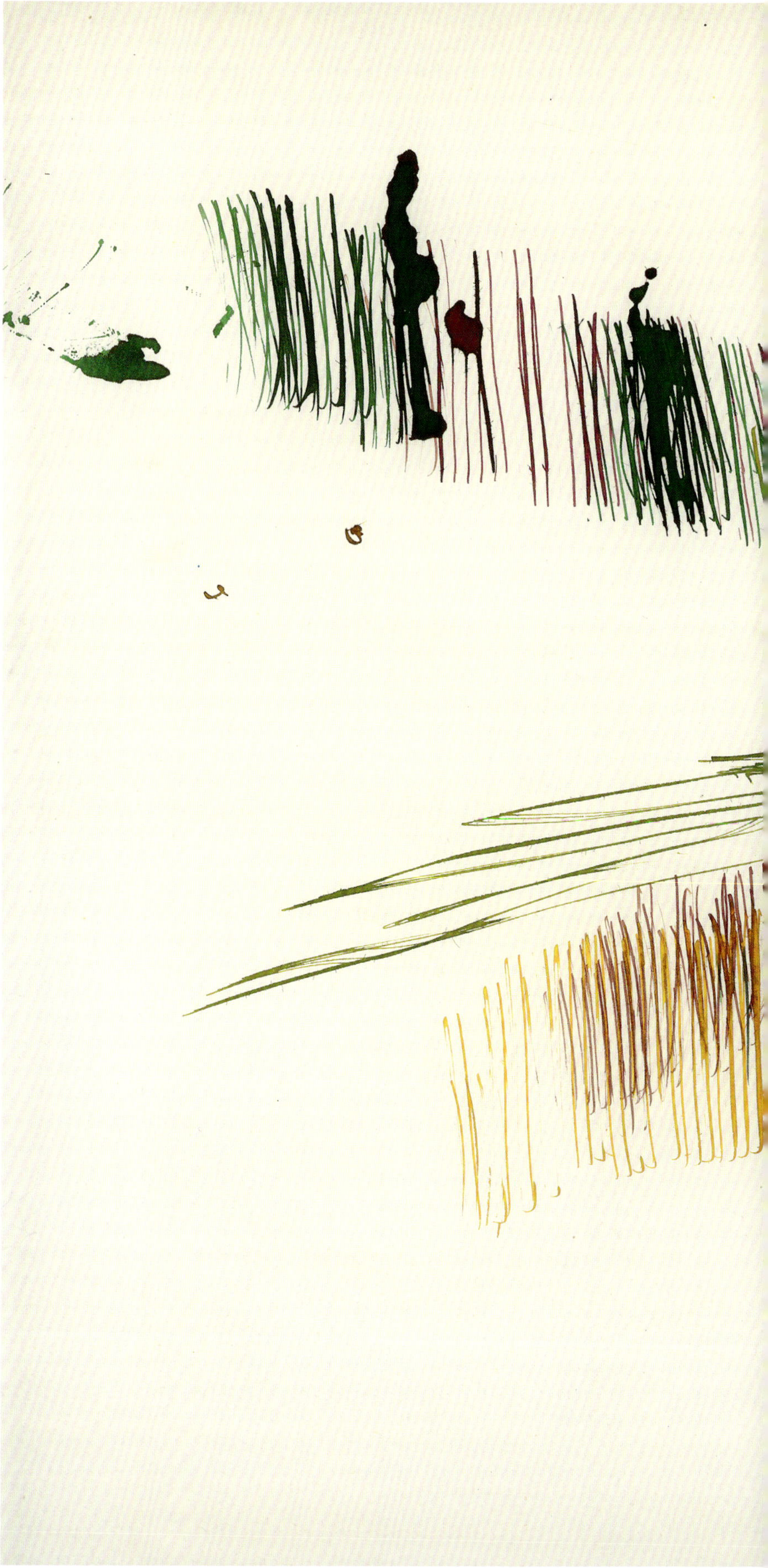

euston

penultimate

cathedral vaults **Lincoln**

The path

Boston

De stuurhut

|||||| Woodland Cabin

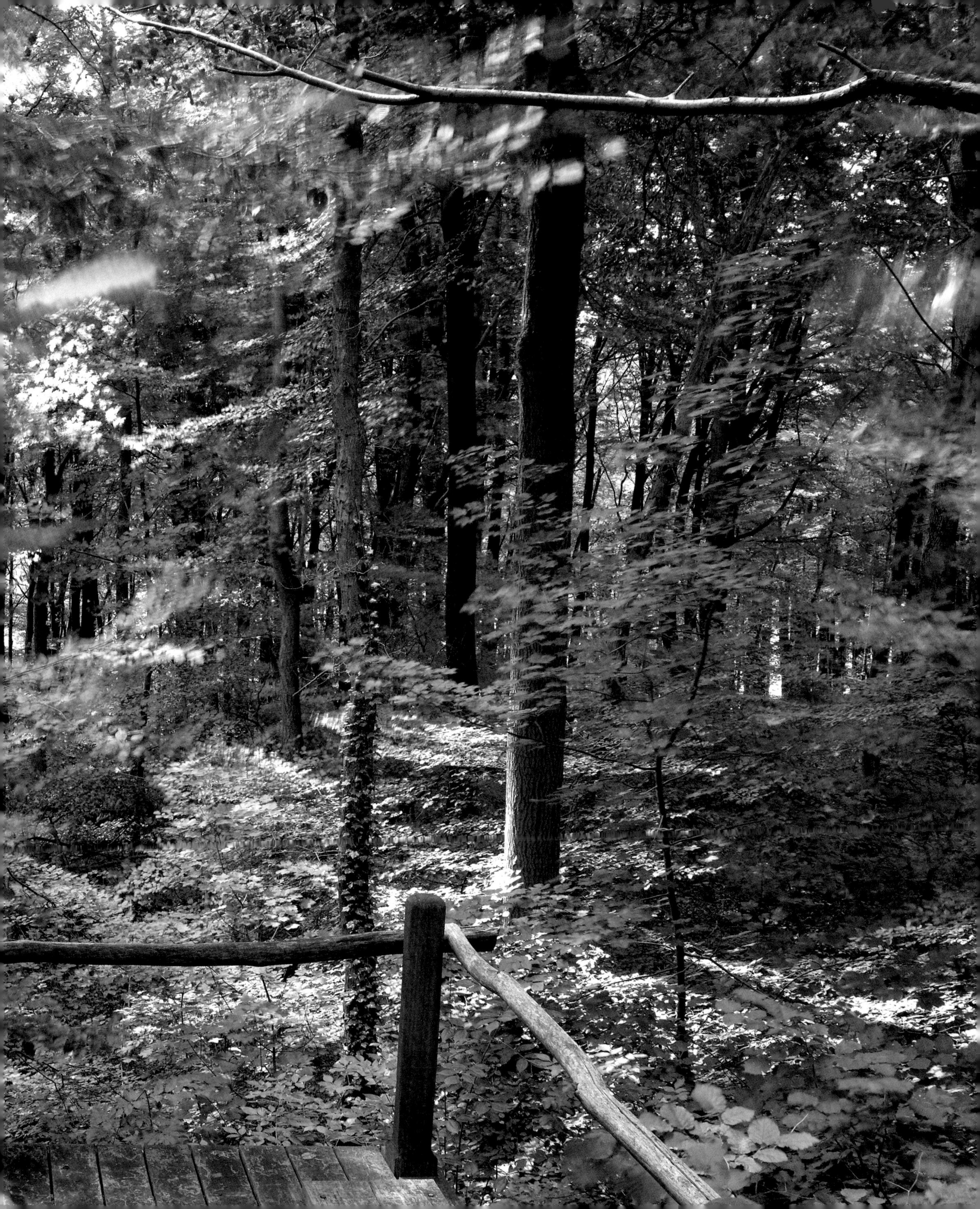

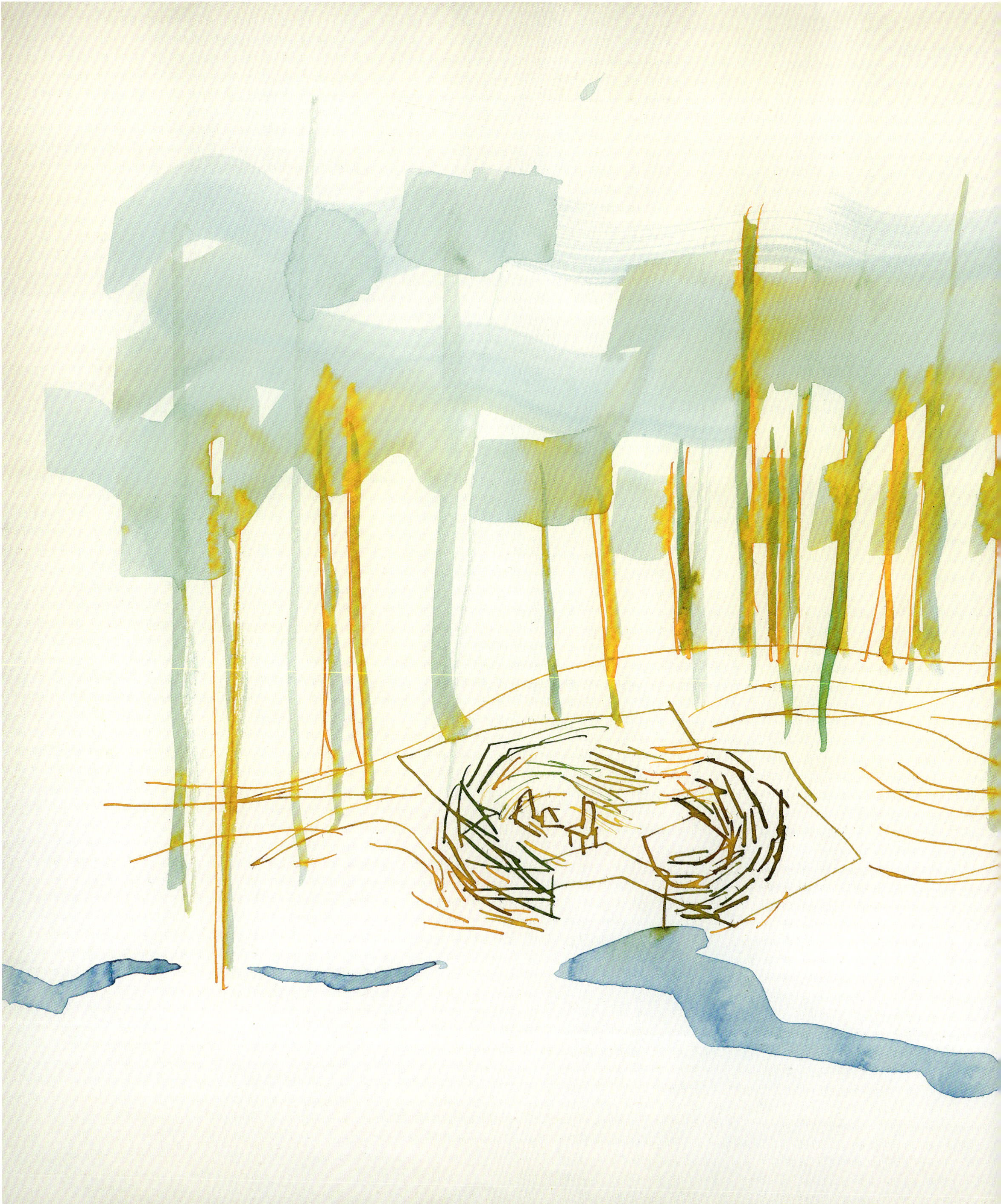

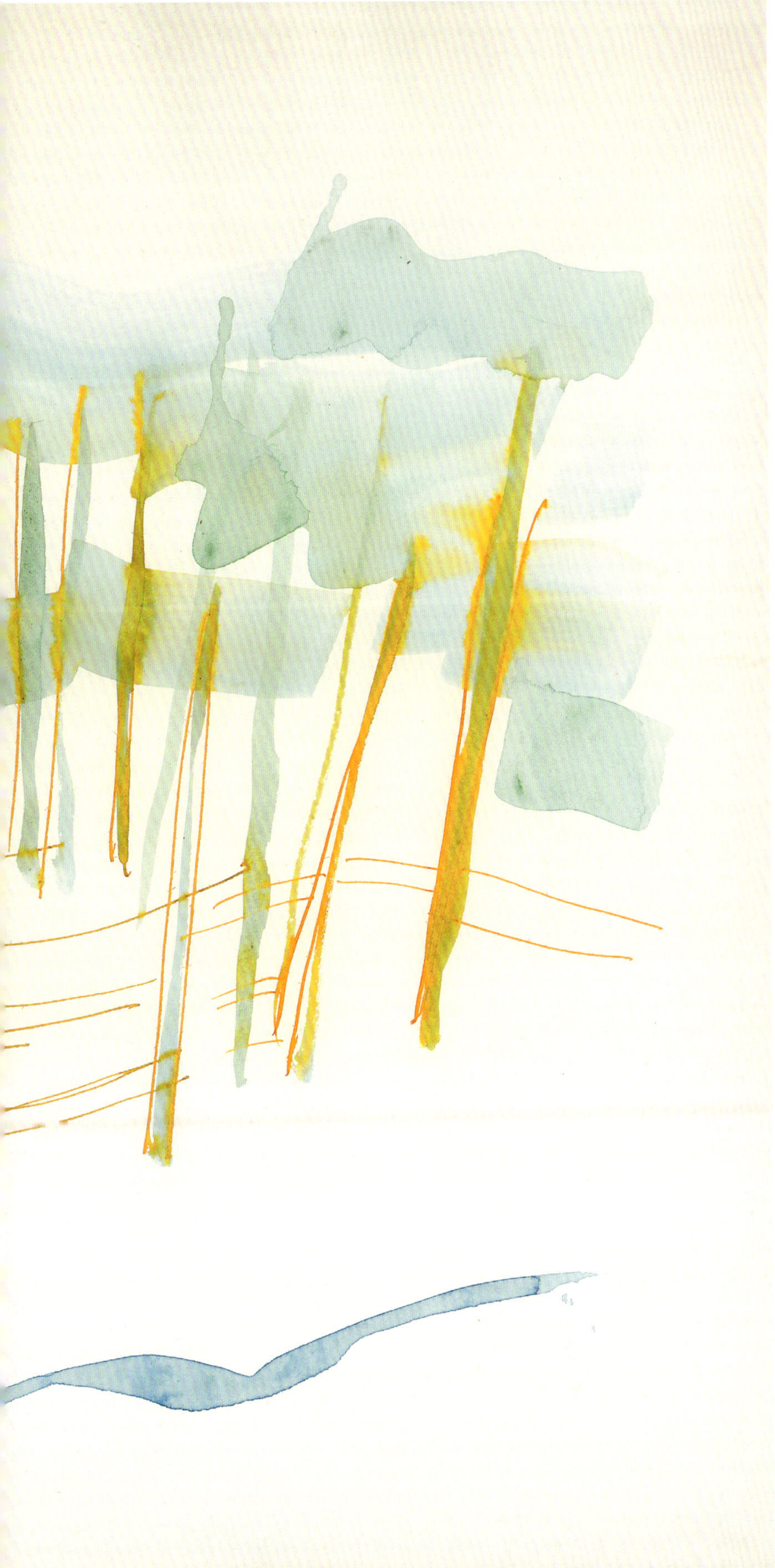

158

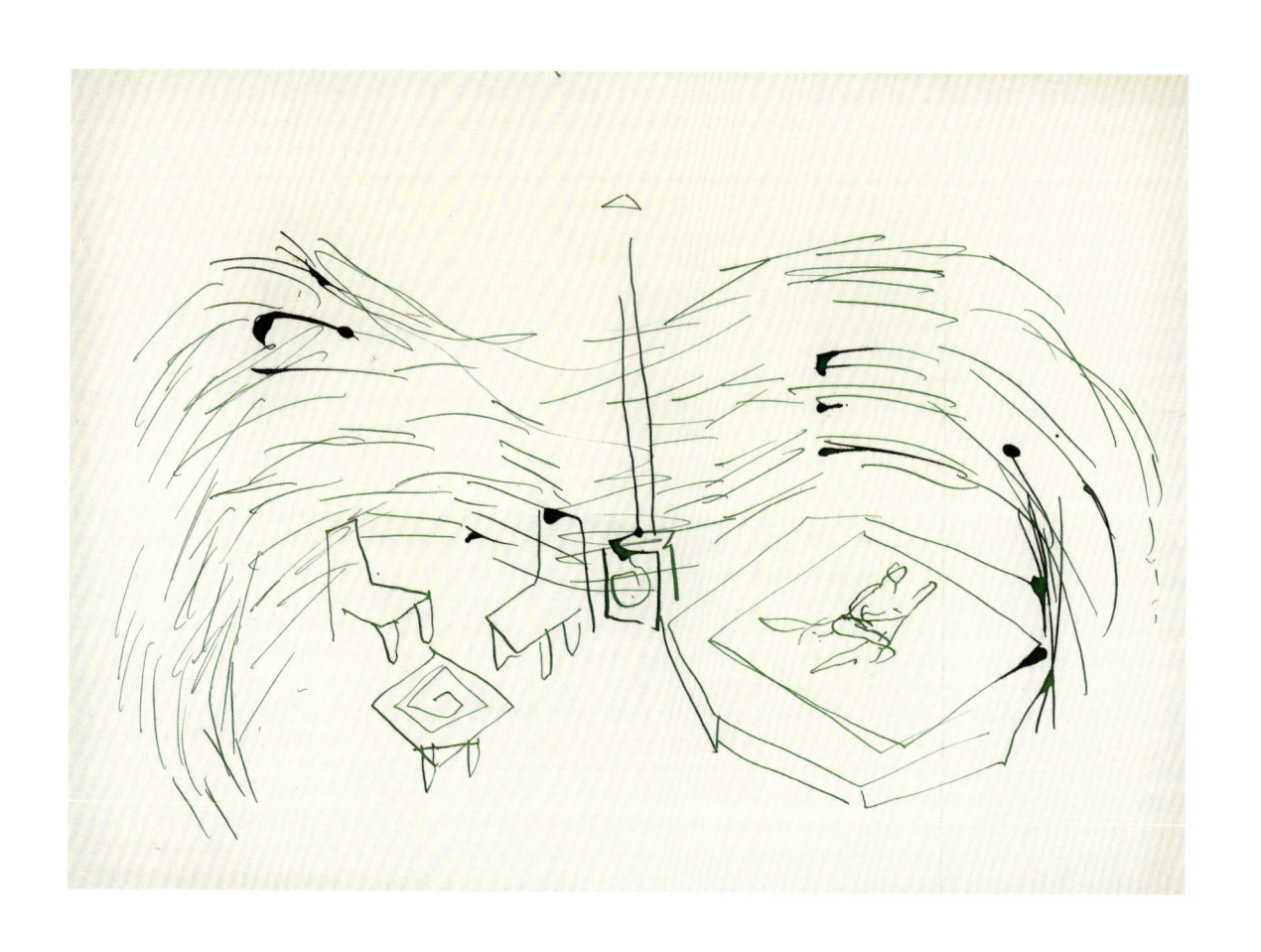

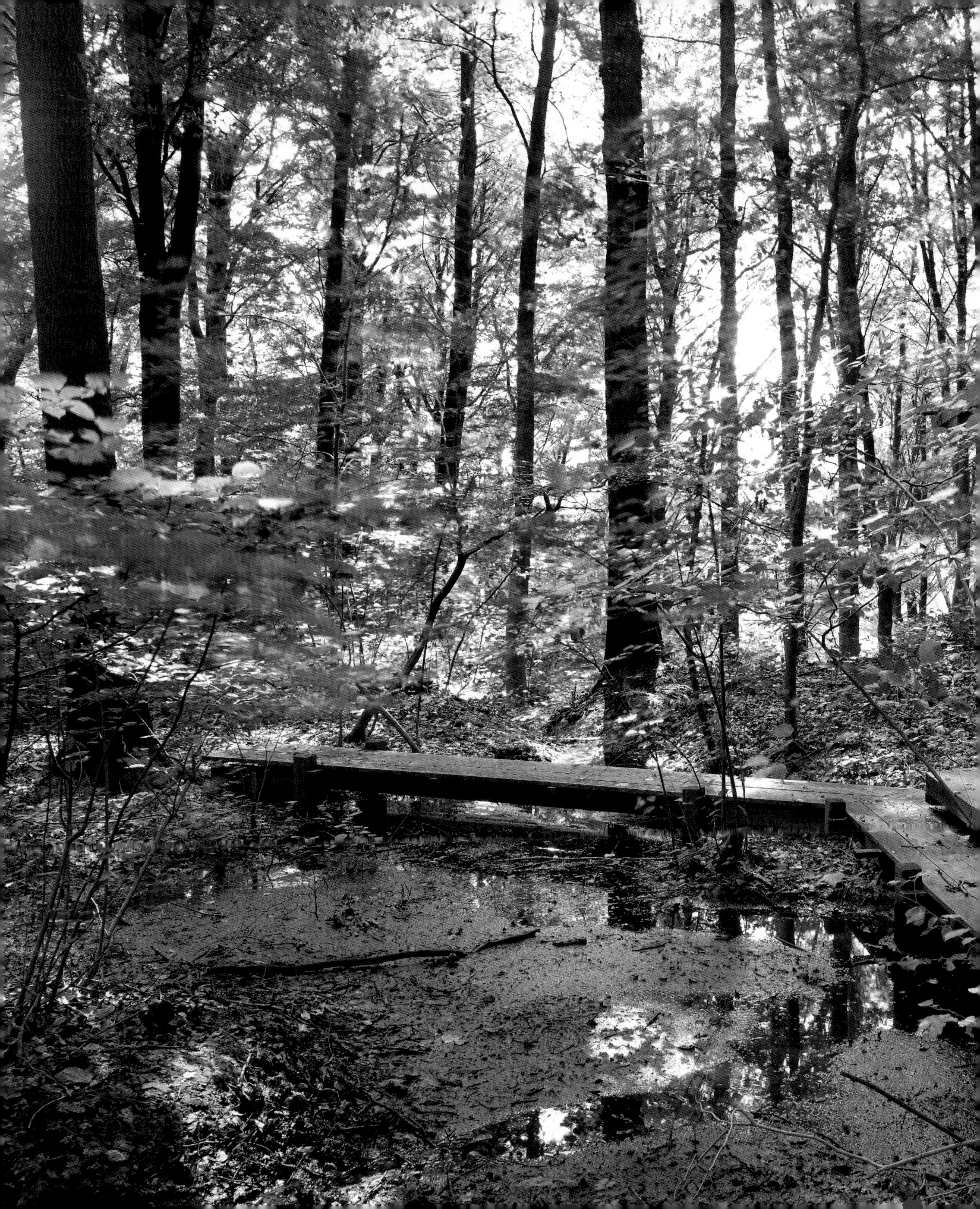

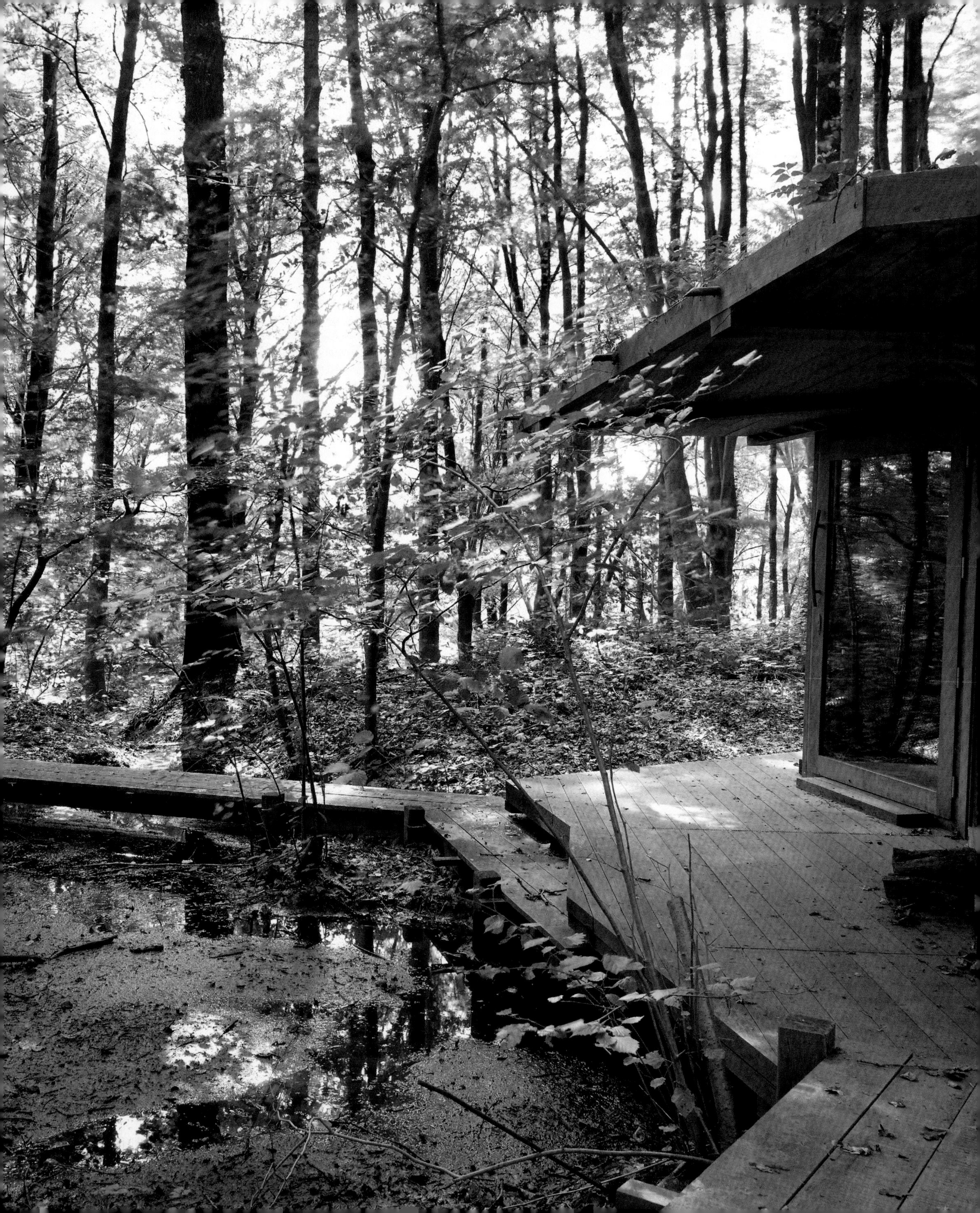

Now only one thing more is needed.....

To reflect the light through the window.

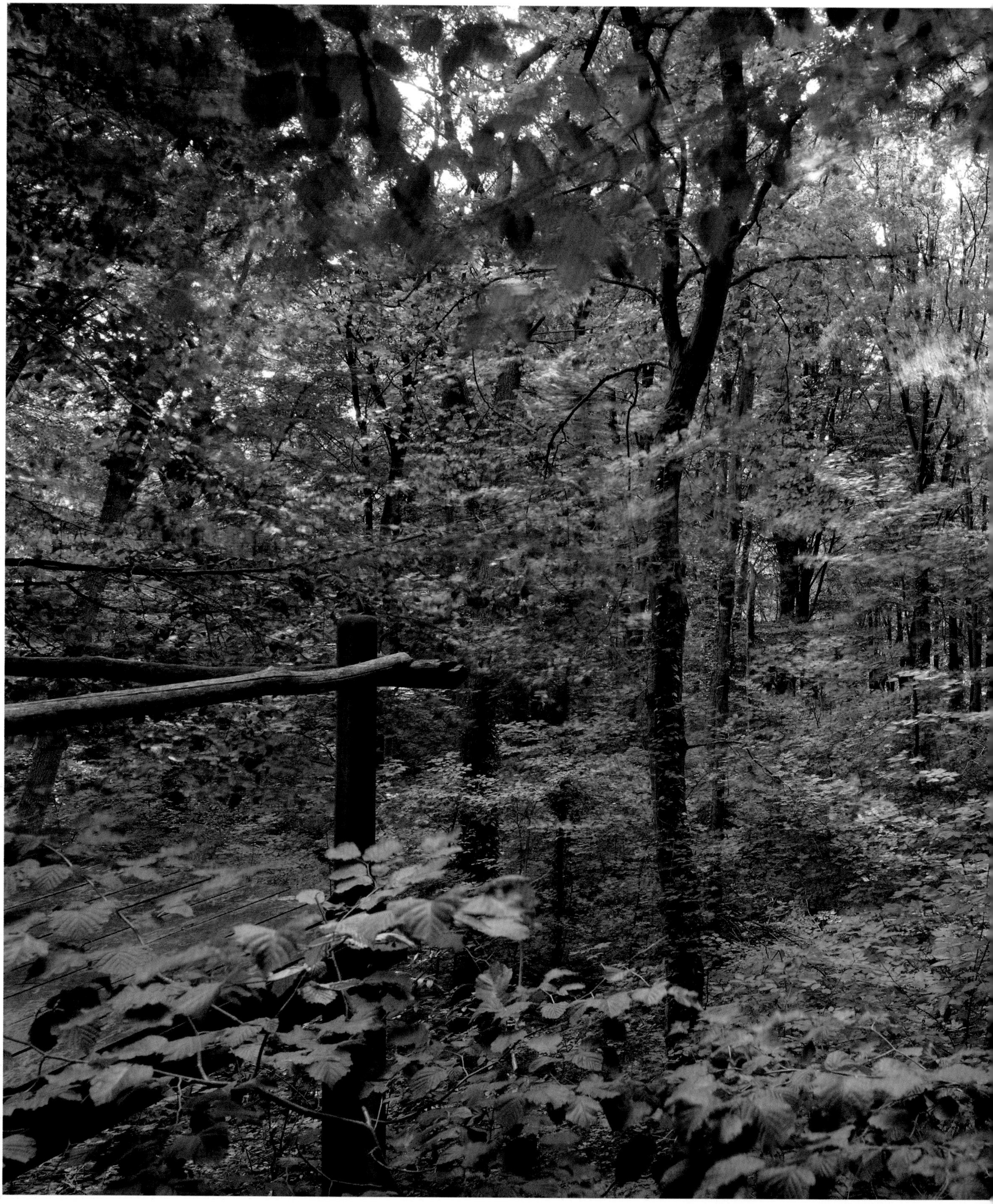

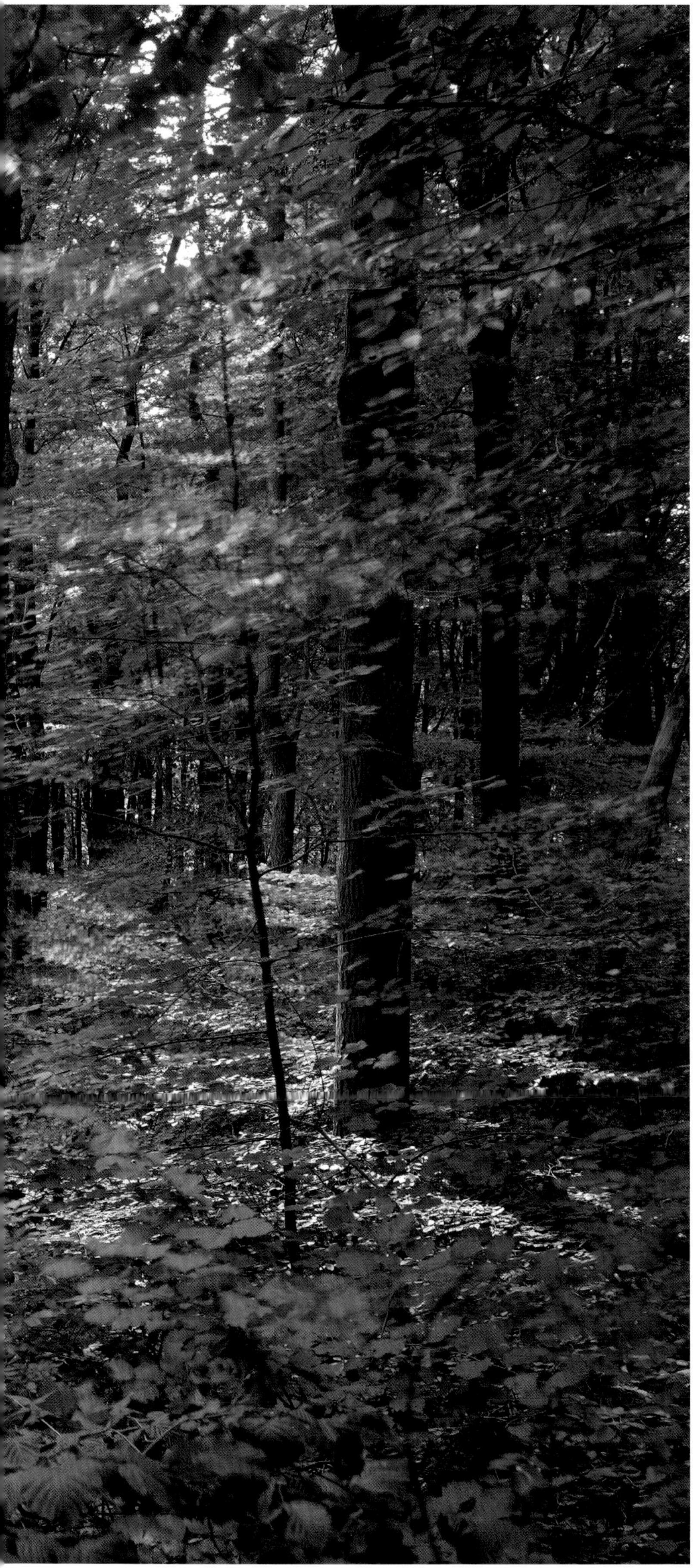
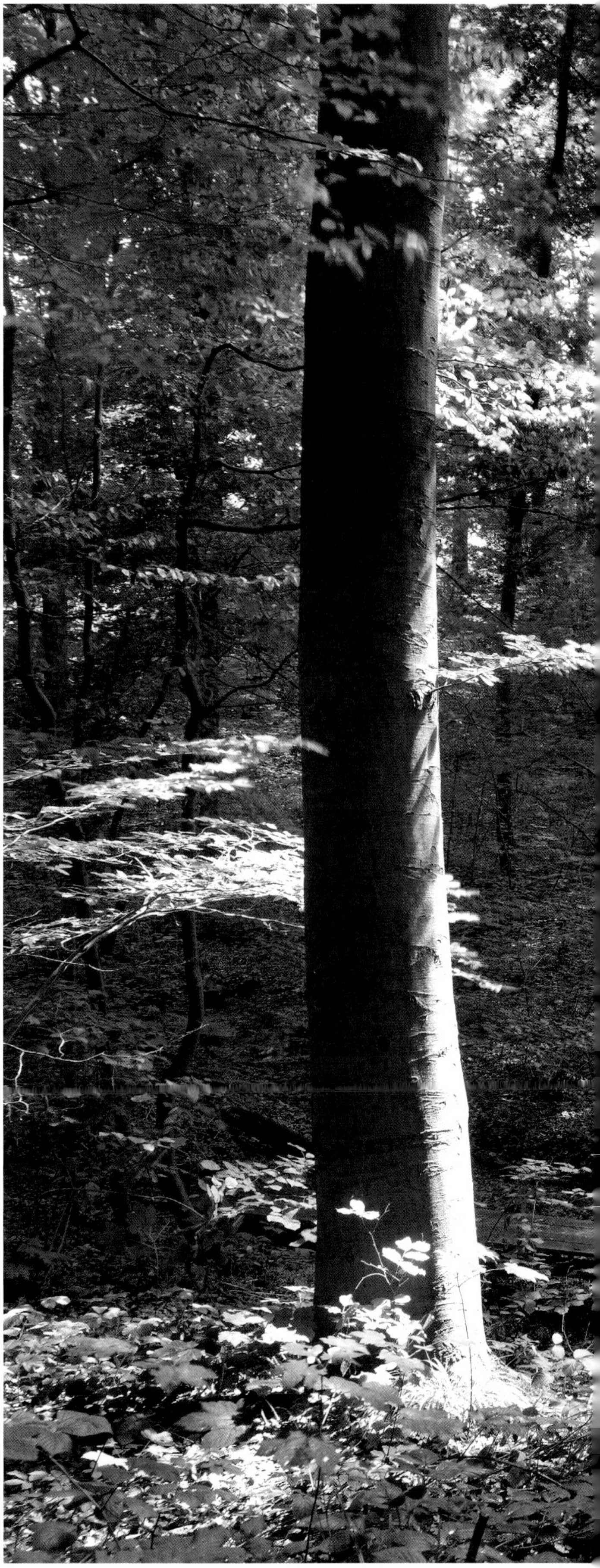

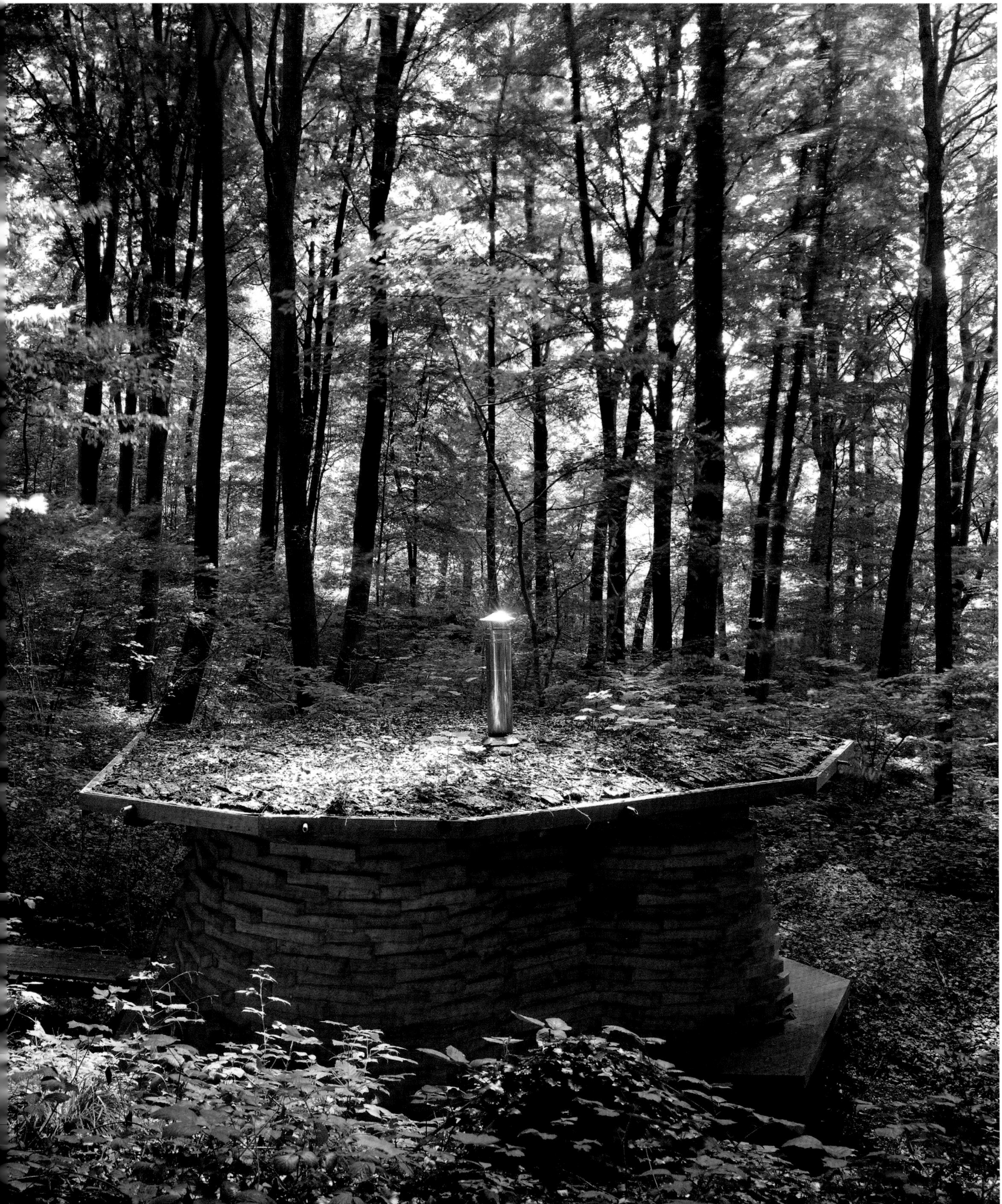

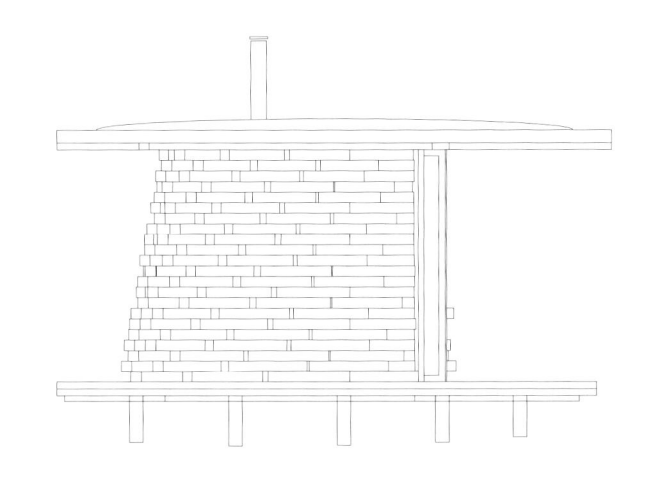

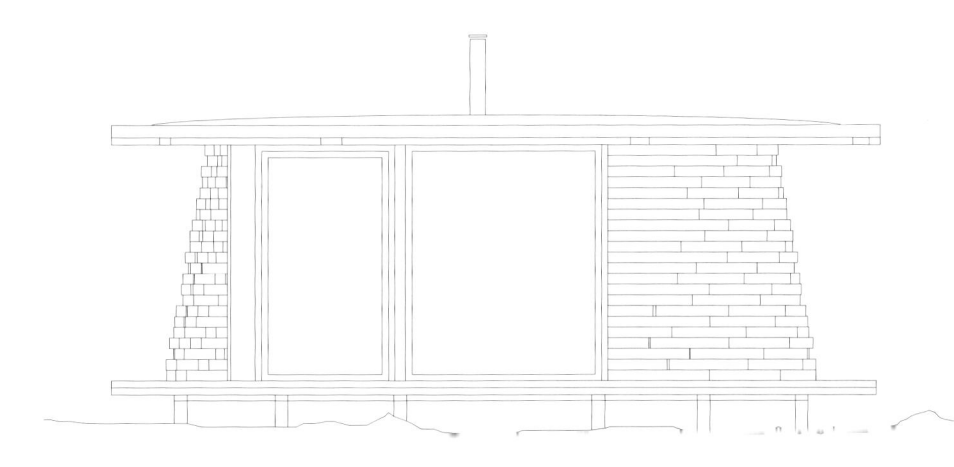

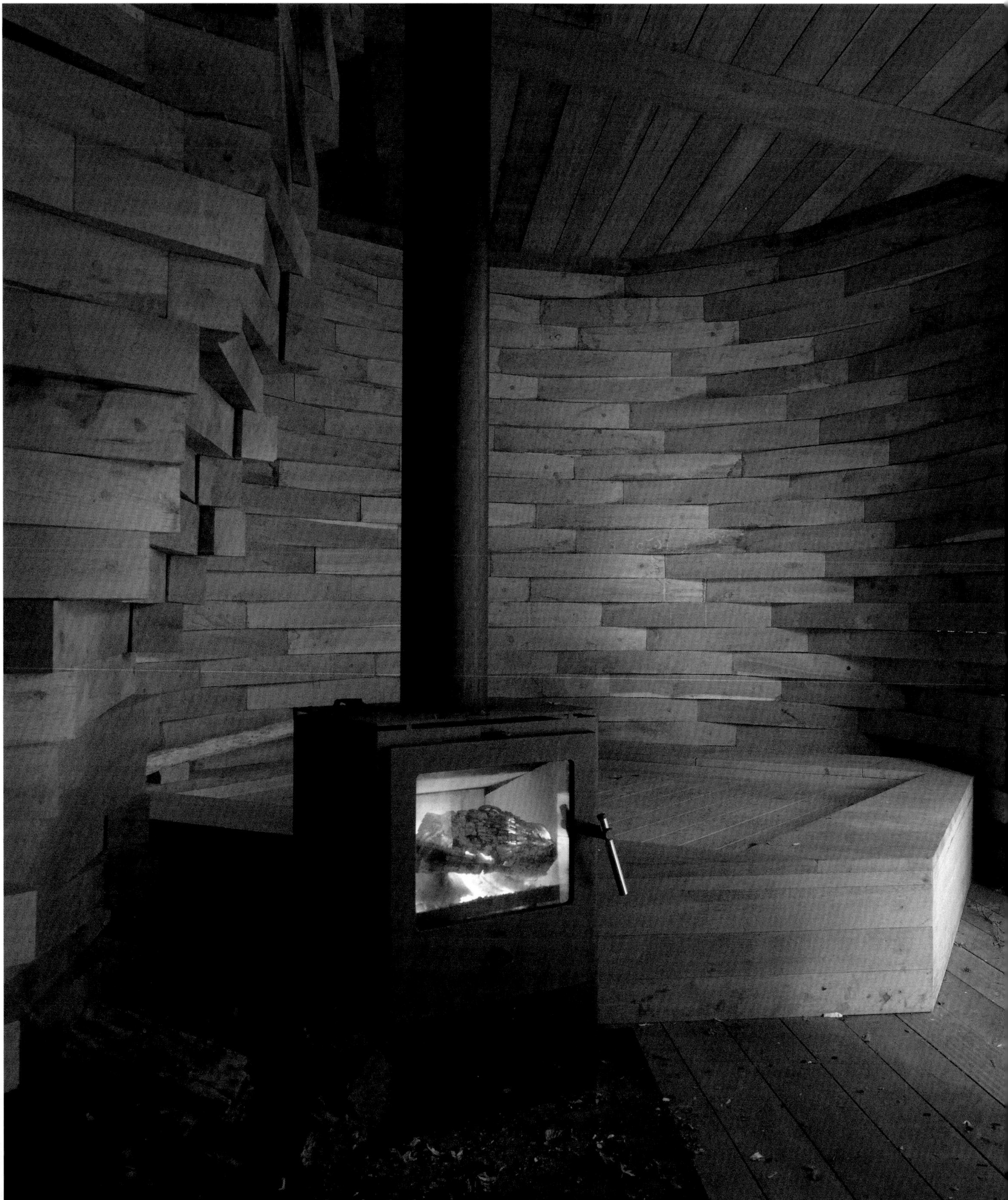

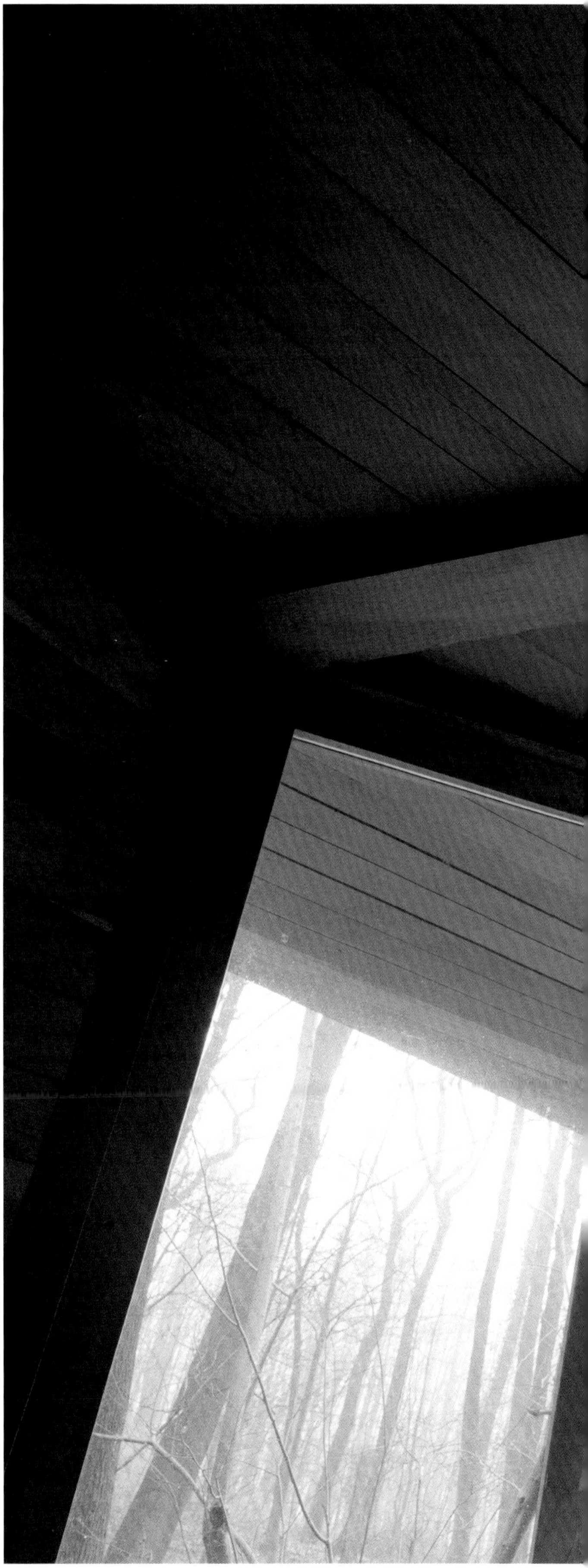

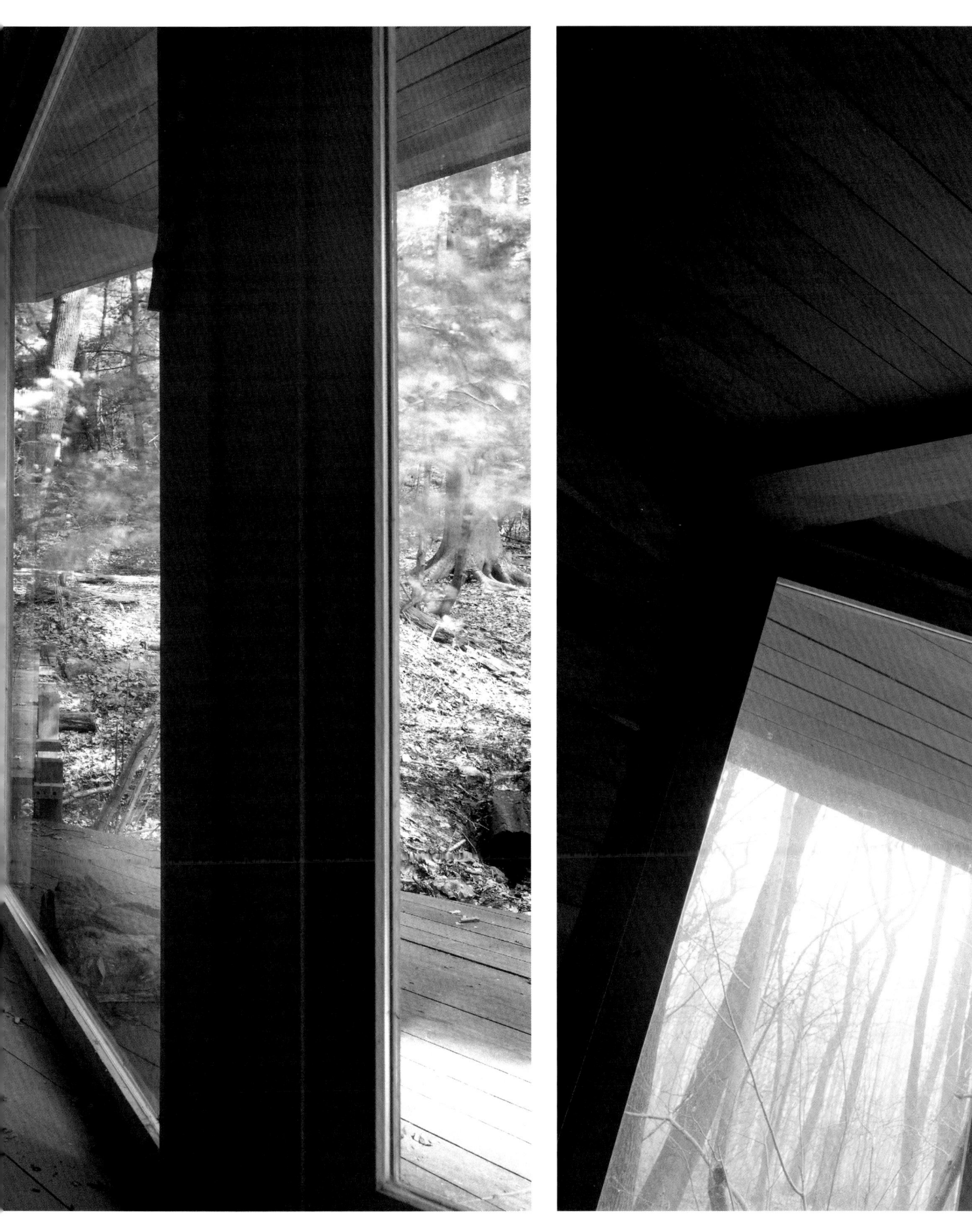

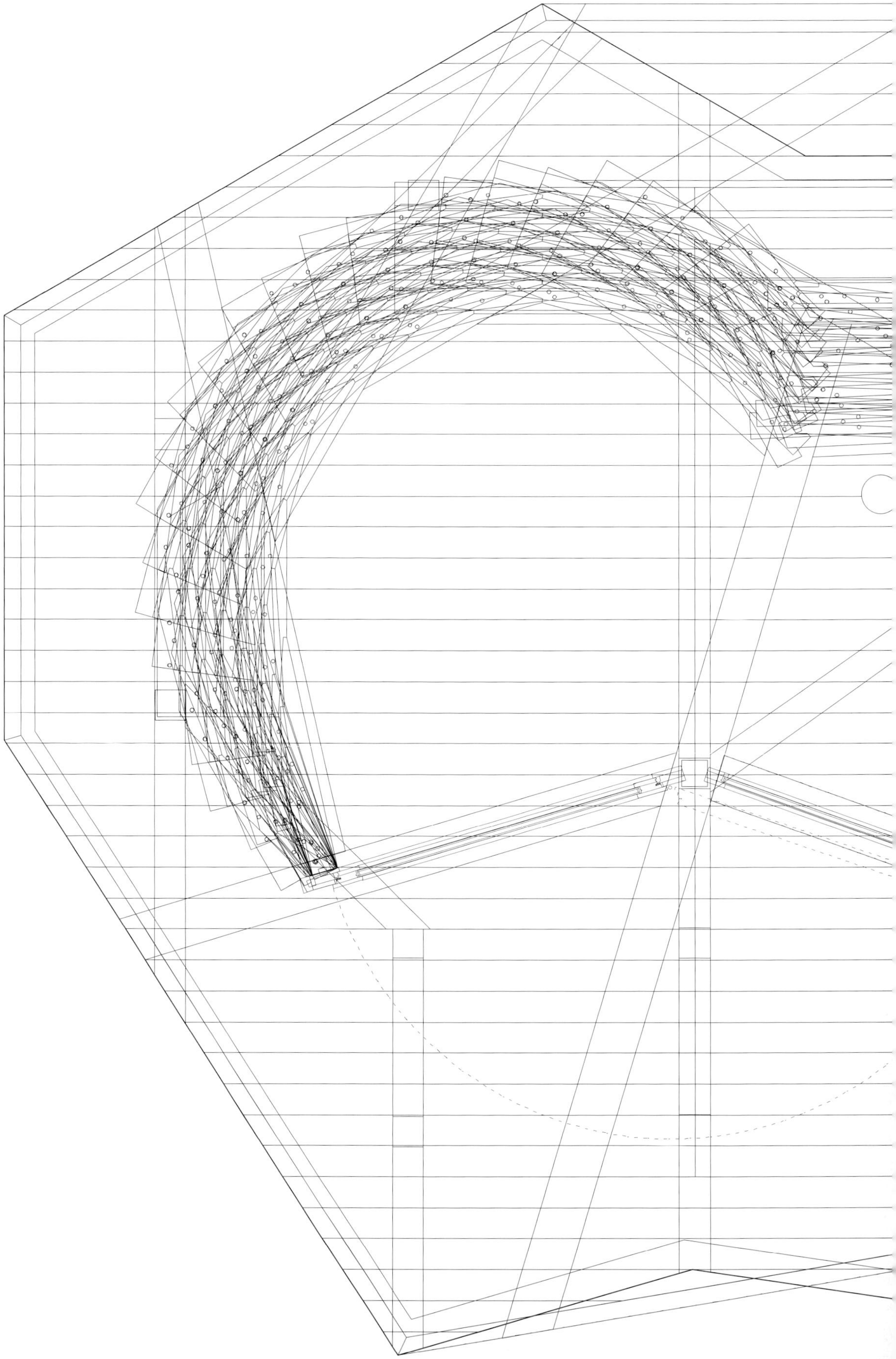

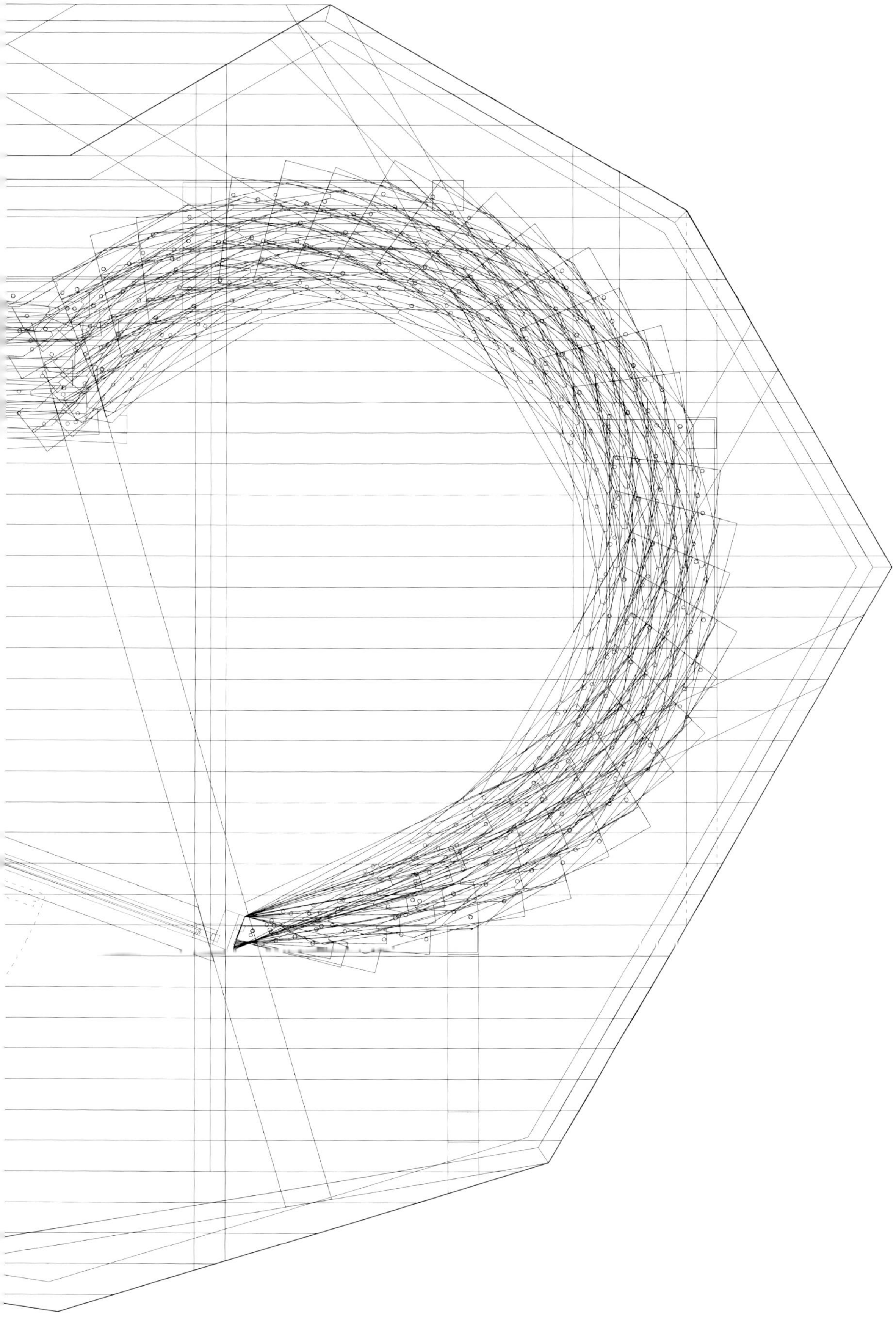

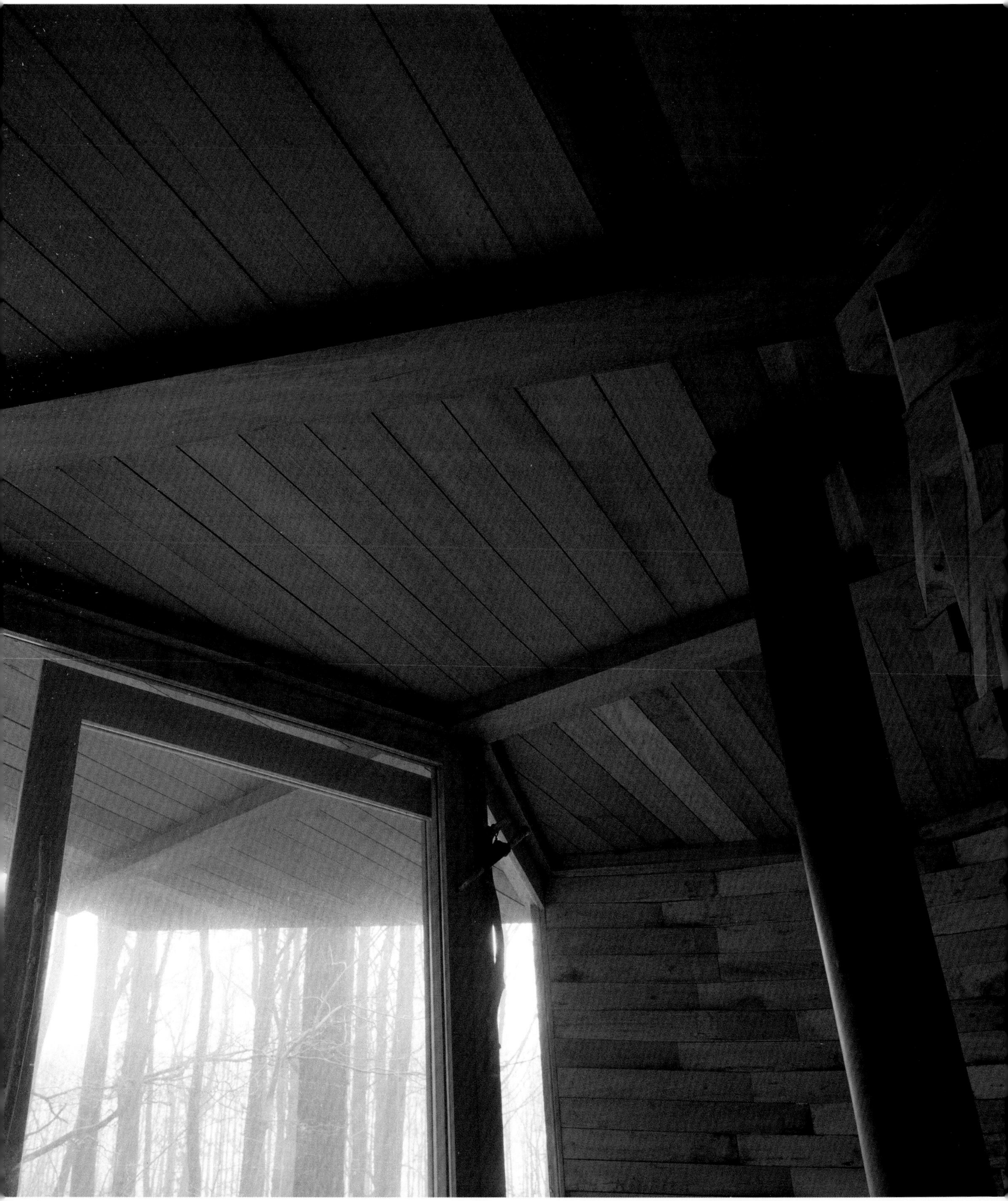

wat vloeit mij aan

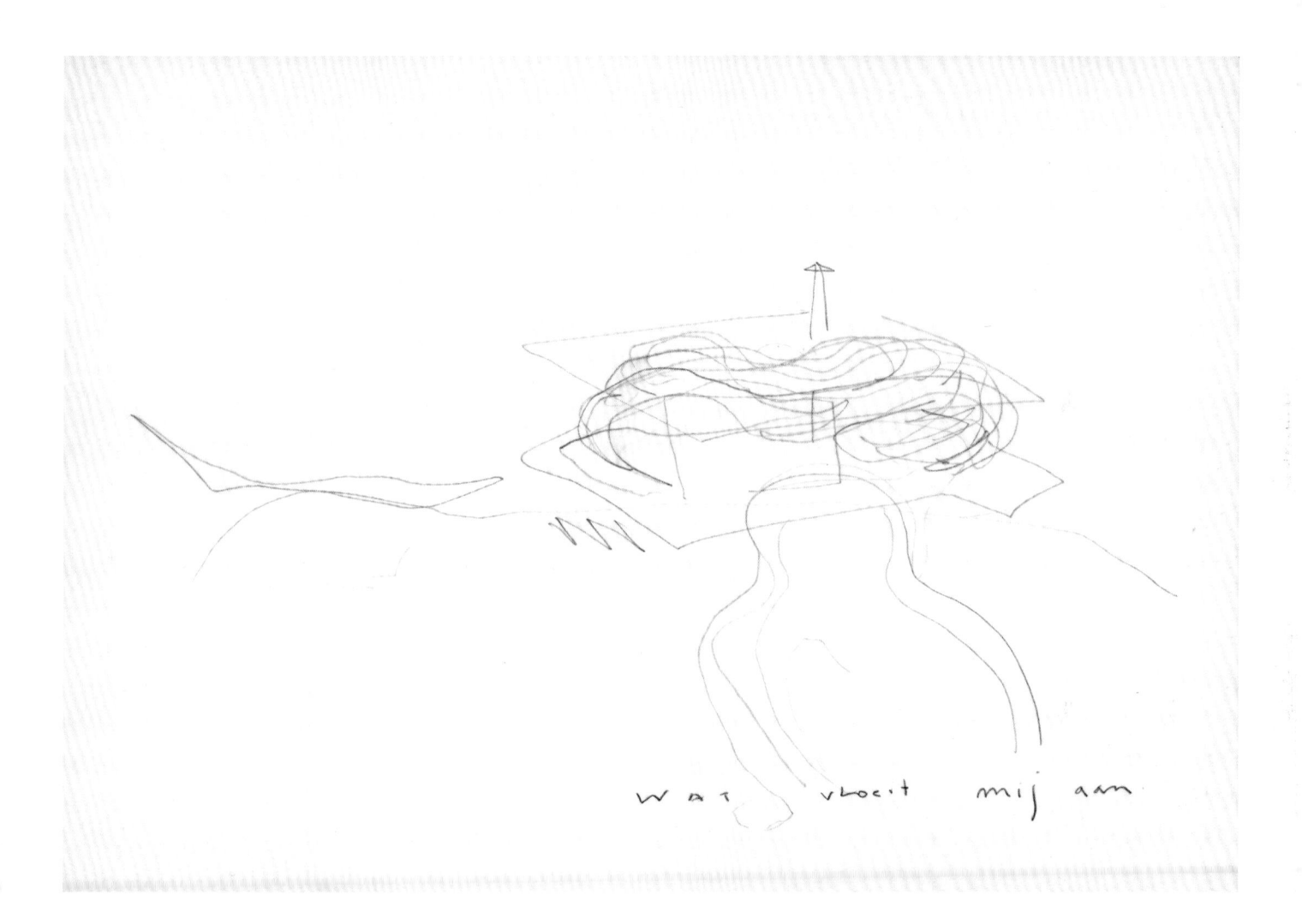

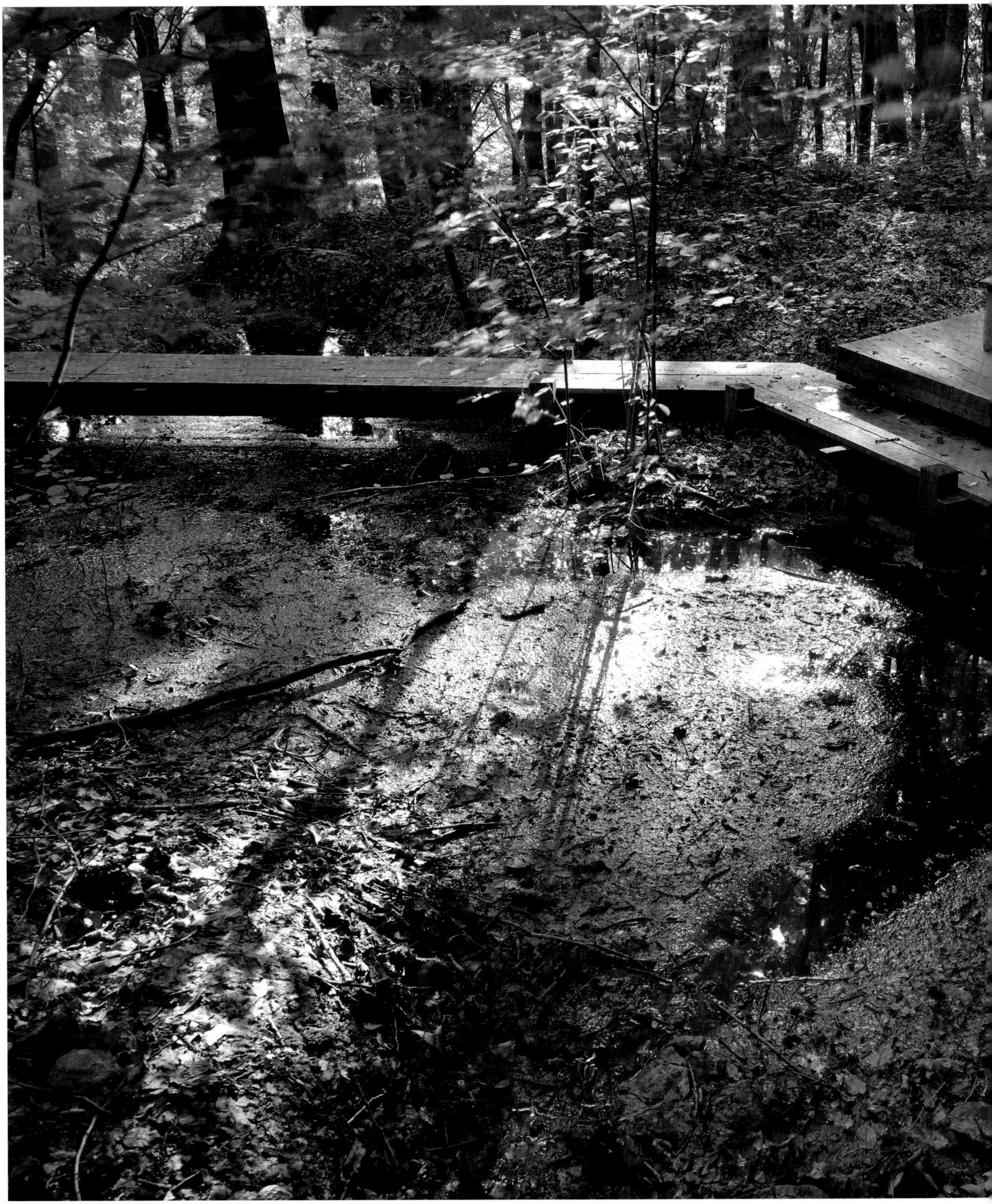

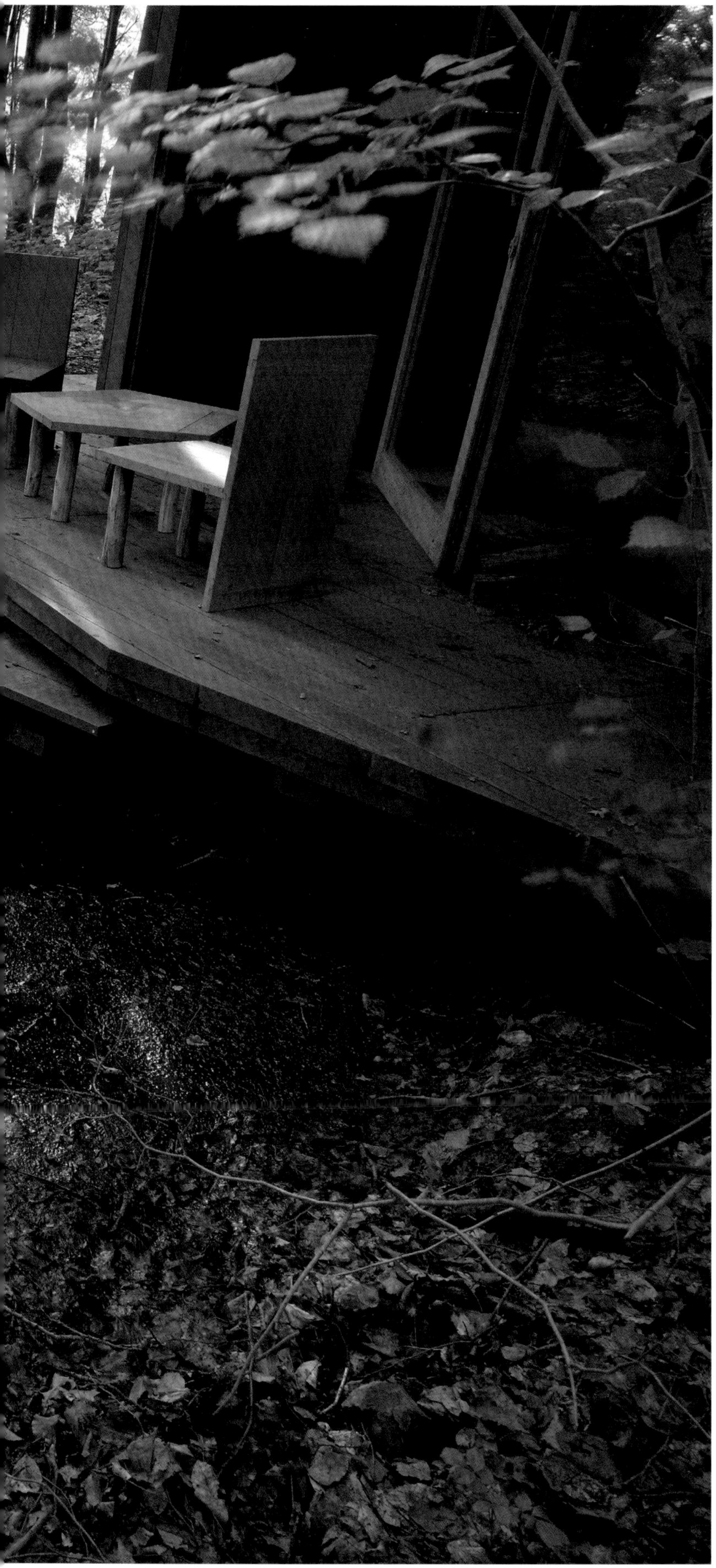

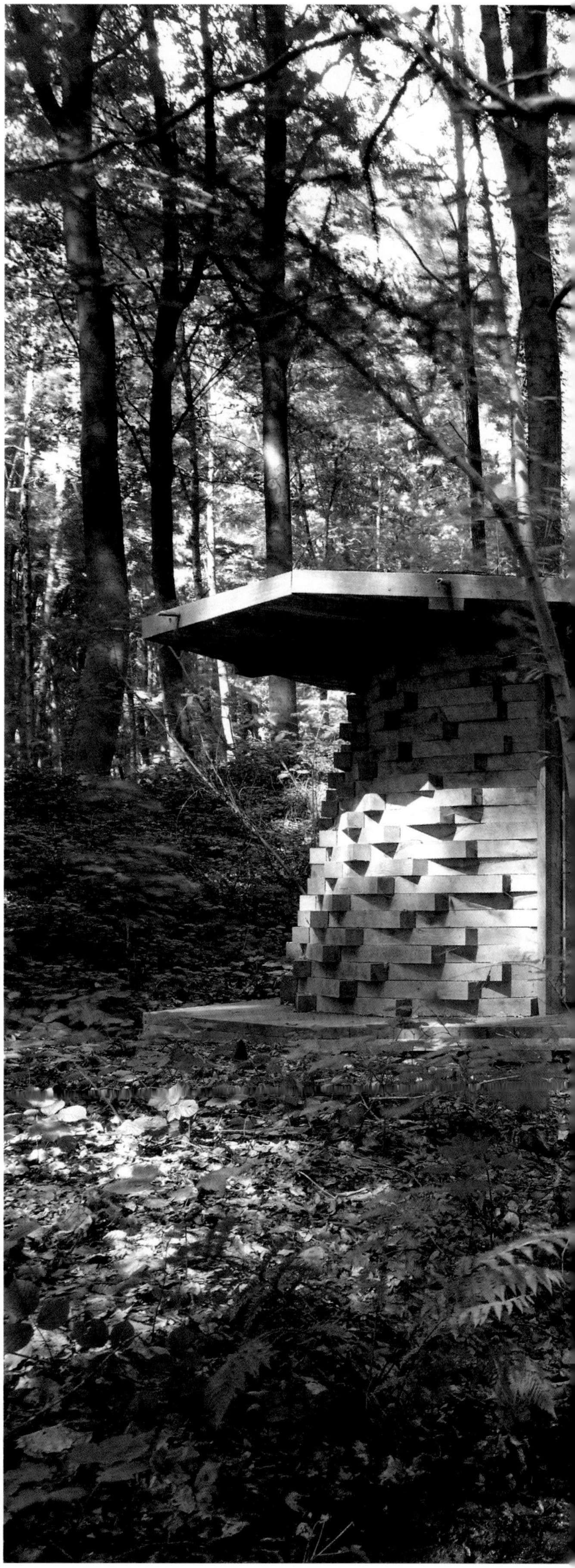

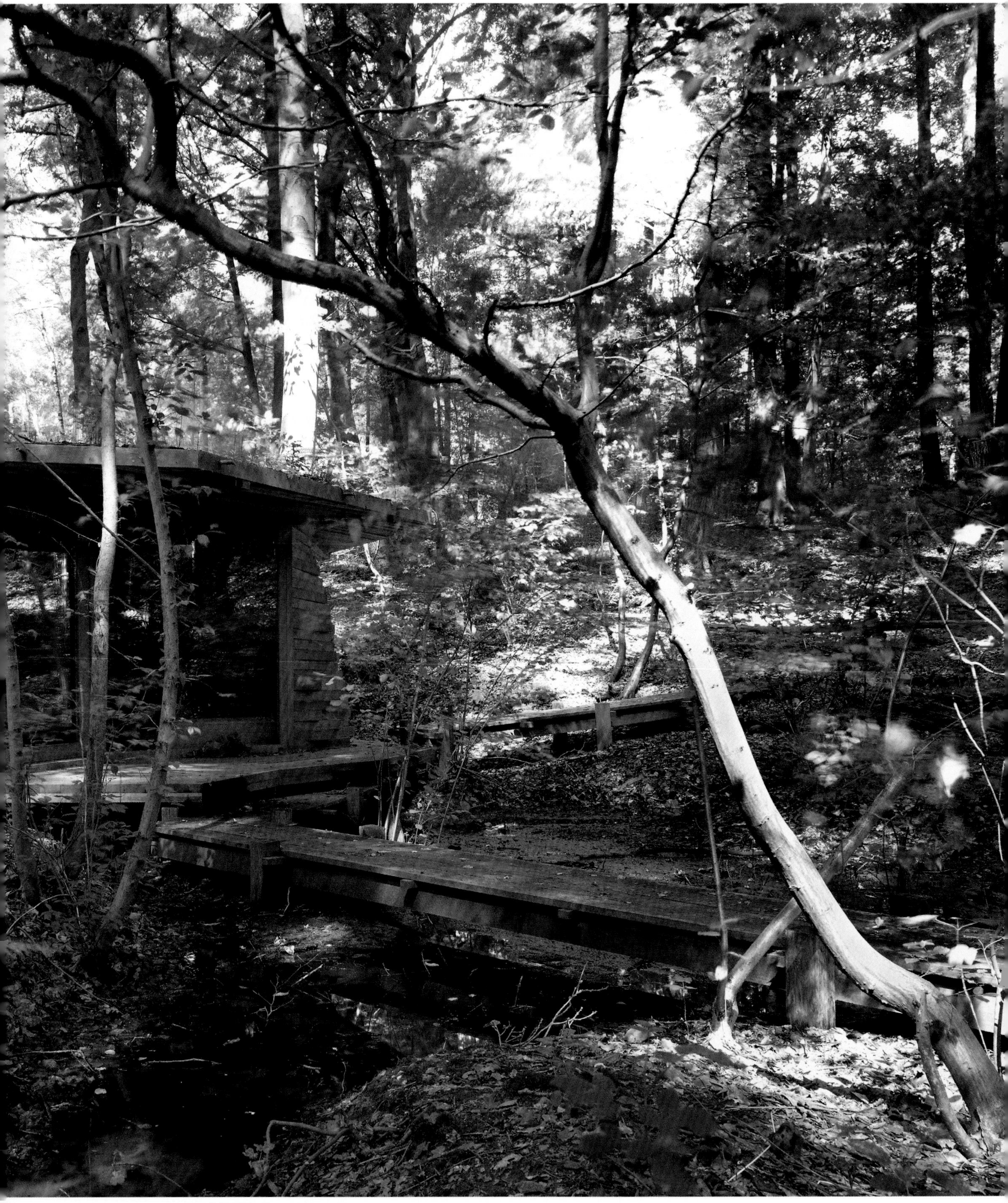

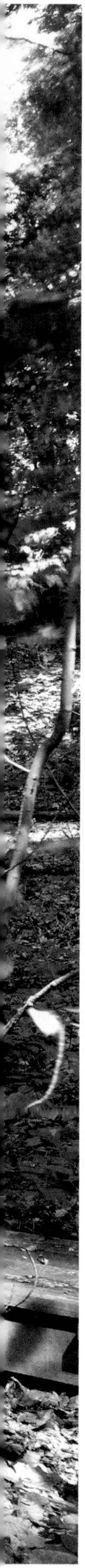

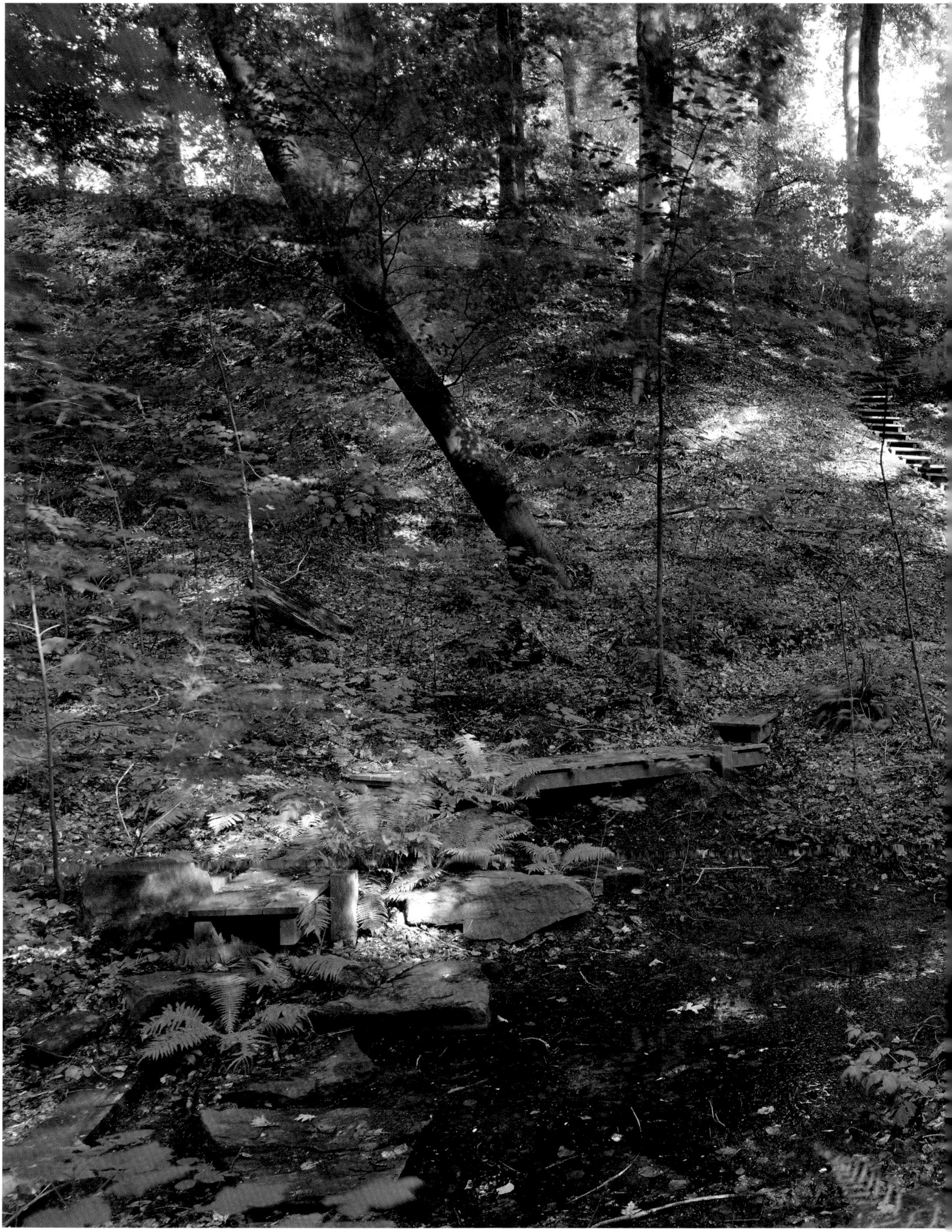

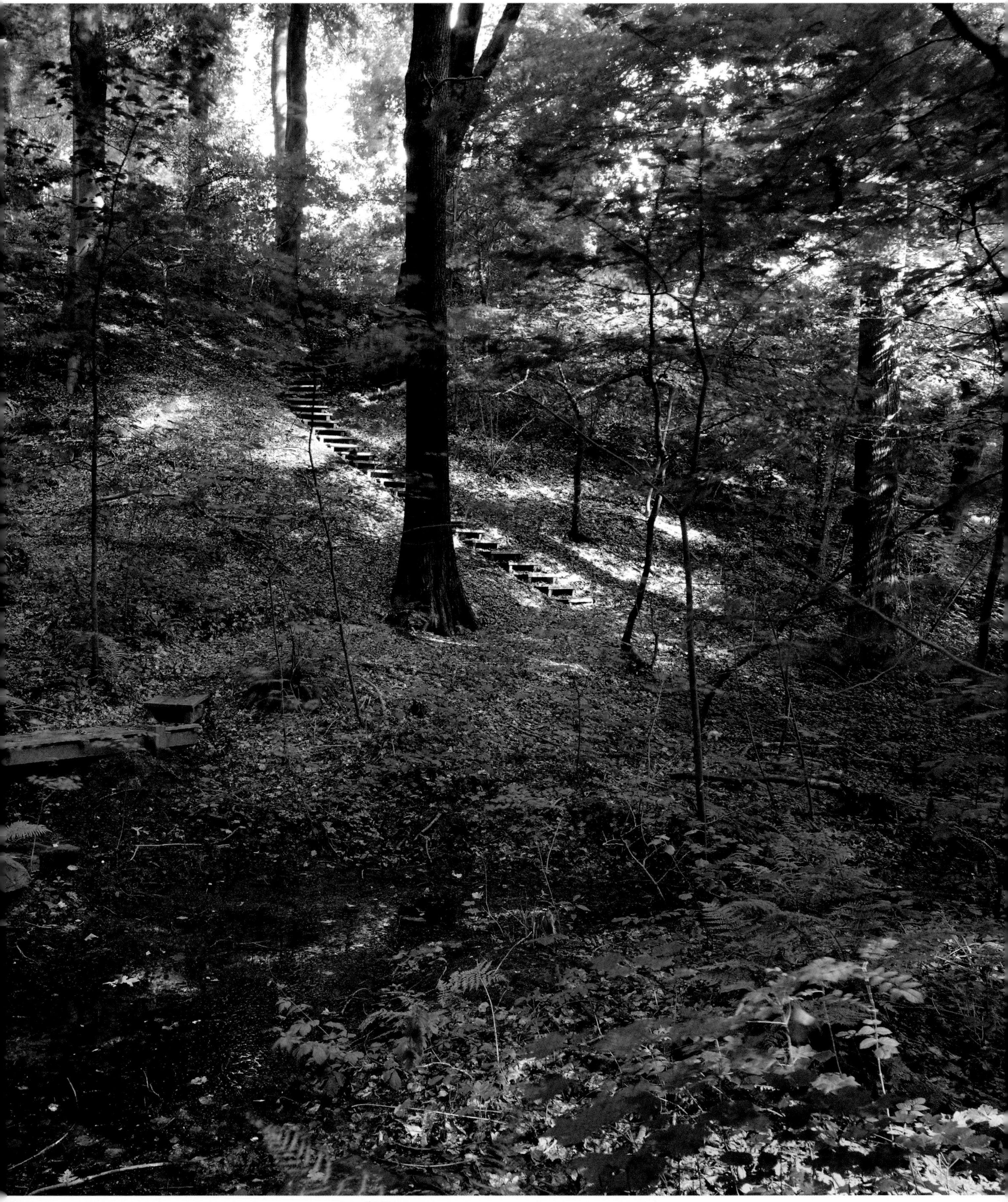

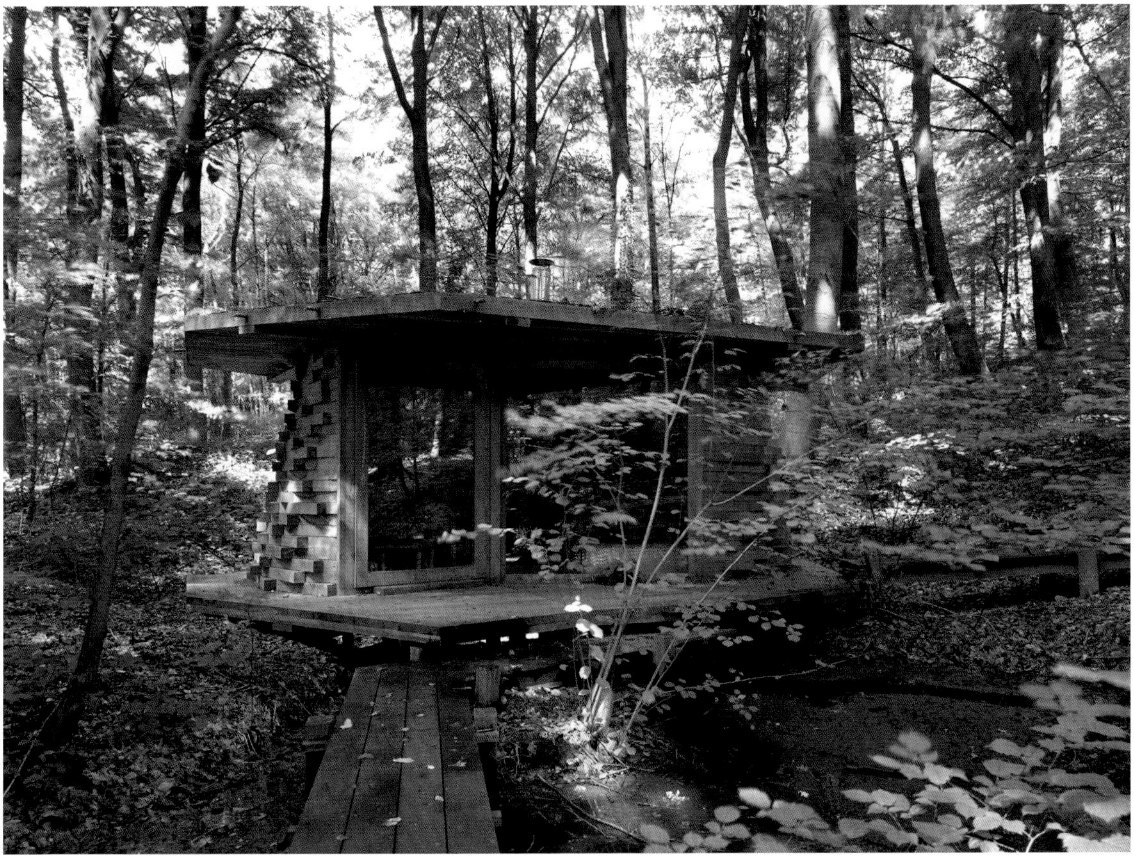

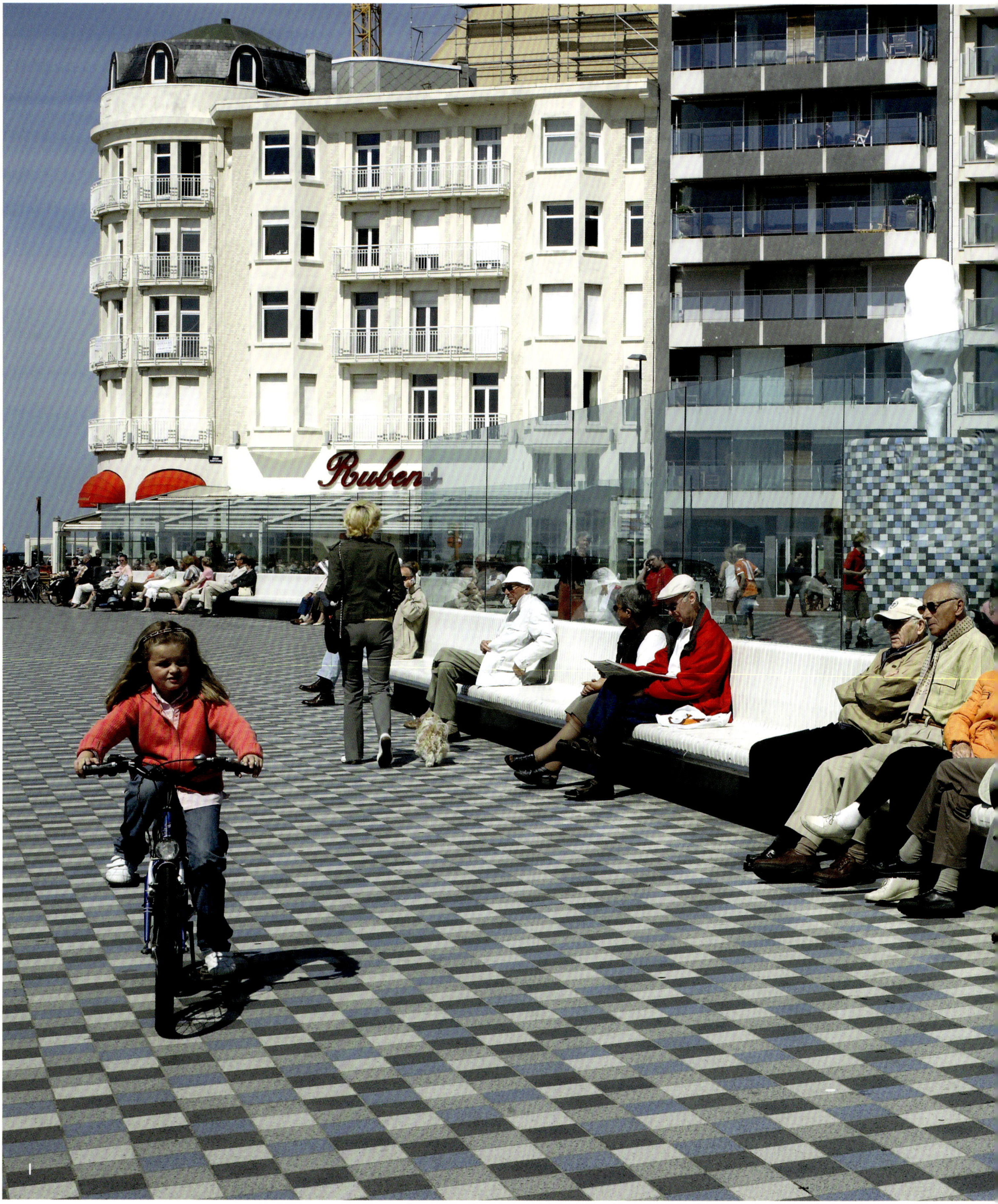
Ruben

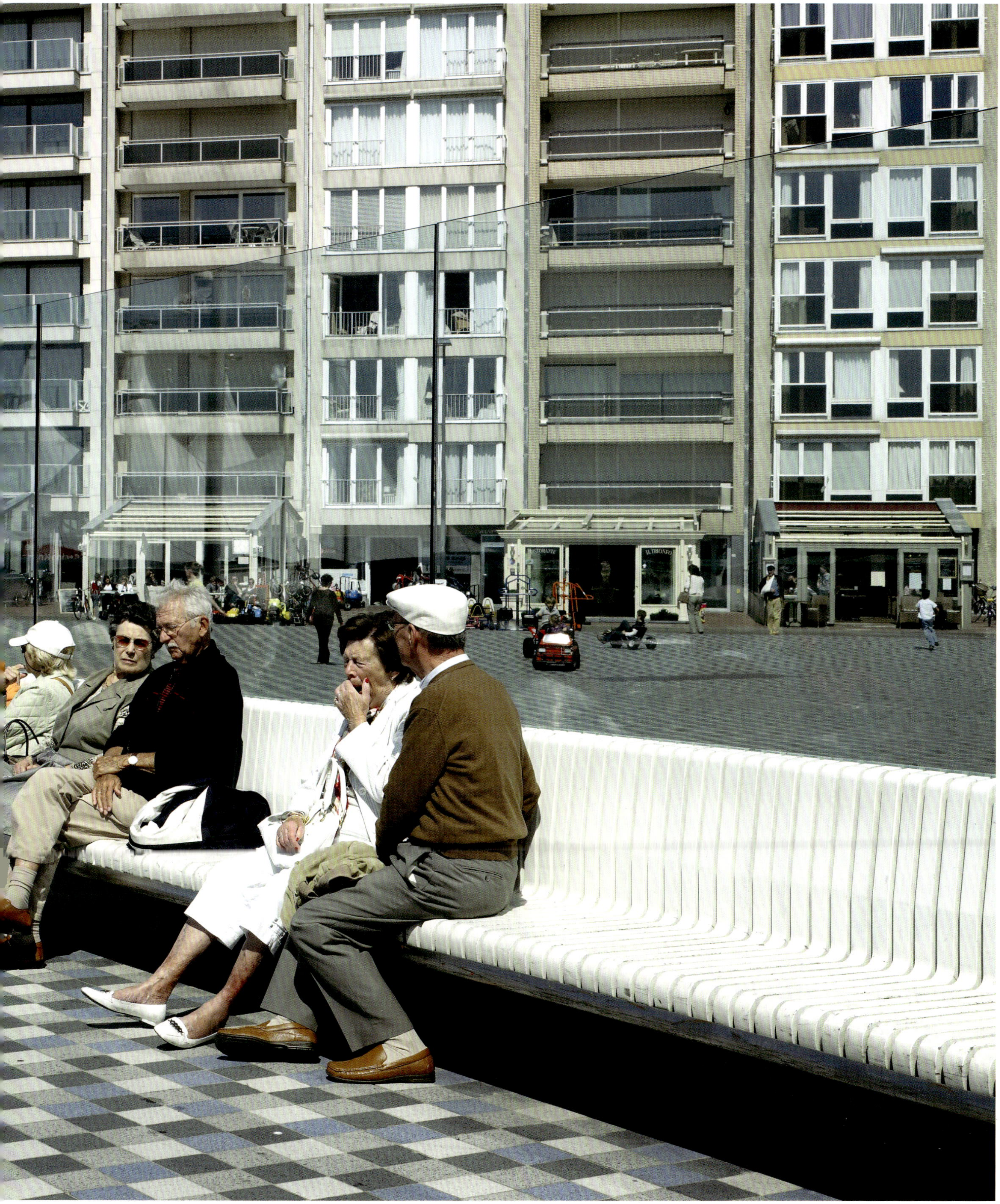

COLOMBIER DORST

Ephemeral principles   Maarten Delbeke

Form and Shape

Architecture is unnatural, building not always. Architecture is an art, a complex practice with its own examples, rules, principles, practitioners and history. The act of building is available to everyone, regardless of their purpose or prior knowledge, as to children making a sandcastle. The importance of the distinction between architecture and building is demonstrated by the tenacious and unrelenting attempts to remove it. Time and again, architects, critics and writers of treatises or theories of architecture try to assimilate architecture with building, and to derive from it all the elements of architecture – design, drawing, construction, thinking, speaking and writing. When, in 1436, the Florentine humanist Gianozzo Manetti wrote to a friend in praise of the newly consecrated dome designed by Filippo Brunelleschi, he did not hesitate to describe the building as something not touched by human hands, but descended straight from heaven as one piece of stone, precisely and elegantly shaped. The dome – then, at the outset of the Renaissance, already an emblem of new times and modern art – is not architecture, Manetti suggested, but a natural *given*, a creation of the same order as a mountain or a river. The assertion that architecture really is building, serves here as the ultimate praise.

Conversely, the primacy of building is declared to challenge and tackle the pretensions of architecture, even today. A famous yet far from isolated example of such a challenge, Bernard Rudofsky's exhibition *Architecture without architects. An introduction to non-pedigreed architecture*, first shown at MOMA in 1964 and published as a book, vaunted the qualities of vernacular or 'natural' architecture as being much better able to accommodate and express the true needs of a community than authored buildings. Rudofsky's enterprise was fundamentally flawed as it celebrated 'architecture without architects' only insofar as it incorporated the ethics and especially the aesthetics of modernism, but nonetheless proved hugely successful. The exhibition was shown at more than 80 venues over 11 years, including the Royal Library of Belgium in Brussels. The allure of the formula proved such that the first important attempt to produce an exhaustive overview of postwar architecture in Belgium was entitled *Bouwen in België 1945-1975* (*Building in Belgium 1945-1975*), thus glaringly discarding the notion of architecture. The authors, Geert Bekaert and Francis Strauven, explicitly took issue with Rudofsky's point that architects are to blame for the poor state of architecture; indeed, they argued that the biggest threat to architecture – in Belgium at least – was the architect's diminishing capacity to participate in design processes exceeding the scale of the individual house. Nonetheless, Bekaert and Strauven – writing at the time when Paul Robbrecht and Hilde Daem graduated – also made it clear that Belgium has little to do with architecture, not only because of political and historical circumstances, but also because Belgium, replete as it is with 'non-architectural' buildings of all sorts and types, might well do without. If architecture wants to stake its claim on Belgium, so the title of the book suggested, it should first state its case.

Regardless of their specific contexts, these examples suggest that building is invoked in order to reconnect architecture with its origins, and as such with its sole essential quality. In other words, comparing architecture with a natural or supra-natural form of building is always an attempt to provide architecture with meaning and even the right to exist. Cast as building, architecture seems to be in touch with something essential that does not pertain to a profession, conventions or play.

If architecture tends to claim its descendancy from building, in the projects of *Robbrecht en Daem architecten* presented here the two notions meet each other as equals. They embrace the mythology of building without turning away from architecture. As objects with multiple origins, between architecture and building, they seem to derive from multiple intentions, or maybe even an interplay between intentionality and unintentionality. In any case these projects pertain to architecture, as artifacts formulating answers to precise if sometimes extremely simple questions: housing pigeons (the Colombier near Dorst), providing viewpoints (the High Views), building a hut (behind a villa in the south of Flanders). In the larger projects, such as the transformation of the Former Dairy in Gaasbeek, Rubensplein (Rubens Square) in Knokke, the architects' office in Ghent and the Concertgebouw (Concert Hall) in Bruges, the question is more complex and demanding, but these projects are, of course, also well-designed answers to a particular demand. Yet such a reading is limiting, since the basic operations of building, such as demarcating, stacking or arranging, are of crucial importance to all of these works. Even the intricate hulk of the Concertgebouw sometimes resembles a huge, partly collapsed pup tent of broomsticks and blankets.

Even so, these projects are not merely structures; they are designed too thoroughly and precisely for that, as transpires from their measurements, geometry, construction, colours and materials. The final product moreover carries prominent traces of the accurate construction and the refined design process, such as the modular stones of the Colombier, the Woodland Cabin and Rubensplein , the meticulous colour schemes of the square, the Concertgebouw and the High Views, or the ever recurring geometrical figures, both in the composition of the plans as a whole or in specific parts, such as the pentagonal chandelier and the similar drain cover in Gaasbeek recalling the little table in the Woodland Cabin and the flowerbed in the open hall of the office building. This is also why these projects are visibly different from their surrounding non-architecture. Even if the extension in Gaasbeek never turns its back on the vernacular buildings in its immediate vicinity, it will never seem one of them. And the transformation of the factory shed into an office with a semi-private exterior space does not betray any nostalgia for the vernacular or everyday qualities of such a construction; the shed has been dismantled to lay bare its architectural qualities.

Furthermore, these projects contain a treasure trove of essential yet often disguised or distant cultural references, ranging from the local bird population that provided the colour scheme for the High Views of Boston and Lincoln, through the ziggurat carrying a staircase, reminiscent of a Renaissance palace, in Gaasbeek, which also surfaces in the Bruges Concertgebouw and – slightly simplified – in the High Views, to possible reminders of Henry David Thoreau's *Walden* in the Woodland Cabin. But these references never claim a prominent or even fixed place in the final result. They range from identifiable, almost iconic formal elements to intellectual raw material that has been transformed beyond recognition. These references, moreover, are never pure and simple: it is equally possible, and legitimate, to read the roof of Gaasbeek as a ziggurat or a mastaba, and the High View in Boston as a great nephew of Tatlin's project for the Monument of the Third International of 1919 or as a poetic answer to the enjambements in the ribbed vaults of Lincoln Cathedral. The meanings attached to these references do not act as a bridge between building and architecture, or as the contents that transform a natural building into a product of culture. They are shades that wander through building and architecture alike.

That building, designing and cultural meaning are at least partly separate is true for every work of architecture that was ever realised, not just for these projects. Only when architects, patrons and critics speak and think about architecture does it become necessary to balance these three components, preferably so that they naturally follow from one another. After all, speaking and thinking about architecture very often serves to legitimize specific projects or architecture in general, and such justifications are only efficient when they are coherent and thus demonstrate the cohesion and necessity of the architectural project itself. When, in *Vers une architecture*, Le Corbusier praises the Parthenon, he points out the origin of its beauty: the temple rises from a single intention. '*D'une unité d'idée allant de l'unité de matières jusqu'à l'unité de la modénature.*' Thanks to this all-encompassing unity, the beauty of the Parthenon seems entirely natural, just as the Duomo of Florence did to Manetti. By linking literally every aspect of the design and the building, Le Corbusier repeats a central tenet of Modernism, that objects carried by a single thought acquire a form untainted by the traces of their laborious manufacture and generate the entire cultural meaning of the building. To Le Corbusier, these unified forms do not carry symbols or stories, but they appeal to a 'categorical experience'.

What Robbrecht en Daem discard is perhaps the Modernist ambition to envisage an architecture where a unity of intention establishes an absolute coherence of design and meaning. Nonetheless, their architecture is deeply indebted to Modernism; for example, Le Corbusier's colour schemes, as collected by Arthur Reugl in the work *Polychromie architecturale*, are an important source of inspiration. But the architects have abandoned the clear and linear relationship between intention, idea, form, building and meaning in favour of the ratio of the collection, conglomerates of shapes and ideas. The collection does not produce a clear story or a clearly delineated shape. Paul Robbrecht's preliminary ink and watercolour drawings consist of outlines with spots, alternating with unfinished points of precision. Details seem to have been scratched into the composition and produce forms that are hard to name, but are still immediately recognizable in the final result. For example, the sketch of the path leading to the Woodland Cabin shows a two-lobed figure with a pair of straight extensions. This shape not only prefigures the final plan, but also indicates what the project is about: a place for two people near the water in the woods. In a second sketch this shape is developed into something that is as reminiscent of a bird's nest as a house, with chairs and a table drawn within the curve of a wall.

A similar polysemy characterizes the presentation drawings as well. The ground plans of the Woodland Cabin, like those of the Colombier near Dorst, consist of rampant lines impeding the recognition and interpretation of established patterns. The brick patterns of the extension in Gaasbeek overwhelm the figure of the ground plan. As a result, the presentation drawings render something of the way these buildings are experienced by the viewer; they oscillate between clarity and confusion, between unity and plurality, between straightforwardness and ambiguity. For instance, the apparently clearly delineated volumes of the two High Views are distorted and multiplied by means of the multicoloured latticework that allows glimpses of the walkers climbing the little towers. The Woodland Cabin is at first barely visible, partly because its roof is overgrown; it does not slowly emerge from the shrubbery, but suddenly appears. A similar effect is produced by the Colombier near Dorst, an appearance between the trees and in the water. Upon entering the Former Dairy in Gaasbeek one simultaneously looks inside and outside, the book-lined wall in the concert room barely separated from the outdoor staircase immersed in fallen leafs or unmitigated sunlight. A similar experience awaits the visitor to the office the architects designed for themselves: the existing industrial shed has been largely reduced to a skeleton containing not only the private exterior space but also the memory of the original spatial boundaries, thus offering an almost unworldly perspective on the surrounding houses and high-rise flats. Even the mass of the Concertgebouw, covered in red tiles, assumes ever-changing shapes depending on one's point of view and interest: from the almost classical composition facing the Zand Square, over the composite and ineffable bulk of the west face of the building, to the facades that look out over the park and announce the scale of the houses surrounding the Zand Square. Its homogeneous skin makes the

Concertgebouw as of one piece – even the Lantern Tower, a distinct entity positioned towards the square, is part of the volume – but it remains hard to describe or even observe: the mass is a conglomerate whose parts and composition are sometimes shrouded or accentuated by its stone cloak.

In other words, if all these buildings have a well-defined form, which of course they do, this form is also released and rendered to the beholder, the environment or nature. Even in the case of a large building like the Concertgebouw this happens with surprising ease, because the final shape of none of these projects can be reduced to a single pronouncement or action. The first intuitions, represented in the sketches and paintings, can be easily recognized in the final result, but they also become complicated along the way. In an apparent paradox, it is the process of elaboration that transforms these projects from designs (or architecture) into structures, less well-defined forms than appearances. To Robbrecht en Daem, naturalness does not mean a kind of perfection that lifts the object beyond its maker and man in order to leave behind randomness and contingency, but the accumulation of facts and meanings that render a building as natural (if not as casual) as the things it is surrounded by.

Shape and conglomerate

To direct this accumulation is a delicate process. The success of the projects collected here perhaps depends on their delicate balancing of indeterminacy and extreme purposefulness. After all, the projects, certainly the smaller ones, deal with simple programmes and could easily have become a single statement; at the same time, they are bound by very few restrictions. Conversely, in the larger buildings, where the programmatic exigencies are far more complex and defining, the architects have wilfully created opportunities to escape determination, for instance by complicating the spatial dimension of the building. There is perhaps a relationship between the means adopted to strike the balance between purpose and randomness, and the degree of freedom found in the design brief: the buildings with the lightest programmes acquire their shape by means of a conglomeration of a limited set of basic elements, whereas the larger projects evolve as an accumulation of different themes. In the latter case, best exemplified by the Concertgebouw, much of the energy is directed into maintaining unity in the accumulation; in the former, the process of conglomeration literally shatters and thus complicates the final form, much in the way of the pointillist paintings of Georges Seurat, a key reference in these architects' work. The High Views, shown in several preliminary sketches as solid volumes, are executed as a fenced staircase (in Lincoln) or a latticework mounted on a metal supporting structure (in Boston); their shape, appearance and iconography results from the way they are made. The same is true for the Colombier: it is built as a stack of two different sizes of stone, arranged on a triangle with sides slightly bulging like the rotor of a Wankel engine. Variations in the length of the sides generate a slowly swelling and sharpening tower. Leaving out several stones in the upper portion allows the doves to enter the tower.

The pavilions on Rubensplein that provide access to the underground car park also look like stacks of stones, in this case cylinders with one corner cut away. Here, however, the stones derive their measurements, colour and arrangement from the tiles of the square itself. The small buildings are three-dimensional applications of its blue, white and grey mosaic. If the conglomerate of the Colombier seems to indicate that the structure is an architectural and hence alien presence in the wood, the building stones on Rubensplein form part of a pattern which, by dint of its tightly controlled repetition blended with randomness, unabashedly refers to the overdetermining elements of the context, the sea and the beach; the benches and the low parapet bordering the square, which occupy the surface like breakwaters and an embankment, only go to reinforce this association.

The pattern transforms the uniform variation of the water and the waves into an architectural theme, and thus intertwines natural with design as in the other projects described here. But on Rubensplein we are made aware of the importance of pictorial strategies in arranging this confrontation. It is, after all, a square, and the treatment of its surface demonstrates that Robbrecht en Daem do not see the application of refined materials as a way of conquering the third dimension, but of complicating the surface. Such intricate surfaces, like those the architects encounter in the works of Seurat, Barnett Newman and Gerhard Richter, establish a parentage between architecture and painting that seems to discard another Modernist tenet – architecture as a composition of volumes and the concomitant parentage between buildings with sculpture – and harks back to a much older notion of creation where art, including architecture, is always to some extent mimetic. Mimesis here does not mean the representation of recognizable forms, but the incorporation of fleeting references to depth, distance and images just beneath the surface of the object, generating an incessant interplay between the solidity of the surface and the transitory illusion of three-dimensionality. If this process, as already pointed out, serves to complicate the sculptural presence of their buildings (including the pavilions on the square), the fluttering of the square's surface moreover recalls old, almost archaic connotations. The mosaic seems to hark back to a tradition with its roots in Byzantium; the floor tiles of the Hagia Sofia, made out of slabs of Proconnesian marble, have been read for more than a millennium as a frozen or congealed sea. This connotation is based on two related associations, between water and stone, as glistening materials produced by the earth itself, and between the sea and heaven, as two infinite and unfathomable spheres beyond the reach of man. Or, as the character Mikkelsen puts it rather awkwardly in Willem Frederik Hermans' novel *Beyond Sleep*: 'Of everything that happens in the world, life beneath the surface of the water is the most invisible to man. The waterworld is least like ours. That is why the waterworld is the most powerful symbol of the hereafter. Heaven is mirrored in the water.'

However, if the design of Rubensplein invites these associations, the project does little to dramatize the relationship between surface and underworld, or earth and sea, but treats them as part of the actual environment of the Belgian coast. On the most basic of levels, the mosaic recalls the long stretches of sand-coloured and grooved tiles that line the promenade over the entire length of the coastline. What is more, the underground car park is not distinguished from the hundreds of similar spaces positioned along the beaches by an exacerbation of the contrast with the outside world. The underground space is bathed in daylight; it is not a dark underworld. In other words, Rubensplein emerges from a collection of related thoughts that allow the project to slide between what things meant in the past and the contingencies of everyday life in a context with many ambiguities of its own, the sea and the Belgian coast.

In the Woodland Cabin too, the basic operation of composition simultaneously produces and disperses the possible forms and meanings of the design. The elaborate walls of the hut, closed by a glass window and door, rest upon a polygonal platform and support a roof with a chimney. These different elements consist of clearly visible and nameable components; for instance, the roof is supported by identical beams that fan out from the supporting walls. Between these different elements, but also within each element internally, the shape of the plan suggests several symmetries and parallels, which are however interrupted just before they give rise to a simple design system. The two enclosing walls start symmetrically from the centre of the building, but are of unequal length. In the resulting opening between the walls the glass surface yields inwards, parallel to the edge of the terrace, so that the smaller lobe acts as the entrance zone. And even if the two lobes follow a similar curve, the two sides of the platform are of a different shape. As a result, the plan as a whole is turned slightly towards the path leading to the civilised world. If it is possible to discern these and similar incidental patterns in the design, which moreover make perfect sense with regard to the programme of the Cabin, there are at least as many incidents that seem to escape these ephemeral principles. The pattern of supporting columns perhaps best illustrates this accumulation of incomplete systems. Although the pattern seems to suggest a grid, verification always shows this impression to be false.

Conglomerate and type

The Woodland Cabin, then, is by no means a primitive construction of columns, beams and roofing. Neither the composition of the plan nor the structure of the design follow from a simple intention or attempt to reveal an essential act or statement. The project is not about returning to an origin or type, or making a model, or realising an idyll. As such, this small building does not correspond to the almost inevitable expectations raised by the situation: a hut for adults, and for what adults do, situated in a wood behind a fine late-modernist villa. The composite nature of the work pushes these expectations aside, but unemphatically, not by excluding references to the idyll or the type, quite to the contrary. As has been mentioned, from the first stages of the design process the building emerged as a nest – a literal imitation of the animal houses which, according to Vitruvius, taught man how to build – and it contains a hearth and a bed that also serves as a cupboard, almost like a house in the hut. But of the Cabin's various components, some – such as the glass window and door – do not at all belong in this pastoral setting. These elements, moreover, appear to have little to do with the first gestures made by the design, such as the small mound and the nest. Several iconographic registers intermingle, and as a result the programme of the hut does not generate a fixed or ultimate meaning. It is rather the other way around; expectations with regard to the original type are slightly deflected in order to free up the possible meanings of the building and connect them with ideas and stories that are perhaps entirely disconnected from pastoral connotations. Maybe the Woodland Cabin is actually a kind of small villa or a roofed terrace.

A similar exploration of archetypes characterizes the library and concert room in Gaasbeek. The project preserves an old milk factory as the facade and front section of a small hall that replaces an old industrial space. Like that space, the hall is as large as the older building and its maximum height does not exceed that of the original volume. Because the extension is partly dug into the hill behind and has a sloping roof, it appears similar in scale to the surrounding buildings. Only inside does the true size of the volume become apparent. Within this envelope, the essentially very simple shape of the plan generates a complicated and ambiguous spatial arrangement: the lowest beam of the exterior slope, which is connected to the front section, runs parallel to the hall, but the second beam, at the rear of the building, cuts into its volume and so becomes the lowest segment of the ceiling that climbs upward in a spiral towards the middle, a movement accentuated by the contrast between the white walls of the room and the brick pattern of the surrounding gallery. Because the plan is not squared, partly out of acoustic considerations, an irregular volume emerges; intentions of different kinds have transformed a limited set of elements into a complicated building.

This effect is enhanced by the impression that different levels of scale intermingle, each of them connected with a different programme or use. The hall incorporates elements of the house and even the room. The wall is lined with an uninterrupted yet by no means monumental bookcase, and the furniture recalls the traditional living or dining room. A similar discontinuity in scale is apparent in the windows. From the inside they appear as monumental incisions in the volume of the hall (except the lowest window, they all give out onto trees and the sky), but from the outside, to those who climb the slope, they frame the interior as an almost domestic space. The pattern of the Lantern Tower at the Concertgebouw in Bruges, which envelopes the upward spiral of the audience gallery, is repeated here but is organised around a sharper antithesis: the encircling gallery is now an exterior space shaping the roof of the interior. A walk to the upper terrace literally crowns the hall. As a result, the building interweaves two very different registers, that of the farm or barn, built of bricks and with whitewashed walls, and that of the almost royal walk and observatory. This hybridity is also apparent when hand-shaped bricks are not only used to cover the walls, but also as an inlay cast into the underside of the slopes, as a kind of pastoral – yet meticulously designed – mosaic. The apparent materiality and weight of the bricks does much to remove the potential predominance of tectonics and sculpturality, in favour of a multiple and composite space made of shimmering surfaces.

If the projects hitherto discussed test the relationship between type and conglomerate through the composite nature of their form (the High Views, the Colombier and the Cabin) or the exploration of an existing or imagined type (the Cabin, again, and the Former Dairy), Robbrecht en Daem's new office building achieves the same purpose by decomposing an iconic building. The shed that houses the office immediately recalls the innumerable similar sheds scattered around the city, the suburbs and the countryside: simple, largely empty constructions of laminated beams housing a small office overlooking the shop-floor. The operation of decomposition is actually quite simple: by removing large parts of the roof and exterior walls, one layer of the separation between inside and outside has disappeared. The glazed wall between the new office spaces and the shop-floor becomes a new facade overlooking a large covered courtyard. By domesticating the unhomely but also iconic structure, whose beams now look like the skeleton of a gigantic tent, this relatively large building, which is moreover not a housing project, probably thematizes the elementary experience of shelter, an effect only enhanced by the high-rises overlooking the plot, more than the Woodland Cabin does.

The image of the tent already came up in connection with the Concertgebouw; just as in Gaasbeek the bricks cover the walls as well as the ceiling, the entire building is covered in a heavy stone cloak or shield made from ceramic tiles whose red colour makes reference to the city's roofs. The sense that the façade is indeed a piece of drapery is reinforced by the scale-like and visibly a-tectonic tiles, the roof's separation from the ground by a strip of colourful panelling, and, inside, by the presence of the heavy concrete structure carrying the burden of the cloak. Despite its apparent weight, this cloak or skin adapts itself to its surroundings and clings, where necessary or possible, to the body it hides. In fact, the synergy between the overall shape, the heavy bare concrete structure and slopes in the interior spaces surrounding the auditorium, and the core of the building, the peculiar yet extremely successful concert hall, generates a sense of temporariness. The entire building provides ample space for wandering, alone or in small groups. The sporadic coloured surfaces one encounters in the interior appear like fragments of an ongoing decoration campaign, an effect much enhanced by the precise composition of the palette and its at once playful and intense application in specific zones. Artistic interventions, like Peter Verhelst's text that runs along the backs of the auditorium seats and the sound collage of Edgard Varèse's *Poème électronique* and Dirk Braeckman's photo in the foyer seem as easily installed as removed. At the same time, the programme is accommodated as precisely as possible within the parameters of the brief. Flexibility in use has been achieved not by designing a number of adaptable spaces but by giving the single auditorium a shape that uniquely manages to combine the acoustic requirements for symphony and opera while still allowing an intimate engagement between the audience of up to 1300 and the performers, with the distance between audience and podium never exceeding thirty metres. But in the auditorium too, the gaze is allowed to wander upward to two light shafts pouring their light over the interior with its coloured plaster grooves, recalling (at least to an ever diminishing part of the audience) those moments when the tedium of sitting through mass was relieved by studying the stained-glass windows of the church.

The ongoing dialogue between permanence and temporariness, determination and vagueness provoked in the building, just as in the Woodland Cabin, Gaasbeek or the architects' office, has much in common with the domestic interior. The interiority of the building gives away how intimately Robbrecht en Daem engaged with the programme – this is a world the architects share with the musicians and their audience, a private and indeed precious universe. From the interior, through the many windows that offer views of the roof, this preciousness spills over onto the tiles covering the building, and from there to the quite spectacular views of the city that one discovers while wandering through the Concertgebouw's interior. The building takes full advantage of its proximity to the centre, enhanced by the height of its location and the relatively low buildings between it and the two nearest medieval towers. From its freestanding position, the Concertgebouw reveals the city and strips it of its paraphernalia. Its interior offers a viewpoint to look Bruges straight in the face: the balance between permanence and temporariness established within the body of the building manages to bring out the city's beauty before it becomes picturesque. The importance of the Concertgebouw's interior as a framing device for the view of Bruges becomes all the clearer when one steps onto the roof terrace of the Lantern Tower, where the big planes of the windows in the interior give way to a panorama intersected by the vertical bars. With its uninterrupted view of the city's 20th-century suburbs to the north and west seamlessly evolving into its iconic image, the roof terrace suddenly treats the visitor as if they were standing on a tower like the Belfry, the Cathedral or the Church of Our Lady, the monuments which the Concertgebouw inevitably engages by dint of its scale and situation. But if the historical towers are three attempts to give unique and perfect expression to religious and civil notions, the roof terrace of the Concertgebouw is part of a building that assembles a plurality of experiences and references into an indefinite whole. That is why it stands comparison with the much smaller High Views, built on places with literally less historical significance and accommodating a much simpler programme: they all lead the beholder to the end of trajectory, without charging that trajectory with a univocal or dramatic meaning.

Type and Body

The architects have compared the Concertgebouw with a recumbent body. This metaphor reveals much about the building's relations with the historical towers. The medieval monuments are standing bodies, and as such also columns, beacons, triumphal pillars or totems. The visibility, proportion, cohesion or tectonics that are essential to these towers are much less prominent in the recumbent body, which is characterized rather by its pose, its place and maybe even the path that was followed or the work that was done just before it lay down. The shift in meaning between the standing and lying figures pertains to the role and meaning of the body in all these projects. Classicist architectural theory, expressed in the previously cited passages from Manetti and Le Corbusier, not only postulates the fundamental unity of architecture, but grounds this unity in an unbreakable bond between man and building, based on the parentage between architecture and the body. By incorporating systems of proportion, establishing an organic unity, or referring to parts like the foot or the head, architecture literally incorporates the entity that adheres most closely to man. This bond guarantees the ability of architecture to signify and be understood without additional elucidation. In these projects by Robbrecht en Daem too, the body is often prominent, but not as the substratum uniting all aspects of design into one coherent system. The module employed by the office, the Loue (a sequence starting with the numbers 3, 5 and 7, which are multiplied with each other to produce 9, 15, 21, 25, 35, 49 and finally 105, the key number), has nothing to do with human proportions. To Robbrecht en Daem, the body is the aforementioned shape, a presence acting less as the security underpinning a satisfying contract between architecture and its users than as a mobile and plural point of reference.

If these projects are anthropomorphic, the body referred to is elusive or even misshapen. Acting as pedestals for the peering heads by Franz West, the two cylindrical pavilions on Rubensplein are highly simplified versions of a torso without hands or feet. As stacks of stones emerging from a scrambled surface, devoid of articulations such as plinths or cornices, they bear no trace of the kind of architectural order that might recall the human body. Such an architectural order is present in the Woodland Cabin, with its clear tripartite construction of platform, walls and roof. Moreover, as indicated, the building proffers a return to the origin of architecture, inevitably evoking the natural inception of building, the shelter that primitive man constructed in imitation of the animals' nests. Countless authors since Vitruvius have stressed that architecture only emerges subsequently, when the primitive and almost thoughtless imitation of animals is regulated by the proportion and arrangement of the human body; the 15th-century author Filarete associated the birth of architecture with the first building in Adam's image. But when the Woodland Cabin leaves the realm of nests and caves behind, it does not do so by incorporating a well-proportioned or even legible human figure, but the strange shape (copulating bodies or Siamese twins?) we saw appearing in the preliminary drawings and paintings.

This distorted trajectory from nest to architecture also takes place in the Colombier, but in the opposite direction. A dovecote generally only becomes architecture when enough money and energy is available to assign even this part of a farmhouse, villa or castle to a designer, or – as was the case here – when landmarks are needed in a park. This situation establishes a kind of parentage between the Cabin and the Colombier. If the hut refers to the human imitation of the bird's nest, the pigeons of Dorst are invited to nestle in architecture, something they are apparently quite reluctant to do. Unlike the Cabin, however, this building, destined for people only as an object to watch or circle, clearly recalls a basic architectural order. Its construction allows us to discern three zones, the lowest section, of six parallel brick layers, then a second zone where the layers are slanted, and finally the crown, where the volume narrows and the layers are again arranged in parallel. This tripartite division is like the base, shaft and capital of the column, and by analogy the human body. But in this project, too, the analogy gets a peculiar twist. The Colombier is still a pile of stones and not a clean shape; the drawings of Paul Robbrecht seem to show a mummy rather than a body, suggesting that the little building, a house for animals at the outer limits of architecture, enwraps an imprisoned entity.

A similar form of anthropomorphism, where the body is not the basis of a design system but quite literally the content of the project, characterizes the High Views. The architects themselves associate these little towers with a detail of a painting by Hieronymus Bosch, where a human being seems to be swallowed by a tree. Here too, the relation of the reference to the project is far from univocal. It touches upon the analogy between body and tree, with its implication of transformation (bodies become trees, or vice versa, through an often violent process of growth, as when

Apollo touches Daphne). The body in the tree also points towards the meeting of man and nature, and thereby of artefact and landscape, important themes in two buildings situated on the border between habitation and a landscape park. But the one-to-one relationship between body and trunk suggested by the painting is transformed into a composition of stairs, lattices and moving figures. As in the projects whose single form consists of many stones, like the Colombier, in the High Views the many bodies constituting the building never become one but remain distinct, individually, in series or in multitudes. In fact, the High Views are cages for one or several guests, separating them not only from the landscape but also from their peers; their composite nature almost reproduces the social configurations they aim to establish, possibly more than anything else. It is certainly possible to read the Woodland Cabin and the Colombier, but also the Concertgebouw and the architects' office in a similar way, if only because they use latticework to define spaces and separations. More essential, however, is to consider what these projects do as cages: to keep wandering bodies in place, even by persuasion, and then to leave them to their own devices.

References
— The cited oration by Gianozzo Manetti can be found in Christine Smith and Joseph F. O'Connor, Building the Kingdom. Gianozzo Manetti on the material and spiritual edifice. Tempe, ACMRS, 2006.
— On the historical association of marble floors with the sea, sea Fabio Barry, "Walking on water: cosmic floors in Antiquity and the Middle Age", Art Bulletin 89 (2007), pp. 627-656.
— The paragraphs on the Concertgebouw are based on Maarten Delbeke, "Myth versus History. The Concert Hall in Bruges by Robbrecht and Daem Architects," Journal of Architecture 11 (2006), pp. 359-373.

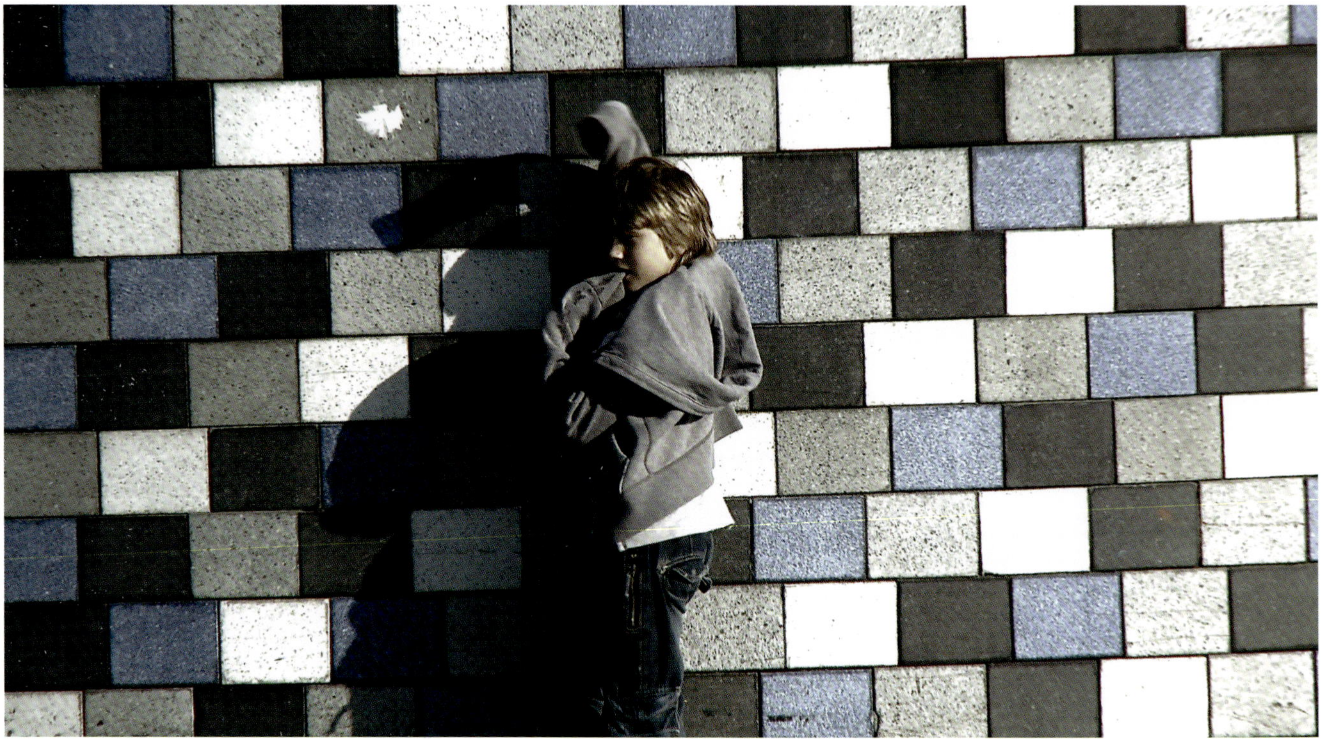

Projects

Initiatief '86
Ghent
1986

Thanks to the exhibitions 'Chambres d'Amis' and 'Initiatief '86', in the summer of 1986 Ghent was transformed into an international centre of contemporary art. For 'Initiatief '86', Robbrecht en Daem created a space specifically to exhibit the work of René Heyvaert. A corridor in St.-Pietersabdij was divided into three compartments that kept their distance from the existing architecture.

This spatial modification laid the foundations for their later exhibition designs.

address: St.-Pietersabdij, Ghent
program: Temporary exhibition space
curator: Kaspar König
status: Dismounted
dates: 1986

Mys House
Oudenaarde
1983-1993

The renovation of the Mys residence in Oudenaarde is not just a simple adaptation of a historical building to the new requirements of the residents. It should more accurately be viewed as a collection of different local interventions in an 18th century structure that has already been touched by a complex history of consecutive renovations. In addition to a new front door, cut out of the historical portal, Robbrecht en Daem's designs include a library tower, a garden shed with a slanting roof, a recess in the wall on the garden side, and a fully glass *loggia* above the *porte cochère* in the façade that offers the residents a lookout over the surroundings.

address: Oudenaarde
programm: Refurbishment of a family house
client: Christian & Martine Mys
assistants: Christian Kiekens, Marleen Dilissen, Wim Cuyvers
stability: BAS
artists: Juan Muñoz, Cristina Iglesias, Lili Dujouri, Thierry Decordier, Jan Vercruysse
status: Completed
dates: 1983-1992

Penthouse Meert
Brussels
1989-1991

A penthouse was built on top of an industrial building with an art nouveau facade. This glass pavilion forms a still-life on the roof together with the technical installations enclosed inside a grating, and Isa Genzken's work of art *Camera*. The frame of the work of art emphasises the role the flat plays as an observatory overlooking the town.

address: Rue du Canal, Brussels
program: Penthouse
client: Greta Meert
assistants: Hugo Vanneste
stability: BAS, Dirk Jaspaert
artist: Isa Genzken
status: Completed
dates: 1989 (project) 1991 (execution)

Aue Pavilions
Kassel, Germany
1992-1994

The Aue pavilions were originally built for the Documenta IX exhibition in Kassel in 1992. Two years later they were moved to the Dutch town of Almere, where they were used as an art centre for temporary exhibitions. The basic idea for these pavilions comes from the combination of painting and nature. Painting returns to its origins, the landscape, and enters into confrontation with it. The pavilions are on poles so as not to harm the classified Aue Park and because they definitely do not want to be rooted in the ground. The building can be expanded by the addition of more pavilions.

address: Friedrichs-Aue, Kassel, Germany and Almere, the Netherlands
program: Pavilions for temporary exhibitions
client: Documenta Gmbh, and the City of Almere
assistants: Wim Cuyvers, Hugo Vanneste, Sofie Delaere, Brigitte D'Hoore
stability: Lamparter Stahlbau, Bauamt Kassel
status: Dismounted and reconstructed
dates: 1992 (project) 1992-1994 (execution)

Kanaalhuizen
Ghent
1993-1997

The 19th century historical mansions of the Coupure in Ghent form the backdrop for the Kanaalhuizen, two stately apartment buildings with classical façades. The two volumes complete the corner of a building block and stand perpendicular to each other, slightly angled vis-à-vis the street. They are connected by a fine cornice that evolves into a perforated awning between the two buildings, over the entranceway to the interior area. The steel-enclosed window openings and the glass *loggias* give the façade rhythm, depth and a layered appearance, reflecting the surroundings with its sycamores and *belle époque* architecture.

address: Coupure Rechts, Ghent
programm: Luxury appartments and office spaces
assistents: Hugo Vanneste, Sofie Delaere
client: Canal Properties
stability: Bureau Gyselinck
services engineering: Bureau Stockman
landscape architecture: Wirtz International
status: completed
dates: 1993-1997

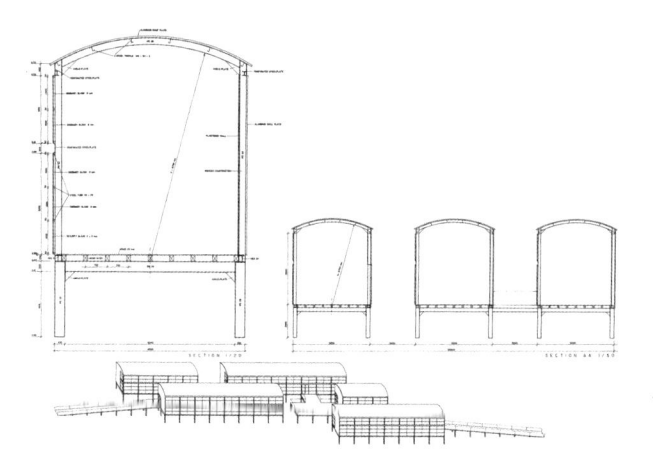

Katoen Natie
Antwerp
1992-2000

Richter Table 1992, Ligeti Bench 2002,
Messiaen Table 2009, Thulin Stool 2009

An extraordinary play of light is to be found in two of the former harbour warehouses that accommodate the Katoen Natie in Antwerp. In one of them, domes in alabaster and leaded glass function as new skylights – designed by the Spanish artist Cristina Iglesias – and on top of the other is a roof of wooden slats through which sunlight slips in many layers. A new four-storey building connects the former warehouses. The ensemble of old and new buildings contains offices, conference and reception rooms and a museum of Coptic textiles.

address: 33, Van Aerdstraat, Antwerp
program: Transformation of former harbour warehouses into offices and museum
client: Katoen Natie
assistants: Frank De Baere, Caroline Vanbiervliet (project architects), Aslı Cicek
stability: Arcade – Herman Mortelmans
techniques: Jan d'Hondt
artist: Cristina Iglesias
status: Completed
dates: 1992-1996 (fase 1) 1993-2000 (fase 2)

The Richter Table is a small writing table in walnut designed on the occasion of Gerhard Richter's 60th birthday. The Ligeti Bench, in veneered chipboard, was developed for the foyer of the Concertgebouw in Bruges. The Messiaen Table is a folding table in plywood, constructed for the 'Pacing through Architecture' exhibition. The Thulin Stool was designed for the foyer of the Cinematek in Brussels.

program: Furniture
client: Various
status: Completed

1. Thulin Stool, 2009
2. Messiaen Table 2009
3. Richter Table, 1992
4. Ligeti Bench, 2002

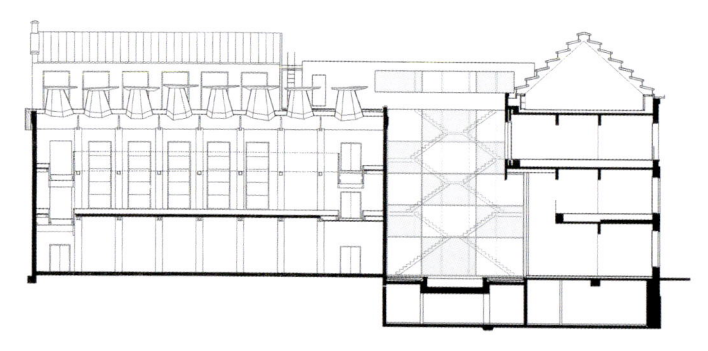

'The House Where it Always Rains'
Barcelona, Spain
1992

'The House Where it Always Rains' is a sculpture erected in Barcelona in 1992 on the occasion of the Olympic Games. Robbrecht en Daem designed a pavilion for five human figures with the sculptor Juan Muñoz. The cage is built of iron slats of varying thickness and is reminiscent of the Aue pavilions built in that same year.

artist: Juan Muñoz
address: Barceloneta, Barcelona, Spain
program: Work of art
execution: Studio Muñoz
status: Completed
dates: 1992 (execution)

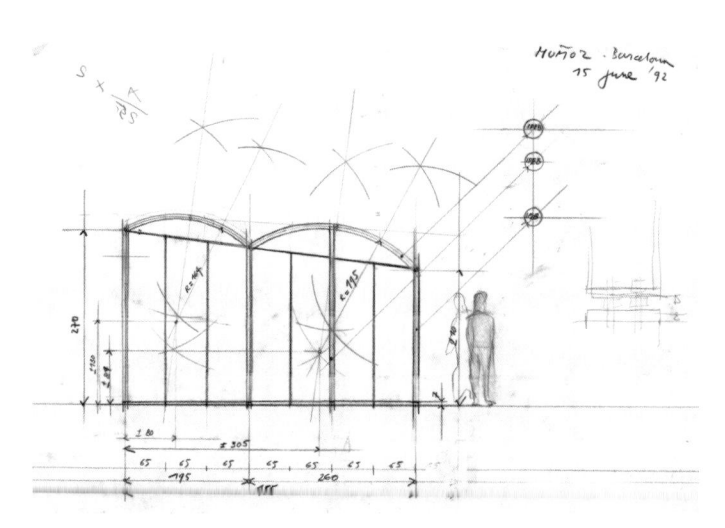

Korenmarkt and Emile Braunplein and surroundings, Ghent
1996-2012

The re-laying of the central squares in Ghent will be completed by 2011. This urban design includes the Korenmarkt and Emile Braunplein and arranges such major monuments as St.-Niklaaskerk, the Belfry and the Town Hall around it. A small urban park provides a green between the historical buildings and is bordered by various facilities. A new Municipal Hall with duplicated roofs introduces a covered public space into the city centre and is a reminder of the former use of this part of the city.

architects: Robbrecht en Daem architecten, with Marie-José Van Hee architect in collaboration with Technum-Tractebel engineering
address: The city centre of Ghent
program: Construction of public squares and streets, including public transport and buildings
client: City of Ghent, TMVW, De Lijn
assistants: Wim Menten, Pieter Vanderhoydonck, Kathy Vermeeren, Arne Deruyter, Bert Callens, Gert Swolfs, Gert Jansseune, Katrien Cammers, Linde Everaerd, Petra Decouttere, Wim Walschap, Tom Broes, Trice Hofkens, Matthias Deboutte, Jan Baes
stability: BAS, Dirk Jaspaert
services engineering: Studiebureau R. Boydens
infrastructural engineering: Technum, Ingenieursbureau France
landscape architecture: Wirtz International
status: In progress
dates: 1996-2012 (project and execution)

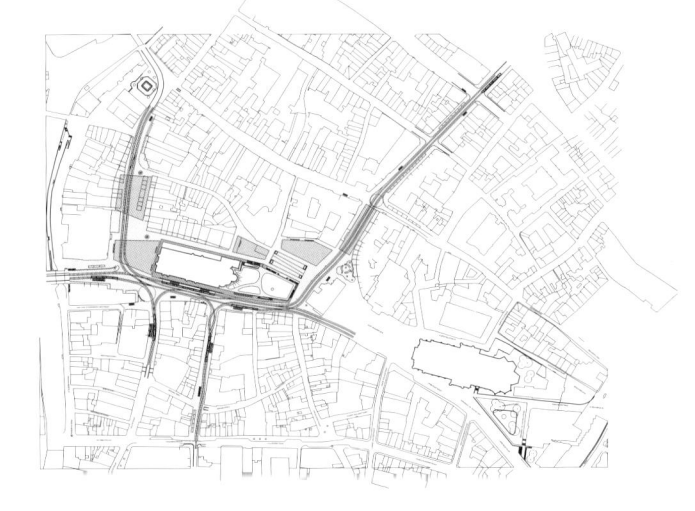

Extension of the Boijmans Van Beuningen Museum
Rotterdam, The Netherlands
1997-2003

The Boijmans Van Beuningen Museum in Rotterdam is a complex amalgam of sections all built at different times. This new building makes the museum into a single entity again. Green-tinted glass sheets introduce a rhythm into the facade that looks austere and elegant, but its layering also gives a hint of the complexity of the building. Inside, there is a striking link between Adrianus Van der Steur's 1935 brick building and the new one: old and new interlock without any brusque movements and turn the museum into a building that is both coherent and flexible.

address: 18-20, Museumpark, Rotterdam, The Netherlands
program: Interventions in the existing museum building and extensions with a new wing with exhibition halls, a library, offices and a storage space
client: Museum Boijmans Van Beuningen and Gemeente Rotterdam
assistants: Kristoffel Boghaert (project architect), Sofie Delaere, Brigitte D'Hoore, Catherine Fierens, Gilberte Claes, Francesca de Fonseca, Shin Hagiwara, Hugo Vanneste
project manager: PKB bouwadviseurs, Diemen-Amsterdam
construction consultant: Tuns + Horsting architecten, Rotterdam
stability: Corsmit, Rijswijk (Pim Peters)
installations: Huisman & Van Muijen, 's-Hertogenbosch
environmental engineer: Dorsserblessgraaf, Den Haag
glass consultant: GTC-Nederland, Delft
status: Completed
dates: 1997-1998 (project) 1999-2003 (execution)

Garden Pavilion
Vosselare
1997

The garden pavilion in Vosselare is the first in a series of small architectural objects. In Paul Robbrecht and Hilde Daem's practice, these small structures give rise to a reflection on their position as architects and the status of architecture as such. In connection with this project, Juan Muñoz wrote 'Estimado Amigo…'

program: Garden Pavilion
client: Bernard Filliers
stability: BAS, Dirk Jaspaert
artist: Juan Muñoz
status: Not executed
dates: 1997

Leopold De Waelplaats
Antwerp
1997-1999

The design for the square reconciles two aspects: on the one hand the heavy traffic is dealt with by two roundabouts, one at each end, and on the other a public forecourt is laid out for the Museum of Fine Art. Several works of art have been installed on the square: recovered fragments of the Loos monument by Auguste Rodin, a bench designed by Ann Demeulemeester and a fountain by Cristina Iglesias. This fountain forms the heart of the forecourt, gives the place depth and imposes a temporal rhythm.

architects: Robbrecht en Daem architecten and Marie-José Van Hee architect
address: Leopold De Waelplaats, Antwerp
program: Public square
client: City of Antwerp
assistants: Tania Vandenbussche
stability: BAS, Dirk Jaspaert
artists: Cristina Iglesias, Ann Demeulemeester, Auguste Rodin
status: Completed
dates: 1997-1998 (project) 1998-1999 (execution)

Concertgebouw Brugge
Bruges
1998-2003

On 't Zand, an open urban space near the station in Bruges, Robbrecht en Daem built a concert hall for Bruges on the occasion of the Cultural Capital of Europe in 2002. Alongside the Halletoren, the Onze-Lieve-Vrouwkerk and St. Salvator's Cathedral, this 'Concertgebouw' has become a landmark when driving into the city. A uniform external cladding in terracotta tiles hangs like dignified drapery over the volumes of the concert hall, fly tower and Lantern Tower, and accentuates the monolithic mass of the building. The concert hall, with its 1300 seats, can be converted into a theatre for musical productions. The Lantern Tower contains a remarkable chamber music hall where about 320 people can look down on the musicians on the floor or look out over the city from seating in a rising spiral.

address: 't Zand, Bruges
program: Concert Hall
client: vzw Concertgebouw Brugge
assistants: Wim Walschap (project architect), Matthias Baeten, William Mann, Pieter Vandendries, Piet Crevits, Brigitte D'Hoore, Sofie Delaere, Els Claessens
stability: Studium NV
installations: Ingenium NV
theatre techniques: GCA Ingenieure, Germany Technics
acoustics: Arup Acoustics, United Kingdom
landscape architecture: Wirtz International
urban surroundings: Lobelle Studiebureau
consultancy: Van Assche & Van Langenhove
building coordinator: Coördinatiebureau De Brock
control: Seco
status: Winning competition project, executed
dates: 1998-1999 (project) 1999-2003 (execution)

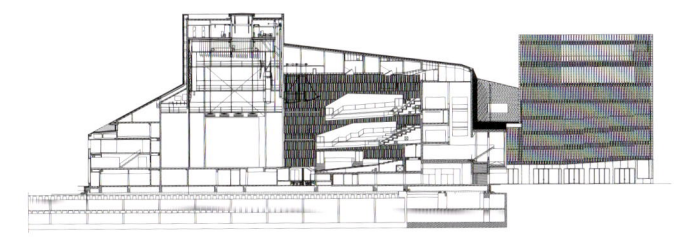

Felix City Archives
Antwerp
1999-2006

The Felix City Archives are housed in the 20,000 m². St. Felix Warehouse, an icon of historical harbour architecture in Antwerp. Concrete containers have been built on its six storeys for the conservation of documents from the city's archives. On the top floor, a new oak roof structure accommodates reading and study rooms around three large, well-lit light wells. Access to the building is via a semi-public internal street.

address: 30, Godefriduskaai, Antwerp
program: Renovation and transformation of a historical warehouse into city archives
client: City of Antwerp
assistants: Caroline Vanbiervliet, Frank De Baere (Project architects), Johannes Robbrecht, Shin Hagiwara, Katrien Cammers, Tinne Verwerft, Wouter Willems
city architect: Danielle Vandervloet
stability: Grontmij Vlaanderen
installations: Grontmij Vlaanderen
building coordinator: Grontmij Vlaanderen
status: Completed
dates: 1999-2000 (project) 2001-2006 (execution)

Lockremise
Sankt Gallen, Switzerland
1999-2000

A former repair workshop for locomotives is fitted out for the exhibition of a private art collection. Within the horseshoe shape of this hall, a succession of enclosed and open spaces is laid out, with walls as individual separate elements.

address: 7, Grünbergstrasse, Sankt Gallen, Switzerland
program: Exhibition space
client: Sammlung Hauser und Wirth
executive architect: Hans-Reudi Wirth
status: Dismounted
dates: 1999-2000

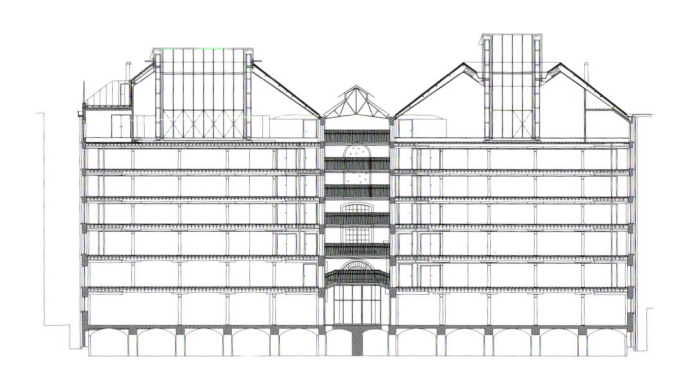

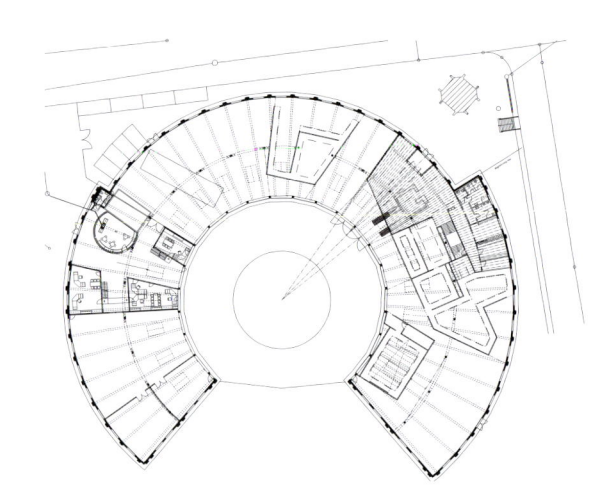

Rubensplein
Knokke
1999-2003

Rubensplein is slightly concave, which gives it a similarity to a skating ramp. The two long benches are screened off with a wall glass. People sitting there can look at the sea. The floor is a mosaic of maritime colours: blue, grey-green and white. The two small buildings at the entrances to the underground car park are clad with the same motif, and the Austrian artist Franz West has placed five-metre-high heads on top: they are primal and somewhat grotesque and are a playful counterpoint to the square itself.

address: Rubensplein, Knokke
program: Public square
client: Gemeentebestuur Knokke-Heist
assistants: Tania Vandenbussche
artist: Franz West
executive architects: Groep Planning (SUM project)
control: Seco, Brussels
status: Completed
dates: December 1999 (project)
2001-2003 (execution)

Conversion of a Former Dairy
Gaasbeek
2001-2004

A dairy at the foot of the historical castle of Gaasbeek has been converted into a guest house for musicians, with a concert hall. The late nineteenth-century front building was transformed into the guest quarters; the concert hall replaces the original small factory shed but adheres to its original outline. The volume is dug deep into a slope into which an open ramp has been cut which then bends over the hall and climbs upwards like a ziggurat and forms the roof of the volume. The vertical and horizontal walls of this construction are clad inside and out with hand-shaped brick. The space is lit by large openings that offer a view in from the ramp.

address: Gaasbeek
program: Conversion of a former dairy into guest quarters for musicians with music room
client: De Eik
assistants: Els Claessens, David Schalenbourg
stability: BAS, Dirk Jaspaert
acoustics: Kahle Acoustics, Brussels
landscape architecture: Eric Dhont
status: Completed
dates: 2000 (project)
2002-2004 (execution)

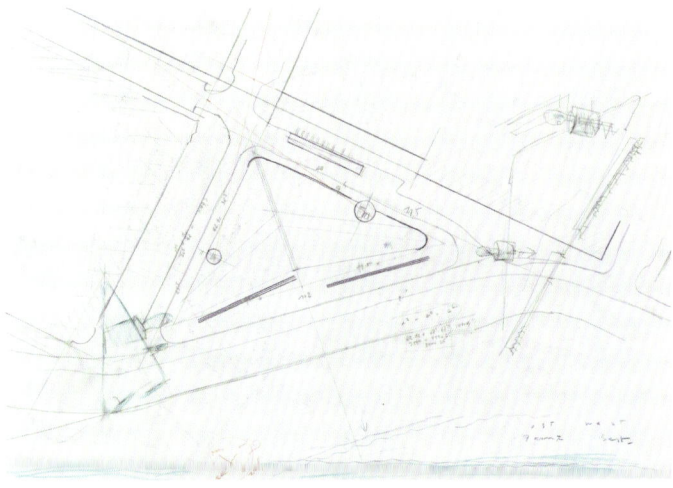

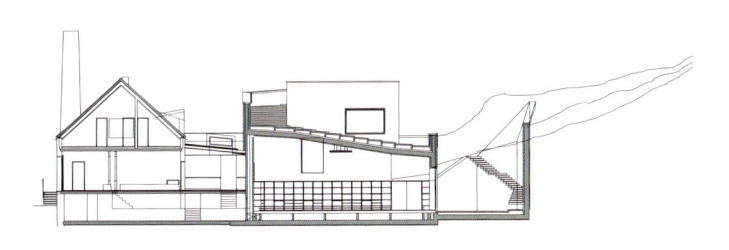

Woodland Cabin
Southern Flanders
2001-2002

A wooden walkway, which descends from a platform to the small valley behind a villa in Southern Flanders, leads to the Woodland Cabin, a distant relative of the igloo and the small buildings one comes across in the mountains throughout the world. On a platform next to a pond, wooden blocks have been stacked to form a two-lobed space that is closed off with a glass wall and door. Beams that fan out support a green roof from which emerges the chimney of the wood stove.

This shelter has a table and chairs and a bed that also serves as a cupboard.

address: Southern Flanders
program: Cabin
assistants: Catherine Fierens
landscape architecture: Herman Seghers
status: Completed
dates: 2001-2002

Garden Pavilion
Sint-Martens-Latem
2002-2004

This garden house with swimming pool is a two-storey wooden structure with an irregular floor plan. The load-bearing wooden beams form a pattern of adjoining triangles. A sculptural hearth element runs up through the volume as a solid supporting pillar. On the ground floor there are changing rooms, a sauna and a hammam, and upstairs a flat with kitchen.

The roof is fitted out as a terrace amidst the tree-tops.

address: Sint-Martens-Latem
program: Garden pavilion with swimming pool
client: Mr. and Mrs. Lannoo-Van Wanseele
assistants: Sofie Delaere (project architect), Gert Jansseune
stability: BAS, Dirk Jaspaert
status: Completed
dates: 2002-2004 (project)
2004 (execution)

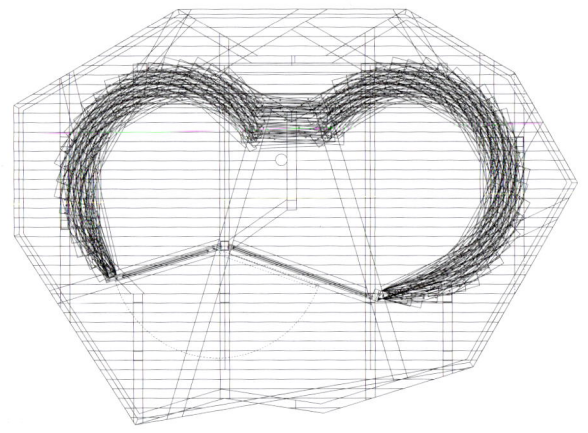

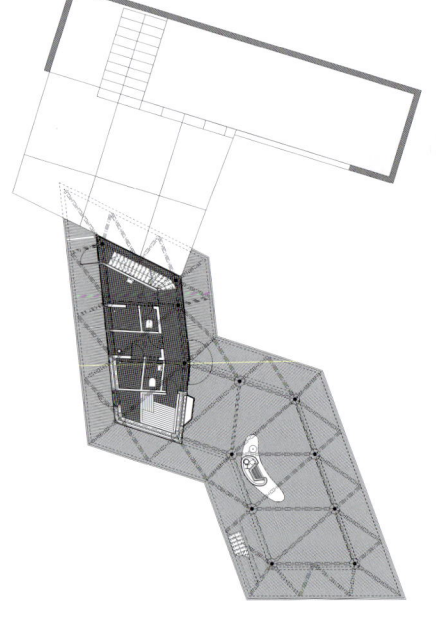

Cinematek
Brussels
2003-2009

Two new projection rooms have been excavated (for the Royal Belgian Film Archives) underneath Victor Horta's Centre for Fine Arts. This makes it possible for the 'Salles des Arts Décoratifs' to be restored, as provided for in the masterplan for the restoration of the building. The collection of film apparatus is rehoused in a Wunderkammer, which stands detached in the room. Rooms for new digital image production were also created.

address: 9, rue Baron Hortastraat, Brussels
program: Architecture, interior architecture of the projection rooms and the film museum
scenography: In collaboration with Voet Theuns architecten
restoration: Barbara Van Der Wee Architects
client: Royal Film Archives of Belgium
assistants: Myriam Rohde, Aslı Cicek, Pieter Vanderhoydonck, Petra Decouttere, Kris Van Buynder
stability: Ney and Partners
installations: Ingenium
acoustics: Mathys Acoustical Adviser, Jan Mathys
production of furniture: Martela, Korhonen (Finland)
status: Completed
dates: 2003 (project) 2009 (execution)

Colombier
Dorst, The Netherlands
2003-2004

The Colombier (dovecote) in the forestry area in Dorst stands in a clearing in the wood, next to a stream in which it is reflected. The way the stones are stacked leaves edges and angles on which the birds can sit. There are occasional gaps too, where a stone has been left out so that the birds can get inside to sit on bars. The dovecote is built in blocks of Pietra di Vicenza, a calcareous sandstone from Italy.

address: Boswachterij Dorst, Breda, The Netherlands
program: Colombier
client: Staatsbosbeheer Nederland
assistants: Tinne Verwerft, Katrien Cammers
status: Completed
dates: 2003 (project) 2004 (execution)

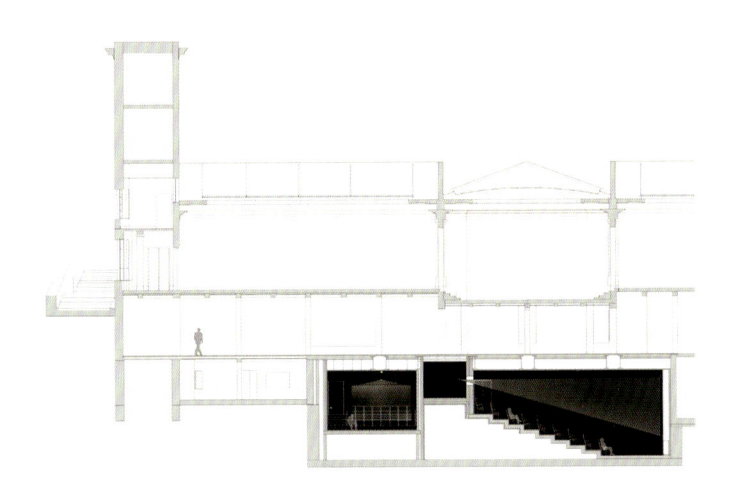

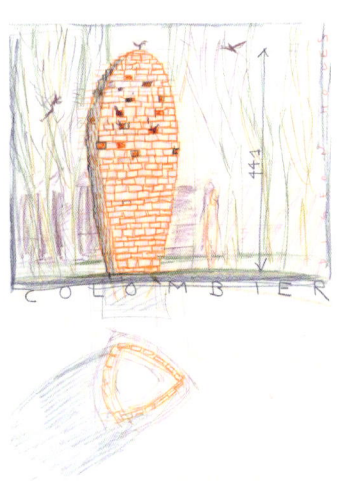

De Kloef
Ronse
2003-2004

De Kloef is a large undeveloped site within the urban fabric of Ronse, next to the heart of the city. Ronse is lacking a city park that can also play an important role on a regional level. A new green lung for a densely populated centre forms a connection between the existing inner city on the one hand and the beautiful surrounding landscape on the other. A cut out groove links the park to the main square of Ronse. Different types of residences will be built in the park itself geared to a varied target public: patio residences on the north side, terraced houses with a garden along the cut out groove, apartment residences connected like a band along the east side and finally, detached residences for the liberal professions.

address: Ronse
program: Urban redevelopment design including park, housing, recreation facilities and hotel
client: Flemish Government
assistants: Tinne Verwerft (project architect), Johannes Robbrecht, Liesbet Vandenbussche, David Schalenbourg
status: Completed (masterplan being executed)
dates: 2003-2004

Whitechapel Art Gallery
London, United Kingdom
2003-2009

The Whitechapel Art Gallery was expanded to incorporate the former Passmore Edwards Library next door. The two classified buildings are joined together, but each retains its own character. This results in a duality of architectural style, between international appeal and local orientation, and between gallery (short visits) and library (long visits). The program includes two large exhibition rooms and several smaller connecting rooms, archive rooms and educational studios. The circulation in between and linkage of the two buildings are a crucial part of the design. The buildings are completely closed in. Skylights and internal open spaces provide daylight and orientation.

address: Whitechapel High Street, London
program: expansion of the Whitechapel Art Gallery
client: The Trustees Whitechapel Art Gallery
assistants: Kristoffel Boghaert (project architect), Wouter Willems, Tinne Verwerft, Gert Jansseune, Matthias Baeten, Miriam Koudmani, Leen Corthier, Chris Watson, Joerg Maier, Henning Roeschmann, Daniela Büter
executive architect: Witherford Watson Mann Architects
stability: Price&Myers
services: Max Fordham LLP
conservation: Richard Griffiths Architects
project manager: Mott MacDonald
quantity surveyor: Davis Langdon
external lightning: Jason Bruges Studio
artist: Rodney Graham
control: HCD Group, London (fire engineers)
status: Completed
dates: 2003 (competition) 2004-2007 (project) 2007-2009 (execution)

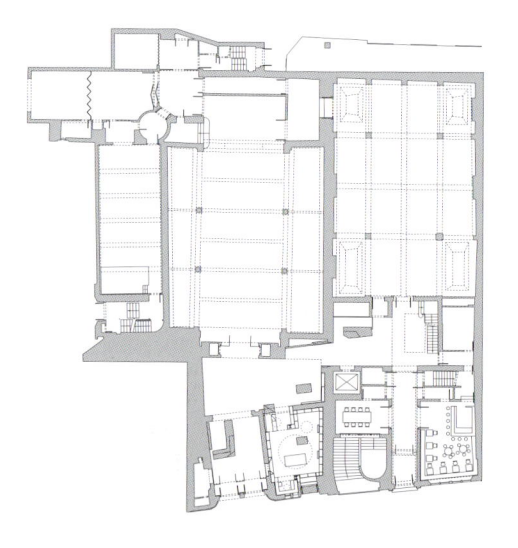

Webber Building
Brussels
2004-

The biggest challenge presented by this well situated but narrow corner plot is to design light and spacious flats without giving up the sense of intimacy. The commercial space on the ground floor has been made as open as possible to keep the transition from public to private space as gentle as it can be. The glazed facade is covered by a woven metal structure that aims for a balance between the outward view and security, between straight and curved lines, and forms a visual link between the living rooms and their outdoor areas. The 'hard' structure in steel and glass is complemented by 'warm' wooden floors and ceilings.

address: 5, Quai aux Barques, Brussels
program: 9 appartments with commercial ground floor
client: Mr. and Mrs. S. Webber
assistants: Bert Haerynck (project architect), Petra Decouttere, Suzanne Desmet and Miriam Rohde
stability: BAS, Dirk Jaspaert
installations: Henk Pijpaert Engineering
acoustics: Daidalos-Peutz
status: In progress
dates: 2004- (project)

Office Robbrecht en Daem architecten, M.-J. Van Hee Architect, Ghent
2005-2007

In an impoverished part of Ghent, against the background of nearby blocks of high-rise flats, Robbrecht en Daem have converted an existing timber yard into new architectural studios. The roof of the shed, built by the wood construction company De Coene in the early seventies, has been partly dismantled. The workfloor has become an outdoor space that will accommodate an arboretum, a swimming pool and a large open area for performances and exhibitions. The generous office spaces, primarily made in wood, are situated under the beams to one side, overlooking the yard.

address: 64, Lieremanstraat, Ghent
program: Conversion of a former wood storage into an architect office
client: Paul Robbrecht and Hilde Daem
assistants: Bert Haerynck (project architect)
stability: BAS, Dirk Jaspaert
status: Completed
dates: 2005-2007

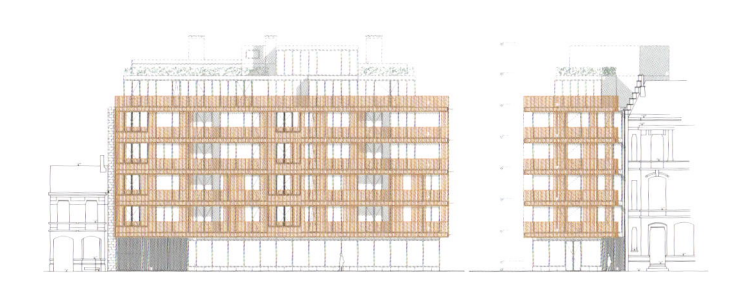

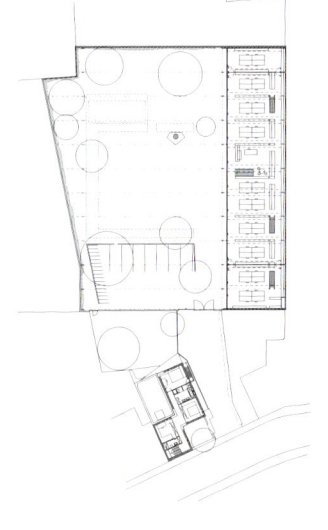

Shopping Mall Sint–Janspoort
Kortrijk
2005-2009

The new shopping centre at Sint-Janspoort covers a whole block in the centre of Kortrijk. With its interiorised street pattern and monumental atrium – the 'garden of light' – this shopping centre forms a diagonal link between Steenpoort and Veemarkt. The tower closes off one end of the Romeinselaan. The volumetry of the block, which contains offices and homes as well as shops, matches the scale of the surrounding buildings.

address: Wijngaardstraat, Sionstraat, Steenpoort, Kleine Sint-Jansstraat, Veemarkt, Kortrijk
program: Shopping centre, parking, appartments
client: Sint-Janspoort NV, Foruminvest Group
assistants: Tom De Moor, Suzanne Desmet, Luc Beckstedde, Griet Ollivier, Mo Vandenberghe, Kristof Keerman, Cliff Reid, Haike Apelt, Wim Walschap, Petra Decouttere, Kris Van Buynder
stability: THV Technum-TDE
acoustics: THV Technum-TDE
status: In progress
dates: 2005-2009

Municipal Archives
Brussels
2004-

The complex of buildings that houses the municipal archives includes the former Jules Waucquez warehouses.
A sizeable new building houses a climate-controlled storage space and makes it easier to read the whole. The new facades are in relief masonry on which the words 'Document' and 'Monument' can be read.

address: Rue des Tanneurs, Huidevettersstraat, Brussels
program: Archives and museum deposits with reading room
client: City of Brussels
assistants: Frédéric De Vylder, Bert Haerynck, Greg Geertsen, Charlotte Pattyn
stability: Bureau d'études Greisch
installations: Bureau d'études Greisch
status: In progress
dates: 2006- (project)

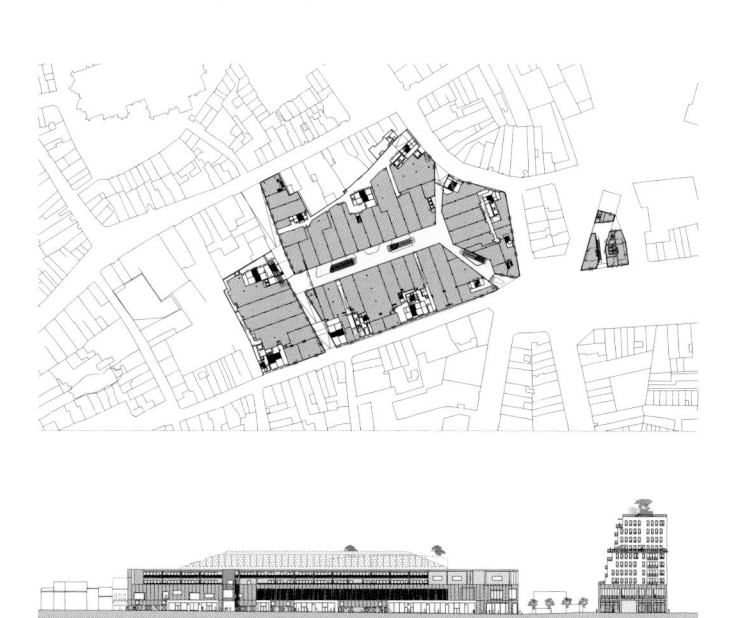

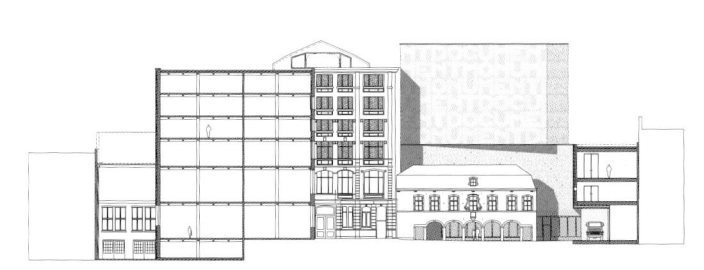

High Views
Lincoln and Boston, United Kingdom
2004-2007

The High Views are two observation towers along a cycling route between Lincoln and Boston, 60 km apart. They mark a place to rest on the banks of the River Witham where one can look out over a landscape that is very varied in its use. The design of the towers is in part based on the churches of the two towns. The meandering vault of Lincoln Cathedral inspired the observation tower in Boston. The stubby parish church of Boston gave rise to the design in Lincoln. Both towers are clad in wooden slats, enhanced by a colour code derived from the colours of the local birds.

address: Lincoln, Boston, United Kingdom
program: Observation towers
client: Sustrans
assistants: Wim Walschap, Wouter Willems
status: Completed
dates: 2004-2007

Le Chai à Pomerol
Pomerol, France
2007-

The storehouse for wine barrels, the 'Chai à barriques', is entirely underground and is the heart of the building. This reduces the overall height of the building, which keeps its impact on the surroundings to a minimum. Wine production is carried on in the 'Cuvier' on the ground floor, a functional area spanned by a vault of inclined roof planes. Light enters through windows at the corners. A separate tower houses a reception area, a small office and the vertical transport system for the barrels. The roof vault of the 'Cuvier' links up with this volume. This creates a covered outdoor area between them where grapes can be sorted at harvest time.

address: Pomerol, France
program: Winery
client: Mr and Mrs Thienpont
assistants: Kobe Van Praet, Caroline Vanbiervliet
stability: BAS, Dirk Jaspaert
building coordinator: Didier Lamouroux
status: In progress
dates: 2007-2008 (project)
2009- (execution)

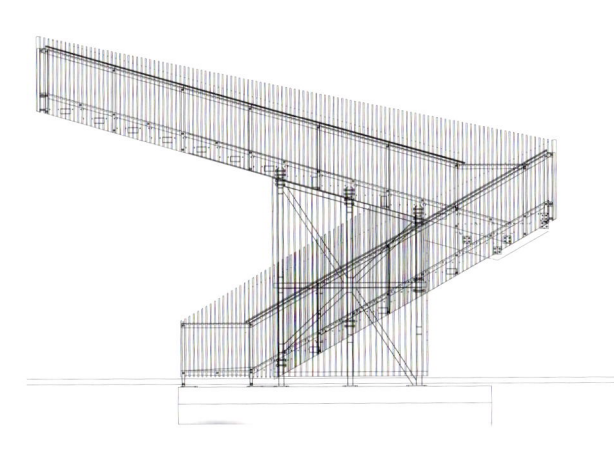

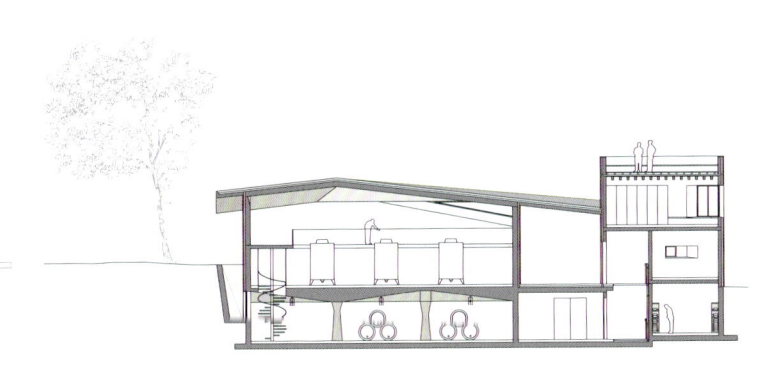

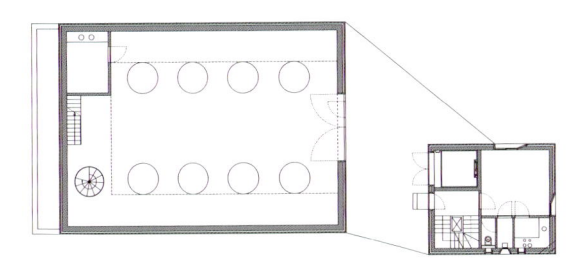

3 Leeuwen
Vilvoorde
2007

The site is located at the pivot of an office area and residential area and park. A green raised plinth connects these various areas and forms the basis for 3 apartment blocks of different heights. The highest volume is constructed against an existing apartment building. The second and third volume are systematically lower. Raising the apartment towers not only assures the privacy of the various residential units but the plinth is also intended, together with the gradual decrease in living volumes to make the link to the varying heights of the residential towers on the one hand and the scale of the surrounding buildings on the other.

address: Tweeleeuwenweg – Medialaan, Vilvoorde
programm: Housing
client: Investvil nv
assistants: Johannes Robbrecht (project architect), Petra Decouttere, Kristof Keerman
status: In progress
dates: 2007-

Renovation University Library
Ghent
2007-

The Central Library of Ghent University, designed by Henry Van de Velde in the 1930s, is being restored and geared to the current requirements of library use and conservation. To this end, an entrance will be built next to the HIKO, which is part of the original complex, that will generate a new sequence of spaces around the inner garden. This includes among other things a café/reading room, a canopied terrace (which Van de Velde had actually designed) and workspaces for handling digital data individually or in groups. Together with the necessary technical modifications, and making the observation room at the top of the tower fully accessible, this clear-up will restore the building's dignity as a place for study and reading.

address: 9, Rozier, Ghent
program: Restoration of University Library
client: University of Ghent
assistants: Gert Jansseune (project architect) Linde Everaerd, Katrien Cammers, Kristoffel Boghaert
stability: Bureau d'études Greisch
services engineers: VK Engineering
consultancy: Barbara Van Der Wee Architects, Baro, Daidalos-Peutz bouwfysisch ingenieursbureau, SumProject Architecture & Engeneering
status: In progress
dates: 2007-2009 (masterplan)

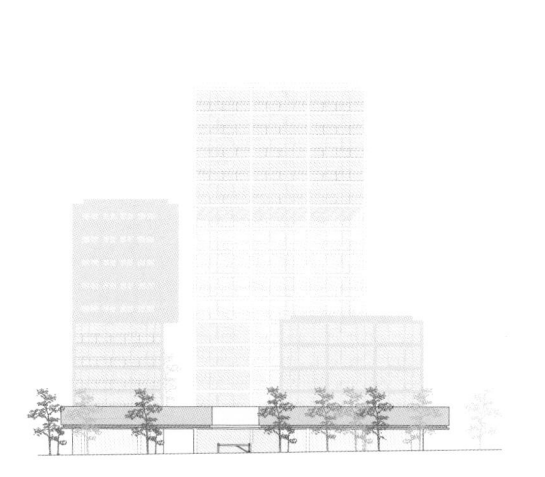

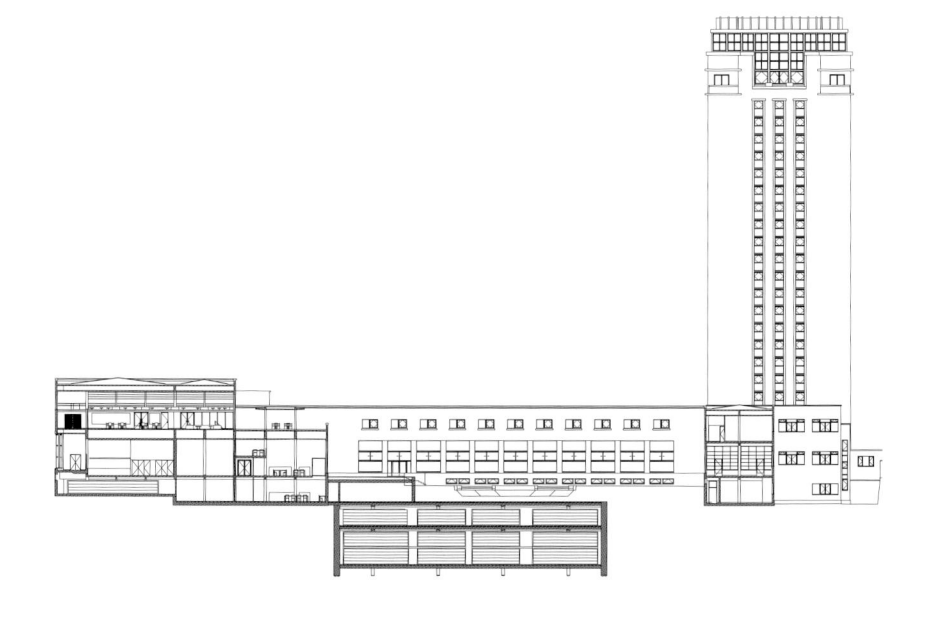

Headquarters Cera
Leuven
2008-

Three buildings were joined together to form the new head office for Cera in the old centre of Leuven, close to the town hall and cathedral. Two of the buildings are of great historical worth and were thoroughly renovated. A new corner building presents itself as a building of its time, but matches its historical neighbours well. The facade is composed like a 'claustra' in stone that filters the light and the view from the surroundings. Three inner gardens provide a breathing space for the staff, light for the exhibition area and greenery inside the street block.

architects: Robbrecht en Daem architecten, with AR-TE / STABO
address: Eikstraat, Boekhandelstraat, Muntstraat, Leuven
program: Headquarters of Cera, meeting rooms and offices
client: Cera
assistants: Sofie Deboutte, Kobe Van Praet
status: In progress
dates: 2008 (project)

Oosterweel Connection
Antwerp
2005-

With a new tunnel under the Schelde and a viaduct with cable bridge over the docks of the old harbour, the ten-kilometre long Oosterweel connection will close the ring around Antwerp. The Flemish government made a reference design and quality specifications that served as the starting point for negotiations between consortiums of contractors and designers. The contract was awarded to the Noriant consortium, whose design team consisted of Bureau d'Etudes Greisch, TV Ney-Poulissen, and Robbrecht en Daem. Robbrecht en Daem assumed responsibility for urban design, landscape design and architectural design of art works and buildings in a close collaboration with the other designers. At scales ranging from landscape design to detailing, the search was to achieve better living experiences and usability. The pillars of the cable bridge, of which there were five in the reference design, were brought back to only two, implanted next to the existing bridges to Antwerp North, thereby transforming the artwork from a barrier to a portal.

address: Antwerpen
programm: Landscape design, urban design, design of civil engineering for a highway link
client: THV Noriant DC
assistants: Marleen Goethals, Greg Geertsen, Charlotte Pattyn, Tom Broes, Trice Hofkens, Arne Deruyter, Bert Callens
status: Under study
dates: 2005-

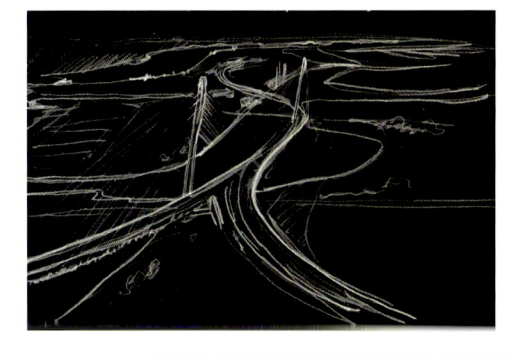

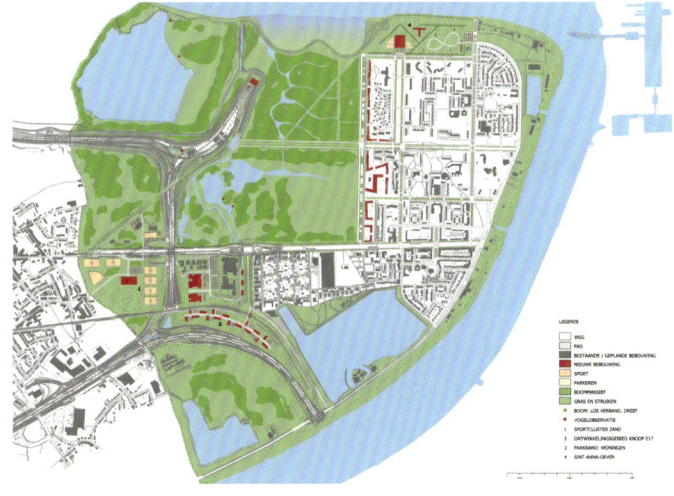

Zoo van Antwerpen
Antwerp
2006-

By purchasing and demolishing the surrounding houses, the Antwerp Zoo is able to expand its area by more than 10%. The aim of the masterplan is to establish the major spatial changes and broad lines of development for the whole of the zoo's eastern flank. The plan includes landscaping, animal houses for okapis, large and small apes, giraffes and elephants, and also a children's pavilion, a brasserie and an orangery. Certain buildings and activities will also be visible or accessible from the street.

address: 26, Koningin Astridplein, Antwerp
program: Masterplan for the Zoo including entrance, animal houses, children's pavilion, brasserie and shop
client: KMDA Koninklijke Maatschappij voor Dierkunde van Antwerpen
assistants: Johannes Robbrecht (project architect), Sofie Deboutte, Bert Haerynck
stability: BAS, Dirk Jaspaert
services: Henk Pijpaert, Engineering
landscape architecture: Ontwerpbureau Pauwels nv
status: In progress
dates: 2006 (competition) 2012 (execution)

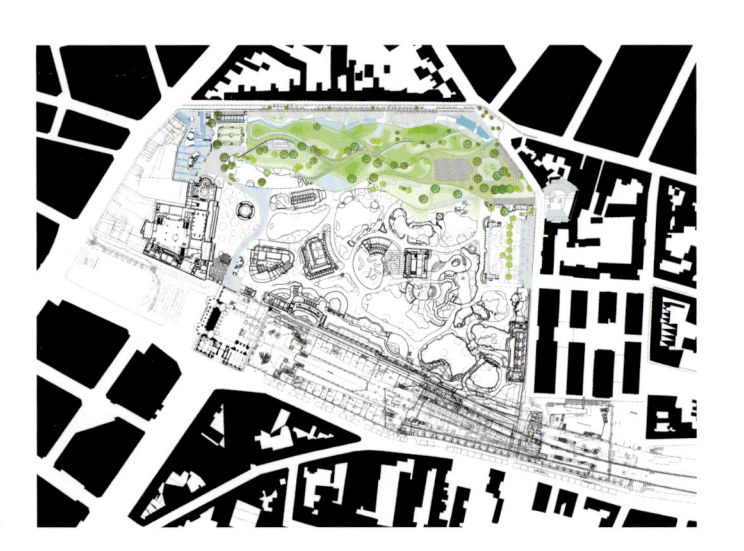

Robbrecht en Daem architecten

Paul Robbrecht (1950)

1974
Degree in architecture
1980
Member of the Centro Palladio in Vicenza, Italy
1978-1992
Lecturer of architectural criticism at KASK Gent
1992-2008
Lecturer of architectural design at HSLI Gent
1997-1998
Lecturer of architectural design at AA School, London
1999-2008
Professor at UGent, TW and A&S department

Hilde Daem (1950)

1975
Degree in architecture and graphic art
2000-2007
Chairman of the Welstandscommissie, Antwerpen

Since 2002 Johannes Robbrecht (1977) joined Robbrecht en Daem architecten

www.robbrechtendaem.com

Selected Prizes and Distinctions

1978
1st prize Godecharle competition for Architecture
1979
1st prize Grand Prize of Rome for Architecture
1994
Premio Zerynthia Dialoghi tra Arte e Architettura
1996
Commercial building of the year: Katoen Natie, Antwerp
1997
Flemish Culture Award for Architecture
1998
1st prize competition design for Concertgebouw in Bruges
2001
Culture award of the Catholic University of Leuven
2001
Awards of Belgian Architecture
2002
Award for the Ligeti Bench, Interieur '02, Kortrijk
2003
Selected for the Premi Mies van der Rohe 2003
2004
1st prize competition design Whitechapel Art Gallery, London
2005
Architecture prize for the Rubensplein, Knokke
2006
1st prize competition design Brussels City Archives
2007
1st prize competition design Masterplan Zoo van Antwerpen
2007
1st prize competition design University Library, Ghent
2007
Renoscripto renovation award for Felix City Archives, Antwerp
2007
Architecture award for Felix City Archives, Antwerp
2008
International Klippan award for the renovation and conversion of a former dairy in Gaasbeek

Exhibitions

1985
Third Architecture Biennial, Venice
1985
Architecture for a Zee-Land, Vleeshalle Middelburg
1988
Architecture and image, deSingel, Antwerp
1991
Architetti della Fiandra, Architecture Biennial, Venice
1996
Katoen Natie, Architectural Association, London
1996
Nouvelle architecture en Flandre, Arc en rêve, centre d'architecture, Bordeaux
1996
The wealth of simplicity, Fondation pour l'architecture, Brussels
1997
Arquitectura de Flandes, Collegi d'Arquitectes de Catalunya, Barcelona
2003
Premi d'Arquitectura Contemporania de la Unio Europea Mies van der Rohe, Collegi d'Arquitectes de Catalunya, Barcelona
2008
Tabularium #7, Nijmegen
2009
Robbrecht en Daem Pacing through Architecture, Brussels

Office Robbrecht en Daem since 1975

Senior Architects
Paul Robbrecht, Hilde Daem

Assistant Architects
Kristoffel Boghaert, Gert Jansseune, Katrien Cammers, Johannes Robbrecht, Bert Haerynck, Suzanne Desmet, Charlotte Pattyn, Pieter Vanderhoydonck, Miriam Rohde, Marleen Goethals, Tom De Moor, Petra Decouttere, Griet Ollivier, Sofie Deboutte, Wim Menten, Kris Van Buynder, Aslı Cicek, Frédéric De Vylder, Mo Vandenberghe, Kobe Van Praet, Leen Corthier, Trice Hofkens, Tom Broes, Linde Everaerd, Bert Callens, Luc Beckstedde, Kristof Keerman, Kathy Vermeeren

Landscape Architect
Arne Deruyter

Visualisation 3D
Gert Swolfs

Photographer
Kristien Daem

Accountancy
Evelien Maes

Administration
Nele Catry

Former Assistants
Caroline Vanbiervliet, Cliff Reid, Haike Apelt, Greg Geertsen, Liesbet Vandenbussche, Tania Vandenbussche, Miriam Koudmani, Wim Walschap, Sofie Delaere, Matthias Baeten, Els Claessens, Gilberte Claes, Piet Crevits, Frank De Baere, Francesca de Fonseca, Marleen Dilissen, Catherine Fierens, Shin Hagiwara, William Mann, David Schalenbourg, Wouter Willems, Pieter Vandendries, Brigitte D'Hoore, Freddy Maenhoudt, Hugo Vanneste, Bas Hage, Maur Dessauvage, Wim Cuyvers, Pascal Van Der Kelen, Tinne Verwerft

About the Authors

Kristien Daem
is photographer of architecture and landscape. Since the beginning of the eighties she has worked with many international and Belgian artists and architects. Time and light are playing a major role in her approach of her personal work.
www.kristiendaem.be

Maarten Delbeke
teaches architectural history and theory at Ghent University and the University of Leiden. His publications on seventeenth-century art and theory include *Bernini's Biographies. Critical Essays*, edited with Evonne Levy and Steven Ostrow (Penn State, 2006). His architectural criticism has appeared in journals, such as *Archis*, *AAFiles*, *A+U* and *A+*, and in books. He co-curated the exhibition *Homeward. Contemporary architecture in Flanders*, shown at the 2000 biennial of Venice.

Stefan Devoldere
is an engineer-architect (Ghent University) and urban planner (University of Leuven). He is currently working as a critic, teacher and curator of exhibitions on architecture. He has presented various guest lectures on the urban landscape and the ordinary, and has been published in *AS, World Architecture Review, Il Giornale dell' Architettura*, among others. Since 2004 he is the editor in chief of *A+*, the Belgian architectural review *A+*.

Iwan Strauven
teaches architectural history at ISACF-La Cambre in Brussels and is co-ordinator of the architectural program of the Centre for Fine Arts in Brussels (BOZAR). He is preparing a PhD on the work of the modernist architect Victor Bourgeois at Ghent University. His publications include a monograph on the Bourgeois brothers, a book on Alfred Hardy and articles in architectural reviews such as *Architecture d'Aujourd'hui*, *Abitare* and *A+*.

This book was published on the occasion of the exhibition *Robbrecht en Daem Pacing through Architecture*
Centre for Fine Arts, Brussels, February 13th 2009 – April 19th 2009
Whitechapel Art Gallery, London, April 24th 2010 – June 20th 2010

Centre for Fine Arts, Brussels

Bozar
Chief Executive Officer, Artistic Director
Paul Dujardin
Deputy Artistic Director
Pablo Fernandez, Gerd Van Looy

Bozar Expo
Deputy Director Exhibitions
France de Kinder
Collaborators
Axelle Ancion, Elizabeth Vandeweghe
Artistic Consultants
Xavier Vandamme

Bozar Architecture
Coordination
Iwan Strauven
Collaborators
Marie-Cécile Guyaux

Bozar Tech
Director Technics, Investments, Safety & Security
Stéphane Vanreppelen
Collaborators
Joris Erven, Nicolas Bernus, Rudi Anneessens

Bozar Customer Services
Director Customer Services
Madelon Van der Hoeven
Manager Production
Erwin Verbist
Collaborators
Cédric Orban, Frédéric Vandervelde, Kim Vloebergs

Bozar Funding
Head of Funding
Elke Kristoffersen
Corporate Development
Annik Halmes

Bozar Com
Director Marketing, Communication
Leen Gysen
Audience Development Expo / Architecture
Geraldine Jonville, Bettina Saerens
Press
Eric Van Coppenolle
Webmaster
Wendy Schuppen

The Whitechapel Gallery, London

The Whitechapel Gallery is grateful for the on-going support of the foundations, individuals, galleries and companies who generously support it's programmes, and

ARTS COUNCIL ENGLAND

Chairman of the Trustees
Robert Taylor
Trustees
Duncan Ackery, Ed Eisler, Ann Gallagher, Runa Islam, Cllr Denise, Jones, Michael Keith, Keir McGuinness, Farshid Moussavi, John Newbigin, Dominic Palfreyman, Atul Patel, Catherine Petitgas, Alice Rawsthorn, Andrea Rose OBE, Sukhdev Sandhu, Nitin Sawhney, Alasdhair Willis
Company Secretary
Tom Wilcox
Director
Iwona Blazwick OBE
Whitechapel Staff
Chris Aldgate, Achim Borchardt-Hume, Jussi Brightmore, Beth Chaplin, Emily Daw, Michael De Guzman, Jo Dunnett, Melanie Dymond, Stephen Escritt, Sue Evans, Elizabeth Flanagan, Michele Fletcher, Annette Graham, James Greene, Gary Haines, Katherine Hart, Kathryn Havelock, Clare Hawkins, Caro Howell, Richard Johnson, Jon-Ross Le Haye, Patrick Lears, Rachel Mapplebeck, Zoe McLeod, Jo Melvin, Patrick Millner, Cassandra Needham, Maggie Nightingale, Rebecca Page, Dominic Peach, Faheza Peerboccus, Chris Potts, Cookie Rameder, Sherine Robin, Shamita Sharmacharja, Nicola Sim, Sarah Smillie, Marijke Steedman, Amy Stephens, Candy Stobbs, Andrea Tarsia, Ros Taylor, Hannah Vaughan, Sarah Walsh, Tom Wilcox, Nayia Yiakoumaki

Exhibition

General Direction
Paul Dujardin
Deputy Director Exhibitions
France de Kinder
Curators
Stefan Devoldere, Iwan Strauven
Coordination Exhibition
Kristien Daem, Robbrecht en Daem architecten,
Iwan Strauven, Bozar Architecture
Director and Cinematography Films
Maarten Vanden Abeele
Assistant of Cinematography Films
Kristien Daem
Film Editing
Gert Van Berckelaer
Sound Design Films
Senjan Jansen
Sound Caption Films
Senjan Jansen, Tom De Widt
Piano Film Gaasbeek
Alain Franco
Text Editing
Audrey Contesse, Lars Kwakkenbos
Technics, Production, Investments, Safety & Security
Stéphane Vanreppelen, Ward Vansteenwegen
Technical Coordination
Joris Erven, Nicolas Bernus
Art Handling & Installation
Aorta

BOZAR ARCHITECTURE

Whitechapel Gallery

Catalogue

Published by
Verlag der Buchhandlung
Walther König, Köln
Ehrenstr. 4, 50672 Köln
T. +49 (0) 221 20 59 653
F. +49 (0) 221 20 59 660
E. verlag@buchhandlung-walther-koenig.de

Project Coordinator
Franz König
Texts
Maarten Delbeke, Stefan Devoldere, Iwan Strauven
Translations
Gregory Ball
Elan Languages nv
Photography
Kristien Daem
Piet Ysabie (Initiatief '86),
Paul Robbrecht (pp. 116-119),
Maarten Vanden Abeele (p. 194)
Coordination
Kristien Daem, Robbrecht en Daem architecten,
Iwan Strauven, Bozar Architecture
Print
Printmanagement Plitt, Oberhausen
Lithogaphy
Kristien Daem
Book Design
Luc Derycke
Graphic Design and Typesetting
Luc Derycke, Jeroen Wille,
Studio Luc Derycke

Special Thanks
Jan De Nul Group

Jan De Nul GROUP

With the support of the Flemish authorities

1st edition 2009
2nd edition 2010

2010 © Paul Robbrecht & Hilde Daem, the authors, the photographer and Verlag der Buchhandlung Walther König, Köln

2010 © Centre for Fine Arts
www.bozar.be

Distribution

Switzerland:
Buch 2000
c/o AVA Verlagsauslieferungen AG
Centralweg 16
CH-8910 Affoltern a.A.
T. +41 (0) 44 762 42 00
F. +41 (0) 44 762 42 10
E. a.koll@ava.ch

UK & Eire:
Cornerhouse Publications
70 Oxford Street
GB-Manchester M1 5NH
T. +44 (0) 161 200 15 03
F. +44 (0) 161 200 15 04
E. publications@cornerhouse.org

Outside Europe:
D.A.P. / Distributed Art Publishers, Inc.
155 6th Avenue, 2nd Floor
New York, NY 10013
T. +1 212 627 1999
F. +1 212 627 9484
www.artbook.com

ISBN 978-3-86560-822-2

The Deutsche Nationalbibliothek lists this publication in the Deutsche Nationalbibliografie; detailed bibliographic data are available at http://dnb.d-nb.de.

Printed in Germany